Lived Isl

Lived Islam in South Asia
Adaptation, Accommodation and Conflict

Edited by

Imtiaz Ahmad
and
Helmut Reifeld

Routledge
Taylor & Francis Group

LONDON AND NEW YORK

First published 2018
by Routledge
4 Park Square, Milton Park, Abingdon, Oxon OX14 4RN
605 Third Avenue, New York, NY 10017

First issued in paperback 2023

Routledge is an imprint of the Taylor & Francis Group, an informa business

British Library Cataloguing in Publication Data
A catalogue record for this book is available from the British Library

Library of Congress Cataloging in Publication Data
A catalog record for this book has been requested

ISBN-13: 978-1-138-09999-9 (hbk)
ISBN-13: 978-1-03-265282-5 (pbk)
ISBN-13: 978-1-315-14488-7 (ebk)

DOI: 10.4324/9781315144887

Typeset in Plantin 10/12
by Eleven Arts, Delhi 110 035

SOCIAL
SCIENCE
PRESS

Contents

Preface

The papers in this book have grown out of a conference titled: 'Lived Islam in South Asia: Adaptation, Liminality and Conflict', held in Goa between 4 and 8 December 2002. Konrad Adenauer Foundation, Germany, initiated and organized this conference, as a part of a world-wide series of seminars and workshops called 'Dialogue with Islam'.

Ever since its inception in the 1960s, Konrad Adenauer Foundation has been interested in initiating dialogues between different ideological positions. There were two main reasons for organizing the present conference. First, there has been an enormous body of literature on Islam in West Asia, largely due to the international focus on that region. By contrast, Islam in South Asia has not received its due attention. We hoped to correct this imbalance in some small way through this conference. It was not our intention however, to enter theological or political debates, but gain better understanding of how Islam was practised by a large section of the world's population.

Second, since September 11, the quest for more knowledge about Islam has increased greatly, specially in the west. But together with this, there has also been a growth in dangerous stereotypes about the connection of Islam to violence. It seemed to us therefore, extremely important to dispel some of these misconceptions about such a large section of people who call themselves Muslims and try to counterbalance negative stereotypes, to find common ground of interests and values, but also to clearly identify differences.

Most of the papers presented at the conference were revised and rewritten for this volume. They address an inter-cultural or inter-religious dialogue, at the level of civil society, and do not try to eliminate differences or directly diminish conflicts. They attempt to broaden our knowledge and thus contribute to a better mutual understanding. On the level of perception of political problems, this might lead to a broader realism, to a reduction of illusions about the 'other' and thus of occasions which may confront us with unexpected surprise. Such a dialogue should, probably, take place more at the level of civil society and individuals rather than at the level of governments. The contributions in this volume provide some understanding of contemporary controversies.

Historically, and in the context of contemporary Islam in South Asia, there has been multi-cultural and multi-religious co-existence. In fact, nowhere in South Asia did Islam develop in a religiously isolated, exclusively Islamic environment. The togetherness and the overlapping spheres of life with other religions was the common pattern. South Asia is probably the largest area in the world where Islam exists within a mixed, composite culture, overlapping with several other religions. No matter how many origins of political conflict one may find in the domain of culture and religion, there are, at the same time, elements of peaceful co-existence as well.

Most of the essays in this volume illustrate how Islam cannot be understood by its own metaphysical postulates and ethical demands alone but has to be seen as a complex religious system, strongly influenced by the circumstances of everyday life and by the policies of the modern world. Islam therefore, like other religions, cannot be fully harnessed to a particular social or economic system of today, nor are Muslims in any way more prone to violence than most other people.

Given the controversial character of some of the issues raised in this book, it needs to be mentioned that all opinions and judgements expressed in the following articles are those of the individual authors and neither of the Konrad Adenauer Foundation nor of any Indian organization. The articles of this book were written with the idea to promote and carry forward the spirit of dialogue rather than end it with a final statement. The present book provides some useful information about South Asia and hopes to contribute to the promotion of a worldwide process of dialogue with Islam.

The spellings of some words have been made consistent within each paper, as per the wishes of the contributors of this volume.

Inputs have come from many sides, in the process of preparation as well as of publication, and it is, as always, impossible to name them all. It is not enough, however, to claim that their effort is reflected in this book. Therefore, the first group to be mentioned is the steering committee which met several times during the summer of 2002. Here, Professor Shail Mayaram, Professor T.N. Madan, Professor Ashis Nandy and Professor Imtiaz Ahmad discussed the focus of the conference. It was agreed, that it should concentrate on syncretic and liminal positions as well as accommodation of Islam in South Asia. After the conference, it was mainly Imtiaz Ahmad who bound the different presentations together, kept in touch with every author, smoothened down worries, and always found the right person. His patience and constant readiness to re-consider, re-plan and re-structure the volume was indispensable for its final outcome. Our greatest gratitude, therefore, goes to him. Sincere thanks are also due to all the contributors, who not only presented their papers and participated in the discussions, but also revised their papers for this volume.

For the implementation of the workshop the Konrad Adenauer Foundation is particularly proud of the collaboration with and grateful to the Fondation Maison des Sciences de L'Homme in Paris, which contributed the air-fares for three French experts. Similarly, we would like to thank the American Centre at the American Embassy in Delhi which provided an air-ticket from the United States. Last and certainly not the least we like to thank the 'anonymous donor' of the flight ticket for Dennis McGilvray who turned out to be McGilvray himself. Our further gratitude goes to Esha Béteille from Social Science Press, her copy-editors, Vidya Sen and Souporno Banerjee, for their understanding, and Meera Juneja for compiling the Index. With their mainly 'invisible' efforts, Ashvini, Manu and Mohita constantly worked behind the scene. Without the help, imagination and friendship of all mentioned, this book would never have come out so quickly.

New Delhi,
May 2003   Helmut Reifeld

Introduction

IMTIAZ AHMAD

S ome forty years ago Professor Wilfred Cantwell Smith, one of the most perceptive and understanding scholars on Islam and comparative religion, undertook a detailed survey of contemporary developments in the Islamic world. He went country by country, examining the nature of the transformation sweeping the different Islamic populations throughout the world and portraying for us the picture of the Islamic world as it strove to remain true to the demands of its faith even as it adapted and adjusted to the power and politics of the mid-twentieth century. Smith's unequivocal conclusion was that the religion was alive and dynamic. 'We have seen them', noted Smith, 'undertaking to refashion their societies, borrowing from the West or introducing from modernity new ways and new ideas, and from their own past, the inspiration and determination to succeed. We have seen them successfully reasserting their independence in national movements and vigorously defending their faith in intellectual endeavour. They have moved far towards acquiring freedom not only politically but internally by substituting activism for passivity, their destiny now significantly in their own hands' (1963: 298).

According to Smith, there was in this also a serious dilemma which the Islamic world faced. While seeking to reaffirm Islam not only in theory but in practice as well, the Islamic countries and populations faced the problem of relating it to the demands of the modern world.

As he put it, 'The question before the Muslim today is no longer simply that of why there is a gap between his convictions and the world in which he finds himself. It is rather the still more searching one as to how, or whether, he himself will or can or should close that gap (or bridge it)between his faith and the world which he has now to construct' (1963: 299). Surveying the developments in the different Islamic countries and populations, Smith indicated that he had encountered varied patterns ranging from attempts to emotionalize Islam into a close system to working for an open one, with a vision for the future. Islam evolved in response to the circumstances of a particular Muslim population. Smith suggested that whatever direction the developments took in any particular Islamic country or population, they would ultimately have to be shaped by Islam or at least some basis would have to be found for them in Islam.

Far-reaching changes have taken place both within Islamic countries and populations and the wider world of which they are intrinsically a part since Smith published the results of his survey. For instance, pan-Islamism has emerged in a reincarnated version. Besides this, the growing wealth of certain West Asian countries, that of Saudi Arabia in particular, has placed them in a position of economic and ideological leadership in relation to other Islamic countries and populations. The rise of ideological and intellectual movements in these Arab countries therefore have implications for other Islamic countries and populations, where they are seeking to penetrate with varying degrees of success. This has transformed the terms of the discourse about Islam and introduced new questions with regard to both the nature of Islam and how it should be understood in an increasingly interactive world (see Hastings and Stokes 2002).

There are broadly two points of view which have dominated the study of Islam (see Ahmad 1980). One sees Islam as the unfolding of a common uniform pattern that as a world religion it is supposed to signify and represent. The other sees Islam as evolving in response to local demands within each Islamic country or population. In the former view, Islam is credited with an autonomous role in which its nature in each country or population will ultimately remain limited within the fundamental orientations of Islam. In the latter view, Islamic societies throughout the world, despite the unity imposed upon them by a common adherence to a universal religion, have both the potential and the possibility of creating a distinctive pattern of belief shaped and ordered by their temporal and environmental conditions. Even if two or more Islamic countries and populations present similar patterns we need to differentiate them in accordance with the varying conditions under which they have to live, which in turn shape in different ways the particular form of Islam which they follow. An adherence to a rigidly formulated faith is not an empirical reality.

Even though this dichotomy of perspective in the understanding of Islam has been quite evident, its analytic implications have not been adequately appreciated and recognized. On the contrary, despite the difference in the way in which Islam is practised in each individual case, there is a predominant tendency to regard it as a unified system. The theologians have been mainly responsible for this. The study of Islam was originally the province of theologians or those who relied on textual sources for an understanding of their faith. Such a mode of study naturally led to a great deal of emphasis being placed on the unity and commonality of beliefs, attitudes and sentiments that were supposed to exist right across the Islamic world. Thus, it would not be uncommon to find in the writings on Islam an assertion of international solidarity with regard to its religious system. In other words, the Islamic world, whether in its collective orientations or in individual Islamic countries and populations, is the product of common attitudes and sentiments which the religion imposes on its believers (see Carré 1989: xiii).

Understanding Islam through the written text alone has been contested by anthropological researches on Muslim societies. Most anthropological studies begin with an assumption of a single form of religious experience and a unity of meaning within the Islamic tradition. Nevertheless, they point out the diversity in the actual content of everyday religious experience of the Muslims. Religious ideology in terms of the anthropological perspective works at two levels: the ideology articulated by intellectuals and the religious elite, and the ideology which consists of local and popular interpretations of a religious tradition. Although they do share certain elements in common, these two dimensions continually come in conflict with each other. Individual societies transform Islam to fit their own unique historical experience. At the local level therefore, there are as many meanings and expressions of Islam as there are historical contexts. The intellectual and religious elite by contrast reflect upon the sacred tradition with its unique experience in order to grasp the eternal essence of Islam. Yet, their superior position, which by definition is one of separation from popular practices, makes it impossible to relate this uniformity of belief and practice to common experience. The Islam of the intellectual and religious elite is highly abstract, formal and legalistic. Theology in this sense is more reflective than popular systems of religious meaning. At the same time it is less ritualistic and less bound to common sense experience and social action.

According to the theological tradition, the notion of Islam centres upon the reading of the Quran and the prophetic traditions which yield meanings intended to transcend any particular idiom. Formal religious education becomes a process of repetition in which meanings are already defined and stabilized. These unchanging formulations of the essence of Islam and the folk concepts which change continually according to social usage in any particular community, exist together in all Islamic societies. One good illustration of this broad pattern is the concept of the Sharia. Originally, the concept of the sharia referred to rules and regulations according to which a tribe lived. It was subsequently used to denote a set of rules and regulations which Islam ordained and imposed for the regulation of society and its ultimate vision. Even though the Islamic scripture did use the sharia in a unitary sense, what constituted the sharia varied widely within the Muslim world and does so even today. Nonetheless, the theological discourse tends to represent the sharia as being fixed and immutable and also binding on all Muslims irrespective of where he might be. One would then like to question if a single true Islam exists at all.

The theological tradition differs also from the view of the anthropologist. An anthropologist is interested in the field view of his subject as oppposed to the book view of the theologist. For the anthropologist, religion as it is practised is more important as a source of knowledge than the written texts. He focuses on the daily experiences, in this instance, of the local Islams and leaves the study of the theological interpretation to the theologian or the Islamicists.

The anthropologist therefore, faces the problem of grasping meanings which are fluid and indeterminate. He stabilizes these meanings into concepts in order to understand them and communicate them to others. These concepts then become finite and well-bounded containers of thought, and the continuous production of meaning and interpretation is brought to an end. They become general (and objective) descriptions which encompass a large number of particular social facts, by which meaning becomes static. By this I do not mean the fluidity of meaning, but the fact that the anthropologist as much as the theologian freezes the meanings of the great variety of everyday practice. Concepts are clearly carriers of meaning and should allow the fluidity of meanings to be captured and represented. However, this is not what always happens. Ever so often, when concepts are formulated they are intended to carry specific meanings and descriptions of a phenomenon which articulate a single meaning. They fail to capture the fluidity of meanings. In order to isolate the objective understanding of subjective meanings, the analyst must regard a concept itself as an objective reality which he can describe without the interference of his own values, in the manner of a scientist. Although the scientist's understanding is still a mode of interpretation which can never be completely free from cultural attitudes, and which can only guess at the meaning of another's experience rather than enter it directly, it nevertheless retains its superior validity by recognizing the process and structure of interpretation itself.

It follows therefore that the very creators of concepts become passive carriers of meaning, while the scientific and supposedly disinterested consciousness takes over the active role (see el-Zein 1977).

Local Islams involve accepted, taken-for-granted experiences, and are not very reflective. Both theology and anthropology claim a higher degree of reflection than folk expressions of Islam. Therefore, they regard these expressions as less ordered, less objective and somehow less complete versions of religious experience. Each, however, looks upon this diversity of experience in different ways. Theologians condemn it in order to enforce their view of the eternal meaning of Islam; anthropologists regard the various expressions as diluted forms distorted by magic and superstition, and thus indirectly imply the existence of a pure and well-defined Islam. This is illustrated in the terminological package that the contributions in this collection bring to the analysis of the existential meaning of local Islamic beliefs and practices. Even if there is no unanimity among the contributors as to the terms to be used, they radiate between two divergent modes of making sense of local religious experiences. As the contributions by Shail Mayaram and Helene Basu demonstrate, they tend to see the local religious expressions as liminal versions. Khan takes popular perceptions of Islam and social practices to be mere reflections of what theology would prescribe. For him, what is practised is not unique or different. It is only a manifestation of the universalistic worldview of Islam. Ute Falash deals with them in terms of ideas of syncreticism implying that the religious practices at the local level are an attempt to integrate the divergent cultural meanings into a coherent whole through integrating them in a common frame. Sharma, Assayag and Gottschalk have sought to deal with this complexity by recognizing different levels within Islam.

Finally, history, because it specifically requires reflection on the past, and science, in this case anthropological reflection on human experience, become the privileged mode of understanding due to their awareness of the processes of human experience. Yet within the total hierarchy.

Both forms of Islam—the formal, textual and the pragmatic and local—coexist in a state of tension. The elite continually contest the local traditions of Islam. People acknowledge the general concepts dictated by the *ulema*, but they choose to live according to more particularistic notions of Islam which relate to their everyday experiences. This particular anthropological distinction appears to reinforce the *ulema's* claim to a superior religious position by treating the elite version as 'religion', and reducing other interpretations to some form of deviance. These distinctions between the elite and popular Islam are obviously derived from the fundamental assumptions defining each anthropological paradigm. Although all positions argue the objectivity and universality of their own premises, the mere fact of multiplicity of possible meanings at the level of everyday existence challenges the notion of a single, absolute reality. Rather than being accepted as a given truth, these anthropological premises might be treated as anthropologists themselves treat the tenets of Islam: as diverse, culturally relative expressions of a tradition—in this case, a 'scientific' one. If versions of Islam must be called ideology, then perhaps these various perceptions of the anthropologists demand the same understanding. In terms of this supposedly scientific distinction between elite and folk Islam, anthropology studies the former, yet its principles of analysis resemble the latter. Thus, the distinction between theology and anthropology of Islam is tenuous beyond a certain point. While they deal with Islam at different levels and focus on different categories of Islam, their method of isolating their version of Islam is the same as that of the theologian. In this sense, anthropology of Islam has yet to take shape.

Like science, the theological positions which are referred to as elite Islam, assume the same detached attitude regardless of how the anthropologists define them in their different paradigms. In science and theology, understanding the real meaning of religious phenomenon comes only through presumed separation from common subjective assumptions and from immediate involvement with the object of study. Both positions agree on the existence of 'folk' Islam as opposed to formal Islam which, in order to be known, demands a greater degree of reflection and systematization of principles than found in popular expressions of belief. Anthropology and theology differ merely in the particular aspects of these local interpretations selected for analysis.

However, the authority claimed by theological Islam is contested by the recognition that in any given cultural system, a folk theology may be found which rivals formal theology in its degree of abstraction, systematization, and cosmological implications. Each form both defines and necessitates the other, the problem of determining the real as opposed to an ideological Islam in this sense becomes an illusion. It can be posited that the difference is really one of emphasis and focus and the terminological package that is brought to bear upon the study of Islam is similar or virtually the same. While the theologian merely focuses upon the ideology and relies upon the textual terminology to expound an understanding of Islam, the anthropologist devices concepts and focuses at different levels at which Islam can and does operate or exists. Not only does the anthropologist not accept the theological picture as axiomatic, he also concerns himself with the dynamics between the theological description with the realities at the ground level. Thus, he either uses the notions of Great and Little traditions or recognizes that there are different levels within Islam. Each of these traditions addresses different needs of the believers and is constituted by entirely different sets of beliefs and practices (see Ahmad 1980). Even so, beyond capturing the range of forms in which the phenomenon occurs in real life the anthroplogical exercise does not clarify which of the traditions or levels constitutes the real Islam.

These contributions do not offer a means for uncovering the logic of culture or the principles which are imminent in culture and which order and articulate the thoughts and actions of culture bearers. In this sense we are not lead to the structure of 'Islam' for it is a contradiction in terms to speak of the systemic 'fit' of an autonomous entity and therefore, meaning is entirely relational. The contributions to this volume, do not select relevant materials according to some standard truth, but consider the systems in their entirety. In this way, a multiplicity of cultural meanings is explored and developed. There are no privileged expressions of truth.

This perspective runs through all the contributions in this book. Peter Gottschalk in his opening contribution shows that, as far as the expansion of Islam is concerned, the conventional perception of the centre and periphery does not apply. He explains why most of the western classifications that follow an evolutionary model grown out of Christian religious categories and European traditions of nationalism should be approached with caution in the context of non-western societies. Gottschalk analyses the specific differences in the evolution of Islam in South Asia as compared to that in West Asia and elsewhere, with the help of the two terms 'routes' and 'roots'. While religious groups in general and Muslims in particular have travelled many new 'routes' by contrast, they have established completely new 'roots' in many of the places they went to. In the case of South Asia, he shows, that the 'roots' that Islam has established in this region have a far greater impact on its position today than those from its Arabic origin. Gottschalk argues that for many, 'Muslim' is a branded community, it actually is 'syncretic', 'hybrid' or 'liminal' because the average South Asian Muslim practices a faith straddling the boundary that separates 'Islam' from 'Hinduism'.

Shail Mayaram and Jackie Assayag dwell further on this theme. Shail Mayaram locates her analysis within the concept of liminility as originally applied to the study of rituals. Her contention is that the concept has potentialities for wider application and can be applied to the study of religious traditions in their entirety. Thus, having laid out her framework of analysis she goes on to examine her own fieldwork among two communities, the Mers and the Meos, in the state of Rajasthan and shows how categorizing them in terms of categorical or exclusive identities is a problematic proposition. The Mers are a bi-religious community having both Hindu and Muslim sections with the possibility of passage from one to the other. The Meos are Muslims and perceive themselves as such but share many rituals, rites and folklore with their Hindu neighbours. Her conclusion is that for those used to thinking in exclusive Hindu or Muslim terms this is problematic but not so for the members of these communities. They do have clear notions of a distinct identity, but are able to live in a liminal space of religious existence. She concludes that this is not a unique situation. In a world characterized by interdependence almost everyone is called upon to live a similar liminal existence.

Jackie Assayag describes some of the roots of Islam in South Asia as a form of 'integrated' acculturation which led, especially in the course of the twentieth century, to increasing 'communal' violence between Hindus and Muslims. Assayag warns us, however, that many interpretations of the assumed 'great' or even universal religious traditions may lead us to over-emphasize the strength of historical notions of 'religion', 'civilization' and 'community'. The contemporary conflicts of certain Muslim groups do not contradict the fact that Islam has developed deep roots in South Asia for nearly a thousand years. Traditions and especially co-existing religious traditions should, therefore, never be interpreted as a fixed or determining heritage but as an open, on-going and competitive relationship between social groups. These groups have to be considered as both different and identical. Their future is therefore open to co-operation as well as to conflict.

Assayag's explanations pave the way for an analysis of the encounter of Islam with other religious groups in South Asia, leading more often to accommodation rather than to conflict. Diane D'Souza describes the religious rituals performed by Shia women in Hyderabad. Coming from an extremely minority position these women discover the collaboration and sympathy of other women with a religious background which is completely different. Through their collective performances, they not only assert the significance of rituals to collective beliefs but strengthen, with the help of these rituals, the belief in the ability to change their lives.

These interpretations are given some historical depth in the essays by Mohammad Ishaq Khan and Sudhindra Sharma. One of the most striking examples of the numerous interrelations of both within and across religions is the intense devotion demonstrated by Muslims and Hindus alike to the shrines of Sufi saints, even though this is seen as contrary to orthodox Islamic interpretations. For centuries, Sufi traditions like their devotional practices and eclectic approach to religion have attracted Muslims as well. The region where Sufis had perhaps their strongest impact in South Asia is the Kashmir Valley. As Mohammad Ishaq Khan explains, the Rishi tradition has predominantly shaped religious and public life in Kashmir for centuries and is the basis of their self-identity as Kashmiris. At the time of Nizamuddin, a Chisti Sufi saint, whose shrine is located in Delhi, Sufism had become a mass movement in north-west India, and was influenced by Hindu traditions of this region. Against this backdrop, Islam emerges not only as a moral but also as a comprehensive socio-cultural resource. Through its syncretic practices the Rishi tradition created a common cultural identity which gradually shaped the way for the assimilation of people belonging to different religions, in this case Hindus and Muslims, into a regional cultural community. Whether this will be transformed into a more reified and exclusive religious identity separating Hindus and Muslims and can provide a resource for coming to terms with the political crisis that has plagued Kashmir in recent years is an open question.

Aparna Rao takes up the discussion of the inter-relationship between normative and practised Islam reflected in the other contributions to the yet academically unexplored area of cyberspace. Perusing the contents of electronic exchanges among a group of Kashmiri Muslims, she demonstrates how there does not exist today, as indeed there has never existed at any time in the past, complete unanimity over what typically constitutes Islam and what it means to be a Muslim. All such questions are deeply contested and the exchanges within the e-community she chose to look at bear ample testimony to this. What is particularly significant is that information techonology has opened up simultaneously two conflicting possiblities. On the one hand, it makes possible for a unified and formal understanding of Islam and self-definition of Islam to be communicated over vast areas and among a large group of believers. On the other hand, the new technology has also rendered it possbile for the divergence of understanding of theological principles and Islamic principles to be reflected. If the new technology allows those committed to a narrow and formal understanding of the Muslim faith to be relayed widely, it has also allowed the peripheral groups whose beliefs are eclectic and clustered to talk back at any effort to popularize a radical and universal understaning of Islam. Within this context of continuing contestation of understandings of Islam, self-conscious dissonances surface and antinomies arise when people are exposed to a sense of insecurity of being treated as 'the Other'. Such tension also reflects the insecurity created over many decades by the Orientalist privileging of religion as the foremost site of essentialized difference directly dependent on modern understandings of religion and its new location in the public sphere. She concludes that in any endeavour to understand Islam one must focus on both the diversity of religious practice and the growing tendency among some (non-Muslims and Muslims alike) to reduce this diversity in order to use religion and religious identity as markers, in order to physically or psychologically target the constructed image of the Other.

Sudhindra Sharma deals with the religiously plural situation in Nepal where three religious traditions—Hinduism, Islam and

Buddhism—have simultaneously existed in harmonious relationship for long. Since Nepal is constitutionally a Hindu State, the pre-eminence of Hinduism was easily recognized without apparent conflict with the other religious traditions until recent times. It is only in recent times that this situation has begun to change, and the Hindus, Muslims and Buddhists are increasingly beginning to define themselves as exclusive communities. The reasons for this are partly internal to the groups and their changing interactions and partly external. Forces from outside and the role of the State become extremely important in this context for understanding the changing relationship among these three communities. The Muslims have reacted by trying to purify their religion and projecting themselves as 'correct Muslims'. This process has been strengthened by the Muslims returning from the Gulf countries and the visiting orthodox clerics from across the border with India. The growing influence of this section of the Muslim population in Nepal has resulted in antagonism between them and those who see themselves as culturally assimilative and resist the more exclusive foreign versions of Islam from Arab countries and across the border with India. Even so, this disturbance of communal harmony has the potential to alienate the Nepali Muslims from the dominant Nepali culture and differentiate them from others.

The tradition of cultural sharing that Sudhindra Sharma outlines for Nepal is described by Yoginder Sikand with reference to the Sufi shrines in South India. His analysis of a large number of shared shrines in Karnataka shows how Hindus and Muslims have shared the beliefs and practices associated with Sufi shrines and through them lived together for centuries. In recent times however, these shrines are being contested by the two communities, Hindus and Muslims, for their own exclusive use. This division has been brought about by the orthodox Muslim clergy and the Hindu nationalist elements. The orthodox Muslim clergy oppose the veneration of Sufi shrines which they consider to be deviations from Islam. They assert that such worship compromises their religious identity. In the same mould, Hindu nationalist elements, seeking to promote a strong Hindu identity, have been asserting their rights of exclusive possession over these shrines. Both serve to erode syncretic traditions that emerged around them. Nevertheless, these shared shrines continue to enjoy a powerful influence which cuts across exclusive communitarian identities and still plays a vital role in strengthening mutual bonds of co-existence.

Asha Rani discusses the semantic and symbolic meaning of Hindu-

Muslim syncretism as reflected in the nationalist discourse about the introduction of Hindustani as the common Indian language. The discourse was both political and communal. Asha Rani illustrates the role of the Hindustani language as a potential syncretic category with an explicit religious and cultural agenda. This might help us in understanding Hindu-Muslim relationships as not being necessarily dichotomous and segmented but mutually commensurate and convergent.

The reality of lived Islam is primarily concerned with social and probably political co-existence. Within this struggle for power, religion often serves as a pretext—not only in the form of inter-religious conflicts but disguised as intra-religious conflicts as well. Mariam Abou-Zahab illustrates how violence marks the recurrent conflict between two Muslim sects, the Sunni and the Shia in Jhang, a small town in central Pakistan. She shows that beneath the apparent cause of sectarian differences powerful economic interests are at work. Sectarianism, thus, serves as a substitute identity and as a vehicle of social change in the peculiar circumstances of Pakistan.

Most puritanical and orthodox Muslims see any form of Sufism or close interchange with other religions as a danger to true Islam. For them, the Sufis lacked the appropriate moral rigour. Others however, particularly the non-Muslims, venerated the Sufi saints for their moral superiority. The great number of voluntary conversions to Islam in South Asia led to a large area of accommodation as well as syncretism and liminal coexistence. Sufi saints, who ignored orthodox expressions of religion, brought about most of these conversions. They did not develop the image of any imperial decree. Sufis put their emphasis on personal piety and it was mainly with the help of their charisma that they won new followers. They showed a love for humanity that was free from communal boundaries and independent from worldly possessions. In this way, they exercised a strong and long-term influence in South Asia.

Based on research on the shrine of Pirana, near Ahmedabad, Dominique-Sila Khan explores the tradition and the impact of the so-called Imamshahis who constitute the core group of devotees around this shrine. Within this group Muslims and Hindus have merged so completely that some of them are not able to state which of the two religions they belonged to originally. For Khan this shrine serves as an example to contest the value of the descriptive categories of syncretism and liminality.

Another group which found accommodation in the context of Sufi traditions is that of the Sidis in Gujarat. The Sidis originated from East Africa and came to Gujarat and other parts of India as slaves, seamen or traders. Helene Basu discusses questions of ritual communication in the context of Sufi religiosity. The Sidis live among the lowest strata of the Indian society and are regarded as indifferent Muslims by the more orthodox Muslims who have been trying to spread an orthodox version of Islam among them. However, they are regarded as Muslims by the State. Basu brings out the role of the State in both defining identities and reinforcing exclusive communitarian identities through a study of the shrine of the patron Sufi saint of the Sidis called Bava Gor. The shrine of Bava Gor was originally a simple thatched roof structure and the rituals that took place there were highly syncretic and heterodox. The *dhammal*, the African drum dance was performed within the precincts of the shrine which also attracted a large number of Hindu pilgrims because of its power to heal psychological disorders. After the State took over the shrine on account of alleged financial irregularities, its administration was put into the hands of orthodox Muslims who belonged to influential groups in the locality, and who reconstructed the shrine to architecturally reflect its Islamic character. Further, they prohibited the performance of syncretic rituals, including the *dhammal*, inside the shrine.

Equally interesting is the case of the Madaris, a Sufi brotherhood spread over large parts of northern India. As Ute Falasch explains, the Madaris have absorbed their Hindu environment to such an extent that the orthodox Muslims found them unacceptable as Muslims. Not being Muslims any more they serve as a fruitful example to explore the fringes of 'lived Islam' and illustrate what Falasch rightly terms as 'multiple identity'. Falash also raises significant theoretical questions involved in treating a brotherhood like the Madaris in terms of the notions of syncreticism, liminality and hetrodoxy. Use of such terms to describe religious beliefs inevitably involves a question of perspectives and raises the question of whose perspective is at work in these descriptions: the analyst's, the outsider's or those constituting the brotherhood. Falasch demonstrates that, while from the perspective of the outsider or the analyst the Madaris may seem syncretic, hetrodox or liminal, their own self-view is that they are Muslims and follow Islam.

Dennis McGilvray deals with the hermitage shrine of Daftar Jilani in central Sri Lanka. Even though Jailani can be seen as an exclusively Muslim shrine it is embedded in a Buddhist environment. Political friction and communal strife between Sri Lanka's Tamil Hindus and their Tamil-speaking Muslim neighbours has been widely recognized as a significant and growing problem, but a more concealed but an equally dangerous ethnic antagonism has long existed between the Sinhalese and the Muslims. It is not the fundamentalist adherents who have posed the serious threat to the hermitage shrine of Daftar Jailani. It is the location of Jailani shrine in an overwhelmingly Sinhala Buddhist district coupled with the fact that the Adam's peak is revered by Muslims as well as Buddhists lies at the root of this conflict. Since the early 1970s, Sinhala chauvinists and politicized members of the Buddhist Sangha have seen this as a seeming violation of the Island's sacred geography.

Each paper in this volume is interesting for providing ethnographic details and offering insights into the problems inherent in dealing with the sensitive issue of religious identity. The religious identities explored in this volume, are located in a region which has not only been a home to adherents of diverse religious traditions but where the believers of these traditions have lived and interacted in close proximity. Taken together the contributions highlight the religiously clustered scene in South Asia which continues to be remarkably diverse and varied though there have been movements among all religious communities to acquire an exclusive identity through symbols. The role of the State and political processes have added complexity to such efforts at inventing images of 'correct' Hindus, Muslims, Buddhists and Christians, not to speak of the many numerically minor religious groups. Ultimately what happens to the multiplex, fluid and shifting identities, which many of the contributions in this book have explored in such depth, will depend upon the direction that the State in each of the countries of the region gives to the elements that are seeking to foster mutually exclusive identities. Meanwhile, the diffused and liminal identities and cultures that cut across communities persist side by side with vigorous attempts to articulate singular, exclusive and antagonistic identities.

References

Ahmad, Imtiaz (1980). Introduction, in Imtiaz Ahmad (Ed.), *Ritual and Religion among Muslims in India*, Manohar Publishers and Distributors, Delhi.

———. (1989). Introduction, in Olivere Carré (Ed.), *Islam and the State in the World Today*, Manohar Publishers and Distributors, Delhi.

Carré, Olivier (1989). Preface to the French Edition, in Olivier Carré (Ed.), *Islam and the State in the World Today*, New Delhi.

el-Zein, Abdul Hamid (1977). Beyond Ideology and Theology: The Search for the Anthropology of Islam, *Annual Review of Anthropology*, 6, pp. 227–54.

Hastings, Donnan and Martin Stokes (2002). Introduction, in Donnan Hastings (Ed.) *Interpreting Islam*, Vistaar Publications, New Delhi.

Smith, W. C. (1963). *Islam in Modern History*, Mentor Books, New York.

PART

I

Concepts and
Interpretations

1

Mapping Muslims: Categories of Evolutionary Difference and Interaction in South Asia

PETER GOTTSCHALK

Recently, a colleague and I hailed a taxi in Toronto, Canada. Once inside, conversation with the taxi driver revealed that, he was from Bangladesh and that we were attending the same conference on religion. 'What do you think of Hinduism?' the driver asked. My colleague gave an answer far less cautious than I would have after I spotted a red plastic sign with an Arabic prayer hanging from the driver's rear-view mirror. I had had experiences in which South Asian Muslims posed this question as a prelude to disparaging remarks about Hindus and Hinduism. This time, however, the taxi driver went on to say how much he appreciated Hinduism and often celebrated Diwali and other Hindu holidays as well as Muslim ones.

Muslims who might disapprove of our driver's ecumenicism would blame the 'Hindu' character of Bangladeshi society as a corrupting influence on so-called 'true Islam'. For many of them, the word 'Muslim' represents a bounded category with a core, a limit, and an outside. To secular scholars, the taxi driver's faith might represent a 'syncretic', 'hybrid', or 'liminal' Islam straddling the boundary with Hinduism. Such terms necessitate not only critical reflection on the categories purportedly transgressed, but the acts of classification that create and sustain them. In other words, because they demonstrate that categories have boundaries and gaps between them, attention must be paid to the human effort that establishes, maintains and values—(positively or negatively)—these positions. It must also be remembered that a group endures classification of itself both by members of that group (who situate 'us' among 'them') and those outside the group (who differentiate 'us' from 'them' and then situate the latter among other classes of 'them'). As I hope to show, western secular studies of religion have borrowed classification processes from evolution theory in ways that aptly prompt caution in the classification of non-western societies, especially in light of nationalist appropriations of religious categories to define the nation inclusively and exclusively.

Although an evolutionary model of classification dominates current humanistic and social scientific research, its Christian roots and nationalist applications are apparent. So, it is useful to unpack the assumptions of this categorical system drawing on the work of Jonathan Z. Smith and propose a complementary model that aims to appreciate—using Paul Gilroy's distinction—not just the *routes* religious groups—particularly Muslims—travel, but the *roots* they establish, especially in India. Through this focus on how Muslims have become entrenched in India and a challenge to the rigid categorization of Islam relative to Hinduism, I hope to demonstrate that syncretic, hybrid, or liminal Muslims in India might perhaps be better described as enrooted Indian Muslims as shown by examples drawn from my fieldwork among the residents of the area around Arampur, a village in western Bihar.

From Morphological to Phylogenetic Classification

Let us begin with categorization itself. This essential human activity associates individuals or individual objects with other individuals or objects based on a shared feature or features. I identify a Tata-brand bus constructed 18,000 kilometres from my home as a bus because it bears the same features as a bus used to transport passengers in my hometown in North America. Similarly, zoologists originally classified the red wolf as a wolf because of the physical traits it shared with other animals identified as wolves. This morphological classification occupied much of the efforts of Carolus Linnaeus (1701–78) who bequeathed to empirical science the foundation of the contemporary taxonomical system.

Such classification practices are not limited to scientists. A number of Muslims in the Arampur area differentiate Muslims according to their practices and beliefs. While discussing the commemoration of Muharram, a significant number of Arampur Muslims make a point of distinguishing the Shia from Sunni as Muslims who ritually immerse themselves in the pathos associated with the martyrdom of the Prophet Mohammad's grandson Hussain and his entourage. In a conversation about Muharram, I ask Waliuddin Khan about the death of Hussain. After saying that he was murdered, Khan continues unprompted with a reflection on the commemoration of his martyrdom. 'People fast in grief. There are two groups among *Mussalman*: Sunni and Shia. Shias greatly observe it. Sunnis less so.' Others made a point of explaining that some Shias lacerate their bodies with chains or blades while Sunnis do not. In doing so, they distinguish two classes based on distinctions in forms of practice within the category of 'Muslim'.

Western biological science has recently advanced a taxonomical system not beholden to such morphologies. By the 1970s, as the red wolf looked as if it were nearing extinction, debate erupted among scientists as to whether it represented a hybrid of two species or a separate species altogether. Whereas a previous generation of scientists classified this animal as a unique species due to its distinctive physical features (or morphology), others regarded the red wolf as a hybrid of the gray wolf and the coyote. In other words, the red wolf as we know it was either the result of its own unique evolutionary development or that of a mixture of the members of two distinct evolutionary stages.

The differences between these two views lay in the differences between two methods of classification—while some scientists measured the differences by uniqueness or shared shapes of skull and teeth, others did so according to the distinct place the red wolf occupies on the evolutionary scale (Freeman & Herron 1998). The former group thus classified the red wolf according to morphology—the synchronic, physical description of the animal based on characteristics such as shape, size and colour—while the latter classified it according to its diachronic mapping in time and space relative to other groups of animals.

This latter, newer system of categorizing living beings is called phylogenetic classification. The displacement of the centuries-old morphological system by the phylogenetic represents the latest in a long series of victories across a number of academic disciplines for the evolutionary paradigm which is itself a product of the new ways of cognizing time in Europe since the Renaissance. This revolution displaced medieval European views of a constant cosmos and insisted, instead, on a cosmos in perpetual change, teleologically leading from a specific origin to a particular end. Each individual no longer existed as itself in the present but, represented instead an ephemeral moment in the present, a link suspended between the past and future on a trajectory of change.

And, so, whereas the morphological classificatory system groups individual members according to morphological characteristics (e.g., shape, size, colour), the phylogenetic first situates each member on a timeline and then groups it with others relative to their position and similarity.

Another case in point is the panda. Is it a bear (which it resembles) or a raccoon, to which it is genetically linked? Paleontologists categorize certain skeletal remains as Homo erectus because of their similarity and situate that species on a timeline as the ancestors of Homo sapiens who are genetically indebted to them. Meanwhile, zoologists view chimpanzees as related, but distantly, to Homo sapiens. Paleontologists have sought not only to plot human remains along this timeline but to also trace the all but vanished trails of human distribution to our place of origin. Scientists commonly hunt for origins as an insight into the nature of the creature as it makes its way along the evolutionary trail.

The Classificatory Challenge of Islam

There seems to me a parallel in how life scientists have situated the red wolf in their fields of knowledge and the ways in which many social scientists treat not only 'syncretic,' 'hybrid', or 'liminal Muslims' but religious traditions as a whole. Faced with the stunning diversity of practices around the globe, of beliefs, ideologies and material products associated with deities and other superhuman agents, scholars of religion have grouped components into categories of 'religion' juxtaposed with one another according to their place of origin and subsequent geographic expansion. Hence, Baal worship and Islam become 'Middle Eastern religions', the Druids and Vestal Virgins become part of 'European religions', and Hinduism and Buddhism become 'South Asian' or 'Indian religions'. The morphological classification of religious elements into categories such as 'sky gods' and 'earth gods', 'axis mundis' and 'sacred spaces' by scholars like Mircea Eliade has also, however, had an influence although it has been largely forsaken in favour of evolution based (phylogenetic) classification.

Current conflicts between evolutionists and fundamentalist Christians notwithstanding, the evolutionary paradigm is indebted to a Protestant Christian teleology. This forged in Europe an expectation for spiritual change that arced in time toward the rise of progressively improving humans under the guiding hand of divine intervention. While many Christians celebrated humanity as the crown of creation and Christianity as the culmination of revelation, scientists often proclaimed humanity as the most complex and advanced product of evolution. The teleological paradigm involved in both these views led to Christian expectations of social and religious development, that the existence of Islam has routinely challenged.

Islam has long posed a dilemma for the Christian-dominated west. It is perhaps for this reason that so many European theorists of religion simply ignored it in their reflections regarding the universal development of religion. Many of these theorists' narratives of this evolution have traced the historical progress of humanity from animism to paganism to religion of the law (Judaism) to the religion of love (Christianity). If animists, pagans, and Jews still flourished after Christianity's ascendancy, many Christians ascribed that to the isolation, ignorance, or resistance of groups soon to be converted to the 'true religion'. Islam posed a problem from its inception. Having arisen after Christianity, it taught a monotheistic message that quickly challenged the latter's dominance in the Mediterranean region, and seemed to threaten the Church in Europe. Moreover, Muslims considered their religion an improvement over Christianity and convinced many erstwhile Christians of the same, leading to their conversion with a success Christians had attributed, when they made similar gains previously, to the God-given truth of their cause. While some Christians tried to accommodate Islam to their teleology by declaring it a heresy or degraded form of Christianity, the Muslims' unwillingness to see Islam as anything less than the superordination of Christianity made such subordination difficult to sustain. Therefore, resisting this teleology, Muslims were cast as deliberately subversive of the divine plan, accounted for as the handmaidens of Satan or the like, and destined for terrible divine punishment as attested by the prophet Mohammad's position in one of the lowest circles of Dante's inferno.

Sayyid Afifuddin exhibited the strength of his Islamic teleology one morning in front of his expansive house. This wealthy landowner makes his rounds in a preaching circuit across North India annually.

He explained how Mohammad was a *nabi* (prophet) who brought the final revelation of the Quran after three preceding revelations: 'One book came, then another was necessary. People wrote according to their own mind. Another became necessary; it came and people did it again a third time. After this God said that no full stop or comma could be changed. If you see a Quran in America, far from here, and one in Hindustan, you will not see any difference'. According to many Muslims, the revelation of these four books—the Torah, Psalms, Gospels, and Quran—became necessary due to the failure of the communities—to whom Allah revealed the first three books—Jewish and Christian, to maintain the integrity of the books. The Jews, Christians and Muslims thus form *ahl al-Kitab* ('People of the Book') among whom Muslims distinguish themselves through their fidelity to the original form of the book as revealed to Mohammad. Although this narrative certainly represents a teleology of Allah's faithfulness to aid humanity despite its repeated failures, it is not one of a successive lineage because one form of the revelation does not give birth to the next. Rather, it is the failure of each of the first three that guarantees a new effort of revelation whose origin resides firmly in Paradise. Jews, Christians, and Muslims inhabit one plane of classification not because of genetic relation to one another but because of the common trust given them by Allah in the form of a book, described as *asman ki kitab* ('Book of Heaven') by one resident. Secular scholars of religion, in contrast, assume a relationship of lineage by which Christianity develops from Judaism and both influence the rise of Islam.

In terms of classification, the medieval and early modern Church, however, historically posited a group of categories hierarchically related to one another according to the progression of humanity to the supposed one true faith. It considered Abraham's rejection of polytheism and idolatry as the establishment of a new category— that of the *Jews*—set apart from and above the *pagans*. *Christians* became a newer and more elevated category. The category *Muslims* challenged this arrangement because Muslims resisted being subsumed into the category *Christians* as they rejected the divinity of Jesus yet agreed on too many other points of Christian theology. Moreover, Western Christian categorization operated under a strict logic that refused members from belonging to two categories simultaneously. The Church developed a stern sorting that required orthodoxy as the measure of membership to a category, bounding the Christian identity within a perimeter of dogma and prescribed practice and excommunicating as heretics those perceived as having crossed this perimeter (Boyarin 2001). Whereas shared devotional practices and rituals in places like South Asia had earlier made definitive identity and community separation uncommon, confessional politics during the early modern period divided Europe into warring Christian denominations.

Consider, as an illustration of this classificatory urge, the example of Friedrich Schleiermacher, the early nineteenth-century German romantic philosopher. Schleiermacher sought to use classification language to distinguish 'religion' from 'religions.' The influence of Linnaeus' taxonomical innovations is apparent as he exhorted readers not to confuse 'natural religion' with its expressions in 'positive religions': 'Divide an idea to infinity if you will, you cannot thereby reach an individual. You can only get less general ideas which may, as genus and species, embrace a mass of very different individuals' (Schleiermacher 1958). In order to convince skeptics not to disparage 'natural religion' because of the deficiencies of the 'positive religions' through which it manifests itself, the author delineates the difference between various levels of classification. The four types of historical religion he identified were naturalism, polytheism, theism, and deism (ibid: 22).

Western scholars organized these categories both historically and geographically, associating each religion with the places of its domi-nance and seeking to trace each back to its place of genesis. Earlier generations of more optimistic scholars sought the origins of religion itself as a phenomenon. Although that project has largely been aban-doned, academicians steadfastly connect religions primarily with their places of origin no matter how transnational the traditions may be.

For instance, scholarship too often fastens upon the Middle East as the 'natural' context of Islam. This seems particularly odd in the face of the fact that more than half of the world's Muslims live east of Afghanistan. Although Indonesia, India, Pakistan, and Bangladesh are home to the world's largest Muslim populations, the academic study of religion has commonly labelled these as 'Muslims on the periphery' or 'Islam from the edge'. Indeed, perhaps the most important American academic meeting for scholars who study Islam is the annual conference of the Middle East Studies Association (MESA). Suggesting that the one religious world is coterminous with these regions, MESA describes itself as comprising those 'interested in the study of the Middle East, North Africa and the Islamic world' (Middle

Eastern Studies Association Website 2003). Certainly the prejudices of some Islamicists and Arabists that Islam is somehow truer in the area in which it germinated has played their part. Clearly, the overall dominance of the genealogy of religions in scholarship privileges the place of genesis even in studies of contemporary Muslim societies.

Roots in Cultures rather than Routes to Nations

Western scholars as well as nationalists often rely on the genetic metaphor in constructing some notion of naturalness in their definition of the nation. Nationalists commonly imagine a self-given nation with the conceit that it and the people who comprise it always existed even if they had not always been aware of their common identity. Those who enter a nation's territory do not become part of the nation until they divest themselves, if they can, of the attributes that are at odds with what are understood to be the essential to the nation's model citizen, specific qualities carried from their old homes or inherited from their ancestors. This expectation manifests itself, for instance, through a tension in the dominant nationalist narrative in the United States. Relying as they do on the 'nation of emigrants' ideal, nationalist narratives must cope with the presence of 'natives' who preceded these emigrants—natives to the land but not to the nation and, so, find little inclusion in the myth of the nation's founding and independence. This myth traces a genesis through the rebirth of the Old World seeds of the Greek and Roman civilizations in American soil as sowed by European Americans, leaving little room, for non-European emigrants. The resulting difficulty of imagining multiple lineages for the nation has meant that the categories of Native American, African American, and Asian American have found less easy and only more recent accommodation within the class 'American' as constructed by European Americans.

Vasu Singh illustrates his sense of a perennially existent Indian nation as we sit on the porch that serves as the sitting room in his father-in-law's large home near Arampur. Following a discussion of the Independence Movement and in response to my question regarding how he knew about the events he had narrated, Singh explains that he studies history and describes it as *parampara* (tradition). He went on to explain that India was the *sona chidiya* (golden bird) during the period of Mauryan rule but that, 'Man Singh and the rajas of the Indian states who fought on Akbar's side were … what does one say?

One who always cheats and betrays? Traitor. This type of people were born'. I ask who Man Singh was against and Singh replied, 'His tradition, his society, against all native Indians. Because the Mughals came from outside, right? He fought with them as a third force and for this reason they were able to expand to the South.' I then ask whether the sepoys who fought for the Mughal emperor in 1857 were also traitors. 'No, no, no! They were not! In 1526, Babar came. So three hundred years passed until 1857. In three hundred years a culture and civilization had appeared. They mixed in Indian culture slowly. They were a separate kingdom for three hundred years. Then, a third force came from outside—the British people came. From the beginning, okay, it was bad. But by the sixteenth or seventeenth century it was established. Sher Shah's people did a lot of development. Akbar did a lot of work. So when a third force comes, the people decide, "I have to live here"'. Finally, when I ask him about his own identity, Singh says *Bharat, Bharati, and Bharatiya*—"India, Indian, Indianization"'.

Singh demonstrated the suffusion of the genetic model into his understanding of Indian history in several ways. First, his narrative assumes an 'India' that exists from the age of the Mauryas until today despite the fact that almost none of the residents of the sub-continent in Ashoka's time would understand what that term meant. Second, he assumes a singleness for India that allows it to be de-scribed in the singular as *sona chidiya*, represented by a single tradition and society that Man Singh, among others, betrays and in doing so, turns 'against all native Indians'. This category of 'native Indians' stands in contrast with two other categories as evidenced by Singh's use of the terms 'third force' and those 'from outside' in the descrip-tion of different groups. The first mention of a 'third force' is in the context of Akbar's rule and refers to Man Singh, who falls out of the 'native Indian' category when he allies with the Mughals, those 'from outside'. In the context of 1857, 'third force' is used as a synonym for the British who arrive 'from outside' India. Of the other two groups, one is composed of those (Muslims) who decide 'I have to live here' and includes those who contributed to India's development such as Sher Shah and Akbar; the other category is, by implication, those who already 'live here'. Note how imperfectly the Mughals/Mus-lims transition takes place from being outsiders who employ traitors during Akbar's time to being outsiders inside, neither Indian nor Brit-ish. Overall, these are in Singh's worldview, 'Indians', 'outsiders', and those who fall somewhere in-between.

The consequences of this geo-genetic classification are readily apparent in the rhetoric and policies of the Hindutva (Hinduness) movement in India. Hindutva rhetoric depicts Muslims and Christians as either inherently non-Indian because they are not Hindu or, conversely, Indian only if they accept that they still are Hindu. Hindu, then, becomes the only indigenous religious category, encompassing almost all religions that originate in South Asia, such as Jainism and Sikhism, while people of other religions are tacitly excluded from the national category by associating them with a foreign religious category. Singh's self-description *'Bharat, Bharati,* and *Bharatiya'* asserts a singular identity that collapses place, nationality, and the propagation of an essential national character. It appears to be a more benign version of the standard Hindu militant mantra, *Hindu, Hindi, Hindutva.* This starkly definitive world-view allows no room for those who demonstrate, if not outright claim, an association with more than one religious tradition.

Because the nation relies on an exclusionary self-definition to distinguish and valourize itself, it defines a boundary of qualities that differentiates members from foreigners. And so the Hindutva leaders of contemporary India hail the supposed Hindu character of India's people and disparage Muslims and Christians as inherently either outsiders or converted insiders. 'Hindu', for Hindutva proponents, becomes the only indigenous religious category. Paradoxically, Hindutva activists harbour great suspicion of transnational identities even as they cultivate one among non-resident Indians (NRIs) throughout the world.

Overall, as Paul Gilroy has pointed out, imaginations of the nation weigh heavily in cultural studies. Secular scholars have too often acquiesced to the conflation of religions to nation. For instance, the electronic version of the *Encyclopedia of Religion*—the standard reference work for historians of religion—contains a synoptic outline table of contents that lists a number of regions and, within each, a selection of religions supposedly of that area. Despite the fact that India represents the third most Muslim-populated nation in the world, Islam does not appear under the heading of 'Indian religions', the implication being that Muslims do not practice an Indian religion. Islam, according to the outline listing, is a Middle Eastern religion, identified as such, one assumes, by its genetic origin (*Encyclopedia of Religion* 1995). As Gilroy suggests, this bias privileges the *routes* of a group rather than its *roots*. Influenced by Sherman Jackson's adaptation of Gilroy's terminology in his reflection on Muslims in America (Jackson 2002). I would argue for a critique of the evolutionary model dominant in religious studies of Islam.

The examples provided earlier demonstrate the dominance of routes over roots. Routes refer to the paths taken from the place of origin to elsewhere. This place by default must be 'outside', 'peripheral', or 'marginal' to the 'core', 'centre', or 'birthplace.' Routes involve migrations through places associated with others and their cultures. Religions, as human expressions, change with time and context and these changes become associated through this paradigm with the spatial and temporal distance from the origin and influence of the 'outsider' locals. As in studies of evolution, scholars track these changes over time and create new categories for groups as they differentiate to fit their environment. The Islamic world becomes divided according to Arab Islam, Indian Islam, Indonesian Islam and African-American Islam. Each represents a stop on the route from core to periphery with unique characteristics through association with those on the other side of local cultural boundaries. Meanwhile, within each of these categories are sub-classifications, including some that claim to be closer to the 'core' of the 'original' religion and others that demonstrate the influence of non-Muslims. Seen as inherently displaced, still from their origin via the historical route, these Muslims appear only as Muslims (albeit in a specific place). They are in a place but not of that place, like passengers in a transit lounge.

A common strategy of explaining Muslim behaviour that fails to conform to the expectations of the western category of Islam is to place it within a historical narrative in which Islam in some essential form becomes exposed to Hinduism and changes, either through mutation, adaptation, absorption, or degradation, depending on one's attachment to the purity of the supposedly essential form. Historicized, it loses its claim to the Islamic roots that offer the legitimacy of that label only, in the minds of many Muslims and scholars, in its association with and imitation of the *umma* of Mohammad. Not restricted to the study of Muslims in South Asia, this academic narrative describes the subcontinent as a massive cultural sponge that absorbs even the most headstrong of invaders until they become less recognizably what they were and no longer fit into the category with which they were associated, whether it be Persian Muslims or Turkish Muslims.

In juxtaposition to this view, scholarship might focus more on Muslim cultural roots. In the world-view of many north Indians, the quality of crops as well as humans depends on the environment in which they take root. Hence some Arampur residents described my complexion as changed after a year in their village due to my exposure to the local water and air. Many, if not most Muslims live amidst other religions and traditions, their cultural roots intertwining, complementing and competing not as isolated transplants but as part of a forest of local character that involves them in the lives of others at a level that transcends religion.

Sayyid Rushd echoes these notions of migration, enrooting, and change, as we sit talking one day with some other men in his courtyard. Nearby, the mausoleum of Rushd's uncle, a locally venerated Sufi, stands opposite the village's main mosque. At the moment, his house is empty of the many supplicants—Hindu, Muslim, and others—who come seeking the gift of healing that Rushd's father inherited from his uncle. I ask Rushd how long his family has lived in Arampur. 'We come from Arabia', he answers. 'The Adivasis were dark and short and uncivilized. The Aryans came and mixed with them. Due to the climate, there was a change in their complexion.'

Mapping Muslims challenges us to transcend the simple two-dimensionality of a roadmap image of routes from genetic centre and embrace a three-dimensional vision of individuals sharing multiple identities. Moreover, in contradistinction to the identities that may appear so clearly and definitively separated from each other, specific practices have long demonstrated the permeability, if not inconsequentiality, of these borders. In his encyclopedic *Things Indian* written in 1906, William Crooke quoted a British observer in Punjab who noted that Muslims there 'observe the feasts of both religions [Islam and Hinduism], and the fast of neither (Crooke 1972)'. A century later, our taxi driver in Toronto also demonstrated the indefinite character of many borders, by identifying himself in the space of a short drive, as a Muslim, Bengali, Bangladeshi, Canadian resident, and celebrant of Hindu holidays. Clearly, humans, including those of displaced origin and contemporary cultural sustenance, often have more than one set of roots.

The lives of the residents of Arampur offer many more examples of the lives of enrooted Indian Muslims. One of the most vivid examples of these emerges in a discussion with Sakin Ansari about the castes of India's independence leaders as we sit surrounded by merchandize in the small niche he calls his store. His white money box has two Indian flag stickers so as to be visible to both passersby and prospective customers. Ansari identifies the *jati* of B.R. Ambedkar, Jawaharlal Nehru, and Mohandas Gandhi but does not know that of Maulana Azad.

Me: '*Musalman* have caste?'

Ansari: 'There are many in India. There are only three in Arabia—Quraish, Hashmi, and Ansari.' When I then ask him if his family comes from Arabia, he replies in the affirmative. When I ask when, he replies, 'At least 1500 years ago. I cannot say. There were conversions'. The Arabs first came to India for business purposes. Then Chishti came, he taps a poster of this Sufi's tomb in Ajmer, 'to teach about Islam'. When asked about Muslim *jati*s, he mentions the Pathans, Oajjams, Shaiss, Dhobis, Dafali, Sabzi Farosh, and Teli before adding, 'There are forty to fifty *Musalman jatis*; all are Mohammedan'. I ask if there is intermarriage among them and he replies, 'No. Among *Musalman* there is no restriction—"In the name of religion, all are one"—but due to caste there is no intermarriage'.

'Why is there caste?'

'After coming to India, *Musalman* took titles.'

'Were there any conversions?'

'The Islamic religion is very old. It started with Adam.'

'Were there any conversions?'

'[The village of] Naugrah converted in Aurangzeb's time'. Referring to a popular local narrative about two Rajput brothers who settled in two villages, one of which converted to Islam. Reaching into a shoe box on one of the goods-laden shelves, he pulls out some Urdu magazines. He opens to an article that describes Aurangzeb's gift of land for a performance of the Ram Lila, and then renders his own English translation of a poem by Mohammad Iqbal:

'Religion does not teach hostility towards others; we are Indian, our home is India.'

Many Indian Muslims, like those of their neighbours, have calendars in their homes and places of work depicting landscapes, toddlers, flower arrangements, etc. Prem Chaudhari, a local cloth merchant, sends his most important customers calendars with pictures selected according to their religion—images of Mecca, Medina, Ajmer and Agra for the Muslims, and pictures of Varanasi and Mathura for the Hindus—every year. Yet, despite the similitude in form, this difference in content feeds some sentiment that Muslims remain foreigners and non-Indians. In a discussion about the 1995 Oklahoma City bombing that devastated a federal government office building in the United States, Ravan Tripathi, while relaxing in conversation on the white divan of Chaudhari's cloth shop concludes, 'It was done by the Pakistanis. It's the same type of bomb that was used elsewhere. Is America your motherland? They do not have a motherland. Only Mecca is their motherland'.

The concepts of 'syncretic', 'hybrid', and 'liminal' Muslims offer important opportunities for understanding Muslim groups that appear to transcend normative expectations of behaviour, belief, and identity as demonstrated in the paper of Shail Mayaram, and others in this volume. Yet scholarship must exercise caution in regard to the assumptions inherent in dominant classificatory schema. These concepts presume a limit that often implies a centre. In religious studies and in some religious movements, the centre often becomes conflated with the place of the tradition's origin. Because categories tend to be defined according to a core characteristic and distinguished from others by heavily demarcated boundaries, it can be tempting to describe members of the category according to a measure of where they stand in relation to the core of their group and outsiders. By relying too heavily on such a model and on the Christian and scientific paradigms from which it is derived, we circumscribe beliefs and practices with impenetrable borders where none may exist. This may unwittingly privilege some positions as 'core' and negatively taint those associated with the terms 'syncretic', 'hybrid', and 'liminal'. Overall, these issues may imply a normative 'essence' or 'nature' for a religion and threaten to draw academics into theology.

In as much as there is an answer to this conundrum, surely it does not lie in the abandonment of categorization or disregard of history—the first would be impossible and the second naïve. Instead, it may be beneficial to complement diachrony with synchrony. Just as a diachronous view may trace the route of a subgroup geographically, a simultaneous synchronous view helpfully allows for a three-dimensional perspective that links individual members not only to one group but to many, sharing identities rooted in their place in the present.

We cannot escape classification systems—they are inherent to our perception of the world. We cannot pretend that people identifying themselves as Hindus or Muslims at various times have themselves not employed concrete classifications. But secular scholars need to be more sensitive to the manner in which a system creates categories of groups, the members of which may be valued differently due to their inclusion in them. Scholars also need more awareness of the roots and impact of Western classification systems. The practice of categorization not only differentiates between individuals but also constructs conditions of differentiation for individuals. The categorization of Muslims according to the cultural roots of their contemporary lives and not simply their historical routes from some distant heartland demands a three-dimensional map that encompasses the multiple identities and diverse layers of individual self-expression and interpersonal relationships.

References

Boyarin, Daniel. 2001. One Church; One Voice: The Drive Towards Homonoia in Orthodoxy (The Arian Controversy and Talmudic Judaism), *Religion & Literature* 33 (2), (Summer).

Crooke, William. 1972 (1906). *Things Indian: Being Discursive, Notes on Various Subjects Connected with India*, Oriental Books Reprint Corporation, New Delhi.

Encyclopedia of Religion (electronic version) 1995 (1987). Macmillan Publishing Company, New York.

Freeman Scott, and Jon C. Herron. 1998. *Evolutionary Analysis*, Upper Saddle Brook, Prentice Hall, New Jersey.

Gilroy, Paul. 1993. *The Black Atlantic: Modernity and Double Consciousness*, Harvard University Press, Cambridge, Mass.

Jackson, Sherman. 2002. African American Muslims and Black Religion in the U.S., Presentation at Presenting & Re-Presenting Islam, The University of Texas at Austin, 22 March.

Middle Eastern Studies Association Website accessed 28 February 2003. <w3fp.arizona.edu/mesassoc/mesainfo.htm>

Schleiermacher, Friedrich. 1958 (1799). *On Religion: Speeches to its Cultured Despisers*, John Oman, trans., Harper & Rowm, New York.

2

Beyond Ethnicity? Being Hindu *and* Muslim in South Asia

SHAIL MAYARAM

Introduction

With the bombing of the World Trade Centre and the wars in Afghanistan and Iraq, Huntington's fault lines seem to have become a self-fulfilling prophecy spurred on as they are by the will to empire.[1] In the South Asian subcontinent, nationalist imaginaries have become viciously real in the last decade as the cities of its nation-states are cleaved into a myriad partitions, signifying otherness. Even as the contemporary globe seems pervaded by

This paper owes its shaping to the lively debate at the Goa seminar on Lived Islam and conversations on this and other occasions with Ashis Nandy, T.N. Madan, Deepak Mehta and J.P.S. Uberoi; to colleagues at CSDS on whom some of these ideas have been tried at the lunchtime 'seminar'; to Daya Krishna who has often been my first reader/listener; and to early discussions with Lloyd and Susanne Rudolph. I also must acknowledge my membership in another fellowship for over a year, that of the Ramachandra Gandhi Seminar (2002–3) where the discussion has ranged from *advaita* to violence and from Sri Ramana Maharishi and Ramakrishna Paramhans to Buddha, Christ, and Gandhi. My thanks apart from Ramachandra Gandhi, to Anjana, Vidya and Punam Zutshi, Fr Devasiya and Shankar Ramaswami. For the argument and all its flaws I alone am responsible.

[1]Eric Hobsbawm points out that the new American Empire has achieved a global reach that no other former empire has ever achieved. *The Guardian*, 14 June 2003.

boundaries, fabricated and otherwise, at no time has there been greater interest in the blurring, transgression, and, indeed, defiance of religious boundaries, in the dissent within religious traditions and the dialogues between them both on the part of theologians and as a constituent of everyday life. This is a relatively new interest but an extremely important one.

My own work began in the broad area of the Hindu-Muslim question investigating modes of conflict and violence, between state and community and between communities. I have, however, gradually realized that what one centrally needs to address alongside the question of ethnic conflict is the project of 'living together' both in the past and in our troubled present. Regrettably what are completely glossed in the burgeoning genre of ethnic studies are the shared mythic and ritual spaces between groups whom we today refer to as Hindu or Muslim; the networks that came into being across religions; the vast arena of interaction that I have elsewhere described as medical pluralism; the political formations and civil society experiences of Hindus and Muslims working together and how human agency can intervene to repair, heal and build bridges even after apocalyptic genocide.

What has been ignored is the large number of communities who are or were simultaneously Hindu and Muslim. The origins of this paper come from a restlessness with the established ways of under-standing religions and cultures exclusively in terms of boundary and closure and from the neglect of a vast terrain of cultural and religious interaction that gets manifest as conflict and competition, but also something more that is quite inadequately referred to as coexistence and in fact, might even involve a celebration of the other.

This paper addresses a question I have visited before in my work which is, as the title suggests, what does it mean to be simultaneously Hindu and Muslim? The partners of the combine can easily be substituted by other combinations involving being simultaneously Hindu *and* Christian or Muslim *and* Sikh/Christian *and* Buddhist/ Jewish and Christian. The early part of the paper will appraise some of this complex ethnic universe in South Asia and elsewhere. The second part of the paper will review the conceptual vocabulary used to describe this universe. I regard this section, to use a Sufi metaphor, as a further *maqam* (station, halting place) in a journey that has time and again negotiated with and interrogated the idea of the syncretic and also attempted to contend with the question of an alternative that will describe states of identity that are seen as mixed, impure, even heretic and most certainly, confused and a source of contamination. I conclude with a more contemporary case from our times of a person whose self-description was of a Hindu-Christian monk. The larger issue I have lived with for some time is, how do these states of living, feeling and being, destabilize boundaries of religion, sect and denomination? In terms of numbers this refers to the cultures of a fairly substantial population since the South Asian population comprises one-fifth of the world's population (Stein 2001). The region is home to the largest concentration of Muslim population in the world.

Three significant themes need to be foreground in the contemporary discussion of religious identities: the consequences of cultural encounter for the histories of castes and communities; the possibility of dual or triple religious affiliation expressed openly or unconsciously; and, dimensions of liminality articulated through varied registers. These manifest as a series of identities that are seen as 'border line Muslims', 'half Hindus' or 'half Muslims', or 'half Christian' (whatever the components of the 'half' may be).

How does one approach the theme of cultural encounter? One obvious way in the subcontinent is to narrate a history of conquest, iconoclasm, conflict and underwrite a politics of writing historical wrong. But there are other ways. The political theorist, Rajeev Bhargava, uses the metaphor of the palimpsest, the idea that something is altered yet bears traces of its original form.[2] One visualizes here a stone that is constantly written over or an artist's palette, witness to the magical play of colours, the emergence of endless new shades through flow and combination. We know of Tibetan civilization that became Buddhist but could not quite overwrite its past of the Bon religion (Snellgrove 1967). The pilgrimage site of Mount Kailash is resonant with the overlapping symbolism that is Hindu and Jain, Buddhist and Bon and is what draws the inveterate Himalayan trekker, philosopher-psychoanalyst Madhu Sarin season after season. Fisher's recent ethnography of the Thakali of Nepal who inhabit the borderlands of central Nepal wryly comments that scholars have seen Hinduism, Buddhism and shamanism together intensifying their influence on the Thakali (Fisher 2001). Sylvain Levi commented in 1905, that the traditions of Hinduism and Buddhism are so closely

---

[2]Presentation, at, International Conference on Living Together Separately: Cultural India in History and Politics, organized by Academy of Third World Studies, Jamia Millia Islamia, New Delhi, 19–21 December 2002.

interwoven in Nepal that it made no sense to see Nepalese gods as either Hindu or Buddhist.

The Indian subcontinent is not unique in this respect. From Indonesia to the Maghreb a range of scholarships have described the fascinating negotiation between Islamic textual models and pre-Islamic worlds. Even as the contemporary Afghan has been frozen into the Taliban terrorist, we know the long tradition in Afghanistan of adaptation to both Islam and Pakhtunwali/Pushtunwali, the legal and moral code that frames the social order and might even be in opposition to the shariah. Ethnographers have described Afghan identity with its blood feud and own interpretation (some would call distortion!) of Islam. The good violent Pathan in Tagore's *Kabuli wallah* (1916), is a case in point.

The coming of Islam and Christianity to the Indian subcontinent resulted in a phenomenal cultural encounter. India's encounter with Islam opened up new connections with West Asia, just as Buddhism linked India with East Asia (Kulke 1990). 'Conversion' intensified the available plurality that had already seen the efflorescence of the *vaidika* and non-*vaidika* religions, the challenge of the *sramana* traditions of Buddhism and Jainism, the many *adivasi* cosmologies, the atheist Carvaka and the *agamika-tantrika* schools as also the wave of devotional traditions that would become such a prominent theme through the medieval period. Friedhelm Hardy refers, in addition, to the somewhat autonomous world of *gramya* or village religion that involved, from the point of view of the *vaidika* Brahman, heterodox vulgarities of village cults involving the consumption of alcohol, smoking opium, shedding blood, killing animals, eating meat, states of possession (Hardy 1995). South Asia has had more complex identities than any other region of the world.

The idea that peoples, regions and cultures have had more than one religious affiliation, however unacknowledged and silenced, has gained some currency. Ashis Nandy reminds us that for a Japanese it is possible to be simultaneously both Shinto and Buddhist. Shintoism, the original religion of Japan, involved the worship of local deities called *kami* that were later introduced into Buddhism so that Buddha and Bodhisattvas were identified with local deities.[3] Similarly in China no absolute boundary demarcated Buddhism from Confucianism

---

[3]A Japanese has been known to respond to the question, are you Buddhist or Shinto? with the mocking answer, Shinto is our religion for times of happiness and Buddhism for times of sorrow!

(the cult of the ancestors). A community in Vietnam continues to incorporate both Hindu Ahier Cham and Muslim Awal Cham sections, representing the yang (male) and yin (female) principles, respectively.

In South Asia, some enumerations relating to India mention 600 odd bi-religious communities and there are even thirty-eight tri-religious communities according to K. Suresh Singh (Singh 1992, cited in Nandy 1995). Describing these groups in terms of bi-religiosity and tri-religiosity, however, presents problems as these categories elude the rather high levels of internal differentiation within these communities. Further, the phenomenon of overlapping and blurring of identities is far more pervasive than has hitherto been suspected and I will merely indicate the range in the subcontinent which requires far greater attention from researchers.

We know today of a large number of identities that have at a historical juncture occupied an interstitial space, straddling two or more religious traditions. My own familiarity is with the Muslim Meos of India and Pakistan, who are today one of the largest Muslim communities of the subcontinent and with the Merat of north-western India. The Rawat-Chita-Merat comprise a complex group formerly called the Mer and were divided into Hindu-Muslim-Christian sections. Significantly the Hinduism of the Hindu Rawat was described as hardly recognizable and the Muslimness of the Merat was viewed as similarly evanescent! They not only intermarried but their cosmologies inhabited by gods, goddesses, spirits, pirs, and ancestors were shared. The psychologist, Morris Carstairs, describes secret cults called *kunda* or *kachli panth* whose practices challenged the dominant discourse with respect to caste, gender and sexuality so that even what is called incest is redescribed as a mode of worship (Carstairs 1961).

Across the subcontinent there are many groups whose cultures suggest that it is possible to be simultaneously Hindu and Muslim. Castes and communities associated with storytelling and the performing art traditions in South Asia have had particularly nubile identities. In western India the Langas, the Manganiyars and the Mirasis also defy categorial classification.[4] In eastern India the role of the Baul singers is particularly illustrative. These singers are classified as Muslim but their identity transcends our simplistic classifications, 'Hindu' and 'Muslim' and is expressed in one of the world's most profound traditions of mystical music. I have a lurking suspicion that Jayadeva's poetry that carries Krishna bhakti to new heights might

[4]See Kothari in conversation with Bharucha (Bharucha 2003).

have absorbed the theme of love that is sensual and adulterous from Baul songs. It is no coincidence that the annual congregation of some 10,000 Bauls takes place where Jayadeva, the author of *Gita Govinda* was born. This twelfth century lyrical masterpiece became crucial to the making of a new literary culture in India as it inspired music, painting, sculpture and drama. Gayatri Spivak writes of the 'poetic counter theology' of the famous Baul singer, Lallan Shah fakir (1774– 1890) in which *advaita* becomes the abstract God of Islam. The *nirakar*, the formless, combines with the dualist urge to *rupa* (manifestation or form) so that Khadija, Mohammad's eldest wife is Allah (*je khodija a sher to khobai*) but also the chief goddess (Spivak 1999). Nietzsche recognizes this impetus as the Dionysian, and Kierkegaard as the 'erotic sensual genius of music' (Kierkegaard 1944). Little wonder that utopias that represented model projects of state engineering preferred to exile poets and musicians! They represent the Khattam-Shud of Rushdie's story, the sinister tyrant who presides over the dark land of Chup, and whose name means 'completely finished', 'over and done with'. Khattam-Shud is 'the Arch-Enemy of all Stories, even of Language itself.'

Like the cultures of performing artists, those of peasant and pastoral tribe-castes have hitherto been 'mixed'. I deliberately use the hyphenated tribe-caste to highlight that these were also not walled-off social formations. The data is telling. The 1921 Census records that there were 47.3 per cent Hindu and 33.4 per cent Muslim Jats (besides others who were Sikh). In this respect they were similar to the Rajputs (27.7 per cent Muslim and 70.7 per cent Hindu) and Gujars (25.3 per cent and 74.2 per cent Muslim) (Edye and Tennant 1923). Wink points out that the culture of Jats and Gujars had a significant Persian component (1990:138). The Ahirs likewise had Muslim branches even as the Mewatis and Mirasis had Hindu populations.

Ruling and warrior castes and the so-called Sudra castes of the subcontinent also suggest significant religious complexity. In the region of Rajasthan, with which I am more familiar, the category 'Muslim' includes the Musalman Rajputs, Khanzadas, Desi Musalman, Kayamkhanis and Sindhi Sipahis (Kothari 1984). In Uttar Pradesh we know of the Malkanas who claimed to be neither Hindus nor Muslims and preferred to be called Mian Thakur. Helena Basu points out that the Jadeja Rajputs of Gujarat who were described as 'half Muslim' employed African (Muslim) Sidi slaves as cooks.[5]

[5]Presentation, International Conference on Lived Islam, Goa, 5–7 December 2002.

Some of this description comes from the early censuses of the twentieth century, that one can see as a dialectic between the imposition of homogeneity by the state and a mirroring of ethnic complexity that emerges from the interstices. Regrettably research on the Census, as Peterson points out, has ignored mixed identities with the exception of the Anglo-Indians (Peterson 1997). The world of scholarship, in general, has not given much cognizance to the phenomenon of overlapping identities, interpenetrating cultures and religions, and the transgression of boundaries. Only now as ethnicity, nationalism, militarization overtake the worlds we inhabit and boundaries are etched in blood and genocidal violence have we woken up to the realization that possibly the world itself, its past and present, needs to be described differently. There is some very significant recent work on South Asia that challenges ethnic faultlines (see, for instance, Silva 2002; Gilmartin and Lawrence 2000; Gottschalk 2001). The importance of these cultures for both the writing of history and ethnography and the larger understanding of religion and cultural encounter can hardly be overemphasized.

This is not to deny that the boundary making enterprise is not also a constant for the worlds these cultures inhabit as also within themselves. State Shintoism is quick to decry the mixing of popular Japanese practice. Official recognition of the Bon religion from Tibetan Buddhism dates only to the current Dalai Lama who has recognized it as a living tradition. Reformist and purist trends in state and civil society have frequently sought to purge the popular of 'corrupt' and 'depraved' practices. Performing artists have been recruited by nationalist ideologues, Hindu, Muslim, Sikh.

The discussion that follows will be an attempt to theorize the notions of syncretism and liminality. It goes without saying that cultures are not static and are constantly changing and shifting in terms of religious affiliation and are highly internally differentiated. While the existential universe will be drawn upon what I elaborate are really ideal typical forms. Actual and living cultures might approximate, but will never conform to this abstraction.

Challenges of Conceptualizing this Universe: Liminality

When I first began my work on the Meos of India and Pakistan a decade ago there was hardly any vocabulary that would capture the complexity of a culture that was simultaneously Hindu and Muslim. The search for a language to describe the phenomenon of blurring and interaction has taken scholars in varying directions advocating varied concepts such as ambiguity, fuzziness, the idea of the border and frontier, the hybrid, and, of course, the age-old syncretic. Some of this work marks a shift of interest from boundary to borderlands, borders being conceived as frontiers that are zones of interaction. This reverses the erstwhile conception of the frontier as a space to be mastered and conquered by an imperial/racial project.[6] Anzaldua asserts, 'To survive the Borderlands you must live *sin fronteras* (without frontiers) be a crossroads' (Anzaldua 1987). Border zones are seen as arenas of partially realized identities, manifest contradictions and deliberate ambiguity. Uberoi (1999) elaborates on this using the metaphor of a revolving door for Afghanistan. Islam comes in through one door and Buddhism goes out through another.

I myself began to play with the alternative formulation of liminality, a term that had up to then been used primarily to understand ritual following van Gennep's conceptualization in his famous *Rites of Passage*. Victor Turner's performative approach that looked at social drama further elaborated the idea of the liminal in ritual contexts (Turner 1974). The state of being liminal, or liminality, refers to being between two statuses. The word is derived from *limen*, the Latin word for threshold that Turner formulated as 'A no-man's-land betwixt-and-between ... a fructile chaos, a fertile nothingness, a storehouse of possibilities ... a striving after new forms and structures.' Liminality became a convenient shorthand to indicate a third space that does not presuppose binarism but seeks to transcend the binary mode of thought and understanding. It might even suggest ways in which binary identities are contested, however, unconsciously.

The current conception of liminality has gone far beyond the anthropological usage of characterizing modes of ritual being and has been used to refer to space and time; and culture and agency. It is not just people in conjunction with rites of passage that may be in a liminal state. There may be time periods that are liminal as well. That is, certain times of day or times of year may be between one state and another. Dawn and dusk suggest rhythms of daily liminal periods. Times that fall between seasons are instances of calendrical liminality.

[6]Elsewhere, I have critiqued the syncretic and the hybrid as inadequately theorized formulations of the subject under discussion (Mayaram 1988).

Liminality has been used to understand geographic space (water and forests), architecture and literary texts, the human body (say, in adolescence) and mythology, folklore and religion. One of the prototypical images of animals in folklore was that of a wolf-headed man, the prototype of the werewolves of subsequent folk belief (Lionarons 1994). In some of the literature it is argued that binarism needs a third component: the liminal space between the two opposites. This space is what myth ultimately allows us to articulate. Liminality is even advertised as not concerned with the old strategies of the edge and the marginal but as offering a kickstart for new performance practices in this new century, as bestowing a new way to experiment and create using the in-between spaces, the interstices.

At the turn of the millennium, liminality has acquired a certain academic respectability and even an avant garde status. Liminality has even been exaggeratedly valorized as fluid, open, unfixed, inclusive, and diverse. Liminal states are often described as occasions for licence, where people are allowed or even expected to do things that would be forbidden during the everyday, organized life of ordinary time or of people who have a clearly defined social status. There is now even in existence a *Journal for Liminal Phenomena*, concerned with the theory and practice of liminal phenomena. But the attendant problems relating to its theorization for cultural practice need to be posed far more sharply.

Since there has been considerable debate on the concept, I use this essay to clarify aspects of my own usage. First, as a concept, liminality is an abstraction and not an empirical description. Second, its application will always have to be historicized and contextualized. Third, the liminal is not another categorical identity such as Hindu or Muslim. Hence, one cannot pronounce on an entire culture or person as liminal, but use it to illumine aspects of being and belonging and suggest at the political location of an identity in relation to the institutional fabric of state and religion. Why does one need such a concept? It helps identify a range of identities and locations across religions and cultures and consider them in terms of a common framework and as facing a set of shared problems.

The following propositions clarify the concept of liminality for purposes of political sociology:

1. That there exist groups, sections of groups, or paths charted by individual identities that relate to one or more religious traditions.

2. That these groups or persons manifest facets of in-betweenness

in their belief and practice (including aspects of their expressive and symbolic culture).

3. That these have been viewed in terms of inferiority and spuriousness from the perspective of institutions, religious and others.

4. That these groups are usually highly creative in terms of their theologies. Since they challenge established theologies they intimate contestations and alternative visions.

5. If this third space may be characterized as one of liminality, its very impurity and capacity to creolize is seen as dangerous from the perspective of state and religious authority.

6. These identities then are often characterized by a marginality that derives from the discourse of both state and religion (both in the upper instance).

7. Historically, liminality manifests itself as a moment that is particularly fragile since it is subject to ruling cultures and hegemonic ideologies that seek to absorb, appropriate and distort their visions and agendas.

8. Liminal identities may appear as weak and fragile, but in fact, they are subject to enormous violence and pressures to conform manifest in the attempt to singularize, reform and domesticate these identities.

9. Their importance lies in just the fact of their appearance and in that they provide fresh and original perspectives on ways of thinking, feeling and being.

10. Liminality does not have to do with vanished, pre-modern identities but also with contemporary quests for selfhood and transcendence.

11. Liminality has crucial implications for intercultural and inter-religious dialogue.

I have elaborated on the concept of liminality in some detail, so as to prepare the ground for the distinction with syncretism that follows. As I conclude this section let me not leave my reader with the impression of a 'good' liminal. Liminality is also the site of violence, patrilineal, sectarian and other. It is also capable of reversal and of transforming itself into an invented 'pure' identity and purging aspects of contaminatinating 'impurity'. It must necessarily then relate to the anthropology of the present.

It is true that we know very little about the inner worlds of these cultures. Often liminality does not arise from a self-reflexive position, but may be quite unconscious. Let me amplify what might be one such inner world with the instance of the Meos. For the last fifty years Meos have been deeply involved in the Tablighi Jamat and have over a period of time come to virtually dominate the Islami Markaz. This is the headquarter of the Tablighi Jamat, from which the global activities of the Islamizing Jamats or parties working in over 150 countries are controlled. And yet one could find tucked away in their oral tradition, in their narratives and in their music, vestiges of a totally different world view.

It is a Meo who composed the Mewati Mahabharata in the early eighteenth century. It continues to be performed by Mirasi and Jogi singers, both Muslim performing art communities, for Meo and non-Meo audiences. The frames of this regional epic prepare the listener for a novel journey into their mythopoetic world as the *bismillah* (the opening sura of the Quran meaning 'In the name of Allah') goes on to invoke the divine feminine. In an episode of the epic, the Mewati poet-composer Sadulla, amplifies the rivalry of the cousins. The mother of the one hundred Kauravas, Gandhari, asks her sons to make her an elephant of cowdung and mud so that she can make an offering of water to the Sun God, Surya. She taunts the mother of the Pandavas, Kunti, who is so envious that she gives up eating. Arjun then obtains a divine elephant from Raja Indra, the king of the gods, to enable Kunti's worship of the sun. This worship of Surya is also a metaphor for the birth of their sixth brother, Karna, begot from the Sun God.

The opening frame of the folk-epic invokes both goddess and guru. The guru is the great medieval ascetic, Gorakhnath. Both goddess and guru we know relate to kingship. In the Meo case, the two figures suggest Meos' self-representation as the warrior caste of Kshatriyas. This Kshatriya status meant claims to entitlements of political power and the autonomy of their polity that was based on an institutional arrangement of dispersed rather than concentrated power (Mayaram 1999). It generated a sensibility that brought them into recurrent confrontation with the Turko-Afghan Sultanate and the Mughal Empire between the thirteenth and eighteenth centuries; with the eighteenth century kingdom of Amber/Jaipur and with the Bharatpur and Alwar kingdoms; and the British Raj in the nineteenth and twentieth centuries. As I have pointed out elsewhere, the Meos have a history of sustained resistance to the state that is unparalleled anywhere in the world and one that is documented by state and community for nearly eight centuries (for details, see Mayaram 1997; Mayaram forthcoming).

A verse from the Meo oral tradition highlights the historical consciousness of the Meos that brought them into conflict with Turkish Sultans like Balban (r. 1266–1286) and Mughal Emperors such as Akbar (r. 1556–1605):

kahañ huñhuñ vahi hasti jo har hamlavaron se takrai
jo shahanshahon se kabhi mat na khayi
kahañ dhundhuñ vahi hasti jo balban se takr ayi
jo jalaluddin akbar se kabhi to mat na khayi

Where can I find those warriors
that confronted every invader
who were undefeated by Emperors?
Where can I find those warriors
who matched swords with Balban
and did not even succumb to Jalaluddin Akbar?

In the early years of my work with Mewati narratives, I was assisted by two Mewati *maulvis* who are currently based in Delhi. Maulvi Subban is now involved with the Tablighi Jamat, but runs a flourishing practice of what is called *ruhani ilaj* (healing through the spirit) using the power of Quranic verses to heal and solve everyday problems. Both he and Maulana Rahim shared the Tablighi aversion to music. Mirasi musicians no longer sang at ritual occasions in their families. To my surprise, however, it was these two 'orthodox Islamists' who managed to improve on my version of the Mewati Mahabharata recorded from a Mirasi. Maulvi Subban told me of how Bhima who has the strength of a hundred elephants, receives from his mother, the strength of ten more. This is to help him fight the Kichak of Bairath whose wicked eye is on Drupada (Draupadi). And Maulana Rahim revealed to me the real identity of Drupada as the goddess. Guru Goraknath and Drupada, the goddess, were the guarantors of Meo kingliness.

The Meo world(s) were extremely dynamic and internally heterogeneous in terms of sectarian influence and affiliation. Elsewhere, I have described how religious sects were considerably open ended and their membership fluid as there was a constant lateral movement of Meos drawn to Vaishavism, the Nath Panth, *nirgun bhakti* (the worship of a formless God) or to various Sufi lineages. Some Meos were also involved with the Rasulshahis and the Madariyyas regarded as heterodox sects given to mystic intoxication and ascetic nakedness as they wore only a loincloth. But Meo identity derived from numerous

sources including from their interaction with states and strong attachment to land; their mythic memory as ruler-warriors and pastoral
and other migration; from gender relations and a religious culture
that was simultaneously Hindu, Muslim, and regional as it shared
in the religious culture of the Brajbhasha speaking area. The sharing
did not necessarily imply an eternal peaceful coexistence. Indeed,
sharing itself needs to be problematized and can be overwritten by
other countervailing interests. It certainly did not preclude violence,
say when two rival communities competed for the benefaction of the
goddess!

From the perspective of state and religious authority the Meos
were 'degenerate' and 'lax Mohammedans'. Colonial ethnographers
commented on the 'spurious character' of their Islam, ignorant as
they were even of its basic precepts. They were said to keep the feasts
of all religions, and the fasts of none! Having been one of the most
insurgent communities in the Revolt of 1857, they were stamped
with the label of a criminal tribe and it was pronounced that they
had added to their original evil disposition the blood-thirstiness of
Mohamaddan fanatics. Race, caste and criminality were the backbone
of colonial anthropology and history that was in aid of the colonial
state.

Liminality and Syncretism

In this section I revise my earlier dismissal of the syncretic and will
attempt to stand the syncretic as usually understood on its head.
(See, for a discussion, Stewart and Shaw 1994). The syncretic is a
concept that emanates from an official discourse whose philosophical
presuppositions involve the idea of the purity of the self and the
impurity of the 'other', that the syncretic is somehow 'out there' in
popular, folk or otherwise low-brow cultural practice. Without denying
the original character of revelation or religion, I would argue that the
syncretic is also constitutive of the theologies of the 'world religions'.
Lest one have delusions of the purity of world religious/civilizations/
cultures, the idea of the syncretic has a limited use, i.e. to reinforce
the idea that there are no original pure situations. Indeed, liminality
can be contrasted with the syncretism of world religions, i.e. the
mainstream of texts, beliefs and practices of the 'world religions'.

A range of new research has brought out the syncretisms of world
religions. There are the hypothesized beginnings of Christianity from

the dissenting Jewish sect of the Essenes; the Jewishness of Jesus; and the derivation of aspects of Christian and Judaic belief such as the worship of the Madonna or the celebration of feasts and festivals from pagan traditions. Hence, Gunkel's description of Christianity as syncretic. The view of the Christian community as separate and distinct from Judaism. Van der Veer has highlighted that the very term syncretism is associated with the rise of Protestantism and the decline of the absolute authority of Catholicism that had pronounced on the syncretic as the heretical (Van der Veer 1994).

The association of Mecca with the pagan ritual involving priestesses of three goddesses has frequently been written about. The Egyptian feminist writer, Nawal El-Saadawi, pointed out that the practice of kissing the black stone housed in the Ka'ba shrine derives from pre-Islamic practice. She has since been accused of heresy and almost forced to divorce her husband in accordance with a law that requires Muslims not to remain married to apostates. Ismailism draws upon Pythagoras and Aristotle, Christianity and the Manicheans and upon Judaism. Sufism grew in Mesopotamia, Eastern Iran, and Khorasan where it was influenced by Buddhist monastic ideals. Later period influences included those of neo-Platonism, Christianity and Central Asian and Indian asceticism (For a discussion, see Schimmel 1992).

In South Asia, Dumont viewed orthodox Brahmanism as syncretic contrasted with a sect. Puranic syncretism has been pointed out frequently (Chakrabarti 2001). Sikh holy scripture incorporated the verses of Kabir and Farid I or Farid II and Bhikan the Sufi (Uberoi 1999). That syncretism is strategically deployed in the history of religions has been demonstrated again and again. Eaton shows in relation to Bengal how syncretism was actually used to further conversion. Distancing himself from the use of orthodox and unorthodox, fundamentalist and syncretic as unproductive terms, Eaton argues that Islam in Bengal absorbed an enormous amount of local culture so that it was never regarded as foreign. Eaton maintains that it is inappropriate to speak of 'conversion' of Hindus to Islam, instead what occurred in the Bengal context was an expanding agrarian civilization whose cultural counterpart was the growth of the cult of Allah. A simultaneous syncretism and anti-syncretism is manifest in movements of social and religious reform such as the Brahmo and Arya Samaj and more recently in the Vishva Hindu Parishad.

In the west the so-called New Age Religion has produced new sycretic combinations. One version combines *tantra*, *wicca*, spirit possession and Christianity. There is in existence a highly syncretic post modern Christianity. Wilson mentions that nearly a quarter of the west's Christian population now believes in reincarnation rather than a realizable Heaven. There is also a new emphasis on Christ's humanity, his role as an ethical teacher rather than merely on divinity. Ideas of the Original Sin (of children having been born of sin) and of damnation have similarly been given up (Wilson 1999). Feminist theologians have been emphasizing the idea of a gender-neutral God who ought to substitute the idea of God as exclusively male. Black cults are similarly syncretic variants of Islam and the Baptist religion. Further, syncretisms have married western ideas of individualism and liberalism with Christianity and socialism with Islam.

The question is how does one theorize these identities? For one thing Asian religions did not stress singularization that was associated with the institutional framework of Christianity and the idea of heresy. For people embedded in a traditional world religious view, liminality followed from a quest for the power of the transcendental. It meant, what has been called, a policy of double insurance: if one's own gods were not powerful enough, others might provide a better guarantee of the fulfilment of desire. For persons located in modernist contexts liminality derives from the quest for a moral life, in which inherited traditions might be drawn upon but are also subject to scrutiny and other spiritualities might become potential sources of insight and guides to living.

Lest it be concluded that liminality relates to only premodern, folk theologies one might mention two particularly well-known contemporary persons of our times. Ramakrishna Paramhans (1836–86), one of the greatest Indian sages and mystics, said to have experienced *moksha* in his lifetime, and who actually lived for brief durations as a practicing Muslim and Christian. *The Gospel of Ramakrishna* brings out how in his state of ecstatic illumination he experienced himself as a woman, Jew, Muslim, Jain and Buddhist as he beheld the varied manifestations of God, as Christ, Mohammad and also as the Divine Mother, as Sita and Rama and Krishna.

Gandhi's life and work illustrates the point. Ramachandra Gandhi points out Gandhi's rejection of exclusivist identities. 'He was a Hindu, but insisted that he was simultaneously also a Muslim, Christian, Jew, Buddhist, Jaina, etc.: a believer in the truth of all faiths' (Gandhi 1994: 9). Madan points out that his Ram Raj recalled no mythic Hindu past, but the Asokan vision of Dhamma (Madan 1998: 230–1). Gandhi also acknowledged the enormous influence of the moral teaching of Christianity on his thoughts particularly the Sermon on the Mount and declared, 'Jesus has given a definition of perfect *dharma*.'[7] Nandy has similarly pointed out that Gandhi's idiom cut across the boundaries of Christian, Hindu and Buddhist world views (Nandy 1992: 35). Saxena demonstrates the influence on Gandhi of the Jain notions of *syadvada* and *anekantada* that theorize the multiplicity of viewpoints (1988).

A keen interlocutor might further ask of this line of argument, may be it is easy to combine identities given a 'pagan', polytheistic worldview. Is liminality also possible for a person deep-rooted in a monotheistic tradition?

Conclusions

Let me conclude with the fascinating story of the French missionary, Dom Henri Le Saux (1910–73) who actually described himself as a Hindu Christian monk.[8] Known by the name Swami Abhishiktananda, he was profoundly influenced by *advaita* (the non-dual experience of the absolute brahman) but remained rooted in the Christian tradition. Indeed, he felt that the insights of the Upanishads helped him apprehend the deepest truths of Christianity. Ordained a priest of the Benedictine order in 1935, Abhishiktananda experienced a 'call of India' around the same period. After having studied Indian religious texts he expressed his desire to live in a hermitage around Tiruchirappalli in consonance with the monks of early Christianity and the traditions of Indian sannyasa. The following account draws from Abhishiktananda's writings (1975; 1988), Visvanathan's ethnography (1988) and Baumer's reflections (2000). Visvanathan maintains that Abhishiktananda came to India in 1948 as a 'missionary' in the conventional sense and a transition began within him soon after. A

[7]Indeed, Gandhi's first biographer commented, 'I question whether any system of religion can absolutely hold him. His views are too closely allied to Christianity to be entirely Hindu; and too deeply saturated with Hinduism to be called Christian, while his sympathies are so wide and catholic that one would imagine he has reached a point where the formulae of sects are meaningless' (cited in Madan 1998: 230n).

[8]Nandy (1995) describes the first case of a Hindu-Christian identity, that of Brahmabandhav Upadhyay, who believed that an Indian did not have to renounce Hinduism to adopt Christianity.

year later he took to saffron clothing abandoning his Benedictine habit and began visiting Hindu ashrams to learn about sannyasa. His encounter with Sri Ramana Maharshi affected a profound transformation in him. His early response to Sri Ramana on his first visit to Tiruvenmalai had been nonchalant (Why had he let himself be enthroned as Bhagvan?). But the chanting also moved him, 'as if the very soul of India penetrated to the very depths of my own soul and held a mysterious communion with it. It was a call which pierced through everything, rent it in pieces and opened a mighty abyss.' He wanted to visit the ashram again in 1952 but Sri Ramana had passed away. Again and again he received the call of Arunachala, the mountain that was also a Siva lingam and visited its caves and hermitages. Codes of vegetarianism, silence and total abandonment of all desire were self-imposed even as he experienced states of exaltation, joy and freedom. At the ashram he participated in the weekly three-hour long puja including the recitation of the many hundred names of the goddess.

Visvananthan points out how the two worlds that are normally seen as mutually exclusive religious universes in missionary discourse were apprehended very differently by him. Arunachala became the 'ultimate symbol of his own non-*advaitic* search. Shiv, the symbol of unity, became *aruna*, the rays of the rising sun, the rising of fire, the burning bush of Moses, the consuming fire of the Hebrews, the Light of the world, the Supreme light, the joyful light. Entering into the heart of Arunachala, was to enter the caves, the heart of the mystery, to enter the depths of the self, to live in the centre of his heart.' Vishvanathan foregrounds the quality of such an experiment, the possibility of participating in another world view, another state of being while holding on to one's own identity and religious faith.

This was no fashioning of a new synthetic order from two religions. Vishvanathan argues that Abhishiktananda sought a syncronicity between two different scriptures using key themes. Through *advaita* he reinterpreted the Trinity and the Eucharist in Christianity and Christ's Awakening. Abhishiktananda identified this moment of Jesus' Awakening that took place on the occasion of his baptism. When he came out of the waters, Jesus saw the heavens 'rent asunder', and thus the separation between heaven and earth, between man and God, was abolished, while the Spirit 'descended' thus filling the whole of space. Jesus then heard a voice, 'Thou art my Son' and responded, 'Abba (Father)'. 'This 'Son'/'Father' is the nearest equivalent in a

Semitic context to *'tattvamasi/'aham brahmasmi'* [Thou art That/I am brahman] which the Spirit utters through the mouth at the time of the *diksha* and the heart of both guru and disciple beyond all duality. This awakening marked Jesus' entire life and consciousness, all his words and actions. Even death did not compromise this awakening. On Easter he revealed himself in a range of human forms. At Pentecost and subsequently, Jesus continued to make his presence felt in the various manifestations of the Spirit. Death was his *mahasamadhi* (Abhishiktananda 1975).[9]

Visvanathan's later work details strands of Abhishiktananda's thought which contribute to a theory of dialogue. *Advaita* and Trinity were the central realities of the Abhishiktananda dialogical method. This offers a very different model of conversion 'as metanoia, as a change of heart and being' that is possible dialogically and 'how through the process of seeking and possible revelation one could begin to understand the other'.[10] Visvanathan goes on to draw a parallel between the 'mystical journeys' of Simone Weil and Abhishiktananda (Visvanathan 1998: ch 2). Simone Weil is, of course, the celebrated Jewish philosopher and trade union activist known for her experience of mystic revelation of Christ's presence. As Vishwanathan puts it, 'both stood on the axes of two domains, two worlds of thought. Simone Weil was a Jew whose encounter with revelation and mystical light came from Christianity; for Abhishiktananda, it was from Hinduism.' Both, however, continued to remain grounded in their own religions. There were, of course, differences in their genders and in their respective pilgrimages. Both were French, born at the same time (Weil was a year older and died prematurely in 1943, aged just 34 even as she was writing her most powerful work and Henri Le Saux had begun

[9]Abhishiktananda maintains that the impetus to monastic order is a universal principle. He refers to 'Hindu sannyasa, despite all the changes and even the times of degeneration through which it has passed', as 'the most radical witness to that call to the beyond which sounds, however faintly, in the heart of every man.' 'The call to complete renunciation cuts across all dharmas and disregards all frontiers. No doubt the call reaches individuals through the particular forms of their own dharma: but it corresponds to a powerful instinct, so deep-rooted in the human heart, nihitam guhayam, that it is anterior to every religious formulation.'

[10]Baumer maintains that Abhishiktananda understood his encounter with Hindu spirituality not just as a question of entering into a dialogue with 'another' but from 'the point of departure that there is an inner challenge within Christianity that is in need of the spiritualities of Asia in order to overcome the deep crisis of western Christianity' (2000).

his Indian studies), deeply affected by the violence of the interstitial period between the world wars, both concerned by the relationship of the human to God, with ideas of love and work, and visions of self and society.

With Marc Chaduc known as Ajatananda, Abhishiktananda experienced the agonizing moment of the Father-Son relationship, the Vedantic 'I am' in the guru-shishya relationship. That spiritually charged moment of self-realization that was also one of Marc's *diksha* left him so profoundly affected that he did not survive it very long.

Abhishiktananda's own self-perception, however, was as a bridge between Hinduism and Christianity. He felt that the binary oppositions of everyday reality, the felt experience of this and that; here and now; he and she; we and they were transcended when one had reached the 'further shore'. Visvanathan points out, 'Abhishiktananda was deeply Christian, but the language of the 'Other', the Hindu, was now his own—not in translation, but in the spontaneity and immediacy of something known and felt as experience'.

In Abhishiktananda's case we have an indication of the ferment and agitation that liminal states can produce. According to Baumer, in his meeting with Ramana Maharshi all the deeply entrenched convictions of Christian superiority seemed to crumble as he encountered that perfect embodiment of advaitic experience. Baumer asserts that at a certain stage he was even shaken and torn apart by two experiences, two 'ultimates', 'two identities', two worlds of religious experience, and 'two loves,' as he put it.

We do not know enough about Dara Shikoh's (1615–59) inner turmoil but possibly Abhishiktananda's responses suggest Dara's seeking and resultant dialogues with Upanishadic scholars and Qadirriya Sufis.

Baumer, interestingly reflects upon her own experience and identification with Christianity and the mystical tradition of Kashmir Saivism with its incarnated spirituality of Siva rather than the acosmic sannyasa that was Abhishiktananda's ideal. In this spirituality, both cosmos and body are taken more seriously and it is thus 'more sacramental since all the acts of daily life are considered to be sacred and means for spiritual realization'. What happens then to one's Christian roots and convictions, she asks. 'There is an entirely inner process of encountering, absorbing, letting the two traditions lead an internal dialogue without too much interference of the mind. It happens at the level of pure consciousness. Where the names "Shiva" and of "Christ" are not important, but the reality lived and experienced beyond those names.'

Abhishiktananda's life and work inspired a community of theologians and scholars. The setting up of a Hindu Christian Ashram contributed to the consolidation of the Christian Ashram movement in India. There were others, however, who questioned his fascination with Hindu renunciation and preferred the path of Dalit Liberation Theology. The polemical text, *Christian Ashrams*, represented his project including the use of saffron and the Upanishads as a manipulative one that lured Hindus under false pretences. On the Christian side, the ideas expressed in his book, *Guhantara*, were perceived as heresy in some Christian circles.

What was it that Gandhi and Abhishiktananda (and Dara Shikoh much before them) represented that was seen as intolerable by sections of Hindu and Christian civil society. The fact that Abhishiktananda wore the cross of St. Benedict over which was also carved the symbol Om? Or that Gandhi was as comfortable with Christian hymns and Biblical myths as the *ram-dhun* and the Mahabharata?

The fragility of these worlds and ways of being have been and are like footprints on sand. State, religion, nationalism are always ready to draw boundaries. But then Dara also asked the significant counter-question, can one draw lines on water? Like the 'dreamtime' of the Australian aborigines that is always and never, so the 'dream' or the liminal is everywhere and nowhere.

Simultaneously, as Baumer suggests, the very idea of 'double belonging' that amounted to a heresy in Abhishiktananda's time, has now become an accepted term. Raimon Pannikar points out in his introduction to Abhishiktananda's diary, 'To live at the meeting point of several traditions is the destiny of a large portion of the human race. For very many people it is hardly possible any longer to feel at home in a single culture' (xvi). The paradoxical promise of our times is that even as the ethnic faultlines of empire and nation-state are deepening, they are being challenged as never before.

References

Abhishiktananda, Swami. 1975. *The Further Shore: Three Essays*, ISPCK, Delhi.
_____. 1988. *The Secret of Arunachala: A Christian Hermit on Shiva's Holy Mountain*, ISPCK, Delhi.

Anzaldua, Gloria. 1987. *Borderlands la frontera: The new Mestiza*, Aunt Lute, San Francisco.

Baumer, Bettina. 2000. Abhishiktananda and the Challenge of Hindu-Christian Experience, *Monastic Interreligious Dialogue Bulletin* 64.

Bharucha, Rustom. 2003. *Rajasthan: An Oral History*, Komal Kothari in conversation with Rustam Bharucha. Penguin.

Carstairs, G. Morris. 1961. *The Twice Born*, Hogarth Press, London.

Chakrabarti, Kunal. 2001. *Religious Process: The Puranas and the Making of a Regional Tradition*, Oxford University Press, Delhi.

Edye, E.H.H. and W.R. Tennant. 1923. *Census of India*, 1921, Government Press, Allahabad.

Fisher, William. F. 2001. *Fluid Boundaries: Forming and Transforming Identity in Nepal*, Columbia University Press, New York.

Gandhi, Ramachandra. 1994. *Sita's Kitchen*, Wiley Eastern, New Delhi.

Gilmartin, David and Bruce Lawrence (Eds). 2000. *Beyond Hindu and Turk: Rethinking Religious Identities in Islamicate South Asia*, University Press of Florida.

Gottschalk, Peter S. 2001. *Beyond Hindu and Muslim: Multiple Identity Narratives from Village India*, Oxford University Press, New Delhi.

Hardy, Friedhelm. 1995. *The Religious Culture of India*, Cambridge University Press.

Kierkegaard, Soren. 1944. *Either/Or*, Oxford University Press.

Kothari, Komal. 1984. Introduction, *The Castes of Marwar*, compiled by Munshi Hardyal Singh, Jodhpur Printing House, Jodhpur.

Kulke, Hermann and Dietmar Rothermund. 1990. *A History of India*, Routledge, London.

Lionarons, Joyce Tally. 1994. Bodies, Buildings, and Boundaries: Metaphors of Liminality in Old English and Old Norse literature. *Essays in Medieval Studies* 11: 43–9.

Madan, Triloki Nath. 1998. *Modern Myths, Locked Minds: Secularism and Fundamentalism in India*, Oxford University Press, Delhi.

Mayaram, Shail. 1997. *Resisting Regimes: Myth, Memory and the Shaping of a Muslim Identity*, Oxford University Press, Delhi.

————. 1988. Rethinking Meo Identity: Cultural Faultline, Syncretism, Hybridity or Liminality, in M. Hasan (Ed.), *Islam, Communities and the Nation: Muslim Identities in South Asia and Beyond*, Manohar, New Delhi.

————. 1999. Framing Epic and Kingdom: The Mahabharata of a Community of Muslims, Workshop On Framing: Narrative, Metaphysics, Perception, Israel Academy of Sciences, Jerusalem.

————. 2003. *Against History, Against State: Counterperspectives from the Margins*, Columbia University Press, New York and London.

Nandy, Ashis. 1992. *Traditions, Tyranny and Utopias: Essays on the Politics of Awareness*, Oxford University Pres, Delhi.

————. 1995. *Coping with the Politics of Faiths and Cultures: Between Secular*

State and Ecumenical Traditions in India. Culture and Identity Project, International Centre for Ethnic Studies, Colombo.

Peterson, William. 1997. *Ethnicity Counts,* Transaction Publishers, New Brunswick, NJ.

Saxena, Sushil. K. 1988. *Ever unto God: Essays on Gandhi and Religion,* Indian Council for Philosophical Research, New Delhi.

Schimmel, Annemarie. 1992. *Islam: An Introduction,* SUNY, New York.

Stewart, Charles and Rosalind Shaw. 1994. Introduction: Problematizing Syncretism, in C. Stewart and R. Shaw (Eds), *Syncretism/Anti-Syncretism: The Politics of Religious Synthesis,* Routledge, London and New York.

Silva, Neluka. (Ed.) 2002. *The Hybrid Island: Culture Crossings and the Invention of Identity in Sri Lanka.* Social Scientists' Association, Colombo.

Singh, Kunwar, Suresh. (Ed.) 1992. *People of India: An Introduction.* Anthropological Survey of India, Calcutta.

Snellgrove, David. 1967. *Nine Ways of Bon: Excerpts from Gzi-Brjid,* London Oriental Series, London, 18.

Spivak, Gayatri, Chakarbarti. (Ed.) 1999. Moving devi, in Vidya Dehejia and R. Shaw (Ed.), *Devi: The Great Goddess, Female Divinity in South Asian Art,* Mapin, Ahmedabad.

Stein, Burton. 2001. *A History of India,* Oxford University Press, New Delhi.

Turner, Victor. (1974). *Dramas, Fields and Metaphors,* Cornell University Press, Ithaca.

Uberoi, Jit Pal Singh. 1999. *Religion, Civil Society and the State,* Oxford University Press, Delhi.

van der Veer, Peter. 1994. Syncretism, Multiculturalism, and the Discussion of Tolerance, in C. Stewart and R. Shaw (Eds), *Syncretism/Anti-Syncretism: The Politics of Religious Synthesis,* Routledge, London and New York.

Visvanathan, Susan. 1998. *An Ethnography of Mysticism: The Narratives of Abhishiktanada a French Monk in India,* Indian Institute of Advanced Study, Shimla.

Wilson, B. 1999. *Christianity,* Routledge, London and New York.

Wink, Andre. 1990. *Al-Hind,* Vol 1., Oxford University Press, Delhi.

3

Can Hindus and Muslims Coexist?

JACKIE ASSAYAG

*'Whatever the infirmities of the concept of 'culture' ('cultures',
'cultural forms'...), there is nothing for it but to persist in spite of
them.'*

Geertz, Clifford, *After the Fact. Two Countries,
Four Decades, One Anthropologist* (1995:43)

The social sciences strive to render intelligible a complex local
situation occurring at a given moment, but we find that history
does not proceed in a straight line and is not a cumulative
process. From 1990 to 1994, I spent a great deal of time studying the
relationship between Muslims and Hindus in a village in South India.
The result of this fieldwork was a book, *At the Confluence of Two
Rivers*.[1] The picture that emerged then was of a fairly harmonious
relationship between Muslims and Hindus, a fact that made it all
the more difficult to accept the politically motivated carnage by
organized groups in Gujarat in February-March 2002. After this
pogrom, the past appears like a veritable utopia.

At the Confluence of Two Rivers was the result of a study of religious
sites, spaces, practices and beliefs shared by Hindus and Muslims
living in close proximity during the 1990s. The picture that emerged
shows quite clearly that the so-called 'war' between the 'Hindus' and
'Muslims' is not the rule but a historical myth rooted in xenophobia
and ethnic nationalism.

[1]Jackie Assayag, *At the Confluence of Two Rivers: Muslims and Hindus in South
India*. First published in French, 1995, English translation: Manohar Publishers,
Delhi, 2003. There are many references to this book in this paper. *Editors.*

Scholars tend to assume that Islam and Hinduism are monolithic or primeval entities. When I talk of 'acculturation' and 'counteracculturation', I do not confine myself to the observation of exclusively sectarian relations or celebrate the supposedly harmonious and communal peace of a Golden Age (to which we could still return if we wanted to). I am certainly not an idealist, only a liberal.

The empirical evidence presented by my fieldwork among Hindus and Muslims in South India during the early 1990s shows that coexistence may be a matter of competition or 'competitive sharing' and that identity may be a product of competitive syncretism or 'antagonistic tolerance'. The supposedly syncretistic nature of the shrines and spaces, practices, powers and cosmologies, historical resources and cultural values shared by the two communities was invariably questioned by social agents involved in local, regional or national politics. The coexistence of groups was very often based on competition and compromise; adjustment did not necessarily signify brotherhood while conflict and sharing were not antithetical. The processes of interaction, identity formation, and conflict pluralize the repertory of language, behaviour, knowledge and power and do not denote distinct groups that define themselves as Muslim or Hindu. Members of both communities must be understood in the context of the historical circumstances in which they lived. These circumstances include the entire range of context-specific interests with which these particular identities interacted, as well as the larger contexts that framed various categories of identity.

This socio-cultural historical landscape was a living testimony to the dynamic exchanges and the periodic cognitive readjustments that took place between members of the so-called 'majority' and 'minority' social groups, which were then presumed to be the constitutive units of South Asian politics. The purpose of this monograph was three-fold: first, to challenge the assumptions underlying the division of Indian society into (Hindu and Muslim) communities in the ever-changing context of post-colonial India; second, to present a critically-informed view of the plurality of histories and diversity of cultures and discourses constituting the Indian social fabric, and third, to illustrate and understand this plurality and specificity as well as the dynamics of this complex interaction between multiple identities that often transcend the simple religious divide in South Asia. This locally based study also throws up some lessons of a more general nature regarding 'tradition', 'community', history and events, and the power of interpretative anthropology.

Integrative and Antagonistic Acculturation

Contrary to the general belief that the terms Hindu and Muslim denote descriptive or analytical categories, membership and belonging cut across religious boundaries. The different cultural forms are not watertight compartments; they are the products of dynamic processes and mutual adjustments whose encounters bear witness to the creative efforts of individuals in a particular area to make sense of an environment that is not always supportive. Thus, when it comes to the notions that oppose Hinduism and Islam, polytheism and monotheism or even hierarchy and egalitarianism, one must be careful not to project them anachronistically in history or consider them as values on which contradictory conceptions are founded.

To understand the social history of Islam and Hinduism (and also Christianity)[2] in the subcontinent, we should not focus our attention on prominent *ex post facto* statements about Muslims being distinct from Hindus and vice versa. We should concentrate instead on the numerous cultural similarities and the 'exchange equivalence' of practices and beliefs within a variety of social arenas.[3] Mutual social, economic and ritual adjustments between social groups of Hindus and Muslims in North Karnataka, especially in Shahabandar village, in Belgaum district, where I collected data (Assayag 2003: Chap. 1),

[2]Though there has been a clear distinction between Muslims, Christians and Hindus in South Asia since early times, it has not prevented various types of exchange, acculturation and cross-fertilization between them at both theoretical and practical levels; for an overview and case-studies, see Jackie Assayag & Gilles Tarabout (1997).

[3]According to Tony K. Stewart (2001), 'exchange equivalence' is the dynamic process of translation that enables those involved in the interaction to appraise the results of the encounter of diverse traditions. This process of seeking equivalence invariably leaves out some elements of the original idea, while introducing new ideas into the equation. There is little evidence that the semantic fields of significant terms were originally conceived as identical, transparent, or literally equal to general mythical constructs such as 'approximate equivalence'. Dynamic equivalence not only accounts for overlapping semantic domains but also gives priority to the cultural context, which can account for the different values ascribed to equivalent terms, e.g. *avatara/nabi, dev/pir, bhuta/jinn, dhikr/japa,* Muslim Yoga literature, etc. Authors and practitioners usually 'translated' notions, concepts, values, models into the closest locally available terminology or practices in their endeavour to describe different kinds of behaviour, beliefs, attitudes, etc.

and overlapping stories about Muslim saints and Hindu goddesses in the region, especially in and around the Yellama temple, a popular pilgrimage site in Saundatti where I carried out fieldwork (ibid: Chap. 5), provide ample evidence in this regard. The Hindus and Muslims of South India must be understood through the notions of 'competitive sharing',[4] 'dynamic acculturation',[5] and 'antagonistic tolerance'[6]— three processes that form the basis of dynamic exchanges, viz. accommodation, cultural innovation and sometimes violence.

To understand and illustrate the complexity of 'competitive sharing', 'integrative/antagonist acculturation', 'competitive syncretism' and 'antagonistic tolerance', i.e. the interactive processes responsible for evolving a culture through contacts, exchanges and conflicts, let us recall our observations in villages and places of worship shared by Hindus and Muslims in North Karnataka.[7]

Worship in Temples and Dargahs

Sacred sites and public spaces have long been shared by members of different religious communities in South Asia. The most striking feature

[4]The concept of 'competitive sharing' developed by Robert M. Hayden (2002) is very helpful in understanding so-called 'syncretism' as a complex social process. This competitive sharing is compatible with the passive meaning of 'tolerance', viz. non-interference, but incompatible with its active meaning, viz. embracing the other. Such places of sharing may even exhibit syncretistic mixtures of the practices of both communities that may be appropriated or destroyed by members of one community to establish their dominance over the other community.

[5]Regarding the sharing of spaces, the Hindu-Muslim relationship often exhibits an acculturation that is simultaneously 'integrated' and 'dissociative', to borrow Devereux's concepts (1975).

[6]See Robert M. Hayden (2002). The presumption that syncretistic phenomena are non-competitive is based on the assumption that a hybrid construction is itself a single identity. The syncretistic nature of practices, beliefs or sites, is always a reflection of the opposition between people who have adopted practices associated with the beliefs of their rulers.

[7]For a short survey of some well-known Hindu-Muslim shrines in Karnataka, and also the recent 'communalization' of some of these shrines—especially the syncretistic Datta *pita*/Dada *pir dargah* located in the Baba Budhan hills in Chikmagalur—by Hindu organizations (VHP, RSS and Bajrang Dal), see Yoginder Sikand (2002). According to informed opinion, since Ayodhya has become 'a dead issue' for garnering popular support, the Sangh Parivar is raising a controversy over the shrine at Baba Budan Giri to keep the communal cauldron bubbling in South India. The Parivar has identified 30 other shrines in Karnataka due for 'liberation' after 'freeing' the Baba Budan Giri shrine from the control of Sufi Muslims. As for public spaces in Karnataka, refer to the article by Satish Deshpande (1998) on the flag-hoisting controversy in Hubli city.

of this so-called 'composite culture',[8] especially in popular religion, is the continuing popularity of shared religious traditions in large parts of the region, bringing together Hindus and Muslims.[9] Many Muslims (usually of a low social status) freely visit temples of the goddess in South India. Conversely, many Hindus (mainly untouchables or from the lower castes) are seen in the precincts of *dargahs*—tombs of Muslim saints—that dot the Indian landscape. At these shrines, official religious affiliation is not as important as the need for divine assistance. Every individual can gain tangible access to the sacred for the fulfilment of wishes or for healing. Both the Hindu deities and the Muslim saints seem to recognize that human distress does not depend on denomination and they seem to recognize that all men and women need their compassion.

Despite borrowing the practices of the other community in specific religious contexts, Hindus and Muslims continue to retain their separate identities. Everyone knows when it is a Muslim who has broken a coconut in honour of the goddess to be distributed later to other devotees or when it is a Hindu who is exorcized of evil spirits by the saint known as *jinns* by the Muslims and *bhuta* by Hindus without any distinction. For these caste Hindus and Muslims visiting places of worship belonging to the other community, acculturation is 'dissociative by differentiation', to use the typology devised by the ethnopsychiatrist Devereux, who explains it as 'the adaptation of the average to the manifest culture, but not the underlying culture' (1975: 383). Hindus perform a Hindu rite to propitiate a Muslim saint as if he were a Hindu deity. Even though they respect the ritual associated with the worship of the Muslim saint, e.g. by offering sugar instead of rice and absorbing a portion of his divine power (*baraka*), they do not touch his tomb as Muslim worshippers would in a *dargah*. By the same token, when Muslims visit a temple, they follow Hindu practices in order to obtain a view (*darshana*) and the blessings of the divine power. Some of these practices are in fact similar to those followed in *dargahs*,

---

[8]The debate on 'composite culture' began in earnest in the 1940s as a reaction to the movement supporting the creation of Pakistan. It resurfaced from 1959 onwards as the result of a series of nationalistic studies published by the Bharatiya Vidhya Bhavan in India and officially supported nationalistic studies in Pakistan. The 1962 Indian History Congress devoted its annual session to the question of India's composite culture. See Achin Vanaik (1997: chap. 4).

[9]A rich and evocative study of the manner in which people understand their position and their multiple identity in a North-Indian village is to be found in Peter Gottschalk's book (2001).

such as ritual circumambulation called *tawaf* (around the *Ka'aba*), in Islam and *pradakshina* in Hinduism, without in any way repudiating their own religious culture. In neither case does the observance of the other religion's rites imply conversion. The divine benefits obtained from these separate forms of worship—paying a visit to a saint after going to the goddess, or vice versa—are generally believed to be duplicated through an increase in the quantity of aura received and, consequently, the benefits from the divine power. In this way cultural duality is respected even though members of both communities behave in a manner that is very similar. When worshipping the saint, it matters little to the Muslims that they are doing it in the Hindu manner. For in this autonomous area of worship, the absorption of techniques typical of the dominant group in no way affects their awareness of being Muslims in the strongest sense.

A perfectly 'integrated' form of acculturation is likely to shock only the zealots of Hindu nationalism or scriptural Islam and surprise foreign ethnologists studying India. Identity is reinforced when Muslims are excluded from a *puja* ritual in honour of a Hindu deity or vice-versa. They translate the label of 'non-Hindu' in a socio-religious sense and attribute their segregation to the fact that they belong to the Muslim community. This defensive isolation defines a 'reactional identity' that may lead to ostentatious differentiation and ultimately to a 'communal' confrontation between Hindus and Muslims.

Reformism

I shall close this short account with a reference to the efforts of Islamic militants to put an end to this situation. For a long time, both traditionalists and reformers have been pressurizing the community of believers, or *Umma*, in India, to 'purify' their faith. Young proselytes, mainly students who are members of an urban branch of the Jamat-e-Islami, organize tours around villages to eradicate superstition, combat polytheism (*shirk*) and remind the people of their creed (*fatiha*)— 'There is only one God, Allah, and Mohammad is his prophet.'

In the village of Shahabandar, for example, they came to strengthen the position of the local leader, a *mullah* of the Jamat-e-Islami, regarding the 'purification' of rites. At village funerals, the Muslims use a bamboo bier that is destroyed after the ceremony. Convinced that this custom resembled the Hindu funeral practice too closely, the militants decided to have standard-sized wooden biers (*doli*) made and transported to the village. With the agreement of the village head, these wooden biers were stored in the mosque. The villagers unanimously condemned this action, claiming that keeping these objects of ill-omen in the house of God would lead to numerous deaths.

There was a violent dispute that was subsequently settled to the satisfaction of both parties. The villagers now bury their dead in wooden coffins manufactured in Belgaum, but the reformers were not totally victorious. Not only did the villagers win their point that coffins should never be placed in the mosque but they also continue to play music and throw flowers during funeral processions—a detail which confirms the thesis of anthropologist Jack Goody (1993), who claims that Islam in India has become a 'flower culture'. Attempts such as these to align local practices with a (supposed) norm of Islam—which has however spurred many orthodox groups to anathematize each other—often lead to equivocal results.[10]

My next example is that of the professionalization or Hinduization of the forms of worship. Members of *mullah* lineage officiate at the *urs*, a festival commemorating the death of a holy man (literally translated as a mystic marriage with Allah), as well as at Muharram, an exclusively Shiite festival that is also celebrated in a playful manner by Sunnis in India. During private ceremonies, families frequently invite a *mullah* to recite prayers (*fatiha*) on their behalf. This practice is typical of Hindu family priests. Similarly, on the occasion of *Bakr-'Id*, the festival commemorating Ibrahim's sacrifice, the *mullah* plays the role of a sacrificer, making the offering in the Muslim way (*zebah*) by cutting the sheep's jugular vein as it is laid on the ground with its feet tied together, reciting prayers all the while, rather than in the Hindu manner by decapitating the standing animal without any accompanying prayers. Nevertheless, the *mullah* performs the sacrifice just like a Hindu manner by priest would on behalf of devotees, a practice common amongst low caste and untouchable Hindus. Sometimes, a village's Hindu inhabitants offer a sheep to the Muslim community on the occasion and a part of the offering is returned to them to be partaken of at a communal feast. People may also ask a *mullah* for amulets to protect them from the evil eye or talismans to ward off attacks from evil spirits. These rituals performed by the *mullah* lie beyond the religious domain normally assigned to him by Muslim orthodoxy in his capacity as a doctor of the Law (*alim*).

[10]Even the sharia, Islam's most powerful marker, has assumed varied political meanings in India (see Muzaffar Alam 2000).

Such liminal traditions of common worship and ritual participation are, by their very nature, ambiguous in terms of clearly defined communal categories and defy the logic of neatly demarcated communities compartmentalized according to a reified, scriptural and essential understanding of religious identity.[11] Following the rise of religious movements for reform or greater orthodoxy, such traditions have increasingly come under attack as powerful organizations seek to define them.[12]

Field Perspectives

Tradition(s)

Attempts to understand socio-religious practices must not be limited to textual norms or to the viewpoint of the so-called great (major) traditions. Some of these traditions claim to be universal, but it must be remembered that before they were written down and even after they became 'traditions', those who created them engaged in a multi-faceted exchange with other systems of thought and action. Moreover, while canons may help locate the boundaries and stabilize the identity of newly founded religious orders, charisma provides the authority to introduce changes.[13]

This observation also applies to those who continued to follow these 'traditions' after they became what they are today. It must be borne in mind that the protagonists are able to create 'traditions', transmit them or destroy them only under the influence of social interaction. Of course, many 'traditions' are distorted by the very persons who are inspired by them or by those opposed to them or even those, usually more numerous, who are either indifferent to them or

[11]For a fascinating study revealing the absence of clearly defined categories between Hindu and Muslim communities in medieval Andhra Pradesh (see Cynthia Talbot 1995).

[12]Nevertheless, the origins of this process may be traced to colonial times, in particular to the introduction of the Census (mapping and categorizing religious communities. *The Politics of Competing Communalisms* (Freitag 1990), and the style of reporting 'communal riots' (Pandey 1990). Actually, the communalization of syncretistic shrines may be seen as a part of a long historical process of the formation of what is called today 'Hinduism' (See Frykenberg 1991 and, more generally, Sontheimer & Kulke 1991).

[13]For historical and conceptual terms of reference to understand the creation and perpetuation of new religious movements, see Vasuda Dalmia *et al.* (2001).

are unaware of them. Ignoring ideas handed down by the history of religions or by civilizations interested in the study of 'religion' or 'civilization' *per se*, amounts to treating these issues in a contextual and pragmatic manner and avoiding identification with the propagandists of either camp.

The composite worship of the popular hybrid figure of Changadeva/ Rajabag Savar (Assayag 2003: Chap. 4),[14] in North Karnataka, who is considered to be an *avatar* of Vishnu as well as an intercessor of Allah is a case in point. His place of worship in Yamanur village is considered to be the temple (*gudi*) of a Hindu guru and the *dargah* of a Muslim saint, where a *pujari* and a *mujawar* officiate side by side.

Community

The indiscriminate use of the notion of 'community' and its corollary, the 'holistic' approach to society presumes what is yet to be demonstrated, viz. the supposed organic unity of the whole and the proper demarcation of groups constituting this whole. As Eric Hobsbawm recently observed, 'never was the word "community" used more indiscriminately and emptily than in the decades when communities in the sociological sense became hard to find in real life' (1994: 428)— just as a community is about to collapse, it acquires an identity!

The use of the term 'community' implies in the first place that it is good and safe 'to have a community'. Secondly, it means that each group has always been cohesive and stable; thirdly, that all its members are sufficiently alike and share long-term common interests because they have the same attitudes and fourthly, that community stands for the kind of world that the group longs to inhabit but which, unfortunately, does not exist any more. We thus tend to represent so-called 'communities' or 'socio-religious groups' according to an ideal formula that we apply to the present, even though we may not go so far as to apply it to earlier cultural forms.[15] A case in point, for example, is the hostility in Shahabandar village between the Lingayats and Hanabars, both Hindu castes, or between the Kasais and Mullahs, both Muslim groups, whose members are not allowed to intermarry (Assayag 2003: Chap.1). This amounts to likening the group to a stable object that can be represented very easily. By merging socio-

[14]A similar example was studied by Ian Duncan & Hugh van Skyhawk (1997).

[15]For a brilliant reappraisal of the concept of 'community' and an explanation of the price to be paid of being a 'community', see Zygmunt Bauman (2001).

logical reality, collective representation and social identity in this manner, we ignore the series of tactical changes taking place within rival groups in a social framework created jointly by them. As the great Norwegian anthropologist Frederick Barth explains, the ostensibly shared 'communal' identities are after-effects or by-products of ever unfinished (hence all the more feverish and ferocious) boundary-drawing. At the same time, we ignore the extreme diversity of practices that are likely to express an identity displayed through more or less institutional channels. This is what is practised day after day by the various groups living side by side in the villages of Shahabandar (ibid.: Chap. 1) and Yamanur (ibid.: Chap. 4). The plurality of lifestyles is determined not by stereotyped behaviour or uniform values, nor is it unified by some vague notion. On the contrary, we may even wager that 'forms of life' are simultaneously singular and plural, composite and conflicting and that they have never been nor are they now exempt from dynamic contradictions. Once again, this brings to mind the idea that whirlpools are bound to exist at the confluence of two rivers or, better still, of the two oceans represented by Hinduism and Islam.

History and Events

This kind of anthropological study of the present does not contradict the historical approach. The fact that Islam has been deeply rooted in India for almost a thousand years stands testimony to this. To support our argument we must not reduce anecdotes (both past and present) to non-events; micro-events may appear fortuitous but they are meaningful. Their significance, however, changes with the passage of time. Anecdotes, like the symptoms of a social crisis, reveal upheavals and social norms. Although they are experienced on an emotional plane, they are necessitated by history. The incident leading to the exclusion of Muslims from the Yellamma goddess' service in the Saundatti temple[16] for example, is a sign of the growing tension between Hindus and Muslims in contemporary India (ibid.: Chap. 5). The fake beheading of the Jalali (Rifai) fakir during a performance in the city of Belgaum (ibid.: Chap. 3) has its roots in an ancient theme that is both mythological and mystical. Since history spans a

[16]For an extensive description of Goddess Yellamma, the temple of Saundatti, the Banajiga priesthood and the methods of worship by pilgrims and devotees (*jogammas/jogappas*), see Jackie Assayag (1992).

long period of time, it is likely to endorse myths going back to times long past.

Today however, the existence of several forms of culture has given rise to another type of historiography in the form of a myriad unwritten 'micro-(hi)stories' interest to the ethnographer. This explains why, the 'little stories' about the relations between a handful of Hindus and Muslims as narrated in *At the Confluence of Two Rivers* allow us to conclude with relative certainty that social and cultural identification can be of a temporary nature, often subject to historical change depending on the context. Many traditions that we believe to be ancient were 'invented' relatively recently. The profile of devotees visiting the goddess' temple or the saint's mausoleum is proof enough of this changeability. It is evident that in the beginning this identification was of a functional nature, even though it tended to persist. In India, of course, this persistence would be transformed into a 'tradition' only too readily. Associating with a set of criteria determining the membership of a religion and the ways of making this membership and exclusiveness manifest, boundaries sometimes change because they are unstable and always contextual. Throughout history, we see that a society where norms are many and there are several rival offers is subject to rifts. Not only do social structures propose a multiplicity of roles, social agents also tend to overlap roles and there is sometimes confusion between various roles. In my book, I have tried to identify the dividing lines according to historically controllable contexts in time and space, i.e. two centuries in an area transiting between the present states of Maharashtra and Karnataka. It so happens that oceans—like rivers—flow across borders.

The reason for drawing attention to the changing forms of culture, while focussing on the context that produced various expressions of identity, is to prevent them from being reduced to an organic model in which all cultural manifestations have a fixed and unchanging place. It matters little whether they are learned or popular because they belong to different levels of the same realm. This is illustrated by the rites of worship (*dhikr*) of a brotherhood of Jalali fakirs in the city of Belgaum (ibid.: Chap. 3; Assayag 1999c) and testified to by traditional *mullahs*. This concept encourages us to imagine culture as a kind of lost world of symbolic coherence but ignores the fact that stories and values change according to the context and contradict one another in different domains.

Behaviour patterns, because they reflect diverse interests, are first and foremost forms of praxis, which need not necessarily constitute a perfectly coherent ideological system. Any attempt to conjugate cultural identity in the singular, whether it is individual or collective, learned or popular, religious or political, fixes and immobilizes the tracks and ruts of communal rhetoric. We cannot afford to ignore the fact that ideological petrifaction sometimes has tragic political consequences. This is evident in India in the functioning organizations of the Sangh Parivar, such as the Rastriya Swayamsevak Sangh (RSS), the Vishva Hindu Parishad (VHP), and its political wing, the Bharatiya Janata Party (BJP), all of which recruit their followers on the basis of so-called 'eternal traditions' (Assayag 2003: Intro. & Chap. 6). Given that contemporary history is inclined towards ideological nostalgia, there is every possibility of the same illusion being used in the near future.

'Tradition' should never be considered only as heritage, patrimony or ethnicity. It should be considered more as a competition or rivalry between open systems establishing a relationship between social partners—partners who are likely to cooperate but may also come into conflict and consider each other both identical and different.

With this perspective in mind, we selected from the vast scale of social interactions (described in detail in ibid. Chapters 1, 4, 5 and 6) those that best convey the interlocking between individuals, groups and sub-groups whose similarity and diversity are expressed at different levels. At each of these levels, whether it be village or the town, rules pertaining to marriage or eating practices, mausoleum or a temple, a festival or daily life, trade or worship, therapeutic methods or political claims, there are experiences and rules through which social agents can redefine themselves and create their own identity, i.e. discuss the links that bind them to others. Even if cultural acceptance often appears to be intermittent and fragmented, we know that it can be extremely dynamic. Social agents improvise as they go along (the French word is 'bricoler'); they are excellent tacticians and they know how to combine even those cultural practices that appear to be the most exclusive.

The ability to find alternatives and stop-gap solutions in social matters, which depend on the intensity of interactions, bears testimony to the skill of these agents in investing them with meaning, especially because the stakes are critically important. Firstly, because it means legitimizing a particular thought or action and secondly, because it discredits all other ways expressed by others as a distinct semantic system. This involves recognizing the importance of cases of interaction wherever it is possible to examine the dialectics of reciprocal sharing between individuals and also between groups that may be either permanent or temporary. Such a statement is also an acknowledgement of the need to give priority to the symbolic arrangements that give rise to these interactions or are produced by them in social life. In other words, it implies that it is possible to study the culture that encircles and embraces them. How does this work today between Hindus and Muslims (in North Karnataka)? What do they seek to achieve when they come into contact, when they share and exchange customs and 'traditions', or even when they share or exclude others?

Behind the diversity of experiences and contexts, it is possible to identify a system that is relatively coherent but never closed to outside influences. On the contrary, it is always unstable because of its extreme complexity and acknowledged singularities. Of course, there is compatibility between cultural subjectivity and dominant cultural values considered to be 'objective'. It is nevertheless impossible to look at collective identity as the sum total of subjective identities because the variability of interactions makes room for inventiveness and, in some cases, for normative dissension.[17] When this is explained using a limited number of examples, the relationship between different cultural behaviour patterns is often criticized and debated, paradoxically strengthening the traditions contributed by each of them. In this sense, formulas for identity have always seemed more flexible, diffuse and problematic. This is true even more so now than in the past because history offers endless temptations. Harking back on past events in Belgaum's Hindu-Muslim history (ibid. Chapter 6) only reaffirms this.

Interpretative Anthropology

These observations justify the use of a hermeneutic plural to define the method employed in this book. While such an approach may appear hesitant and uncertain at times, it is better suited to the cultural heterogeneity and peculiarities of different types of Indianness. This approach suggests provisional descriptive grids suited to the hazardous process of the crystallization of identities undergoing permanent

---

[17]On the 'invention of tradition', see the path-breaking collection of articles edited by Eric Hobsbawm and Terence Ranger (1983). For a critical approach to the notion of 'invention of tradition', see Ranger's later works and also Jackie Assayag (1999a).

restructuring. The cult of the Muslim saint, *Dudhpira Baba,* for example, has developed around demonology and possession in a hamlet near Sankeshwar (ibid. Chapter 2) and is not just the actualization of pre-existing elements but a particular method used to control crucial situations subject to rapid change. Its representation is not the simple affirmation of what is already established; it is a creation that generally seeks refuge in the sanctuary of 'tradition' but cannot be totally equated with it. Nor is it possible to compare the expression of a cult to the transhistoric identity of the person who performs it, because of the danger of losing the specific character of the idiom through which it is put into action. This is particularly true when intercultural contact is involved, and whatever we may claim, it is doubtful if strictly demarcated cultures have ever existed—the cult functions like a show performed against a backdrop where divergent expectations are integrated and synchronized. When the worshipper finally realizes that the Hindu and the Muslim cognitive universes are too different to be brought together, he resorts to the mechanisms of borrowing, reinterpretation and accumulation, moving freely from one to the other without necessarily mixing them even when circumstances demand it. We must view Hindus and Muslims as a part of history and not as two separate histories connected only by violence and trauma—as religio-political demagogues would have it at present.[18]

There is no static representative relationship between cultural traits, agents and social groups. In the universe of social relationships studied by anthropologists, it is necessary to recognize the articulate expression of cultural sociogeneses and dynamic changes having their own rhythm. Of course, these changes are subject to external constraints but field studies show that they are shaped in equal measure by the action of agents or groups. Individuals must compromise and reconcile contradictions in order to survive. It is these methods of readjusting the imposed order for the right purpose and the reciprocity of historical exchanges that cannot be dissociated from power relationships that is a part of Indian society, what Claude Lévi-Strauss so eloquently called 'the delicate flowers of difference'. But we all know that these flowers are threatened today by political and communal conflicts that are shaking the subcontinent.

[18]According to David Gilmartin & Bruce Laurence, 'it is because the distinction between Islamicate and Muslim, Indic and Hindu, has been repeatedly obscured that scholarship on South Asia has been mired in controversy' (2000: 2).

Conclusion: Identity and Otherness

Some well-known literary examples and a few cursory sociological studies have given rise to the belief that Hindus and Muslims have either fought incessantly in the past or lived together in perfect harmony according to syncretistic principles of thought and action. This syncretism is predicated on the assumption that pre-existing and discrete doctrinal or ritual systems and practices are mysteriously combined to form an unnatural admixture.[19] Field studies, on problems related to the translation of cultures and cultural contacts, carried out in the early 1990s remind us that there is a tendency to idealize references to past events. Without succumbing to either of these two views, we may point out that neither the Hindu and nor the Muslim communities can be understood and defined for all time. Understanding the endless nuances of acculturation and counter-acculturation, competitive sharing, antagonistic tolerance and cognitive reorganization in day-to-day life demands that we mistrust conceptual schemes that are manipulated in the rarefied atmosphere of hypothetical scenarios or pure imagination. We must therefore be prepared to suspend the ideological debate and concentrate on cultural dynamics and sociogenetic aspects that have created the communal mosaic or 'composite culture' peculiar to India and shaped by bilateral relations between Hindus and Muslims.

The study of the modes of thought and action of thousands of people living in a small part of South Asia has led me to conclude that Hindus and Muslims have not been living in separate compartments over the past century. On the contrary, they have thrived on the constant exchanges that have developed over the years. This is obvious because Hinduism and Islam, as they were practised until recently, continue to show a great deal of flexibility and a spirit of accommodation in their mutual relations. In fact, they display an understanding that is infinitely richer than the limited sectarian approach adopted by dogmatic, fundamentalist and neotraditionalist circles on both sides.

All said and done, it is possible that the relationship between

---

[19]An apposite and sophisticated application of the problematic concept of 'syncretism' to Islam in India can be found in Asim Roy (1983). For more generally useful reflections on 'syncretism', see Peter van der Veer (1994) and Richard Webner (1994). Also see Richard Eaton's study (1989; 2003) on the shift from models of syncretism to more historically nuanced and contextual studies.

Hinduism and Islam has been—and may still be, in some regions—an open cultural system, i.e. a codification of the similarities and differences between neighbouring groups, a set of changing relationships within configurations that are constantly adapting themselves to the changing circumstances. What is most remarkable is that the continuous process of integrative and antagonistic acculturation has allowed each tradition to preserve its peculiarities and maintain a demarcating line between Hindus and Muslims. Better still, despite the existence of a network of exchanges and reciprocal actions and the absence of a clear and definitive conceptual boundary between them, this process allows members of these communities to periodically withdraw into themselves whenever the situation (dramatized by social agents) requires them to affirm their social identity *vis-à-vis* the other community. Hindus and Muslims have been able to achieve this not by enunciating basic spiritual truths but through seemingly insignificant though decisive signs, by cobbling together 'little bits of truth', as observed by Sigmund Freud, during the displacement and readjustment of traditions (1975:115).

Today, the best purpose to which this monograph could be put is to convince ourselves that the cost of intolerance is too high. But 'the times they are a-changing'. My last book, published in French, in 2001, was an attempt to explore the '*longue durée*' Hindu/Indian desire for a lasting nation. Its aim was to study how the xenophobic relationship between Hindus and Muslims in South Asia was seen in the past and is experienced in the present. In India today, as everywhere else in our fast globalizing world, there is a growing fear that far from disappearing, religious and cultural boundaries are being erected at every street corner in every neighbourhood of the subcontinent. 'The times they are a-changing' but is that reason enough to fear the worst? Following Friedrich Nietzsche instead of the path of the Nazi swastika it may be exhilarating to think that time could be a circle...

There is good reason to imagine the course of history as the movement of a pendulum. Inspired by Paul Klee's drawing, Walter Benjamin tells us that the Angel of History moves with his back turned to the future and his eyes fixed on the past.[20] What keeps him moving

---

[20]Walter Benjamin describes the 'Angel of History' in the following words, 'his face is turned towards the past. Where we perceive a chain of events, he sees one single catastrophe which keeps piling up weckage upon weckage, and hurls it in front of his feet. The angel would like to stay, awaken the dead, and make whole that has been smashed. But a storm is blowing from Paradise; it has got hold of his wings with such

since he left Paradise is disgust and repulsion for what he sees: the horrors of the past and not the lure of the future, which he can neither see clearly nor fully appreciate. Progress then, is a frantic urge to fly away from the corpses scattered over battlefields of the past, including those of Gujarat.

References

Alam, Muzaffar. 2000. *Sharia* and Governance in the Indo-Islamic Context, in David Gilmartin & Bruce B. Lawrence (Eds), *Beyond Turk and Hindu: Rethinking Religious Identities in Islamic South Asia*, University of Florida Press, Gainesville, 216–45.

Assayag, Jackie. 1991. Documentary VHS: *Islam soufi: Un culte de saint et sa confrérie de fakirs dans le Sud de l'Inde* (Belgaum, Karnataka), Paris, IRESCO/CNRS, 30 mn, colour.

———. 1992. *La colère de la déesse décapitée. Traditions, cultes et pouvoir dans le Sud de l'Inde*. CNRS-Éditions, Paris.

———. 1999a. Introduction: The Past is not (always) a Foreign Country, in Jackie Assayag (Ed.), *The Resources of History: Tradition, Narration, and Nation in South India*, Presses de l'École française d'Extrême-Orient et Institut de Pondichéry, Paris-Pondichéry, 21–38.

———. 1999b. How Can One be Hindu and/or Muslim? The Resources of the Hagiography Exemplar in South India, in Jackie Assayag (Ed.), *The Resources of History. Tradition, Narration, and Nation in South India*, Presses de l'École française d'Extrême-Orient et Institut de Pondichéry, Paris-Pondichéry, 173–87.

———. 2001. *L'Inde. Désir de nation*, Odile Jacob, Paris.

———. 2003. *At the Confluence of Two Rivers: Muslims and Hindus in South India*, Manohar, Delhi, (1st French ed. 1995).

——— & Gilles Tarabout (Eds). 1997. *Altérité, identité: Islam et christianisme en Inde*. Éditions de l'École des Hautes études en sciences sociale (Coll. '*Purusartha*' 19), Paris.

Barth, Frederick. 1969. Introduction, in Frederick Barth (Ed.), *Ethnic Groups and Boundaries: The Social Organization of Culture Difference*, George Allen & Unwin, Bergen-Oslo, Universitetforlaget, London, 9–38.

Bauman, Zygmunt. 2001. *Community: Seeking Safety in an Insecure World*, Polity Press and Blackwell Publisher, Cambridge-Oxford.

Benjamin, Walter. 1969. *Illuminations*, edited by Hannah Arendt. Schocken, New York.

violence that the angel can no longer close them. This storm irresistibly propels him into the future to which his back is turned, while the pile of debris before him grows skyward' (1969: 257).

Dalmia,Vasudha, Angelika Malinar & Martin Christof (Eds). 2001. *Charisma and Canon: Essays in the Religious History of the Indian Subcontinent,* Oxford University Press, New Delhi.

Deshpande, Satish. 1998. Hegemonic Spatial Strategies: the Nation-Space and Hindu Communalism in Twentieth Century India, *Public Culture,* 10(2): 249–83.

Devereux, Georges. 1975. Acculturation antagoniste (1943), in Georges Devereux (Ed.), *Ethnopsychanalyse complémentariste,* Flammarion, Paris.

Duncan, Ian & Hugh van Skyhawk. 1997. Holding the World Together: Lokasamgraha in the Cult of a Hindu/Muslim Saint Folk Deity of the Deccan, *Zeitschrift der Deutschen Morgenländdischen Gesellschaft,* 405–24.

Eaton, Richard M. 1993. *The Rise of Islam and the Bengal Frontier, 1204–1760.* University of California Press, Berkeley.

———— (Ed.). 2003. *India's Islamic Traditions, 711–1750,* Oxford University Press, New Delhi.

Freitag, Sandria B. 1989. *Collective Action and Community: Public Arena and the Emergence of Communalism in North India,* University of California Press, Berkeley.

Freud, Sigmund. 1975. *Moïse et le monothéisme.* (1st. German ed. 1939), Gallimard, Paris.

Frykenberg, Robert E. 1991. The Emergence of Modern 'Hinduism' as a Concept and as an Institution: A Reappraisal with Special Reference to South India, in Günther-Dietz Sontheimer & Hermann Kulke (Eds), *Hindusim Reconsidered,* Manohar, Delhi, 29–49.

Gilmartin, David & Bruce B. Lawrence (Eds). 2000. *BeyondTurk and Hindu: Rethinking Religious Identities in Islamic South Asia,* University Press of Florida Press, Gainesville.

Goody, Jack. 1993. *The Culture of Flowers,* Cambridge University Press, Cambridge.

Gottschalk, Peter. 2001. *Beyond Hindu and Muslim: Multiple Identity in Narrative from Village India,* Oxford University Press, New Delhi.

Hayden, Robert M. 2002. Antagonistic Tolerance: Competitive Sharing of Religious Sites in South Asia and the Balkans, *Current Anthropology,* 41(2): 205–31.

Hobsbawm, Eric. 1994. *The Age of Extremes,* Michael Joseph, London.

———— &Terence Ranger (Eds). 1983. *The Invention of Tradition,* Cambridge University Press, Cambridge.

Pandey, Gyanendra. 1990. *The Construction of Communalism in Colonial North India,* Oxford University Press, Delhi.

Roy,Asim. 1983. *Islamic SyncretisticTradition in Bengal,* Princeton University Press, Princeton, N.J.

Sikand,Yoginder. 2002. The Changing Nature of Shared Hindu-Muslim Shrines in Contemporary Karnataka, South India, *South Asia,* XXV, 1, 4967.

Sontheimer, Günther-Dietz & Hermann Kulke (Eds). 1991. *Hindusim Reconsidered*, Manohar, Delhi.

Stewart, Tony K. 2001. In Search of Equivalence: Conceiving Muslim-Hindu Encounters through Translation Theory, *History of Religion*, 40(3): 261–88.

Talbot, Cynthia. 1995. Inscribing the Other, Inscribing the Self: Hindu-Muslim Identities in pre-Colonial India, *Comparative Studies in Society and History*, 37(4): 692–722.

Vanaik, Achin. 1997. *The Furies of Indian Communalism: Religion, Modernity and Secularization*. Verso, London/New York.

van der Veer, Peter. 1994. Syncretism, Multiculturalism, and the Discourse of Tolerance, in Charles Stewart & Rosalind Shaw (Eds), *Syncreticism/anti-syncreticism: The Politics of Religious Synthesis*, Routledge, New York, 196–212.

Webner, Richard. 1994. Afterword, in C. Stewart & R. Shaw (Eds), *Syncreticism/anti-syncreticism: The Politics of Religious Synthesis*. Routledge, New York.

PART

II

Lived Islam and
its Historical
Context

4

The Rishi Tradition and the Construction of Kashmiriyat

MOHAMMAD ISHAQ KHAN

Introduction

A meaningful discussion on the evolution of the Kashmiri identity demands prior definition of two concepts, namely, Rishi and Kashmiriyat, often but vaguely, used for stressing the importance of the pluralistic heritage of Kashmiri culture. Rishi, as we know, is undoubtedly of Sanskrit origin, meaning 'a singer of hymns, an inspired poet or sage'. According to the Hindu belief, the Rishis 'are inspired personages to whom these hymns were revealed', and such an expression as "the Rishi says" is equivalent to "so it stands in the sacred text" '. In common usage among the Hindus, however, the Rishi meant 'a saint or sanctified sage ... an ascetic anchorite'. (Monier Williams 1964: 227)

Kashmir is reputed to have been the abode of Rishis centuries before the establishment of the 'Muslim Sultanate' in 1320. For this reason the Valley was termed Rishi Vatika a term that suggests 'unmistakably ... an order of emancipated recluses rehabilitating man on his lost glory' (Kashi Nath Dhar: 6). A strong folk tradition still persists, particularly in a number of villages of Kashmir, about the existence of Rishis in ancient times, and that several forests in the Valley are even named after them gives credence to the oral sources of the Rishi tradition.

Nothing explains the crucial issue of Kashmiriyat or Kashmiri identity as explicitly as the gradual transition of Kashmiris to Islam over a period of five centuries, thanks to the role of the Sufis and Rishis. True, the advent of Sufi missionaries from Central Asia and Persia in the Valley from the fourteenth century played an important role in the dissemination of Islamic teachings within the broader framework of the Quran and Sunnah. But what is important, from the standpoint of history, is the creative response of Kashmiris to the belief structure of Islam at the societal level in the Hindu–Buddhist environment of the Valley during the fourteenth and eighteenth centuries. Such a response was intrinsically inspired by the Kashmiris' urge to understand or experience 'the divine' in terms of love rather than as an abstraction. This is the reason that all the Muslim shrines in the Valley continue to play a significant role in constituting a means of communication between society and faith not only in terms of emphasis on the performance of the prescribed five times prayers in the mosques attached to them but, also, through continued fostering of certain traditions rooted in the regional ethos. Thus the loud recitation of benedictions on the Prophet Mohammad (*durud*), invocatory prayers (*award*), and a variety of prayers in Arabic, Persian and Kashmiri at special assemblies on the eve of the *urs* of the local Sufis and the Rishis continue to be the distinctive features of Islam in the Valley. A tiny, but a vocal, minority of the Ahl-i-Hadith and the Jamat-i-Islami, however, regards the celebrations and rituals connected with the *urs* of the Sufis as a reprehensible innovation (*bida*). Undaunted by such criticism, the devotees of the shrines, nonetheless, consider the abodes of the Sufis and the Rishis to be the impregnable fortresses of Islam in Kashmir. Taking pride on calling themselves *Ahl-i-itiqad*,[1] they highlight the historical role of the Sufis and the Rishis not merely in the spread of Islam in Kashmir, but more importantly, in the formation of the Kashmiri Muslim identity. Thus the daily practice of loud chanting of litanies and invocatory prayers on the loud speakers

---

[1] *Ahl-i-itiqad*. The term *i'tiqad* is both a belief and a firm conviction that what they believe or what they firmly accept in the mind is true. As against faith (*iman*) which concerns action (*amal*) and the confession (*iqrar*), *i'tiqad* is related to three degrees of certainty in the Quranic context: known, verified and evident (*ilmu'l-yaqin*), manifest and witnessed (*ainu'l-yaqin*) and the witnesser, the witnessed, the looker on, the looked on (haqqu'l-yaqin). Believing that the Sufis were gifted with all forms of both *iman* and *i'tiqad*, therefore, the Kashmiris calling themselves Ahl-i-itiqad distinguish themselves from those who those who do not see beyond the literal interpretation of the Quran and the Sharia.

after the prescribed prayers, or particularly on the eve of the *urs*, is not simply a matter of ritual but the cultural manifestation of Islam in a regional setting. What is integral to the collective consciousness of the devotees is their determined will to preserve the heritage of the Sufis and the Rishis in the face of ideological,[2] rather religious, threats to the Kashmiri Muslim identity from 'outside'. It is, indeed, the idea of self-definition and self-preservation that permeates the consciousness of a people living in what they call the Valley of spiritual masters (Pirwaer) or the Valley of Rishis (Rishwaer), the same as Rishivatika.

That the concept of Kashmiriyat has evolved out of the yearning of the Kashmiris, both Hindus and Muslims, to situate their mother-land (Mouj Kashir) in something unique is not merely reminiscent of their preoccupation with self-definition but also with certain his-torical contradictions. For a Kashmiri Pandit, the Valley is a land of *tirthas* or pilgrimages. Numerous ancient pilgrimage sites continued to be visited by the Pandits before the onset of militancy throughout the year on particular days. Remarkably, in recent times, despite the continued trouble in the Valley, Pandit migrants have not totally severed their spiritual links with their motherland. A considerable number of them make it a point to visit the shrine of Khir Bhawani at Tulmula annually. It is somewhat a rewarding experience to find local Muslims embracing their compatriots on such an occasion, notwith-standing the seeming divide between the two communities.

Kashmiri Muslims' devotion to the shrines of the Sufis and the Rishis is deep-rooted in the local context rather than Islam alone. It is not just the famous shrine of Hazratbal or that of the most prominent Sufis like Mir Sayyid 'Ali Hamadani, Shaikh Nuru'd-Din Rishi, Shaikh Hamza Makhdum, etc. that attract a multitude of Muslim devotees on the eve of *urs* but also innumerable shrines of the known or unknown Sufis that form objects of their veneration.[3] Kashmiri

[2]The ideological threats emanate from political politico-religious organizations such as the Ahl-i-Hadith and Jamat-i-Islami. Although their reformist zeal has revitalized the concept of *tawhid* among many a devotee of the shrines, nonetheless, their attempts at undermining the importance of the regional Islamic culture vis-à-vis celebration of the anniversaries of the Sufis and the Rishis have met with very little success. True, the concept of *umma* as preached by these organizations holds fascination for many. But, significantly, the Kashmiris as whole are not prepared to break their ties with the shrines on account of their strong belief in what may be described as spiritio-historical pre-eminence of the Sufis and the Rishis in the local Islamic context.

[3]During my recent field work in the Valley in connection with the compilation of a Dictionary of Sufism in South Asia, I have discovered numerous shrines and holy

Pandits' reverence for the well-known shrines of the Sufis and Rishis in the Valley is well known.[4]

Kashmiriyat has therefore been defined more and more in synthetic and syncretic terms by the official and semi-official media to serve the ideological interests of the Indian state. As a matter of fact, the term Kashmiriyat is not of local origin. When and where was it coined needs to be explored; but it is certain that in the aftermath of the Indira-Shaikh Accord of 1975, the National Conference leadership sought to vindicate and reinforce its faith in Kashmiriyat also against the background of the emergence of Bangladesh. While Kashmiriyat began to be used in the Indian press in the post-Accord period to establish the ideological credentials of the Indian state's sovereignty in the Muslim dominated state as against the two-nation theory, the state government, headed by Shaikh Mohammad Abdullah, lent full support to the Jammu and Kashmir Academy of Art, Culture and Languages to debate and define the concept in a specific historical and cultural context. The Academy in its several publications in Urdu and Kashmiri bolstered the claim of the National Conference leadership that Kashmir was a distinct cultural and linguistic identity and that the main source of this culture personality consciousness was the legacy bequeathed by the Muslim Rishis in terms of syncretic and synthetic Kashmiri culture. Shaikh Nuru'd-Din,[5] the illustrious

sites of local importance that attract several thousand devotees in the rural areas on the eve of *urs*. Notwithstanding the fact that the abundant *tazkira* literature nowhere refers to such abodes of popular veneration, nonetheless, their role in the formation of regional identity can hardly be ignored. In the recent past, the Indian Army has almost launched a drive to protect such holy sites.

[4]The reverential attitude of the Kashmiri Pandits towards the lesser known Sufis and the Rishis deserves some mention in the context of their mass exodus to the plains as a consequence of militancy. During my recent travels across the Valley, I was particularly struck by the reverence in which the shrine of one Usman Raina, popularly known as Rishi Baba, is held by the Pandits of the village of Parnewa in the modern district of Badgam. Not long ago, they, along with the Muslim residents of the village, used to celebrate the anniversary of the Sufi by distributing cooked rice coloured with tumeric (*tahar*) among the poor. The lone family of Pandit Brij Nath, a school teacher, that has not migrated to the plains continues to keep alive the traditions of coexistence prevailing in the Valley over centuries past.

[5]Born in 779/1377, Shaikh Nuru'd-Din Rishi and a host of his disciples played a significant role in the formation of Kashmiri Muslim identity. The title of 'Aamdar-i Kashmir' bestowed on Nuru'd-Din is significant for two reasons as it elevates him to the position of the champion of Kashmiri identity and, it also signifies that his role has been much more important in the religious and cultural history of Kashmiri society

founder of the indigenous order of the Muslim mystics in the Valley, known as the Rishi, was eulogized for his contribution to Kashmiri language and culture. The year-long celebrations connected with the six hundredth birthday of Kashmir's 'national saint' were marked by cultural shows, seminars and mushairas in the Valley. One redeeming feature of the efforts at propagating Kashmiriyat was that the Kashmiri Muslim and Kashmiri Pandit litterateurs worked hand in glove with each other in order to define Kashmiri culture on the foundations of unitary concepts of cultural identity originating not merely in the rich cultural heritage of the Rishis but, also, in the relationship between culture and politics that marks the ideology of the Indian state.

Consequently, as a result of the glorification of the past, Kashmiris were portrayed as peace loving people committed to their rich traditions of religious tolerance and non-violence. Certainly, during 1975–87 or so Kashmiri Muslims and Kashmiri Pandit literateurs produced a version of Kashmiriyat that was not merely rooted in the ethos of their culture, but which was, more subtly, the outcome of their perceived threats to their own identity from forces within and outside. That Kashmiri writers were both self-conscious and socially conscious in their endeavours to preserve what may be considered of permanent and abiding value in their own culture and to assimilate from the outside forces what was necessary for building up a new society was highlighted by this author as early as 1983 (Ishaq Khan 1983: 18–26). Paradoxically, however, such was the impact of the events of the post-1989 period that Kashmiriyat entered a crucial phase in its history of chequered evolution. The emerging point is that except for a few Kashmiri Pandit families living in the Valley, Kashmiriyat now began to remain the sole concern of such Kashmiri Muslims who continued to remain wedded to the shrines of the Sufis and the Rishis, in spite of euphoric drive for what I would call militant Islamization. True, under the influence of the so-called 'fundamentalists', the ideological version of Islam decried veneration of the shrines; but what is of significance to emphasize is that the Kashmiri

---

than that of Mir Sayyid 'Ali Hamadani, popularly known as Shah-i Hamadan. The latter title suggest that Kashmiri Muslim masses never regarded the pious missionary from Hamadan in Peris as more than a venerated Sufi or a religious preacher who left Kashmir for good after securing a firm basis for further development of Islam in the Valley.

tradition of celebrating the anniversaries of their saints has never reasserted itself in such robust and meaningful terms as in the contemporary situation. An important question that, therefore, strikes one's mind is whether Kashmiriyat merely represents the attitudes of Kashmiris towards the shrines. Is it that the veneration of the saint and its varied cultural dimensions form an important component of Kashmiriyat?

Notwithstanding the fact that Kashmiriyat occupies a long-existing cultural space, a careful examination of the tradition that sanctifies it particularly brings to focus a set of perceptions of a society in transition during six centuries of Islamic acculturation. Of these the most important is an understanding of Islam promoted by the Rishis and their adherents against the backdrop of the social and cultural context of Kashmir rather than merely against the *Tawhidic* universalism. This paper is therefore focused on Shaikh Nuru'd-Din Rishi[6] who founded the Rishi order in response to the teachings of the Sufi missionaries from Central Asia and Persia.

There is a direct and fundamental relationship between the evolution of Shaikh Nuru'd-Din's religious career and the gradual development of what may be called the Kashmiri Muslim society. The fact is that during the Shaikh's period the Muslim population of the Valley was a minority (Ghazi, Ms. No. 795: f. 205) or perhaps a very small majority of the entire population of the Kashmir region. From a careful analysis of his verses, it would appear that society in the Kashmir Valley was not purely Islamic in form, nor did it experience a radical transformation overnight on its contact with the great tradition of Islam. Indeed the Shaikh's verses represent not only certain basic facts about the gradual transition of Kashmir to Islam, but also something of the crisis which he was himself passing through and its impact on the social norms and meaning of Islam in the regional context. So central is the new sense of crisis and self-awareness evident in his verses that his poetry assumes the pervasiveness of a vital tradition.

It must be pointed out that for Nuru'd-Din, the term Rishi is a perspective, a standpoint, an archetype of certain dominant historical personalities and even dominant images to which he wanted his followers to orient themselves. His use of the term is a way of looking at experience as a whole, a way of interpreting certain elemental features

[6]See for greater analysis, Ishaq Khan, *Kashmir's Transition to Islam: The Role of Muslim Rishis*, Manohar, New Delhi, paperback, 2002.

of human existence. Thus in a number of verses (Kulliyat, 2nd ed. 1985: 33, 77, 149, 152, 187) he uses a vocabulary and a mystic technique which imbue the word Rishi with an universal value. He wants to convey something more valuable than an elementary historical definition of the term. However, it should be borne in mind that his attempt is to lodge the material—taken from history and folk traditions—in the human soul, which knows no chronology. It is thus frivolous to argue whether the 'legendary' Rishis mentioned by him in various verses (Kulliyat: 33) existed or not; what is of importance is to remember that he uses popular figures in the folk consciousness as empty vials into which he could pour his own conceptions. Doubtless, then, his eulogization of the 'legendary' Rishis is not an exact description of a certain band of Rishis but a profound and illuminating portrayal of some living and comprehensible pious men who practiced asceticism in their everyday life. A careful analysis of the following verses of Nuru'd-Din on the family tree of the Rishis is, therefore, essential for understanding the most profound dimensions of the subject under reference.

The first Rishi was the prophet Mohammad;
The second in order was Hazrat Uways;
The third Rishi was Zulka Rishi;
The fourth in order was Hazrat Pilas;
The fifth was Rum Rishi;
The sixth in order was Hazrat Miran;
The seventh (me) is miscalled a Rishi,
Do I deserve to be called a Rishi? What is my name? (Kulliyat: 33)

It will be seen that Nuru'd-Din traces the family tree of the Rishis back to Muhammad and not to any saint of the Valley belonging to pre-Islamic times. From the Prophet are descended Uways and the 'legendary' sages of Kashmir, such as Zulka, Miran, Rum and Pilas. Chronologically, Nuru'd-Din is separated from a spiritual master by several centuries. But as Henry Corbin remarks, 'the events of the soul are themselves the qualitative measure of their own characteristic time'. A synchronism impossible in historical time is possible in the tempus discretum of the world of the soul or of the *alam-al-mithal*. And this also explains how it is possible, at a distance of several centuries to be the direct synchronous disciple of a master who is chronologically 'in the past' (Corbin, 1969: 67). Nuru'd-Din thus presents a kinship with those Sufis who received guidance in the spiritual path directly from the Prophet Mohammad without having a visible guide (murshid) like Uways. The Sufis, known as Uwaysis, owed their name to the first pious ascetic of Islam, Uways al-Qarni of Yemen, a contemporary of the Prophet Mohammad (Ishaq Khan, 1987: 283). Viewed against the deeper implications of the term Uwaysi in the history of Sufism, the hagiographers' attempt at tracing the spiritual links of Nuru'd-Din with the Uwaysi Sufis does not seem to be unwarranted.

The earthly existence of Zulka, Miran, Rum and Pilas defies historical analysis, but it may be argued that unless we situate them in the world of analogies (*alam-al-mithal*) we will not be able arrive at even an approximation of the truth. The fact is that their repeated mention in Nuru'd-Din's verses partakes a different synchronism, whose peculiar qualitative temporality cannot be doubted. However, nothing would be more dangerous than to apply 'objective' historical methods in proving the temporal existence of the 'legendary' Rishis. Nuru'd-Din's main aim seems to have been to show the unchanged significance, authority and universal relevance of the Rishi tradition. Judged by the rules of historical criticism, his claim may seem highly precarious, but its relevance is to another, 'transhistoric truth' which, to use the phraseology of Corbin, 'cannot be regarded as inferior (because it is of a different order) to the material historical truth whose claim to truth, with the documentation at our disposal, is no less precarious' (Corbin, 1969: 36).

Although Nuru'd-Din's euologization of the 'legendary' Rishis may seem to be incomprehensible to many a rationalist, it is not totally beyond the reach of historical realism or objectivity. True, the Rishis mentioned by him do not fall within quantitative physical time, nor can their supposed one-time existence be measured according to homogenous, uniform units of historical time, but from a strictly historical standpoint, three main points emerge from Nuru'd-Din's attempt at invoking their spiritual ascendancy across generations of mankind which obviously culminates in his person:

First, in his recreation of the role of Sufi Shaikh and the founder of a mystic order, Nuru'd-Din defended the social authenticity of the Rishi tradition and its continued capacity to make sense of the world in the face of the challenges posed to it by the Great Tradition of Islam as represented by the *ulema* (Kulliyat, 1985: 33, 77, 107, 152). In order to save the local tradition from oblivion, he sought to raise it by giving it an Islamic content. As a result, the Hindu ascetics retained the essential elements of ancient popular Kashmiri religious culture, e.g. meditation in the caves, celibacy, vegetarianism, etc. even after their conversion to Islam. In fact, the inner religious life of a number of Muslim Rishis, as it manifested itself outside the systematic teachings of the *ulema*, differed according to the degree of the combination of Islamic elements and existing pre-Islamic traditions and practices. Though rarely capable of acting as an effective organized group, the Rishis still became a framework for associational life within a common social, normative, and ritual order, at a time when the very bases of Kashmiri society were coming under increasingly severe stress consequent upon the advent of Sufi missionaries and the *ulema* from Central Asia and Persia. The vital role played by the Rishis in maintaining a balance between the Sharia and Tariqa on the one hand, and on the other paving the ground for the gradual assimilation and absorption of the local ascetic practices in the wider system of Islam undoubtedly gave their movement enormous authority and social importance.[7]

Second, in his poetry, Nuru'd-Din seems to have given a positive response to the ossification of the *ulema* on a spiritual, emotional and social level, wanting to impose a pristine model from above without a thought for the warm, earthy, mystic religion of the Valley. He also seems to have seen in the dogmatic rigidity of the *ulema* an inflexibility fatal to the cause of Islam, which was by all accounts still in its infancy during the heyday of his struggle against the caste-ridden Brahmanic society. By making Islam respond to the social mores of the Kashmiri people Nuru'd-Din enabled it to develop a resilient tradition of its own, which of course one still finds deep-rooted in the ties of Kashmiri peasant society to a great number of the shrines of the Rishis spread in every nook and corner of the Valley. Thus, the old practice of setting a certain share of his rice in every village as an offering to the local shrine by most cultivators in the Valley continues to exist. Not long ago, 'one walnut tree in every village was donated to some saint.' (Lawrence, 1967: 289).

Third, Nuru'd-Din's verses about the Rishis of yore were definitely rooted in homogenous body of folk consciousness. His mention of the 'legendary' Rishis does not necessarily point to their Muslim origin, but in extolling their virtues, he reinterprets the old traditions through new points of appreciation. Nuru'd-Din's eulogization also helps us to understand the inexhaustible history of the popular mystic tradition in the Valley which, in spite of having travelled through

---

[7]Dr Khan, 2002, pp. 47 and 111 sqq.

vast tracts of time, had still kept itself alive. True, it had developed certain dislocations during its long journey as is evident from his condemnation of the false Rishis (Kulliyat, 1985: 33, 77, 107, 152), but under his inspiring leadership it did restore and invigorate itself, though within a broader framework of Islamic mysticism.

It is important to remember that mystic movements have always exhibited analogous tendencies in certain respects. There were, indeed, both borrowings and innovations. The Rishi concept of 'peace with all' was borrowed from Mahayana Buddhism which originated and flourished in the Valley. The Muslim Rishis also shared traits such as wanderings in the forests, vegetarianism, controlling the breath, etc. with the Hindu–Buddhist ascetics. Notwithstanding the social impact of such similarities, one needs to stress that Nuru'd-Din's greatest contribution lies in making the popular language a vehicle for waging a crusade against the Brahmanic pretensions and their claims to possess wisdom and virtue. His compositions in the popular Kashmiri dialect, particularly addressed to the peasants and artisans, point to the plebeian character of his movement. It is not, therefore, surprizing that the conscious feeling that dominates the minds of the authors of Rishinamas of Chrar, written in the nineteenth century, is that Nuru'd-Din's movement opened the path to God for the poor.

Looking at such information as we possess about the social classes affected by the Rishis, we notice that the peasant classes were uniformly involved, though with the gradual success of their movement, petty tradesmen, artisans, dambael-maets, dombs, tanners, sweepers and men and women belonging to other down-trodden castes were also influenced in due course. The reason why the peasants in general and men of other professions rejected conventional Hinduism has been discussed at some length elsewhere;[8] here it will suffice to say that in Nuru'd-Din's religious thought the term 'Rishi' began to have deeper social implications than it did within the system of Hindu philosophy. When we pass from the realm of speculative philosophy to the actual history of the Rishi movement, we can see the inherent weakness of seeing it only as the off-spring of a marriage between Hinduism and Islam. And what particularly gives sustenance to our argument is Nuru'd-Din's attempt at utilizing the concept of avatara *vis-à-vis* Lalla, though diametrically opposed to his monotheistic faith, to the advantage of Islam in Kashmir.

[8]Dr Khan, 2002, pp. 49, 125–33, 180–3, 187–8, 194–6.

It is important to know why the memory of Lalla or Lal Ded, a senior contemporary of Nuru'd-Din Rishi and a wandering woman mystic, was preserved in the folk consciousness as a rebel against Brahmanism rather than as an exponent of Shaivism.[9] True, modern scholarly attempts at resuscitating Lalla as an ardent protagonist of Shaivism are admirable; but the intriguing question that needs careful examination is why the Muslim hagiographers extolled her virtues as a woman Sufi par excellence. Before this question is probed, it must be emphasized that the Rishi tradition arose at a period of great social crisis. In fact, the tradition came to be modelled after a cultural pattern which was in direct conflict with the decadent Brahmanic order, its agents and its doctrines. It would, therefore, be a form of amputation to study the Rishi tradition outside the context of the new cultural trend. That Islam steered Brahmanism in Kashmir out of its narrow waters into the broad sea of humanism is evident from the historical role that Lalla played in the popular perceptions of the folk. It is doubtful that Lalla would have thought of causing sacrilege to idols while entering a temple, but the fact that an argument of this form could be propounded in a subtle way in the hagiological literature points to a substantial change in the intellectual climate.[10] For now, not only was the Brahmanical view challenged but also those two qualities, wisdom and virtue, which were considered to be their monopoly. In fact, Lalla did not preach Islam, but her *vaakh*[11] which was not in conflict with ontological teachings of the Sufis, served the cause of Islam in Kashmir. Lalla, indeed, propagated the mystic idea of divine unity in simple language which had a deep and direct appeal to the common man. For her, true devotion did not imply various rituals and practices evolved by the Brahman but meant seeking God within oneself, and also in the routine of daily life:

[9]Neither there exists any grave nor *samadhi* of Lal Ded in Kashmir. Of course, a tomb supposed to be the burial place of Lal Ded, situated in the vicinity of the shrine of Baba Nasibu'd-Din Ghazi in the town of Bijbehara is an object of veneration for a small number of Muslim women. What, however, need to be emphasized is that none of the Muslim admirers of Lal Ded has mentioned her tomb in the *tazkira* literature.

[10]Baba Nasib is the first hagiographer to relate the incredible story of Lal Ded's entry into a temple for purposes of easing herself; nonetheless, the dialogue recorded by him concerning the Brahman priest of the temple, Lalla and Shaikh Nuru'd-Din clearly reflect the protestant trend in the religious situation of Kashmir in the seventeenth century. See Rishinama, Ms. N0. 795, f. 99b.

[11]A word: *vaakh* is equivalent of the Sanskrit vakya, i.e. Lal Ded's sayings (Lalla-Vakyani), or the verses composed and recited by her.

Siva abides in all that is, everywhere
Then do not discriminate between a Hindu and a Musalman.
If thou art wise, know thyself
That is true knowledge of the Lord. (Jayalal Kaul, 1973: 107)

Lalla's approach to religion, based on mysticism, was fundamentally humanistic and individualistic. By rejecting formal and organized religion which was based on the supreme authority of the Brahman, she helped the common accept the Sufi ideas of equality and the brotherhood of man:

I renounced fraud, untruth, deceit,
I taught my mind to see the one in all my fellow-men,
How could I then discriminate between man and man,
And not accept the food offered by brother man. (Ibid)

Lalla vehemently criticized the worship of idols:

The idol is but stone,
The temple is but stone,
From top to bottom all is stone. (Ibid: 110)

In her criticism of the ritualistic practices of the Brahmans, Lalla remarked:

He does not need the kusa grass, nor sesame seed,
Flowers and water He does not need,
He who, in honest faith, accepts his Guru's word,
On Siva meditates constantly,
He, full of joy, from action freed, will not be born again. (Ibid.)

Again, castigating the Brahman's greed for making animal sacrifices obligatory,
Lalla remarked:

It covers your shame,
Saves you from cold,
It's food and drink,
Mere water and grass,
Who counseled you, O Brahmin,
To slaughter a living sheep as a sacrifice,
Unto a lifeless stone. (Ibid: 104)

Lalla was disgusted by the hypocrisy of the Brahman and thus exposed his pride for claiming to be the learned:

The thoughtless read the holy books
As parrots, in their cage, recite Ram, Ram,
Their reading is like churning water,
Fruitless effort, ridiculous conceit. (Ibid: 104)

Lalla's spirit of revolt against the social inequalities of her age is manifest in these verses:

When can I break the bonds of shame?
When I am indifferent to jibes and jeers.
When can I discard the robe of dignity?
When desires cease to nag my mind. (Ibid: 103)

Some verses of Lalla have been translated literally to describe her semi-nude condition. In fact, these verses have been read and interpreted out of the social context. The historical term of reference to such a context is the sense of revolt generated in her mind by the iniquitous social order and, above all, by her spiritual preceptor, Sayyid Husain Simnani:

The Guru gave me only one word;
Enter into thyself from the outer world;
The guru's precept came to me as God's word;
That's why I started dancing nude. (Parimoo, 1978: 12–13)

Lalla's ascetic self-discipline, therefore, certainly inspired her junior contemporary, Nuru'd-Din, in the days of his youth. True, she was critical of penance and fasting, but her exhortations for choosing the life of poverty had unquestionably its desired effect on the Rishis:

In life I sought neither wealth nor power;
Nor ran after the pleasures of sense;
Moderate in food and drink, I lived a controlled life;
And love my God. (Kaul 1973: 98)

The example of Lalla's vegetarianism surely influenced the Rishis:

Whether they killed a large sheep or a small one,
Lalla had her round stone (as her usual fare). (Parimoo, 1978: 7)

As a true precursor of the Rishis, Lalla was a wandering ascetic engrossed in God-consciousness, yearning to see God everywhere (*Shiv tshorn thali thale*).[12] The prevalent caste taboos about food and

---

[12]Abdu'l-Ahad Azad, 1959. Kashmiri Zuban aur Shairi II, Srinagar, p. 113.

a drink did not impress her (*anas khyanas kyah chum dvesh*);[13] nor was she bothered about the performance of the ceremonial rites. (Kaul and Nandlal Talib, 1984: 41, 43, 110, 112, 136–41)

It is not therefore difficult to understand why Nuru'd-Din Rishi described Lalla as an avatara.

That Lall of Padmanpore
Who had drunk to her fill the nectar
She was an avatar of ours
O God, grant me the same spiritual power. (Kulliyat, 1985: 21)

Undoubteldy, Lalla gave a unique orientation to the evolution of a new cultural pattern in Kashmir. The influence of her *vaakh* was substantial on Nuru'd-Din during the formative stage of his mystical career; likewise the impact of her revolt against social and religious discrimination was tremendous on the folk for whom, even from the point of view of Hindu scriptures, she was the saviour in 'the hour of calamity and enslavement'. Lalla actually shot into prominence in an age of social ferment when Hinduism in Kashmir, as a result of its declining strength, was exposed to the radiant influence of Islam through the egalitarian spirit of the Sufis. That Lalla herself presents a dismal picture of the collapse of dharma is amply borne out by the foregoing discussion. That Lalla, as an ardent lover of Siva, succeeded in reviving Saivism is an argument belied by the very silence of our Saivite chroniclers and poets of her near-contemporary and later times. What is, however, of significance to remember from the viewpoint of social history is the historical dimension of her elevation to avatar by a devout Muslim like Nuru'd-Din Rishi.

According to the Hindu scriptures, avatars are born for the purpose of re-establishing dharma, but as Bhagavat Purana repeatedly stresses they also emerge on the social scene 'for teaching the mortals the wisdoms of the ages. They have taught and given right perspectives and direction to human beings. They have set through their lives an example of right conduct and instilled hope and courage.' (Pandey, 1979: 8–9). It is obvious, then, why Nuru'd-Din described Lalla as an avatar, since Lalla, in a true spirit of an avatar, assumed the role befitting the situational demands, and reshaped the anomalies and derangements into a progressive adjustment and harmony. Lalla

---

[13]Jayalal Kaul, Lal Ded (Sahitya Akademi, New Delhi, 1973), p. 107

wanted that man should become 'more of a man' and swim across darkness into light.

The impact of Lalla's eulogization as an avatar of Kashmiris contributed a great deal to her romanticization, so much so that a Suhrawardiyya Sufi of the seventeenth century, himself influenced by the Rishi movement, extolled her in the following terms:

Passion for God set fire to all she had,
And from her heart rose clouds of smoke,
Having had a draught of adh-e-alast,[14]
Intoxicated and drunk with joy was she,
One cup of this God-intoxicating drink,
Shatters reason into bits,
A little drowsiness from it is headier than
Intoxication from a hundred jars of wine. (Kaul, 1978: 1–2)

Significantly, Lalla was well aware of the success of her role in contemporary society:

Whatever I uttered with my tongue, became a mantra. (Ibid: 59)

Again:

I burnt the foulness of my soul;
I slew my heart, its passions all;
I spread my garments, hem and sat;
Just there, on bended knees,
In utter surrender unto Him;
My fame as Lalla spread afar. (Ibid: 117)

The aural value of Lalla's verses and their profound impact on Kashmiri society is not simply illustrated by Nuru'd-Din's and the hagiographers' eulogization of her role, but also by the fact that her teachings were translated into action by the socially oppressed people rather than by the Brahmans. The very interpolations in Lalla's verses suggests that each word that she uttered became a precept, a maxim of conduct for her Muslim followers with their roots in the local culture. Although most modern writers have been at pains to emphasize interpolations in both Lalla's and Nuru'd-Din's mystical poetry (Ishaq Khan 1986: 187–205), unfortunately, they have failed to grasp the

---

[14]*Alastu bi Rabbikum, qalu bala* (Am I not your Lord? Asked Allah. 'Yes', answered they). For the Covenant between Allah and human souls, see the Quran: 7/12

similarity of the context in which these verses were produced. In fact, the language which Nuru'd-Din spoke was not an individual inheritance but a social acquisition from the environment in which he grew up. The poetry of Lalla and Nuru'd-Din came to be the daily bread of many Kashmiris of the period, who formed their Weltanschauung in accordance with the picture presented to them by their two spiritual teachers. The important place, therefore, occupied by Lalla in the lives of the various strata of the Kashmiri people as well as her role in the formation of a regional culture, can hardly be overexaggerated. Such a culture drew its essential vitality from a conflict, a division, turmoil and a struggle created in the individual psyche by the challenges posed to the social order by Lalla. That the founder of the Rishi order was a spiritual heir to the legacy of Lalla is amply borne out by his animadversions against caste system. However, his criticism of the superiority of caste can also be better appreciated against the Quranic verses proclaiming all men descended from one and the same pair.

Adam is the progenitor of the human race,
The Mother Eve has the same primordiality,
(So) from where have the 'low-castes' descended?)
How can a 'high born' deride his own ancestry? (Kulliyat, 1985: 206)

The contempt in which the Brahmans held the common man certainly touched the sensitive soul of Nuru'd-Din. In order to tame the ferocity of their pride he challenged the concept of purity of the Brahman's birth in terms of the *tawhidic* humanism and universalism. It was Muslim's commitment to an ethic of action which was valued by Nuru'd-Din vis-à-vis the unethical egocentrism of the Brahman:

One who harps proudly upon one's caste,
Is bereft of reason and wisdom,
Here the good alone can claim noble descent;
In the Hereafter 'caste' will be extinct,
Were you to imbibe the essence of Islam,
Then no one would be purer than you. (Ibid.)

Significantly, some of the verses of Nuru'd-Din seem to have functioned as an effective medium of satire and social commentary on the hollowness of the notion of caste in the masterly use of metaphor and allegory:

(By) displaying the caste in the world,
What will thou gain?
Into dust will turn the bones,
When the earth envelopes the body:
To utter disgrace will he come
Who, forgetting himself, jeers at others. (Parimoo, 1978: 226)

It is not, therefore, difficult to understand the continual social discontent among the common folk against Brahmanic supremacy as reflected in the literature on the Rishis. In particular, interpolations in the verses attributed to Nuru'd-Din are crucial to our understanding of the role of the converts themselves in perpetuating the memory of his greatness, singling him out as the hope of the downtrodden and, therefore, a perpetual object of veneration. The popular perception of Nuru'd-Din is not only that of a saint but also of a champion of the commoners, including even menials like sweepers and tanners, who prominently figure in the discussions of the saint with the Brahmans. Certainly, Nuru'd-Din's denunciation of the caste system prompted the so-called castes and the weaker sections of Kashmiri society to break off their ties with a caste-ridden social structure. As the lower-caste Hindus were attracted to Islam, though in stages, over the centuries, the *urs* celebrated at the shrines of the Rishis somewhat solemnly in the early phase of their evolution began to assume festive colour with the passage of time. It was the repetition of the dialogues attributed to Nuru'd-Din and Brahman ascetics by the so-called low born like the village dancers and acrobats (*hand, dambael maets* and *faqirs*) that played a significant role in transmitting the values of the Rishis in the traditional Kashmiri society.

The performances of the folk dancers have a symbolic significance for assessing the role of the Rishis in drawing the peasants and farmers to their fold. But, more importantly, the conspicuous presence of the folk dancers on the eve of anniversaries and the villagers' age-long interest in them imply that it was a social rather than mere religious conversion that created the pressure for change which, in turn, also affected the course of Islamic religious development in the Valley. The issues raised by the folk dancers through their acts concern the relation of the individual believer to God, and equally important, contact between the ordinary believer and the saint, who is in direct contact with God. It was through such contacts that the use of the Kashmiri language as a religious vehicle was fostered and Islam opened up to people who were not educated in classical Arabic and Persian. The overall impact of the Rishi movement was that through the performances given by the folk dancers Islam was brought to the masses in a meaningful way. Since at that time the only education for the illiterate folk was that which was transmitted orally, there arose groups of acrobats and singers who assumed the role of teachers. This also explains why the festive occasions at the shrines of the Rishi saints are days of rejoicing and thanksgiving. They commemorate the formative stage of conversion when the commoners entered the fold that proclaimed the equality of all men. Although the above discussion suggests the existence of a world of syncretism of beliefs and conduct in medieval Kashmir, the ground paved by it for gradual conversion of the people to Islam should not be lost sight of. This is also reflected in the changing pattern of naming the people undergoing the process of Islamic acculturation. True, many converts retained the tribal *nisba* or occupational affiliation as a last name, but what is of interest is the immense popularity of names with strong religious connotation, e.g. 'Abdu'l Rahman, Ghulam Ahmad, Ghulam Muhammad, Ghulam Hasan and so on. The assertion of ones identity by defining a relationship to Allah and the Prophet Mohammad through the assumption of distinctive Muslim names signified an important development in the conversion process. It is true that in spite of this development, the *domb, dambel maets, hanjis* and other so-called lower castes of the Kashmiri Muslim community were (and still are) discriminated against in marriage, but in contrast to their ancestors' position in the Brahman-dominated Hindu social structure, they were not socially ostracized or reviled. It was this group, however, that initially by its very existence, posed questions about the social character of Islam (Ishaq Khan, 2002: 196). This is also the reason that over centuries of social conversion numerous Muslim families could arrogate such high titles as Pandit, Shah, Khan, Shaikh, and even Sayyid to themselves. The extent to which the social matrix has loosened in our own times is now illustrated by the religious leadership provided to Kashmiri Muslims by some respectable men whose leadership followed traditionally despised occupations such as bakery. The emergence of Islam as a social religion among the Kashmiris was bound to give to birth to institutions that eventually assumed pre-eminence in the developing Muslim society. What actually brought about the need to develop such institutions was the process of acculturation itself which influenced their growth, partly through conflict, but mainly through a

peaceful and orderly evolution. Indeed, the emergence of social institutions like the *asthans* of the Rishis in every nook and corner of the
Valley covered a far broader horizon than the asthapans of the
Hindus. In fact, the unlettered folk began to see their community as
socially distinct, complete with its own religious infrastructure in the
form of mosques adjacent to the shrine. It is in the time of the later
Rishis like Baba Nasib and some of his followers that we are able to
understand how the converts spontaneously but cautiously acted upon
the perception of being members of an Islamic community. Gradually
the need for participating in congregational prayers, particularly
on Fridays, began to be felt keenly by the converts—a practice which
decisively separated the Muslim community from the Brahmanic.
It was at the congregational prayers, through the loud recitation of
invocatory prayers and litanies that the converts proclaimed the
universality of their religion in radical contrast to their ancestors'
deification of the priest or an ascetic in the pre-Islamic cosmological
structure.

From a careful examination of the source material, including
innumerable songs composed by the common folk in praise of the
Prophet Mohammad and a number of prominent Muslim Rishis, it
would also appear that the Kashmiris themselves perceived their
conversion more in terms of a social process than a sudden or a dramatic change felt by them in their lives. Of course, conversion of a
certain individuals in the latter sense did take place owing to their
intimate contacts with the Sufis, but it would be unwise to propound
a general theory of spectacular mass conversions on the basis of such
exceptional cases. What seems more reasonable to suppose is that it
was only in the wake of the construction of mosques that the preliterate
people of an agrarian society were absorbed into Islam. However, it
need to be emphasized that even in the mosques the *tazkiras* of the
Rishis and other Sufis remained the medium of instruction in the
values of Kashmiri Muslim society.

Remarkably, men deep-rooted in theological learning generally
wrote *tazkiras*. Notwithstanding the fact that such kind of literature
presents fundamental paradoxes and contradictions in terms of their
authors' emphasis on the role of miracles or supernatural, it would
be worthwhile to evaluate the hagiographical literature through the
perceptions of the hagiographers rather than the perceptional world
of our century. In their world, things do not seem to have preserved
their separateness and their identity; they deeply realize in the core

of human being a homogeneity between their individual life-process and the rest of the cosmic order. Thus while turning stones into living beings, elevating dogs to sainthood, making springs pray for the pious and look askance at the wicked, with wild animals bowing before the Rishis, the hagiographers nevertheless do not indulge in fancies, but point symbolically to the unity of man and the world of man as possessing as pantheism; nor should such descriptions move us in the direction of presenting a theocentric view of history. Both history and Islam would lose their meaning if either of them is divested of its intrinsic relation to the other. Neither Islam nor history can acquire an objective meaning and propose if they are presented respectively as wholly sacred or wholly profane. Does religion corrupt historical thinking? Or have the so-called secular movements in history corrupted religion? Our purpose in raising such questions is to broaden and deepen our own understanding of the dual and reciprocal function of religion and society in not only generating but also easing inner conflicts and social tensions of the human soul and mind respectively.

Conclusions

Against the background of the Rishi movement, Islam in its historical manifestation in Kashmir emerges as a socio-religious and moral force radiating significance to life and thought of the people at the crossroads. The so-called syncretic tradition of the Rishis was a necessary concomitant of the process of Islamization rather than its culmination. The seeming syncretism of Islamic beliefs and local practices, in fact, concurrently marked the beginning of a movement for the realization of the ultimate, if not immediate, objectives of Islam at both the individual and social levels. While apparently accommodating local Hindu-Buddhist practices to the Islamic framework, the Rishis gradually paved the way for the assimilation of the people in the Islamic identity. What is, however, unique about this identity is not merely the assimilation of the Kashmiris in Islam over a period of six centuries but, more importantly, their urge to live with their Pandit compatriots in symbiotic rather than syncretic relationship.

The mass exodus of the Kashmiri Pandits to the plains following the onset of militancy in Kashmir should not, therefore, lead us to believe that Kashmiriyat has a hollow ring. The fact is that an unforeseen event or an accident cannot disarrange the ethos of a people in spite of their different attitudes in their quest for identity. True, the structure of their society or even societies is complex and marked by myriad and untold interrelations. But history bears witness to the fact that complex relations have often found a mutual and workable adjustment in the face of challenges posed to the common cultural identity or even avowed distinct religious identities of the people. How long will it take Kashmiri Muslims and Kashmiri Pandits to recover from the shock of sudden blows and even mutilations remains to be seen. However, what is remarkable about them is that they have not yet broken sharply with the past. Their collective consciousness in terms of Kashmiriyat lies in their urge to keep alive certain unique traditions confined within the sacred boundaries of their asthans and asthapans. The vital social and religious processes of history that separate yet unite the Kashmiri Muslims and Kashmiri Pandits in a search for deeper spiritual identity is best reflected in the verses of the founder of the Rishi movement:

Among the brothers of the same parents.
Why did you create a barrier?
Muslims and Hindus are one
When will God be kind to His servants? (Kulliyat, II, 1981: 33–4)

References

'Abdu'l-Ahad Azad. 1959. *Kashmiri Zuban aur Shairi*, II.
Baba Nasibu'd-Din Ghazi, Nurnama. (Research and Publication Department, Jammu and Kashmir Government, MS. no 795: F: 205), Srinagar.
Corbin, Henry. 1969. *Creative Imagination in the Sufism of Ibn 'Arabi* (Eng. Tr.), R. Manheim, Princeton.
Dhar, Kashi Nath. 1981. *Nund Rishi: A Rosary of Hundred Beads*, Jammu and Kashmir Academy of Art, Culture and Languages, Srinagar.
Ishaq Khan, Mohammad. 1983. *Perspectives on Kashmir: Historical Dimensions*, Gulshan Publishers, Srinagar.
_____. 1986. Impact of Islam on Kashmir in the Sultanate Period, 1320–1586, *The Indian Economic and Social History Review*, 23 (2) Delhi School of Economics, New Delhi, p. 187–205.
_____. 1987. Sufism in Indian History, *Islam in India*, Christian W Troll (Ed.), Oxford University Press, p. 283.
_____. 2002. *Kashmir's Transition to Islam: The Role of Muslim Rishis* (3rd edition, Manohar, New Delhi), p. 197.
Kaul, Jayalal. 1973. *Lad Ded*, Sahitya Akademi, New Delhi, p. 107.
_____ and Nandlal Talib. 1984. *Lal Ded*, 3rd ed. Jammu and Kashmir Academy of Art, Culture and Languages, Srinagar, p. 41–141.

Kulliyat-i Shaikhu'l-'Alam, 1985, 2nd ed. Jammu and Kashmir Academy of
    Art, Culture and Languages, Srinagar, 19.
_____, 1979, 1981. Compiled by Moti Lal Saqi, 2 vols. Jammu and Kashmir
    Academy of Art, Culture and Languages, Srinagar.
_____. 1985. Revised edition by M. L. Saqi, Jammu and Kashmir Academy
    of Art, Culture and Languages, Srinagar, p. 33–187.
Lawrence, Walter. 1967. *The Valley of Kashmir* (reprinted in Srinagar), p. 289.
Nund Rishi: Rosary of Hundred Beads, Jammu and Kashmir Academy of Art,
    Culture and Language, Srinagar, 1981.
Pandey, R.K. 1979. *The Concept of Avatars with special reference to Gita.* Delhi,
    p. 8–9.
Parimoo, B.N. 1978. *The Ascent of Self,* Delhi, p. 12–3.
Willams A. Monier. 1964. *Sanskrit-English Dictionary,* Oxford University
    Press, p. 227.

5

Debating Religious Practice in Cyberspace: Lived Islam and Antinomian Identities in a Kashmiri Muslim Community

APARNA RAO

Introduction

The relationship between prescription and practice—between concepts of the 'ideal' (or normative) and the 'lived' (or 'actual')—has for long been a topic of ethnographic investigation. While in certain areas of research, the former has been stressed (e.g. kinship prescriptions), in others (e.g. the study of religion), the latter has been accorded primacy. Obviously, a great deal of discourse concerning practice takes place among religious specialists and scholars of the scriptures, and hence, the question of similarities and differences between (often scriptural) prescription and practice in a variety of religions has also engaged many ethnographers. Debates about such differences among South Asian Muslims have also engaged many scholars (see notably for India, Ahmad 1981; Robinson 1983, 1985, 1986; Das 1984; Minault 1984). While considerable information exists both about discourse and practice, there are few studies on the discourse that goes on about this practice—on what

I would like to thank the moderators of the virtual community which accepted me as a member and gave me permission to use the communication for research purposes.

The on-line material has been reproduced as it had appeared, without any editorial correction. *Editors.*

Bourdieu (1977) referred to as 'objectified practice'—among lay people and non-specialists. Few studies engage with the ideas and emotions of the vast majority of Muslims regarding the relationship between their normative and lived religion. As an anthropologist, my point of departure is what the people concerned do and say about their actions, since this impacts further action. In this paper, I attempt to briefly discuss such ideas and emotions among a community of Kashmiri Muslims.

The relationship between scriptural, normative Islam and lived Islam has been a subject of reflection among Muslims in Kashmir ever since the notion of Kashmiri Muslim identity as a communitas emerged some decades ago (e.g. Ishaq Khan 1998; Chadha-Behera 2000: Ch. 3; Zutshi 2000, 2008; Sikand 2008). Such reflection and discourse—especially concerning the role of mystic traditions and Sufi shrines—has unquestionably increased, both in intensity and geographical extent during the last decade-and-a-half.[1] Even in far-flung villages, Kashmiri peasants and shepherds now discuss their beliefs and practices and compare these with what they are told about Islam by preachers of the Kashmiri Jamat-i-Islami and the Ahl-i-Hadith, Islamic movements which, in spite of their mutual differences, shun and criticize popular Sufism. Since the early 1990s, discussions about the role of shrines has impacted most Kashmiri Muslims: in 1990 the leaders of the then united Jammu and Kashmir Liberation Front vowed before some 300,000 people at the shrine of Baba Nur-ud Din Rishi to lead Kashmir to independence. Shortly thereafter, however, activists of the Hizb-ul Mujahidin (the then united armed wing of the Jamaat-i-Islami in Kashmir) prevented thousands from participating in their traditional festivals at Sufi shrines and even destroyed some of the buildings. Yet resistance was equally rapid, and thousands of peasants defied the Hizb-ul Mujahidin at the shrines of Baba Zainuddin Rishi, Baba Payamuddin Rishi, Zain Shah Sahib, and even in Srinagar, at Batmoal Rishi. In old Srinagar neighbourhoods, while many young men became critical of the traditional shrine culture, women continued to gather there to find solace, and physically and mentally differentially abled little boys

[1]This period witnessed, not only violent turmoil in the Valley but also unprecedented rise of state-sponsored violence in the name of 'the Hindu religion' in India, notably against the constructed image of the Muslim Other. In Kashmir, the combination of these two phenomena tend to increase such reflection (see Ishaq Khan 2001: 6ff. for an example of earlier reflections on such themes).

continued to be dedicated to specific shrines. In early 2002, similar discussions centred around the video cassettes of Sharaf-ud-din Al-Khalifa, a Tanzanian child, born into a Christian family, but said to have recited verses from the Holy Quran and spontaneously offered namaz from the age of about one. While this was widely accepted as a miracle, many strongly disapproved of these cassettes being kept by some, respectfully wrapped up in a green cloth.

Discussions on the relationship between normative Islam and lived Islam in Kashmir take place, not only in the private and public spheres, but also in cyberspace. Indeed, new communication technologies are contributing in a major way to discussion inputs, and the materials I draw upon here are discussions among Kashmiri Muslims that are taking place on the internet. Drawing on certain methods used in cognitive anthropology (Quinn and Holland 1987: 16; D'Andrade 1991: 282; Strauss 1992: 15f.), I investigate ordinary discourses and conversational materials among a relatively small sample of informants. Following the cognitive anthropological approach, I also apply the concept of schemas, which are considered hierarchically linked building blocks of cognition, capable of triggering action (see Boeck 1998). The uppermost schema in these hierarchies are taken to function as implicit or explicit goals to be attained. In the discourses examined here being a good Muslim and/or being a good Kashmiri emerge as the uppermost goal-schemas, implicit for some, explicit for others. It will be shown first, how the concerns about the relationship between normative and lived Islam are closely bound with one or both of these two goal-schemas; second, how, for some, these two goals, when examined in the light of this relationship are coming to be perceived as dissonant and even antinomian,[2] and how conjunctive practice is being severed to form disjunctive alternatives, with the two goals situated at the two ends of a conceptual continuum.

The Internet, Ethnography and the Community Studied

The community of Kashmiri Muslims focused on in this paper is located in cyberspace and is hence, what is known as a virtual, or online

---

[2]I use the term 'antinomy' to describe a situation in which a person judges two phenomena or possibilities, which are reasonable and rational in themselves to be mutually contradictory and conflicting. In a recent work, Béteille (2000: 1) has defined the term thus: '... contradictions, oppositions and tensions inherent in the norms and values through which societies regulate or seek to regulate themselves ...'.

community. Over a decade ago, it was observed, '... people anywhere ... inevitably build virtual communities ... as more and more informal public spaces disappear from our real lives.' (Rheingold 1993: 6) There can be many reasons for such 'disappearances'; a complete disruption of the earlier public culture in the Valley and a partially diasporic situation are two reasons applicable to Kashmiris.

As part of the inevitable trend towards multisited fieldwork, there is a rapidly growing body of literature based on research conducted in cyberspace (e.g. Turkle 1995; Lyon 1997; Markham 1998; Hakken 1999; Kirchner 2007; Gomes 2001; Morton 2001; Wilson and Peterson 2002). Computer-mediated communication has become a major vehicle of interaction throughout the world, especially among the relatively affluent sections of society (for a critical analysis of its impact in a global economy, see Castells 1996). Members of the South Asian diaspora in particular have initiated and manage a plethora of, often community/language/region-specific—(e.g. Goa-net, KHASI Group, Sindh-Int, TamilNet)—e-mail based internet sites that aim at establishing and encouraging contacts among members of these communities, language groups and regions wherever they may reside (see also Mitra 1997).[3] Membership of such communities is usually restricted, and, in addition to news postings about various subjects, these spaces are also the sites of prolonged dialogues and wider discussions (or netcussions) about specific topics raised by one or more members.[4]

Considerable feedback exists between these virtual and non-virtual communities and much of the discourse that takes place online both reflects and constructs the concerns of the non-virtual, wider society. As already mentioned, online communities are not only translocal, but also transnational, both in operation and membership,

[3]According to a Gartner India survey report of 2000, '... the pace of growth in the Indian Internet user community was the highest in the entire Asia-Pacific region— over 3.1 million Indians surfed the Net regularly, that is, at least one hour a week.' (*Frontline*, 13.10. 2000)

[4]Such e-groups must be clearly distinguished from more general (USENET) newsgroups and websites, whose aim is to disseminate what they consider to be important information. While many newsgroups and websites are not anonymous, unlike e-groups, they do not allow for spontaneous discussions or the exchange of views. There are roughly 1,500 Islamic sites (for an overview see Bunt 2000). Unconnected with Jammu and Kashmir and some 50 sites focusing on the problems and history of Jammu and Kashmir. Some of the latter belong to political organizations such as the Jammu Kashmir Liberation Front (or one of its factions) or to militant groups active in the area, such as the Lashkar-i-Tayyeba (Sikand 2007).

thus enabling quick and intense communication between diasporic and local communities. And as many scholars have noted for South Asia, migration to the west in particular has greatly impacted their notions of what constitutes their identity (e.g. Jain 1998, Uberoi 1998). The diasporic status has also largely contributed to the construction of a new understanding of religion (e.g. Mukta and Bhatt 2001; Van der Veer 2002) and to its practice back in South Asia. Further, new communication technologies have helped place religious content and the awareness of religious identity at the centre stage of what Van der Veer (2002: 174, 183–4) refers to as the 'dialectics between nationalism and transnationalism'. Indeed, increasingly, the internet has become a site of and for information and discussions about a variety of religious doctrines and practices, and a major medium of communication on related topics across the world.

Some still question the use of internet materials as primary ethnographic sources and undoubtedly certain methodological approaches still need refining (cf. Berger 1977: Ch. 8 for similar objections concerning the use of fictional materials). Two concerns sometimes raised relate to the selective use of language and the identities of the personae involved.[5] Face to face interaction—as opposed to written or telephonic communication—makes use not only of the spoken word, but also of a series of other, often subtle, voluntarily or involuntarily non-verbal cues that add to the content of the message, clarify its contextuality and indicate its degree of veracity. In addition, the spoken language is often, though not always, more spontaneous than the written word. While the gaps of non-verbal communication can never be filled in non-visual interaction, fairly frequent e-mail users tend to compose their mails with a linguistic spontaneity whose expressiveness (and errors) seem to belie concerns regarding the selective use of language. The second concern, about the identity of community members, is also only partially valid. While the invention of identities is technically feasible, most online community members either introduce themselves or refer to their professional, family or home identities, and most of these are easily verifiable, both 'on the ground' and often again via the internet. Some even meet in flesh and blood and then recount these meetings. Remaining on the margins,

[5]I would especially like to thank Asha Rani, T.N. Madan, Deepak Mehta, Sudhindra Sharma and Ashish Nandy for raising these questions and for their helpful comments on an earlier version of this paper which was presented at the conference 'Lived Islam: Liminality, Accommodation and Adaptation', in December 2002 in Goa. I am grateful to the community's moderators for giving me permission to use all discussion materials.

the ethnographer cannot thus become a target of propaganda, any-more than she can in a 'real life' field setting.[6]

The virtual community I focus on was founded in 1995 by Kashmiri students in the US, and is not ostensibly connected to any organization.[7] Its members (as of writing roughly 500[8]) came together through their common interest in Kashmir and their topics of discussion vary widely. Most refer at some point of time to their professions and these point to the community consisting mainly of middle (and lower middle) class urban Kashmiri Sunni Muslim men, aged between roughly 20 and 45, some living in the Valley[9] and some outside it. A few young Kashmiri Hindus living in the valley till around 1990 are also members; so too are a handful of men from Azad Kashmir, as also a few non-Kashmiris, both Muslim and Hindu from India and Pakistan. In as far as its members live outside the Valley, the community reflects the diasporic nature of middle-class Kashmiri Muslims—of an estimated few thousand men abroad, almost 1000 live in USA. The community is obviously far from representative of all Kashmiri Muslims, but I contend that it well represents the urban intelligentsia in terms of family background, religious convictions and professional and political aspirations.

In keeping with the ethics of ethnographic research, I sought permission in June 2001 from the community leaders, i.e. the group's

[6]Indeed, Gomes' (2001: 51) observations about Goa-net are probably valid for most virtual communities, including that discussed here:

'... my observations indicate that the majority of the people involved ... do not disguise their identities. Involvement in real-life projects and extensive computer-mediated interactions have facilitated the transformation of most members from anonymous cyberbeings into personalities, with peculiar characteristics and habits. After several months of 'observation', I was able to quickly recognize the personae mentioned ... participants begin to take on distinctive identities ... social relationships are formed and a certain sense of intimacy is developed ... This is revealed in the personalized way some members write their messages as well as the way members refer to or address some of their fellow members ...'

[7]In August 2001, 136 such e-groups were identifiable in a single search engine (Yahoo), simply by keying in the term 'Kashmir'; there were also a few sub-regional e-groups (e.g. Zanskar-online, Kupwara-online), but most of these were either moribund, or had very few members. There also existed internet directories that gave various details about their members, in a clear attempt towards community bonding.

[8]As in all such e-groups, membership fluctuates.

[9]In late November 2002 there were 804 internet connections in Srinagar; Sopore and Islamabad had nearly 100 each. There were 6 servers in the Valley, of which 3 functioned. Srinagar University had 2 servers, and Srinagar had 40 internet cafes. By spring 2003, with the entry of several private firms, faster service and a tremendous drop in prices, the number of connections has risen sharply.

moderators, to join the community and draw on it for teaching and research purposes; permission was readily granted. Again, in keeping with widespread ethnographic practice, I respect the privacy of the community and its members, and refer to these here anonymously.

Given the constraints imposed by space, I now draw on only two[10] of several discussions within this community that relate explicitly to the practice, nature, and contents of Islam in Kashmir. These two[11] were chosen because only Kashmiri Muslims participated, they came from the Valley and the diaspora, and there was no overlap in participants. These discussions serve to illustrate the nature of the current discourse on lived Islam in the Valley, and touch upon many issues of related interest referred to above—practice and prescription, the diaspora, issues of identity, and the antinomies that many grapple with in a rapidly globalizing world.

> 'Men go to mosques. We go to the ... shrines ... We cannot face God on our own, so we ask the Pir buried there to intercede on our behalf .... I find great peace there. What are these men thinking when they burn down our shrines? ...'—Abida, Srinagar (in Butalia 2002)

> 'I asked the jailer [in Tihar] if I could go ... and touch the grave [of Maqbool Butt] .... I wanted to visit the grave to pay my obeisance to my leader ... I prayed to God for the opportunity to be near it.'—Yasin Malik (www.geocities.com/jklf-kashmir/tribute.html)

The Discussions

Typically, discussions are initiated when someone asks for information on a particular topic, and/or forwards printed (or visual) material. All discussions have one or more titles under the heading 'subject'.

Discussion 1

Keeping Islamic Tradition of Tolerance Alive/Puritanical Wahabi Ideology (October–November 2002)

[10]The discussions are reproduced verbatim and indicate the use of language. As mentioned earlier, a variety of topics are discussed in this community—including its very nature. Thus, for example, on 29.04.2003 one member wrote, 'One had ... an idea that one could convey a wish to a friend; initiate and dwell on meaningful themes, particularly in respect to our motherland ...'.

[11]Certain dimensions of these can be better grasped when embedded in their wider socio-political setting, but this exceeds my present mandate. My purpose here is also, neither to discuss whether the views expressed by the Mirwaiz in this interview conform

This discussion took place between five men, and began when one of them, TM, circulated an item published in the newspaper, *The Hindustan Times* (13.10.2002):

Can someone verify and confirm the accuracy of the information of this article?
'The laid-back Islam is part of the heritage of the Himalayan region, where Sufi verse is passed on from generation and generation.'
'These sounds and words which go deep in the soul have saved me from despair,' said Ahmad Qureshi, a tailor, who lost his two sons in the Kashmir conflict.
'Sufis who are found across the Muslim world, mix traditional Islamic rites with a focus on spiritual experience, practicing solitary meditation and following the quest for divine love lauded nine centuries ago by the Farsi poet Rumi.' (does this sound right? (*TM, 17.10.2002*)

HindustanTimes.com > Project Kashmir > The Factfile
Keeping Islamic tradition of tolerance alive

Steeped in the Sufi mysticism they embraced some 500 years ago, Muslims in Kashmir appear to have succeeded in keeping their tolerant religious traditions in the face of a fundamentalist onslaught from Pakistan, Afghanistan and Arab states.
'Islam came to Kashmir from Persia, it came through preaching and teaching rather than conquest and battles,' said Omar Farooq, the 14th 'mirwaiz' (emir) of Srinagar. Farooq's Persian ancestors, leading Sunni Muslims, were among the earliest to preach in the Kashmir Valley following the arrival of Shah Hamadani, revered as a saint in the summer capital of Srinagar.
'Our Islam is one of tolerance and brotherhood, based on the teachings of the Prophet but also on an exchange of ideas, mystic music and poetry', said Farooq, the young political-religious leader who founded the Hurriyat separatist alliance in 1993. 'It has more in common with Central Asia than South Asia or Arab countries', he added. In the streets of old Srinagar, filled with mosques boasting unique pointed wooden roofs, the women's way of dress shows the diversity of Kashmiri Islam. Some are clad in head-to-toe burqas, some in colorful veils, while others keep their heads uncovered. The laid-back Islam is part of the heritage of the Himalayan region, where Sufi verse is passed on from generation and generation.
'These sounds and words which go deep in the soul have saved me from despair,' said Ahmad Qureshi, a tailor, who lost his two sons in the Kashmir conflict.
Sufis, who are found across the Muslim world, mix traditional Islamic rites with a focus on spiritual experience, practicing solitary meditation and

---

to other statements made by him elsewhere (but see Chadha Behera 2000: 190), nor to analyse his political views, or the political aspirations of other Kashmiri Muslims.

following the quest for divine love lauded nine centuries ago by the Farsi poet, Rumi.

This brand of tolerance has formed the identity of many Muslims in Kashmir where Sufism has melded with Hinduism and Buddhism over generations of successive rule by the Mughals, Afghans, Sikhs and Dogras.

'This is the reason why the Hindu minority had been safe in Kashmir until the arrival of foreign fighters,' said Noor Ahmad Baba, chairman of Kashmir University's political science department.

Soon after Kashmir's insurgency against Indian rule broke out in 1989, the ranks of guerrillas who were fighting for independence became overtaken by 'jihadi' fighters from the Arab world, Afghanistan and particularly Pakistan, which controls one third of Kashmir. At the same time, Islamic seminaries financed by Saudis have multiplied in Kashmir, propagating the desert kingdom's puritanical Wahabi ideology.

'Sunni Wahabi militants supported by Pakistan repress Kashmir's culture, the Sufi arts and lifestyle,' said Baba. 'But this type of Islam has not developed any roots here. Sometimes it is imposed on people through terror or attracts young, hopeless Kashmiris, but it is not in the hearts of the people of this land.' Farooq, a critic of both nuclear states that claim Kashmir, agreed. 'Some vested interests in Pakistan and India have attempted to promote extremism in Jammu and Kashmir, but I honestly think that the deep nature of Islam in Kashmir has remained the same,' he said. Farooq does not deny the presence of extremists among the Kashmir guerrillas, but considers it all too convenient for India 'to present the fight for the identity and rights of Kashmiris as part of fundamentalism or terrorism.'

'You have to draw a line between a freedom struggle and terrorism,' he said. 'India is feeding extremism by refusing to negotiate a political settlement,' he said.

dear all,
hello.
The concept of WAHABBISM has rather inadvertently been mixed with the true spirit of ISLAM.as far as my knowledge goes,upon the formation of saudi arabia(earlier najd), king saud called upon a leading cleric of Riyadh and wanted a true basis of a functioning Saudi Arabia.saud was told by the cleric to enforce sunnah and shariah strictly.this began to known as wahabbism,which infact is the way Islamic state ought to be run (*ASF,* 17.10.2002)

Asalamualikum,
    I am not sure if there is anyone who would identify with so called 'Wahabi ideology'. The Saudi and many others who are accused of belonging to this school of thought consider themselves more of 'Salafi'—i.e. the ones who follow the tradition of our Prophet (saw) and his great companions. The word 'wahabism' is being used to create divisions within muslims in order to keep them subjugated.

As far as how the Salafi thought differs from most of muslims in our sub-continent, they believe that any innovation in our religion is a 'biddat' i.e. something that is not part of our deen. Furthermore, every 'biddat" leads to 'Zalalat' i.e. take us outside the fold of Islam.

An example would be the veneration of many of our 'peer'. Many of us pray at their graves, ask them for favors and intersession etc. Such form of worship, in the Salafi school of thought, would be considered as 'Shirk'—i.e. attributing qualities to people, dead or alive, that only belong to Allah (swt).

As with any school of thought, the Salafi had their extremist who did engage in physical violence in order to enforce their view. The other end of this Islamic Sunni spectrum is populated by Sufi school of thought. These are the people who belive in a more 'mystic' form of Islam. Some of them have added singing and dancing as part of the worship—something that is completely opposed by the Salafi.

In our part of world, we usually refer to Salafi as 'Ahl-Hadeeth'.

Many countries, including Russia, India and now USA, are using the term 'Wahabi' to describe the muslims who have taken up arms against them. I am not sure if Imam Wahab, who proposed the Saudi doctrine of following the Salafi school of thought, wanted his name to be used in such a manner.

Wasalam (*AS, 17.10.2002*)

for them, who make differentism
when i born i heard God is greate. God means humanity which is always great now what is this people are claiming
their believe is greate now i'm seeing their believe converts in hate they thinks they are greate, which makes them selfish for each others, (*HHH, 17.10.2002*)

AA

i have been to many lectures where puritanical Wahabi ideology is mentioned, but when i ask the speaker to give me 5 differences between puritanical Wahabi ideology and islam i encounter DDD (deflect, dodge, drible). So is this just a superficial label given to whoever it is attributed to or is there something called wahabism? i feel that we are talking about smoething that may not be existing, unless someone can enlighten here on our great kashmiri treasure; The [online community].

regards (*T, 17.10.2002*)

Dear A
AA

Thank you for your excellent and to the point answer. i get to understand that Wahabi is just another label for Sunnis. I did find many Ahadeeth in the books of Bukhari that were very anti Biddah or Biddat. Kashmiries do have many Biddahs that are forbidden and denounced by our prophet (PBUH).

I am glad that we have Kashmiries among us who have deep knowledge of Islam. (*TM, 30.11.2002*)

Discussion 2

Worship one God (March 2003).

This discussion took place between six persons (including one woman), and began by IKM sending the first mail:

An example of Shirk is the commemoration of certain fixed days of Islamic months in the name of certain great Holy men or Auwlia. This practice also leads to Shirk and is thus a pathway to hell. Many people commemorate certain days of Islamic calendar as special ones. Different people give different reasons in their defense for this practice of theirs. The most common reasons given by most of the people is that some Auwlia or holy men had such and such number of attributes so we commemorate such and such days of every Islamic month and so on. But, by saying that Allah Subhana Wa Tala has no less than ninety nine attributes to his name which are verified by Holy Qur'an, so why don't these people keep a specific day for the commemoration of these ninety nine attributes of Allah. When this question is put to such people they don't speak a word, they remain silent as if they do not possess tongue. All their arguments and explanation fail at this point. They think that by commemorating these days they add to the dignity and glory of these holy men or Auwlias but they don't know that they are spoiling the image of these great people instead. If these have such affection and respect for the Auwlias like Sheikh Abdul Qadir Jeelani (RA) and others then they should not do acts like these which lead to Shirk. If these people want to really pay tribute to these great people then they should look towards the way of these great persons and lead the life as they did. These people should understand that these great men spent their life in the same way as Islam directs us.

Another commonly noticed practice seen among most of the Muslims today is a misconception which most Muslims have developed in their minds about the great men of Islam or Auwlias. People think that these great men have the powers to grant anything therefore, when they visit some shrine they raise their hands and ask not to Allah for favors but they instead ask directly to these great men for favors. The power to grant favors and the power to cure is all with Allah and with no one else. But these people argue saying that since they were great people so we can ask them for favors and thus it is allowed in Islam but I say that if this practice would have been allowed by Islam then the first place where it should be permitted should be near the grave of Prophet Mohammad (PBUH), who himself said that 'whoever comes to my grave should not put flowers on my grave nor should he ask for favors. Even Quran clearly states that Prophet Mohammad (PBUH) had no powers to favor even himself. As Allah says in Holy Quran 'say: it is

not in my power to cause you harm or to bring you to right conduct (72:21)'.
Also in the same Sura in the very next verse (verse 22) it is clearly mentioned
that 'say: no one can deliver me from Allah (if I were to disobey Him), nor
should I find refuge except in Him.' Again in Sura Aaraf the 7th Sura in
Verse 188, Allah orders Prophet to say; 'say: I have no power over any good
or harm. To me except as Allah willeth. If I had knowledge of the unseen I
should have multiplied all well and no evil should have touched me. I am
but a warner and a bringer of good tidings to those who have faith.'

So, I appeal to the whole the Muslim community that they should not
follow these practices as they are just pathways to Hell. And whosoever follows
them should repent as soon as possible so that he may be saved from the
Hell whose fuel is men and stones. Also Allah says in Holy Quran:—'If you
ascribe partners with Allah all your good deeds shall be in vain and you
shall be among loosers'. So we should keep in view all these things and be
careful not to indulge in activities like these which lead us to Shirk. We should
have faith in the same way as it is mentioned in Kalma-i-Shahadat which
states 'Allah is the one and there is none besides him who is worthy of being
worshipping and Prophet Mohammad (PBUH) is his Messenger.'

So, I once again appeal to all Muslim community to abstain from this
dangerous sin which can be the cause of disaster for them. May Allah grant
all of us the power to understand and implement Islam in our lives (Ameen).
(*IKM, 14.3.2003*)

I think an e-mail on debates within Islam coming fron the JKLF hqs, an
avowedly secular and political organization, fighting for a goal which cannot
be construed as religious is anamolous. Please don't see this observation as
polemical. I'd appreciate similar postings if they come from an individual's
e-mail account. (*AB, 14.3.2003*)

Mr. B ... if JKLF hqs can help all of us improve our life and remind us about
the ideal way of life there is no harm in it. Moreover islam doesn't encourage
any comunalism or extremism so there is no question of it not being secular.
Warm Regards, (*IKM, 16.3.2003*)

AS-salamuakum wahrahmatuulah,
What brother Abir is stating is totally correct.
Glorifying anything and everything other than Allah azawa jal is haram.
All these shrines and saints that the indo-pak people go to is stictly biddah
... I fail to see the reasoning of people doing such things which actually makes
it shirk ... and shirk is one of the most major sin in islam. Glorifying is totally
prohibited, thus we are not even allowed to celebrate our birthdays, as most
muslims do not know. Actually the prophet (pbuh) even prohibted people
from celebrating his birthday ... so I really don't know how people come up
with that concept. Also I dont understan how its always the indo-paks who
are going to the saints, shrines or whatever. or celebrating the prophet's (pbuh)

birth day ... I have never seen an Arab doing such things .... I am not saying
the Arabs are the best of muslims, Allah hu Alam, nevertheless, they dont
engage in such activity. Also, every year as I make Umrah, I always see the
indo-pak people kissing and ka'bah and hugging it ... at the same time I see
the mufti's yelling 'Haram Haji' 'Haram Hajjah' ... my point is that I think
we tend to interwine our indopak culture with islam ... this is wrong ... Islam
is our culture and the only culture for muslims ... for those of you who think
that we should learn urdu, kashmiri, or other languages you are wrong. It is
our duty to learn arabic as a mother tongue first. then we may go on to learn
other languages. so basically I think we really need to let go of our indo-pak/
kashmiri culture and concentrate on being a 'better muslim/muslimah' ...
and for those of you who continually talk trash about india side or pakistan
side ... let me mind you that nationalism is forbidden in islam ... so please
grow up ...

> wa-salamuakum wah rahmatallah
> If ALLAH touch thee with affliction, none can remove
> it but HE; if HE touch thee with happiness HE hath
> power over all things ....
> (*FKA*)

ye ye ye ... this is how a comment is acknowledged positively in the
British parliament, and since this was a discussion about secularism I chose
to respond accordingly. But. Islam isn't secularism. It has similarities. In
Islam, the rulers and the ruled, the majority and the minority, the black and
the white are asked to be subservient to a Law supra-human and thus effacing
the subjugation of the ruled by the rulers or of the minority by the majority.
As it should be. No man has a right to rule over another. If any man should
question a directive of another, the one directing should respond with the
words, not my directive, my friend, but God's. If the one directing can't respond
thus, the one who is being asked to accept has no obligation to accept. And
the aim of the administrators is to churn out the good men and women can
produce, as a good gardener seeks to churn out the good from the flowers
and trees that are under his/her care.

And also ... we all know about the 'secularism' being practiced currently.
I don't know if you understand the term 'sucker'. Its a slang used in the U.K.
for someone who has been deceived. So, 'suckeralism' is perhaps a better
term for what is shown to be secularism today.

WaSalam (*AR, 16.3.2003*)

Dear all,

Arabic is NOT my mother tongue. My mother tongue is Kashmiri and
that is it. If someone else has illusions about their mother tongue being Arabic,
so be it.

Our culture is ancient and that is a fact. And it is not something to be disowned. It is something to be remembered, taught and cherished. Anybody who thinks otherwise has lost their bearings. Being Kashmiri is my identity and so is being a Muslim and these two are not mutually exclusive. I love my faith and I also love my culture.

As regards going to shrines is concerned, the sufi movement is not of Kashmiri origin. It originated in central Asia and survives there to this day.

All of us have different ways of percieving our great faith. No one idea can be said to be truly better than the others. It is best to leave people to form their own equation with the maker.

Forcing religious ideas down their throat and pronouncing them apostates is in very bad taste indeed.

Regards, (*NQ, 17.3.2003*)

Dear NQ Sahib Aslamo Alaykam

On this point I totally agree with you; and I am sure silent majority of [Community] members also agrees with this.

Culture and religion are two distinct things and its best they are kept like that; and we should also avoid issuing fatwa's with our mypoic and limited knowledge of Islam. (*SC, 18.3.2003*)

AA

Culture religion, religion culture. There seems to be some confusion. Life is one, we cannot separate one from the other. How can one person do something and then treat that thing as separate from the another thing he/she does? Its the same person doing both things. There is good and bad in all cultures. Islam does not seek to negate the existence of cultures, only seeks to perpetuate and enhance the good in all cultures and to abandon and perish the bad from all cultures.

WaSalam (*AR, 20.3.2003*)

Dear Dr C ...,

This is what I had pointed out in my original e-mail ... that e-mails which open up debates on religious identity shouldn't be circulated from the JKLF headquarters, as JKLF is a political organization.

What I recieved by way of a reply is that why shouldn't JKLF show the way to an 'ideal life' ... I don't need to go into the dangers of such a fascist and totalitarian argument made unfortunately in the name of the JKLF ... we must not forget that Stalin's gulags and Hitler's concentration camps were supposed to pave the path for an 'ideal life'. JKLF could be inspired by Islam but it should not be identified with a particular religion as its goals are political rather than religious.

Such tendencies have become possible because of a lack of democracy which we have witnessed in our struggle over the last decade. (AB, 20.3.2003)

Br A ...,
Islam encompasses all, including politics.
WaSalam (AR, 23.3.2003)

Well Said AR ... Saab;
I just want to point to Brother A ... that islam introduced Democracy
where the rulers were subjected to any inquiry by his people. A ... Saab does
this kind of democracy prevail in the contemporary world ? Than in a country
like US the head of the state would have never opted for a war against the
will of its people!!!
In the existing world there is not a single democracy as chaste as prescribed
by Islam !!! As ar ... said islam encompases all; right from etiquittes to running
a govt ....
Warm Regards, (*IKM, 23.3.2003*)

An Analysis of Discussions 1 and 2

Both discussions represent two mutually related and major aspects
of lived Islam—debating what Islam constitutes and consists of, and
for some, the related endeavour to be a good Muslim and/or a good
Kashmiri. But a closer examination reveals the antinomies involved
for some, the disjunction in goal-schemas that were once apparently
conjunctive. For analytical purposes, I shall examine the discussions
at two levels. The first is that of the denotations used in the discussions;
the second relates to their connotations.

First Level: The Denotations

Discussion 1

At the first level, the nature and contents of Islam are set forth. The
Mirwaiz begins by at least implicitly distinguishing between different
types of Islam.[12] He both defines and distinguishes Kashmiri Islam
as one of 'tolerance and brotherhood', that spread through 'preaching

---

[12]In South Asia, this perennial topic continues to engage many intellectuals, as the
recent exchange between Zakaria (2003: 16) and Ishaq Khan (2003) in the *Times of
India* demonstrates: To Zakaria's 'Indian Islam is very different from Islam in the Arab
world ... Likewise, Malaysian and Indonesian brands of Islam are also different ...'
Ishaq Khan responded in a letter to the Editor: 'Mr. Zakaria has ... failed to distinguish
between religion and culture. Not only does he dramatize polarity between the so-
called "Arab Islam" and "Indian Islam", but he is also at pains to convince his readers,
in the true fashion of Western Orientalist scholarship, about the existence of what he
calls Malaysian and Indonesian "brands of Islam" ... it would be wrong to argue that
Islam of the converts is "different" from Islam in the Arab world.'

and teaching rather than through conquest and battles', forgetting perhaps, that in large parts of the world, including South Asia, Islam was and is just as tolerant and was likewise largely spread through 'preaching and teaching'—forgetting also, that in Kashmir too there have been periods of religious intolerance and extreme brutality. According to the Mirwaiz, 'mystic music and poetry' are an important part of Islam in Kashmir. It is this music and poetry that the grieving tailor refers to. The Professor cited goes further to link Sufism, the Kashmiri lifestyle, and the relations between the Muslim majority and the Hindu minority (this is also done by a number of persons cited in Sikand and Hamdani 2001).

But if Sufism, mystic music and poetry are so much an integral part of Islam in Kashmir, why then, does any Kashmiri require the accuracy of these statements to be 'verified'? Does it point to the heterogeneity of religious practice even within this small online community? Could it be that among all the multiple voices in the Valley, (especially male) urbanites with a modern education are ignorant of such traditions? Or do they wish to negate them? Or does the query reflect the questioner's uncertainty about the nature of Islam in the Valley? Alternatively, does it imply a rejection of such practices, paralleling perhaps what Saktanber (1991: 171) has observed of Turkey— that it is precisely this '... new type of elite raised traditionally but educated in the new secular universal educational institutions ... [who] brought their cultural baggage into the political and socio-cultural environment ... that ... became the producers and supporters of the new Islamic ideologies'? Given the ex-colonial context of Kashmir, does such an elite perhaps unconsciously even echo the contemptuous attitude of colonial powers towards local forms of lived Islam? These issues were not raised in this discussion, but they were indirectly answered by the criticisms of many practices as condemnable innovations, and the remark that 'Kashmiris do have many Biddats' indicates the emotional conflict among many community members between the two goal-schemas—between the deep longing to be a good Muslim and part of the universal Muslim community and simultaneously remain a good Kashmiri, adhering loyally to what the Professor cited refers to as '... Kashmir's culture ... and lifestyle'. These antinomies are apparent in the second discussion too.

Discussion 2

Notably the Sufi shrine traditions of Islam are criticized as being opposed to the way 'Islam directs us', and hence as 'pathways to Hell', and Allah is beseeched to '... grant all of us the power to understand and implement Islam in our lives ...'. Some responses state the nature of Islam ('the ideal way of life', 'Islam ... seeks to perpetuate and enhance the good in all cultures ...', 'Islam isn't secularism', 'Islam encompasses all ...'), and its prohibitions ('activities ... which lead us to Shirk', 'glorifying anything and everything other than Allah ...', 'nationalism is forbidden in Islam'); others raise political issues (the nature of secularism and democracy). The terms 'culture' and 'religion' are used, synonymously by some ('Islam is our culture'), and distinctively by others ('Being Kashmiri is my identity and so is being a Muslim ...', 'culture and religion are two distinct things'). Again, the issue of identity arises (Kashmiri, Muslim). While some cherish the two goal-schemas (being a good Muslim and being a good Kashmiri) and see no disjunction or dissonance in these, for others they are mutually incompatible, and the latter is even sinful.

Second Level: The Connotations

The conflict between the desire to preserve perceived local cultural identities and the universalistic ideals of the Muslim ummah with its monolithic normative identity is widespread among Muslim communities in Asia and Africa. While for centuries the central role played here is the theological debate about *tawhidic* or unitarian concepts, with the rise of western colonialism, and the dominance of neo-colonialism and continued discrimination and racism, theological considerations acquired political dimensions, which in turn led to certain cognitive dilemma.

Discussion 1

Locally lived Islam at the various individual, household and community levels is necessarily part and parcel of local cultures, and hence also of cultural identity. By setting off 'Our Islam' against Islam in South Asia and Arab countries, and in speaking of greater similarities with Central Asia, the Mirwaiz clearly touches upon this issue of identity. Islam—their Islam—is an essential component of the understanding of local cultural identity that for many, if not most, Kashmiris forms the basis of their conviction and concept of an independent Kashmiri nation. The Mirwaiz spells this out more clearly still when he says that India is presenting the fight for '... the identity ... of Kashmiris as part of fundamentalism ...'. He also refers to attempts by both Pakistan and India to promote and feed extremism for their respective vested interests. This 'extremism' and 'fundamentalism' are said to be represented by the 'foreign fighters, the Wahabi militants', but the Mirwaiz at least is sure that lived Islam in Kashmir continues to provide space for resistance to understandings of monolithic Islam. Yet this first discussion also shows that this space must continuously be renegotiated, and that the framework for this negotiation is not, and cannot be, just the Valley of Kashmir, but the globalizing world that is impacting peoples' lives at a rate many find hard to cope with.

Discussion 2

Perceptions of Islam, of anyone's right to enforce these on others, observations on normative and lived Islam and views on cultural and religious identity inform this discussion. For some, normative Islam—as opposed to lived Islam—has become what Serif Mardin (1989) called a 'second culture', the very nature of the primary culture, inspired by western ideals of secularism and democracy being increasingly questioned. Others wish to rid themselves of this primary culture, adopt normative Islam as their only culture, and perceive these two as antinomian. Yet others continue to cherish their multiple cultures and identities, and perceive no antinomies between these. We thus have a kind of continuum. At one end are the first two categories with a single goal-schema: aspiring to be a good Muslim, whereby this goal is implicit for the first category and explicit for the second. At the other end we have those with two more or less implicit goal-schemas: aspiring to be a good Muslim and a good Kashmiri.

Conclusion

> ... You speak of God's Wrath, I speak of His Mercy.
> Your Quran is a Weapon, My Quran is a Gift.
> You speak of the Muslim brotherhood,
> I speak of the brotherhood of Man ....
> You worship the Law, I worship the Divine ....
> Yet there might be one thing
> On which we see eye to eye
> You want Justice'
> So do I
> —a community member (MB, 6.12.2001: You and
> I, a poem for my extremist friends)

Religious practice is inevitably and always a site of culture dynamic processes. Islam, when it first reached Kashmir, had already gone through long years of accommodation and adaptation in the Arab world, in various parts of Iran and Central Asia, picking up myriad concepts and practices that went back to a variety of Semitic, Buddhist, Zoroastrian, Greek, Roman and even earlier times. As it spread, it logically and indispensably integrated or adapted certain local, or more widespread, earlier elements that represent and cater to basic emotions that humans share the world over—fear and sorrow, the need for comfort and protection.

Praying at shrines, celebrating the Prophet's birthday, wearing protective amulets, and notions of the evil eye are major features of Muslim religious practice not just in Kashmir, but also in South and Central Asia, Afghanistan, Iran, Turkey, the Maghreb and almost throughout the Arab world. In some areas closer to Kashmir, such as Hunza, major shamanistic practices go hand in hand with Islam, just as rites of possession and Zar cults do in Sudan, Somalia and Saudi Arabia. Most people simply do not ask themselves whether specific practices make them more or less Muslim. They have, I submit, a pragmatic, problem-solving approach—something which Sheryl Daniel (1983) referred to as 'a tool-box approach'. Such an approach accommodates multiple goal-schemas and identities, and is too subtle and sophisticated to perceive these as polarized, binary sets. It is this un-selfconscious pragmatism within lived Islam that makes such cultures resilient. They are flexible enough to be largely immune to doctrinaire and anti-pluralist impositions, while simultaneously drawing strength from these doctrines or rather the perception of these as essential and axiomatic—the Holy Quran, the Hadiths and the Sharia provide this axiom. But even these perceptions are not static, and thus there are moments when this flexibility wears thin, when this resilience snaps. This happens when a self-conscious questioning of religious practice takes place in a major way. Axiomatic religious practice is then examined and broken into conceptually disjunctive alternatives. To borrow Ahmad's terminology (1981: 15), the 'ultimate and formal' and the 'proximate and local' cease to complement each other and form the 'common religious system' they had once been. The fear of morally wrong practice takes over, and with this feelings of insecurity and vulnerability arise, or increase.

In this paper I have discussed data on a community, many of whose members appear to be losing this resilience, or have already lost it. These data indicate that, when goal orientation becomes explicit, rather than implicit, self-conscious rather than natural, dissonances surface and antinomies arise. This self-consciousness itself is related largely to political factors, to being treated as 'the Other' (cf. Van der Veer 2002). The tension in the relation between normative and lived Islam that is evident in these online discussions also reflect an insecurity that has been created over many decades by the 'Orientalist privileging of ... religion ... as the foremost site of essentialized difference ... directly dependent on modern understandings of religion related to the nationalization of religion and its new location in the public sphere' (Van der Veer 2002: 173).[13]

Simultaneously, this insecurity is inextricably intermeshed with the impact over the last several decades of different forces of change in Kashmir. The fifty-year old conflict with India and subcontinental politics have largely moulded Kashmiri Muslim identity. Indeed, in their intent, these online discourses closely resemble some of the debates that accompanied the early articulations of Kashmiri Muslim socio-political identity in the last decades of the nineteenth and the first two decades of the twentieth century (Zutshi 2000). Both then and now we have periods of tremendous local and regional, political and economic transformations that translate into an overall sense of unpredictability. Then and now we have scenarios where power bases are shifting. The then Mirwaiz[14] tried to preach a 'pure Islam' and criticised the shrines, while his opponents accused him of importing Wahabi doctrines from India and of denigrating Kashmiri Islam. Over the next decades the nuances of such discourse changed, so did their protagonists, but the overall framework remained the search for a Kashmiri identity, alongside a Muslim identity.

The current violent conflict with India and the rapidly globalizing economic and political world order are also increasingly leading to many norms and values being questioned, to overlapping tool boxes and multiple schemas being perceived by many as antinomian. This dialectic between power structures and value systems makes many long for clear-cut behavioural prescriptions and sanctions that require little or no negotiation. One model of such an orderly and clear-cut

[13]Increasingly, the Kashmiri Muslim habitus is also impacted by interactions with fellow Muslims from regions categorized by western Orientalist scholarship as the 'core' or 'heart lands' of Islam. Such interactions between what Anderson (1986) calls 'the determiners' and 'the determined' tend to underline a sense of marginality, and increase diffidence in a community which, on the one hand, largely sees itself as 'enslaved' (by non-Muslims), and on the other, tends to be convinced of what Evans (forthcoming) refers to as its, notably intellectual, 'exceptionalism'.

[14]As opposed to the Mirwaiz Hamadani.

framework is provided by another cognitive system with a global ethos—the world Muslim community, which is increasingly being projected by the global presence of a monolithic Islam. But this framework brings other problems with it—the perceived contradictions between on the one hand, normative identity as a Muslim and moral and singular loyalty to a wider Islam and on the other, the wish not only to preserve, but even defend (above all vis-à-vis India, but for many even vis-à-vis Pakistan) what is perceived of as a unique Kashmiri culture. Again today, the problem remains one of reconciling moral loyalty to this global community with cultural loyalty to the Kashmiri nation. The endeavour must inevitably then, continue.

Our endeavour must remain one of studying both the diversity of religious practice and engaging with the growing tendency among some (non-Muslims and Muslims) to reduce this diversity. Understanding such politically embedded emotional impulses might help prevent religion and religious identity being used as markers to physically or psychologically target the constructed image of the Other.

References

Ahmad, Imtiaz. 1981. (Ed.), *Ritual and Religion among Muslims in India*, Manohar, Delhi.

Anderson, Jon W. 1986. Popular Mythologies and Subtle Theologies: The Phenomenology of Muslim Identity in Afghanistan, in Phyllis P. Chock and J.R. Wyman (Eds), *Discourse and the Social Life of Meaning*, Smithsonian Institute Press, Washington DC, pp. 169–85.

Berger, Morroe. 1977. *Real and Imagined Worlds: The Novel and Social Science*. Harvard University Press, Cambridge (Mass.).

Béteille, André. 2000. *Antinomies of Society: Essays on Ideologies and Institutions*, Oxford University Press, Delhi.

Boeck, Monika. 1998. Experiential Flexibility of Cultural Models: Kinship Knowledge and Networks among Individual Khasi (Meghalaya, N.E. India), in Thomas Schweizer and Douglas R. White (Eds), *Kinship, Network, and Exchange*. Cambridge University Press, Cambridge, pp. 113–36.

Bourdieu, Pierre. 1977. *Outline of a Theory of Practice*, Cambridge University Press, Cambridge.

Bunt, Gary R. 2000. *Virtually Islamic: Computer-Mediated Communication and Cyber Islamic Environments*, University of Wales Press, Cardiff.

Butalia, Urvashi. 2002. *Speaking Peace: Women's Voices from Kashmir*, Kali for Women, Delhi.

Castells, Manuel. 1996. The Net and the Self: Working Notes for a Critical Theory of the Informational Society, *Critique of Anthropology* 16(1): 9–38.

Chadha-Behera, Navnita. 2000. *State, Identity and Violence: Jammu, Kashmir and Ladakh*, Manohar, Delhi.

Daniel, Sheryl 1983. The Tool-Box Approach of the Trail to the Issues of Moral Responsibility and Human Desting, in C.F. Keyes and E.V. Daniel (Eds), *Karma: An Anthropological Inquiry*, University of California Press, Berkeley.

Das, Veena. 1984. For a Folk-Theology and Theological Anthropology of Islam, *Contributions to Indian Sociology* (n.s.) 18(2): 293–300.

D'Andrade, Roy G. 1991. The Identification of Schemas in Naturalistic Data, in Michael Horowitz (Ed.), *Person, Schemas, and Maladaptive Interpersonal Patterns*, Chicago University Press, Chicago, pp. 279–301.

Evans, Alexander. 2008. Exceptionally Kashmiri: The Changing Nature of Kashmiri Identity, in T.N. Madan and Aparna Rao (Eds), *The Valley of Kashmir: The Making and Unmaking of a Composite Culture?* Berghahn/ Manohar, Oxford/Delhi.

Gomes, Alberto G. 2001. Going Goan on the Goa-Net: Computer-Mediated Communication and Goan Diaspora, *Social Analysis* 45(1): 53–66.

Hakken, D. 1999. *Cyborgs@Cyberspace? An Ethnographer Looks to the Future*, Routledge, New York.

Ishaq Khan, Mohammad. 1998. Kashmiri Muslims: Social and Identity Consciousness, in Mushirul Hasan (Ed.), *Islam, Communities and the Nation: Muslim Identities in South Asia and Beyond*, Manohar, Delhi, pp. 201–28.

———. 2001. Rationale for Re-orientation of Attitudes towards Islam in Medieval India. Presidential Address to the Medieval Section of the 33rd Session of the Punjab History Conference, Punjabi University, Patiala, 16–18 March 2001.

———. 2003. Islam in India, *Times of India*, 27 February 2003.

Jain, Ravindra K. 1998. Indian Diaspora, Globalisation and Multiculturalism: A Cultural Analysis, *Contributions to Indian Sociology* (n.s.) 32(2): 337–60.

Kirchner, Henner. 2007. Proudly Serving Palestine and Al Quds—Structure and Functions of the Online-Presence of HAMAS, the Movement of Islamic Resistance in Palestine, in Aparna Rao, Monika Böck and Michael Bollig (Eds), *The Practice of War: The Production, Reproduction and Consumption of Armed Violence*, Berghahn, New York.

Lyon, D. 1997. Cyberspace Sociality: Controversies over Computer-mediated Relationships, in B. Loader (Ed.), *The Governance of Cyberspace: Politics, Technology and Global Restructuring*. Routledge, London.

Mardin, Serif. 1989. Culture and Religion towards the Year 2000, in *Turkey in the Year 2000*, Turkey Political Science Association, Servinç Matbaasi, Ankara, p. 163–86.

Markham, A.N. 1998. Life *Online. Researching Real Experience in Virtual Space.* AltaMira Press, Oxford.

Minault, Gail. 1984. Some Reflections on Islamic Revivalism vs. Assimilation among Muslims in India, *Contributions to Indian Sociology* (n.s.) 18(2): 301–5.

Mitra, A. 1997. Virtual Commonality: Looking for India on the Internet, in S. Jones (Ed.), *Virtual Culture. Identity and Community in Cyberspace.* Sage, London.

Morton, Helen (Ed.) 2001. *Computer-Mediated Communication in Australian Anthropology and Sociology: A Special Issue of Social Analysis,* University of Adelaide, Adelaide.

Mukta, Parita and Chetan Bhatt (Eds), 2001. *Hinduism and the Politics of Diaspora: Ethnic and Racial Studies* (Special Issue) 23(3).

Quinn, Naomi and Holland. 1987. Culture and Cognition, in Holland and Naomi Quinn (Eds), *Cultural Models in Language and Thought,* Cambridge University Press, Cambridge, pp. 1–40.

Rheingold, H. 1993. *The Virtual Community,* Harper Perennial, New York.

Robinson, Francis. 1983. Islam and Muslim Society in South Asia, *Contributions to Indian Sociology* (n.s.) 17(2): 185–203.

———. 1985. Islam and Muslim Separatism: A Historiographical Debate, in M. Hasan (Ed.), *Communal and Pan-Islamic Trends in Colonial India,* Manohar, Delhi, pp. 344–81.

———. 1986. Islam and Muslim Society in South Asia: A Reply to Das and Minault, *Contributions to Indian Sociology* (n.s.) 20(1): 97–104.

Saktanber. 1991. Muslim Identity in Children's Picture-Books, in R. Tapper (Ed.), *Islam in Modern Turkey: Religion, Politics and Literature in a Secular State,* pp. 171–88. I.B. Tauris & Co., London/New York.

Sikand, Yoginder S. 2008. Popular Kashmiri Sufism and the Challenge of Scripturalist Islam (1900–1989), in T.N. Madan and Aparna Rao (Eds), *The Valley of Kashmir: The Making and Unmaking of a Composite Culture?* Berghahn/Manohar, Oxford/Delhi.

———. 2007. Islamist Militancy in Kashmir: The Case of the Lashkar-i-Tayyeba, in Aparna Rao, Monika Böck and Michael Bollig (Eds), *The Practice of War: The Production, Reproduction and Consumption of Armed Violence.* Berghahn, London/New York.

——— and Irfan Hamdani. 2001. *Voices from the Valley: Contemporary Kashmiri Sufi Perspectives,* Y. Sikand, Bangalore.

Strauss, Claudia. 1992. Models and Motives, in Roy G. D'Andrade and Claudia Strauss (Eds), *Human Motives and Cultural Models,* Cambridge University Press, Cambridge, pp. 1–20.

Turkle, S. 1995. *Life on the Screen: Identity in the Age of the Internet.* Simon & Schuster, New York.

Uberoi, Patricia. 1998. The Diaspora Comes Home: Disciplining Desire in DDLJ, *Contributions to Indian Sociology* (n.s.) 32(2): 305–36.

Van der Veer, Peter. 2002. Religion in South Asia, *Annual Review of Anthropology* 31: 173–87.

Wilson, Samuel M. and Leighton C. Peterson. 2002. The Anthropology of Online Communities, *Annual Review of Anthropology* 31: 449–67.

Zakaria, Rafiq. 2003. Fundamental Fallacies, *Times of India*, 24 February 2003.

Zutshi, Chitralekha. 2000. Relgion, State, and Community: Contested Identities in the Kashmir Valley, c.1880–1920, *South Asia* XXIII(1): 109–28.

———. 2008. Shrines, Political Authority and Religious Identities in Late-Nineteenth and Early-Twentieth Century Kashmir, in T.N. Madan and Aparna Rao (Eds), *The Valley Of Kashmir: The Making and Unmaking of a Composite Culture?* Berghahn/Manohar, Oxford/Delhi.

6

Lived Islam in Nepal

SUDHINDRA SHARMA

Introduction

The image of Nepal as a harmonious country where various religions peacefully co-exist was severely undermined during the political changes that took place in 1990. The formulation of a new constitution, which sought to ensure the freedom to profess and practice one's own religion, instilled confidence in various sections of the society, including among adherents of minority religions. Though the Constitution of Nepal (1990) that was finally promulgated retained Hinduism as the state religion, the religion-based social mobilization that had taken place when the new constitution was being drafted in 1990 set precedents in a land that had hitherto not experienced such awakening.

During the 1990s adherents of various faiths increasingly turned to what they considered to be the essential teachings of their respective religion, with prevalent accommodative practices and customs being looked down upon as inauthentic. In the case of Islam, this generally meant the abandoning of the locally-rooted syncretistic practices as well as allegiance to the traditional Barelvi and Deobandi

Discussions with Hamid Ansari on different facets of Muslim life in Nepal have enriched the paper considerably. His input is gratefully acknowledged.

denominations and replacement of the Wahabi and Quadiyani orientations. In Buddhism, this has led to the traditional Mahayana
and Tantric Buddhism prevalent in the country being perceived as
'decadent' and to the importation of Theravada Buddhism from
Burma, Thailand and Sri Lanka. In the case of Hinduism, adherents
increasingly turned towards more puritanical and less tolerant variants, making their way into the country from India, in place of the
local plural or syncretistic variety. In each of the religions, the trend
is the movement away from living practices to the search for the
'fundamentals'. Needless to say, the new orientations making their
way into each of the religions in the country have strong international
financial backing.

While right to religious freedom was restricted earlier than 1990,
the traditional Hindu kingdom had guaranteed the life and property
of all its citizens. Ironically, the openness after 1990 led to religious
distrust, and the state was increasingly unable to guarantee the citizen's
life and property. As Nepal enters the twenty-first century the old
equilibrium with deference to the state religion no longer guides inter-
religious relationships. There seems to be increasing rivalry and
confrontation between and among various faiths in the country. This
trend has been accentuated by the inroads made by the World Hindu
Federation in Nepal.

This paper provides an overview of the history of the various
groups of Muslims resident in the country, including those living in
the Tarai. It explores the rifts and undercurrents in Nepali Islam,
and discusses the new variant of Islam that is increasingly making
inroads into the country. The Hindu-Islamic interface is then explored
followed by the security/insecurity present among Nepali Muslims.
The paper subsequently explores the inroads made by global militant
Hinduism and its implications.

Early Muslims and Latecomers[1]

Nepal's Muslims, while being predominantly Sunni, constitute a
heterogeneous group. The ancestors of the various groups of Muslims
presently living in Nepal arrived in the kingdom from different parts

[1]The various groups of Muslims residing in Nepal and their history is discussed
by S. Siddika (1993), S. Sharma (1994), M. Dastidar (1995) and M. Gaborieau
(1996).

of South Asia and Tibet during different epochs, and have generally lived peacefully amidst the numerically-dominant Hindus.

According to the *Gopalraja Vamshavali*, the chronicles of the dynasties of Kathmandu Valley (akin to Kalhana's *Rajtarangini* which chronicles the dynasties of Kashmir), Muslims of Kashmir arrived in Kathmandu during the reign of King Ratna Malla (AD 1484–1520). In the land granted by the king, they built a shrine that is known as the Kashmiri Takia today. During the period when the Valley was ruled by the Malla dynasty, the Kashmiri Muslims engaged in different occupations—as scribes to correspond with the Delhi Sultanate, and as scent manufacturers, musicians and bangle suppliers. Some were even admitted as courtiers to the Malla durbar, while many traded with Tibet. The descendants of these migrants live in Kathmandu, and this group tends to be well-educated. They speak a mixture of Nepali and Urdu rather than Kashmiri. While many work as businessmen, some have joined government service or entered politics.

The second group of Muslims to enter the Valley were of 'Hindustani' origin, meaning people from northern India. They arrived during the reign of Pratap Malla (1641–74), who allowed them to erect a separate mosque in the southern part of the property belonging to the Kashmiri Takia. This Hindustani mosque, now known as the Nepali Jama Masjid, is originally said to have been a Shia mosque, an *imambara*. According to oral traditions it was converted into a Sunni mosque by Maulana Sargaraz Ali Shah, a mufti of the last Mughal Emperor Bahadur Shah Zafar, who arrived with the entourage of Begum Hazrat Mahal of Lucknow when she took shelter in Kathmandu after the suppression of the Indian Mutiny by the British in 1857. The old structure of the Nepali Jama Masjid was demolished during the early 1990s and in its place a sparkling new structure was erected by mid-1990s.

The third group of Muslims to settle in Nepal came from different parts of northern India during the sixteenth and seventeenth centuries, invited by the rulers of the small hill kingdoms to manufacture military armaments including canons. They remained in the hills as makers of agricultural implements, utensils and ornaments. Though the descendants of these migrants are known as the Churaute, or bangle-sellers, a majority survive as farmers. There is a fair sprinkling of these Muslims in Nepal's central and western districts of Gorkha, Tanahu, Kaski, Syangja, Palpa, Argakhanchi, Pyuthan and Dailekh. Though the exact number of these Muslims has not been ascertained, they probably do not exceed a few thousand.

Muslim migrants of Tibetan origin include both Ladakhis and those from Tibet proper. The latter arrived mostly after the Chinese takeover in 1959, along with their Tibetan Buddhist counterparts. Today, many are engaged in the trade of Chinese consumer durables and selling curios. On the whole, this group tends to be the most affluent among the different Muslim groups inhabiting Nepal. They own prime property in downtown Kathmandu, including in and around the Durbar Marg. Their population does not exceed a few hundred.

While the smaller groups enumerated above provide diversity, the largest community of Islamic adherents—probably more than 95 per cent—are the Muslims of the Tarai region, the southern part of the country bordering the Indian states of Bihar and eastern Uttar Pradesh. While some of the Tarai Muslims inhabited the area even earlier than the period of Nepal's unification, others have been migrants from British India from the nineteenth century onwards. The Tarai Muslims too are not homogenous.

Demography and Geographical Spread

According to the 2001 census, Muslims constitute 4.20 per cent of the total population, up from the 3.53 per cent recorded in the 1991 census. The community constituted 2.6 per cent of the total population in 1954. There has been a gradual increase in the number of Muslims in both absolute and relative terms *vis-à-vis* other communities. The increase in the number of Muslims is, however, primarily due to their high fertility rate and migration from India and Bangladesh and not conversions from other religions to Islam (By way of contrast to the Muslim community's moderate growth rate, the Christian population which numbered around 50 persons in 1951 and a figure that was statistically insignificant, grew to 0.45 per cent of the total population in 2001, comprising around 101,976 persons.)

In the 18 districts of Tarai region, the population of Muslims is numerically preponderant in Kapilvastu, Parsa and Rautahat. In Bara, Mohatari, Dhanusha, Siraha and Sunsari districts, Muslims as a group (in contrast to other groups such as the Tharu or the Yadavs), constitute the second largest community. In Rupandehi and Sarlahi districts these constitute the third largest group. In the remaining seven districts of Jhapa, Morang, Saptari, Nawalparasi, Bardia, Kailali and Kanchanpur, their presence is nominal.

While the Muslim community makes up a significant population in several Tarai districts, the community generally has not voted en bloc and therefore are not treated as vote banks by political parties. Neither do Nepali Muslims have a separate political platform to articulate their demands—there is no Nepali Muslim League or Nepali Jamia Islamia, for example. With the reinstatement of multiparty democracy, the Muslim electorate has generally voted for mainstream political parties, and this is clear from the sprinkling of prominent Muslim personalities across the political spectrum during the 1990s—from Sheik Idris of Nepali Congress to Salim Ansari of Nepal Communist Party, and Mirza Dilshad Beg of the Rastriya Prajatantra Party. No specific political party is perceived as being 'soft' towards the Muslims and wherever Muslim candidates have won they have done so in mixed constituencies.

During the transition to multiparty democracy, there were some Muslims who believed that their community would be wooed, especially when they listened to the media carrying Id greetings by political leaders. Muslim leaders, particularly those of the Left, lobbied for a secular constitution. The document that was unveiled in November 1990 maintained Nepal's status as a Hindu kingdom under Hindu monarchy. While for some sections of the Muslim community, euphoria gave way to soul searching, other sections were pleased that Hinduism was retained as the state religion. Said Mohammad Samu, the then President of the Islamic Yuva Sangh, in an interview to the author in 1994, 'We have seen what goes on in the name of secularism in other countries'. Salim Ansari, was more vocal, 'The fact is that Nepal is de facto secular' (Sharma, S. 1994).

In the 1990s, Muslims in Nepal, living in the Tarai and elsewhere, increasingly turned towards Muslim welfare organizations, such as the Ittehadual Muslimean Committee, Iqra Modal Academy, Islamic Yuwa Sangh, Nepal Muslim Sangh, Bajme Adab and the Muslim Seva Samiti to further their interests.

The Tarai Muslims: Variations Within

Muslims of the Tarai region could be divided into four groups based on the period of their entry into the kingdom. The oldest constitute those people who were residing in the locality even before it was amalgamated to the present state of Nepal. An example of this would be the Muslim residents of Nepalgunj, which before its amalgamation into Nepal was under the Nawab of Oudh. The second and third group constitutes the zamindars and the tillers brought to Nepal during the late nineteenth century and early twentieth century. This group had been invited by the Rana rulers and provided incentives (such as tax exemption for a few years, etc.) for clearing forests and expanding cultivable areas. While the zamindars were invited through various fiscal initiatives and to facilitate the collection of revenue that would accrue once forestlands were transformed into fields, the latter brought in the tillers, many of them landless, to do most of the work. The bulk of the Muslims residing in the Tarai, who continue to remain as poor labourers or have graduated into small proprietors, belong to this third category. The fourth group constitutes tailors, weavers, embroiders, blanket makers, dyers, mechanics and other artisans located in small urban centers in the Tarai. The movement of these artisan peoples is related with the growth of small towns in the Tarai and the requirements for skilled and semi-skilled labour these towns have generated.

Apart from the groups enumerated above are the Bangladeshi Muslims who entered the country during 1970 and 1971. These were Bangladeshis of Bihari origin who preferred to migrate to Pakistan once the new state of Bangladesh came into being. While many of these refugees have been repatriated to Pakistan, many continue to stay in Nepal, though their number has not been properly estimated.

Among the different groups of the Tarai Muslims, though the distinct groups migrated into the country at different periods in history, as far as their culture and lifestyle is concerned, there isn't any substantial difference among them. Moreover, the Tarai Muslims of Nepal have many things in common with the Muslims in the adjacent Indian areas of Bihar and Uttar Pradesh. In terms of language, there is variation among the Muslims inhabiting various parts of the Tarai. While Awadhi is spoken as the mother tongue in western Nepal, Bhojpuri is the mother tongue in central Tarai. Maithali has that status in eastern Tarai. None of these groups have Urdu as their mother tongue though the more literate sections of the community can read and write Urdu.

What separates the Muslims of the Tarai from one another, as in the case with their Hindu neighbours, is the hierarchic divide. There is a hierarchy that prevails among the Nepali Muslims though this hierarchy is not based on notions of ritual purity and pollution as in the case of Hinduism but is based on origin and access to power (historically). While those who have Arab, Turkish, Afghan or upper caste Hindu (i.e., Brahmin and Rajput) backgrounds and have had long-standing associations with seats of power in the subcontinent constitute the Ashraf, local inhabitants and converts from low caste make up the Ajlaf. The differences between the Ashraf and the Ajlaf are still wide and pervasive in Nepal as in other parts of the subcontinent.

Islamic–Hindu Interface in Nepal

The Churaute hill Muslims have been greatly influenced by the Hindu hill milieu. As Gaborieau notes in his study, they follow circumcision and ritual burial of the dead, but other practises like *nikah* (bride price) and *zakat* (charity collected during religious festivals) are unequally observed (1996). The daily namaz and month-long fasting during Ramadan are lightly dispensed with. The Churaute speak Nepali, as do the Kashmiri Muslims of Kathmandu, many of whom are also fluent in Newari; while in their dress, food habits and some customs the Churaute are indistinguishable from their Bahun-Chettri neighbours. However during the past one and a half decade, *moulvis* from the Tarai and from India have increasingly visited the hill majids in the course of *dawa* and the hill Muslims are gradually conforming to what these *moulvis* regard as authentic Muslim practices.

For ordinary Hindus of the hills, Islam appears as *ulto dharma,* or reversed religion, and few are aware of its theological underpinnings. What strikes them are the details of ritual observance, particularly those features that are strange to them. Muslims appear to do just the opposite of what Hindus consider normal, such as washing their feet first and moving towards the face during ablutions rather than the other way around. Hindus face east while performing puja, while South Asian Muslims face west towards Mecca during namaz.

The Kashmiri Muslim lifestyle resembles the upper middle-class urban Hindus. Living in the Nepali state for a longer period of time and sharing common historical experiences, the group has developed a stronger identification with the Nepali state.

The Tarai Muslims, on the other hand, like other Tarai commu-nities, continue to have strong ties across the border and receive cultural sustenance from the large Muslim population of Uttar Pradesh and Bihar. Even though the gulf between the hills and the valley on the one hand and the Tarai on the other has been wide, some of it is being bridged as educated Tarai Muslims marry into Kathmandu's

Kashmiri Muslim families, and *moulvis* from the Tarai take to visiting hill *madrasas*.

In order to explain the concept of liminality existing among the vast number of Muslims who populate the Tarai, I have used an ethnographic case-study of Purushottampur. Purushottampur is a village located in Kapilvastu district in the Tarai of western Nepal, close to a town called Krishnanagar on the Indo-Nepal border.

Local Muslims are adherents of Sunni Islam. Within Sunni Islam, they adhere to a school of thought and practice known as Barelvi founded by the theologian Al Hazrat Ahmed Raza in northern India during the nineteenth century. Many of the *sufi* practices that adherents of Barelvi practice such as visiting the tombs of saints, are opposed by adherents of another school known as Deobandi which regards such practices as being unIslamic. Another group of Muslim seminarians who lived and taught in northern India during the nineteenth century inspires Deobandi. Because of doctrinaire proximity of Deobandi to Al Hadith or the Wahabi school of Saudi Arabia, there has been some Saudi funding flowing into Deobandi *masjids* and *madrasas* in Krishnanagar, an important border town near Purushottampur. The Deobandi or the Wahabi, however, has not made inroads in Purushottampur and the local *masjid/madrasa* Islamia Razai Mustafa, continues to remain affiliated to Barelvi denomination. The school, which remains in a dilapidated condition, is run mainly through local charity.

With regard to daily lifecycle, the canonical prayers (namaz, also known as *salah*), which is undertaken five times a day breaks the day into specific segments. Each of the namaz is undertaken during specific times of the day such as just after getting out of bed, before lunch, before noon, during sunset (before the evening meal) and before going to bed. Since these occur during specific times of the day, the names of the namaz also refer to the time of the day (Sharma 2001).

Common Pilgrimage Destinations

For the common folk of Purushottampur as for other Muslims of the Tarai, the following constitutes the main pilgrimages in the order of priority:

1. Khwaja Garib Nawaz: Also known as Ajmer Sharif, the *mazar* of Moinuddin Chisti and is located at Fatehpur Sikri. Known as the

place where the poor get what they ask for, all the people who can afford it, make a point to go there.

2. Kichocha Sharif: This is located in Faizabad district in the state of Uttar Pradesh in India. Some five hours away from Gorakhpur, one needs to get off at Akbarpur station to reach there. People go there to visit the tomb or *dargah* of Sufi saint Mukhdoom Shah and ask for his blessings. Hindus regard him as a tantric siddha. It is said that those who are possessed or have mental illnesses are immediately cured after reaching Kichocha Sharif.

3. Gazi Baba: This lies in Bahariach district also in the Indian state of Uttar Pradesh. This pilgrimage site is also known as Masaud Gazi. It is said that at Gazi Baba even leprosy patients are cured.

4. Gause Bangala: The Kathmandu-based Kashmiri Muslims are the followers of this *pir*-institution. His *urs* is fixed according to the Gregorian calender on February 5. The *dargah* of Gause Bangala is located in the West Bengal state, in the district of Ranigunj. The Sufi mystic Gause Bangala lived during British times. He had a great respect for Nepalis. Apart from Kashmiri Muslims of Kathmandu he has a great following among Muslims of eastern and central Tarai. His sister's son, whose *dargah* is located in Patna in Bihar, was also a *siddha*.

5. Bareilli Sharif: This is the place where the scholar Al Hazrat Ahmed Raza lived and taught. This scholar founded the Barelvi school of thought, one of the important South Asian denominations of Sunni Islam. Tarai-based Nepali Muslims living west of the Narayani river visit his *urs*.

6. There are specific Nepal-located special religious sites as well. The famous among these is the *dargah* of Malang Baba after which the town of Malangwa (the headquarters of Siraha district) derives its name. Hindus regard Malang Baba as a Tantric Siddha.

7. Delhi: There are a few religious sites or *mazars* in old Delhi that people visit.

Mazars and *dargahs* dot the hills and the Tarai. It is generally the Barelvi people who go to these sites. The Deobandi, in times of distress, go there as well. This in spite of the fact that doctrinally they refute these elements.

For the people in Purushottampur, undertaking these pilgrimages, a bus is usually reserved. A 15-day trip is undertaken during which all of the sites are covered. This allows a few days at each of the sites. However, it is only the men who undertake the trip and the women are excluded because of the purdah system.

What the above account reveals is that the religious universe of the Muslims of Purushottampur is located mainly in northern India. Visiting the main centres of Islam or undertaking a Haj (pilgrimage) to Mecca is beyond the means of most in Purushottampur. Only one person in the entire village has gone for a Haj to Mecca. For the rest, pilgrimage means visiting the tombs of saints to ask for blessings and to cure specific ailments.

Religious Minorities in a Hindu Kingdom

Historically, though the Hindu kingdom has provided the Muslims with the freedom to practice their religion, it has also imposed restrictions. While providing land grants for the construction of mosques and *madrasa* and establishing cemeteries, for example, it has issued a strict ban on proselytization and on slaughter of cows.

The old Civil Code (Mulki Ain) of 1854 ordered all communities living in the country into a single hierarchy based on notions of ritual purity and pollution. In the process, the state assigned the Muslims a caste status towards the bottom end of the hierarchy. As with Christians, they were listed among the 'impure but not untouchable castes'—in the same category as oil pressers, butchers and washerfolk. With the enactment of the new Mulki Ain in 1964, the legal backing to the caste system was withdrawn.

As a proselytizing religion, Islam is in an incongruous situation in Nepal where the state forbids conversion. Unlike Christian missionaries who proceeded to gather a flock despite the state's injunction, the Muslim community has by and large complied with this restriction.

Within the Muslim community, however, there is a different kind of 'conversion' taking place. A Nepali Muslim who has studied elsewhere in South Asia or visited the Gulf countries is influenced by puritanical sects, and returns a more 'correct' Muslim. He then tries to indoctrinate the culturally assimilated Nepali Muslims. At the same time, non-Nepali clerics are invited for *Dawa*, or propagation of the faith.

While this activity is not directed at people outside the faith, there is the danger that this trend would differentiate the Muslims from the national mainstream, which could be detrimental to their interests.

Such activities could lead to Muslims being alienated from the dominant Nepali culture and society.

There is already considerable hostility among those who see themselves as 'correct' Muslims towards the culturally more assimilative Muslims of the hills and Kathmandu. In fact, the brunt of their polemics is directed towards the traditionally liberal Kashmiri Muslims who, being more educated and articulate than others, have traditionally been leaders of the Nepali Muslims. Moreover, these Kathmandu Kashmiri Muslims follow Sufi precepts, which the neo-fundamentalists condemn as un-Islamic. The shift towards becoming more 'correct' Muslims is accelerating among the Tarai Muslims.

The rift between the 'traditional liberals' and the 'neo-fundamentalists' is neatly divided between the two mosques in downtown Kathmandu, the Kashmiri Takia and the Nepali Jama Masjid, which follow different branches of Sunni Islam. The Jama Masjid has remained a strong platform for the Deobandi school, which calls for a literal adherence to the Quran and its adoption in the daily lives of the community members. The Kashmiri Takia follows the Barelvi school, which provides a more liberal interpretation of the Quran and accepts the authority of Sufi holy men as mediators of Allah. In practice, the Barelvi schools tend to be more accommodating of local customs and practices.

Besides the traditional rivalry between the Deobandis and Barelvis, prevalent elsewhere in the subcontinent, the entry of other forms of global Islam tends to be changing the equations. The Wahabi (also known as Al-Hadith) and Quadiyani (or Ahmadia) are aggressively proselytizing within the community as a consequence of which a section of the Muslim community is moving away from locally-rooted denominations like the Barelvi and the Deobandi to those centered in Saudi Arabia (in the case of Wahabi) and in the Punjab (in the case of the Quadiyani or the Ahmadia).

For instance, Wahabis sponsor young Nepali Muslims who generally come from poor families and thus lack modern education to go to institutions like the Madina University to have a Quranic education. After receiving degrees they are sent back to Nepal to give religious education in Nepali *madrasas*. They even receive a generous monthly salary for their services. These religious teachers trained in Saudi Arabia are however, ineffective in communicating their messages to the masses. The excessive Arabic they use is incomprehensible to the lay Muslim folk. Nevertheless because of their rich

lifestyle made possible by their high income (according to local standards) and by virtue of having received education from prestigious
Saudi Arabian Universities, they command a formidable respect from
the local community.

The Quadiyanis, have a different way of preaching their faith. To
the young people they have brought into their fold, they provide not
simply a religious education, but one that is integrated with technical
education. The young converts (whether from other denominations
within Islam or from Hinduism) are sent not to the Gulf but cities
within the subcontinent, such as Chandigarh, for receiving technical
education.

The ideological debates and rivalries between Deobandis and
Barelvis are paling into insignificance as Wahabis and Quadianis make
inroads among the Muslims in Nepal. If Wahabism is a puritan Saudi
Arabian theology, the Quadianism is a reformist-syncretist Punjabi
export. Both developed as a response to and a reaction against Western
colonial missionary activity. Both are backed by rich endowments
and the local Nepali denominations are unable to counteract externally
funded prosetelization within the community.

It is not that there is no resistance by local Muslims against
the inroads made by foreign variants of Islam. For instance, in
Krishnanagar, the activities of the Siraj-ul-Uloom *madrasa* associated
with *moulvi* Abdullah Madani, was looked upon with disapproval by
local Muslims. The Siraj-ul-Uloom *madrasa*, and its Saudi Arabia
educated clerics were often objects of ridicule by local Muslims
and clerics alike. A similar attitude of resentment is articulated, for
instance, by people like Maulana Abdul Rauf Rahmani of *madrasa*
Sarajullum, an institution of Barelvi denomination at Jhandanagar,
Krishnanagar. However, with stronger financial clout and international
connections, Saudi Arabia educated clerics like Moulvi Abdullah
Madani (whose title signifies that he attended the university in Madina)
would probably continue to increase their influence in the future and
local clerics could soon become irrelevant for the community.

Growth in Religious Antagonism in the 1990s

If the absence of religious riots is an index of communal harmony,
the 1990s unfortunately witnessed increasing religious antagonism.
While there had been few outright Hindu-Muslim conflicts before

1990, the number of Hindu-Muslim conflicts has risen abruptly in the 1990s.

There have been few outright Hindu-Muslim conflicts in the Nepal Tarai. According to the All Nepal Anjuman Islaha (ANAI), a committee appointed by the late King Mahendra to resolve communal problems, there were 12 recorded instances of communal riots between 1954 and 1977. These riots were mostly provoked by allegations of cow slaughter, religious processions such as the tajia, or the building of mosques.

The most serious communal flare up during the pre-1990 period was a riot in Bara and Rautahat in 1971, when some Hindus murdered a Muslim on the charge of cow slaughter. The two Tarai districts were unstable for two weeks and the situation of the Muslims seemed extremely vulnerable. King Mahendra, arriving from a trip abroad, mobilized armed police and suppressed the riot. This use of state machinery for their protection seems to have bolstered the Nepali Muslims' confidence in the Hindu state in general and the monarchy in particular.

Marc Gaborieau is of the opinion that the Muslims of Nepal are protected because they constitute a small minority and maintain a low profile (1996). Mohammad Mohsin, a sociologist by training and former Speaker of the Upper House, feels that the atmosphere is not highly charged because the hill and Kathmandu Muslims do not react quickly to communally motivated events and tend to trust the state machinery. It may also be that the Hindu majority does not feel very hostile towards Islam because Nepal has never been subjected to Muslim rule. And, Nepal has not undergone the trauma of a Partition based on religion as has a large part of the subcontinent.

While resentments which have been dormant for a long time may exist among some, having to do with Gayasuddin Tuglaq's raid on Simraungad or Samsuddin's pillage of the Kathmandu Valley kingdoms during the thirteenth century, and the oral tradition that recounts the flight of Rajputs and Brahmins from the Indus-Ganga plain to the mid-hills, these are not recent-enough historical experience for them to affect present-day inter-community relations.

The communal harmony seemed to have been affected detrimentally after 1990, and particularly so with the demolition of the Babri Masjid in Ayodhya in India in 1992. Soon after the demolition of the Masjid, bricks of the same were brought by Hindu extremists and distributed in Tarai towns located close to the Indian border (viz.

towns like Birgunj, Janakpur, Nepalgunj, etc). Simultaneously, several leaders of the World Hindu Federation visited these border towns in Nepal and made provocative statements against Muslims. The entry of extremist Hindu elements from across the border, increase in the number of religious riots, and the inability of the state to punish the elements inciting and engaging in violence against Muslims has generally meant that the trust of the Muslims on the state apparatus rapidly eroded during the 1990s.

Nepalgunj, a town in the western Tarai is experiencing increasing numbers of religious riots over the past few years. As mentioned earlier, the area has a high concentration of Muslims; the latter having lived there from the time of the Nawab of Oudh. Hindu hill migrants and people elsewhere from the Tarai are settling in increasing numbers in Nepalgunj. In December 1994, some scuffles took place between Hindus and Muslims regarding the rehabilitation of a well in a temple, which soon led to riots along religious lines. Several people were injured and a curfew had to be imposed to bring the situation under control. Further, religious riots shook Nepalgunj in 1994–5 on the eve of the national election. In May 1997, during the local elections in Nepalgunj 27 people were injured and curfew had to be clamped for three days due to religious riots. Nepalgunj has, due to these events, unfortunately gained notoriety as the place where the eruption of religious scuffles has become commonplace (Gaunle 1997).

Hinduism in Nepal

The type of Hinduism that prevails in the 'world's only Hindu Kingdom' at the level of the common people tends to be different on several counts from that encountered in the adjoining Gangetic plains of northern India. Though it may be difficult to generalize given the internal regional variations on both sides of the Nepal-India border, Shaktism, or the worship of the Devi, in her various forms dominates in Nepal's midhills, where the self-identity of the state is located. This means that animal sacrifice is widely practised among the lay population, and the people at large are meat-eaters. Also, there is a great deal of syncretism between this variant of Shakti-worshipping Hinduism, folk religions and shamanism/animism to the extent that it becomes virtually impossible to distinguish between them, and in some cases even with Buddhism as practised in the midhills and Kathmandu Valley.

Another significant aspect of Hinduism in Nepal relates to its not having been used so far for political mobilization. While mobilization based on religion or religiously-inspired ideas played a crucial role in certain periods of India's freedom struggle, this trend has been conspicuously absent in Nepal's recent history. On the other hand, Hinduism has had a symbiotic relationship with the state in Nepal since its very formation in the late eighteenth century, primarily through the institution of Hindu kingship. In India, during the British times and after, no single religion has had a privileged relationship with the state. The movement of the late 1940s against the autocratic Ranas or the popular uprising in the late 1980s against the king-led Panchayat regime did not use Hindu religious symbols, nor did they derive inspiration from religious sources. In India by contrast, Hindu religious symbols, idioms and imagery played a major role in galvanizing the masses against British rule during the earlier part of the twentieth century. In its more recent history, the Hindutva agenda, including the proposal for constructing Hindu temples in contested religious sites, has been used as potent symbols for mobilizing the Hindu majority in a constitutionally secular India. 'Hindu' Nepal, it seems, does not need such mobilizing.

Thus, though Nepal may be constitutionally a 'Hindu' kingdom, it is difficult to delineate the Hinduness the Constitution of 1990 so boldly asserts. In circumstances where the laws of the land are not derived from the *dharmashastra* and the state has in principle withdrawn support to the caste system (the premier Hindu governing framework), the Hinduness of the state may be manifested only in certain signs and symbols. At present, the symbols of Hinduism enshrined in the Constitution or pursued in statecraft include the ban on cow slaughter, the promotion of Hindu religious festivals, the sponsorship of Hindu religious discourses, including the use of Sanskrit, and a ban on proselytization. Though these symbols are inextricably linked with the Nepali state's claim to Hindu-ness, there has been a weakening of these elements, and now it is only kingship that remains the core Hindu institution.

One of the strengths of Shaktism in an ethnically and culturally plural country like Nepal is the affinity of Shaktism to local folk religions or beliefs. Both involve animal sacrifice as part of their rituals. There are locations spread all over the country, generally hilltops, which are considered sacred sites for Hindu castes like Bahuns and Chettris and 'marginal' Hindu ethnic communities such as the Gurung,

Tamang, Rai and Limbu.[2] While the former associate the sites with stories of Durga or her multifarious incarnations, the latter link them with their own pre-existing deities. In fact, drawing deities from folk religions or 'little traditions' and incorporating them into the Hindu pantheon has been the mechanism through which Hinduism has spread and brought non-Hindus into its fold.

Dussera, which in Nepal is known as Dasain, is the premier Hindu festival in the kingdom. The importance of Dussera in pre-colonial Hindu kingships and the worship of the *gaddi* (perceived as a deity) and the sword, including other weapons of warfare during the occasion has been noted by scholars. In addition to these, Dasain dominates other Hindu festivities in Nepal because of its association with Shaktism. Moreover, the ruling dynasty of Nepal has the goddess as its titular deity. The culmination of the festival occurs on Vijaya Dashami. Unlike in northern India where Vijaya Dashami tends to be associated with the victory of Ram over Ravana (symbolizing the victory of good over evil), in Nepal it has very much to do with the feats of the Devi in defeating the assuras or demons. Another more important feature of Vijaya Dashami as it is practised in the hills of Nepal is the coming together of family members to accept *tika* (specially prepared for the occasion with curd mixed in uncooked rice and red powder) and blessings from elders and from those deserving respect. Goat which has been sacrificed to the goddess is generally consumed on this occasion.

Caste Hindus as well as ethnic people celebrate Dasain. Certain sections of the *janajati* are, however, boycotting Dasain which they claim to be a 'Hindu' festival imposed upon 'non-Hindus'. Generally Muslims of Kathmandu, and to some extent those living in the Tarai, visit the people they respect and accept *tika*. However, since the goat meat is not duly prepared (i.e., is not halal) they do not generally eat meat. The custom of putting *tika* is reinforced by *miteri* (known in Hindi as *yari*) or ritual relations, which in the past tended to be quite prevalent though among the new generations such relations have become rare. Earlier it used to be commonplace for a Muslim family in the valley and in the hills to have a *miteri* relation with a Hindu family.

[2] Among the various ethnic communities, Magars have been quite extensively Hinduized (with Magars officiating in certain temples, for instances) and for that reason it would be misleading to call them 'marginal' Hindus.

The role of Vijaya Dashami in Nepali society, its different connotations and whether or not to accept it is something that religious
minorities seem to be grappling with. The debate occurring among
recent Christian converts is illustrative in this regard. To put or not
to put *tika* during Dasain (a short-hand for Vijaya Dashami) has
become a fundamental issue among Nepali Christians. Trivial as the
issue may appear, it is at the heart of the debate among converts
because for some *tika* is a symbol of 'pagan' Hindu religion and thus
something to be condemned, while for others it is local culture and
therefore something that Christians can and should accommodate.
Articulating the first position are some evangelical sects while holding
the second view are the Catholic Church and mainstream Protestant
denominations. Thus at the heart of the debate among Nepali Christians are issues of culture and religion (Lama 1999). The importance
that the state attaches to Dasain can also be gauged from the fact that
out of the 13 or so religious holidays, 6 happen to be in Dasain alone.

The census of 2001 reckoned 80.62 per cent of the population
to be Hindu, down from 86.5 in 1991. What goes for 'Hinduism' in
a religiously plural society such as Nepal's where Hinduism, Buddhism,
folk religions, shamanism/animism fuse into one another to produce
a syncretic belief-system is difficult to identify. The reason for the
number of those who profess Hinduism as their religion being large
until now is because the enumerators automatically identify as
Hindus those belonging to specific communities. The awareness of
this tendency, and a campaign among the ethnic groups to describe
themselves as Buddhists meant that the number of Hindus in the
2001 census went down compared to the 1991 census.

Another peculiarity of Nepal has to do with the type of Buddhism
that has prevailed in the country, particularly the capital city of
Kathmandu and the blurring of sectarian differences between the
two religions.

The Buddhist-Hindu Interface

The 2001 census classified 10.74 per cent of the population as
Buddhist, up from the 7.8 per cent classified as Buddhists by the
1991 census. As in the case of Hinduism, what counts as Buddhism
in a religiously plural and syncretistic society like Nepal is difficult to
define. This is particularly so among the *janajatis*. (This term is used

for the various ethnic groups of Nepal whose language is classified as belonging to the Tibeto-Burman family of languages in contrast to the Indo-Aryan of the high caste Hindus. However, in practice 'janajati' tends to be a very permeable category.) While certain communities that have been living in close proximity with Tibetans and have had minimum interactions with the Nepali State (until recently), such as Sherpas can easily be identified as Buddhists; others, who have had a longer and a deeper contact with the Nepali state, such as the Thakalis, can be less easily identified as such. Among the Tibeto-Burman communities inhabiting the midhills, some like Magars have had a longer contact with Hinduism, while others like Gurungs and Tamangs have had less. Still others like Limbus and Rais have a proto-religion of their own besides having come under strong influence from Hinduism.

Among the Newars of Kathmandu, some groups identify them-selves exclusively with Hinduism, others with Buddhism, while still others have a problem with identifying exclusively with either. Among the latter communities, it is difficult to say who are Buddhists and who are Hindus because they participate in Hindu, Buddhist and their own festivities as well as worship Hindu, Buddhist and local deities. One of the parameters for identifying religious adherence in such conditions of ambivalence could be the type of priests people employ and the type of lifecycle rites they follow. But even this pre-sents problems because such groups could employ both Brahmins and Bajracharyas (married Buddhist priests) and follow lifecycle rites that show influences of both. Among the Newars one such 'synretistic' group is the Maharjans.

The Maharjans, who constitute the traditional peasantry of the Kathmanu valley, do not exclusively identify themselves as Hindu or as Buddhists; they accept both Buddhism and Hinduism as equally valid and practice rituals of both. While in the past, during census enumerations, they had identified themselves as Hindu, in recent years they are increasingly identifying themselves as Buddhist.

In the anthropological literature, various terminologies have been used to understand mixed cultural and religious traditions exemplified by communities such as the Maharjans. One such concept is 'liminality'. Introduced by van Genneps in understanding rites of passage, the concept has been further refined by Victor Turner who explains liminality as a state characterized by ambiguity, transformation and reflexivity. Scholars studying South Asia during the 1960s and 1970s had used concepts such as 'folk' traditions or 'little' traditions to understand how local forms of religion diverge from the canonical versions and include other accretive traditions as well. Scholars, in grappling with a similar phenomenon elsewhere in the globe, have also employed concepts like 'hybridity' and 'bricolage'.

What David Gellner (2001) has to say in the wider discussion on the identification of boundaries, margins and what has been called 'in-betweenness', and in a context where various terminologies like 'hybridity', 'liminality', 'bricolage', etc. have been used to understand the phenomenon, is interesting indeed. This becomes apparent in his discussion on the Maharjans of Kathmandu valley.

Gellner explains the 'syncretistic' cultural and religious practice of the Maharjans without resorting to concepts like 'hybridity', 'liminality' or 'bricolage'. Drawing upon the ideas of Emile Durkhiem, he provides a framework that lists several purposes for which a religion may be employed, for example: (1) the legitimation and expression of the household (2) the legitimation and expression of the locality (3) the legitimation and expression of the ethnic group or nation (4) the sanctification of the stages of life-cycle (5) the socialization of the young and the provision of a moral code (6) the provision of psychological and practical help in case of illness and misfortune, and (7) the provision of a path to salvation, i.e., soteriology. Buddhism, unlike Christianity has generally not covered all of these needs of the adherents and neither has it exhibited exclusivism towards other religions.

For the Maharjans, Buddhism provides a framework for lifecycle rituals, ritual assistance in worldly problems, and for those who seek it, a soteriology. The cultural and religious practices of Maharjans appear to be 'syncretistic' simply because the Maharjans derive their other needs from other extant traditions. Drawing further upon this framework and making a comparison with Japan, David Gellner argues that Buddhist monks and priests, through their involvement in the spheres of death and the after-life, provide soteriology, and through worship of ancestors symbolize continuity of the household and have largely ceded other tasks to Shinto cults, to Confucianism, and to Taoism. It is this phenomenon where a particular religion addresses some concerns and leaves to other traditions and belief-systems other concerns that appear as 'syncretistic'. It is this insight that Gellner comes up while discussing 'syncretism' that could inform the wider contemporary debate on the permeability of boundaries and the mechanisms that mediate cultural and religious pluralities.

The concrete situation of the Maharjans illustrates the point that terms such as Hindu or Buddhist become stumbling blocks in explaining the 'in-between groups or situations' faced by many communities in Nepal. It comes as no surprise that in such an ambiguous situation, identifying one's religious adherence through a mutually exclusive blanket category such as a Hindu or a Buddhist is more of a political statement than one that reflects one's true beliefs and practices. It is with this in mind that one has to read the call by the *janajati* leaders to their community members to identify as Buddhist in the 2001 census.

Though neo-Buddhism is a late starter, Buddhism has had a long, albeit a chequered history in Nepal. Some three centuries after the birth of Sidhartha Gautam in the Lumbini gardens of Kapilvastu in 563 BC, Buddhism made its way to the Kathmandu valley, through the emissaries of Emperor Ashok. Not much is known about the Kiratas who ruled the valley at that time but early Buddhism probably spread during the time of the Kiratas. Among the Lichchavi rulers who replaced the Kiratas, King Vrsdeva (AD 350–90) patronized Buddhism, while many other Lichchavi rulers were generous towards it, helping construct many Biharas in the valley. While Mahayana Buddhism was strong during the Lichchavi era, Tantric Buddhism or Vajrayana came into dominance during the Malla era. The eleventh to the fourteenth centuries were particularly important because of the influx of Buddhist-Tantric scholars from Nalanda and Vikramashila seeking refuge in the valley after the destruction of the citadels of Buddhist learning in India.

One significant contribution of Tantrism in Nepal, through its emphasis on esoteric practices in contrast to doctrines, was the blurring of sectarian differences between Shaivism and Buddhism, resulting in religious synthesis. Some of the *mahasiddhas* (great adepts) were Shaivist while others were Buddhist, and so the impetus to forge a common network was shared practices rather than outward religious allegiance. An outstanding example of religious synthesis among Tantric Buddhists and Shaivists is the cult of Matsyendranath. Originally known as 'Bungadya', a local deity from Bungamati, a small urban settlement in the valley, the deity was looked upon as a manifestation of Avalokiteswara, the Bodhisattva of abounding compassion. With the ascendance of Shaivism, the deity was said to be a *natha* ascetic and guru of Gorakhnath. In the story regarding the origin of the deity, Buddhist and Hindu narratives intermingle. The cult of Matsyendranath (as the Hindus prefer to call the deity) continues to remain strong in Kathmandu valley and the festival is attended by both Buddhists and Hindus in large numbers.

'Hindu' State: Changing Meaning and Changing Audiences

Though the state continues to identify itself as Hindu, the meaning of the term and the audiences to whom this message is intended have changed over time. The category 'Hindu' in the political discourse in Nepal has simultaneously played a double role. Whether it be 'Hindupati' (c. 1700), the builder of '*asal* Hindustan' (1774), preserver of 'the world's only Hindu kingdom' (1866), 'the ruler of a Hindu Kingdom' (1960) or ruler of '... Hindu, constitutional monarchical kingdom' (1990), the state by deploying the term has sought to differentiate itself from the surrounding regions on the one hand and to exercise some form of internal autonomy on the other (Burghart, R. 1996).

In an era when Hindustan—the Hindus and their land—was being ruled by Mughals and then the East India Company, followed in turn by the British Government, the concept of 'Hindupati' who was the builder of '*asal* Hindustan' or preserver of 'the world's only Hindu kingdom' had a dual purpose. Vis-à-vis the local population, it underlined the rulers' link with the traditional centre, while vis-à-vis the Hindu population at the centre, it emphasized a region unsoiled by foreign invasions. Construction of a religious difference from the centre allowed the local ruler some measure of political autonomy, while internally allowing for the imposition of an order appropriate for the perpetuation of dynastic rule. Designation of Nepal as the 'real Hindustan' by the local rulers enabled the pursuance of a policy of isolation—political as well as cultural—from the 'polluted' centre while simultaneously following an aggressive Hinduization of local communities within.

Likewise, in an era when the framers of the modern Indian constitution professed their faith in secularism, the declaration of Nepal as 'a Hindu Kingdom' or 'a Hindu, Constitutional Monarchical Kingdom' also tapped the sentiments of those in India who harboured hopes of their own country turning into a Hindu state. This reference also sought to highlight a nostalgic cultural continuity (in a hitherto marginal land), with the traditional centre of Hindu civilization—one that was displaced by Muslim, Christian and modern-secular value-orientations—and nostalgia for that bygone era (Sharma, P.R. 1991). Designation of the country as a Hindu kingdom enabled the rulers to continue with the policy of cultural isolation, in this instance, isolation of those who profess and practise their own religions from proselytizing foreign religions, while simultaneously bolstering the position of the Hindu King.

Not only is the Hindu king regarded as the enforcer of the *dharma* (however the term may be defined), rituals associated with Hindu kingship such as the coronation, mortuary rites and others are derived from the *dharmashastratas*. The Constitution, in the section titled 'His Majesty', echoes the *dharmashastric* view of the king as embodying the territory and its peoples (enacted during rituals such as the royal coronation) when it says 'His Majesty is the symbol of Nepali nationality and the unity of the Nepali people'. It would not be far from the truth to say that Nepal is in *de facto* terms a secular state with the kingship the sole Hindu institution as far as the state is concerned.

The Inroads Made by Global Militant Hinduism in the Traditional Hindu Kingdom

After 1990, Nepal is no longer the religiously peaceful kingdom that it once was. As mentioned at the outset, during the 1990s adherents of various faiths increasingly turned to what they considered to be the essential teachings of their respective religion, with prevalent syncretistic practices and customs being discredited as inauthentic. In the case of Hinduism, adherents increasingly turned towards more puritanical and less tolerant variants making their way into the country from India (i.e. the type of Hinduism as advocated by the World Hindu Federation) in place of the local plural or syncretistic variety. In the old dispensation, the majority Hindus had been tolerant in their own way towards other minority religions. This traditional outlook and amicability is rapidly eroding due to the inroads being made by a new type of Hinduism from abroad.

As Nepal enters the twenty-first century the old equilibrium no longer seems to be holding with increasing rivalry and confrontation between various religions within the country. In a land where rights to freedom had been restricted and the traditional Hindu state had guaranteed the life and property of all its citizens, the openness is ironically leading to religious distrust, which could easily manifest itself as physical violence and the state seems increasingly unable to guarantee citizen's life and property. Though the conflict that is currently engulfing the Hindu Kingdom is a Maoist guerrilla insurgency, given the dynamics among and between religions, violent religious confrontation is certainly not far behind.

The World Hindu Federation made significant inroads into Nepal during the period when the constitution was being drafted and consolidated its position further after that. The Federation mobilized public opinion in favour of retaining Hinduism as the state religion in 1990, and once that was achieved, began targeting Christians involved in proselytization as well as the minority Muslims.

Though the people's movement for the restoration of multiparty democracy launched during the early 1990 did not have a religious flavour, with the dissolution of the single-party Panchayat regime and an interim government in place to oversee the drafting of a new constitution, Nepal soon witnessed mass mobilizations based on religion. For instance, Nepal Christian Fellowship organized a public meeting to express the grievances of the Christians in Nepal on 7 May 1990. The very next day the World Hindu Federation wrote a scathing article in a national daily criticizing the release of religious prisoners. Achyut Raj Regmi, a Minister in the interim constitution, and a member of the World Hindu Federation, declared that he would wage a hunger strike if the state were not made Hindu. Very soon, Nepal Buddhist Association organized a demonstration and Buddhist leaders and scholars addressing the gathering spoke about the suppression of Buddhism in Nepal. On 11 August 1990, leader of the Bharatiya Janata Party, Mr L. K. Advani came to Nepal and expressed his sentiment that Nepal should continue as a Hindu state.

Finally on 9 November 1990, King Birendra unveiled the new constitution, which retained Hinduism as the state religion. But even after the broad contours of the new dispensation had been sealed, the Federation did not lessen its activities in Nepal. In May 1998, its President, Mr Ashok Singhal while on a visit to Nepal said that the kingdom was becoming a victim of religious aggression. He also alleged that NGOs had become willing agents in propagating Christianity. Singhal called for the formation of a ministry of religion and culture to deal with the proselytizations and to propagate Hindu religion and culture.

The rapid increase in the number of Hindus converting to Christianity threatens ordinary Hindus. The vernacular media is replete with the polemics by hard-line Hindus, who tend to brandish the threat of imprisonment, as laid down by the laws of the land, for those converting or found to be actively proselytizing. Hinduism in contemporary Nepal has lacked reformers to meet the challenges posed by missionary religions and other belief-systems. The World Hindu Federation has taken advantage of the situation and has played on the fears of ordinary Hindus.

Recent literature has brought to light the importance of kingship in organizing Hinduism (Inden 1990). This focus on kingship has redressed to a certain extent the notion of Hinduism being an un-organized religion. Though Hinduism may not have structures that organize religion as comprehensively, as say the Catholic Church, there are institutions that provide order to the polity. If Hindu kingship is one of these institutions, what Max Weber calls 'secular Brahminhood' is another (Weber 1958). 'Secular Brahminhood' is something that has been little studied and understood. The importance of this in-stitution in organizing Hinduism becomes clear from the case of Nepal, the only remaining Hindu kingdom in the world. The insti-tution of 'secular Brahminhood' refers to Brahmins who provide their services as advisers in the functions of statecraft. In the Nepali con-text, 'secular Brahminhood' primarily consists of two institutions: that of the *raj guru* (royal religious adviser) and *mool purohit* (the king's chief priest).

The institutions of Hindu kingship, *raj guru* and *mool purohit* have to be better understood since these institutions have the potential to engage with global militant Hinduism. Along with monarchy, not only do these institutions represent the more organized aspects of traditional Hinduism, but are sanctified by tradition and recognized by the laws of the land. With the onslaught of modernization, the importance of these institutions has declined and scholars have generally not been interested in institutions that have been considered the epitomes of 'traditionalism' and 'backwardness'. With new forms of global Hinduism that increasingly seek to reformulate traditional Hinduism and with the growth of intolerance, it has become urgent to understand these institutions and ensure that Hinduism in Nepal retains its tolerance and pluralism as it enters the twenty-first century.

References

Burghart, R. (1996). *The Conditions of Listening: Essays on Religion, History and Politics in South Asia* (Edited by Fuller, C. J. and Spencer, J.), Oxford University Press, Delhi, 1996.

Dastidar, M. (1995). *Religious Minorities in Nepal: An Analysis of the State of Buddhists and Muslims in the Himalayan Kingdom*, Nirala Publications, Delhi.

Gaborieau, M. (2001). Muslims in the Hindu Kingdom of Nepal, in T.N. Madan (Ed.), *Muslim Communities of South Asia: Culture, Society and Power*, (Third Enlarged Edition), Manohar Publishers, Delhi. pp. 205–27.

————. (1996). Varying Identity of Nepalese Muslims, *Comparative Studies of South Asia, Africa and the Middle East*, Volume 16 Number 2.

Gaunle, S. (1997). Nepalgunj: Dharmic Kachingal ko Visphotak Thalo (Nepalgunj: The Place Where Religious Scuffles Erupt), *Himal*, Volume 7 Number 2. pp. 8–16.

Gellner, D.N. (2001). *The Anthropology of Buddhism and Hinduism: Weberian Themes*, Oxford University Press, New Delhi.

Inden, R. (1990). *Imagining India*, Basil Blackwell, Oxford.

Lama, S. (1997). Nepali Christian: Kohi Dasain Manauchan, Kohi Manaudainan (Nepali Christians: Some Celebrate Dasain, Some Don't), *Himal Khabarpatrika*, 18 October–16 November 1999, pp. 90–1.

Ramirez, P. (Ed.) (2000). *Resunga: The Mountain of the Horned Sage*, Himal Books, Kathmandu.

Sharma, P.R. (1991) Secular India and Hindu Nepal: Convergences and Divergences, in Ramakanta et al. (Ed.) *Nation Building in South Asia Volume I*, Manohar Publishers, New Delhi. pp. 125–41.

Sharma, S. (1994). How the Crescent Fares in Nepal, *Himal*, Volume 7, Number 6. pp. 35–40

————. (2001). *Procuring Water: Foreign Aid and Rural Water Supply in Nepal*, Nepal Water Conservation Foundation, Kathmandu.

————. (2002) The Hindu State and the State of Hinduism, in Kanak Mani Dixit & Shastri Ramachandran (Eds), *State of Nepal*, Himal Books, Kathmandu. pp. 22–38.

Siddika, S. (1993). *Muslims of Nepal*, Gazala Siddika, Kathmandu.

Weber, M. (1958). *The Religion of India: The Sociology of Hinduism and Buddhism*, Translated and Edited by Hans H. Gerth and Don Martindale, The Free Press, Illinios.

Conflict and Accommodation

7

The Sunni–Shia Conflict in Jhang (Pakistan)

MARIAM ABOU ZAHAB

Introduction

Although sectarian[1] issues were not prominent in the course of the freedom movement in Pakistan, these identities surfaced soon after independence. Violent clashes were isolated and mostly happened during Muharram when the Shias perform mourning rituals (*azadari*) in public and take out huge processions. Since the mid-1980s, parties and violent groups, often sponsored by Islamic states, have emerged with a narrow sectarian agenda and, thanks to the easy availability of weapons and to the training facilities in Afghanistan and in Kashmir, the level and intensity of violence has tremendously increased, claiming hundreds of lives. Every region of Pakistan has been affected—Sunnis and Shias have killed each other in the name of religion in the Punjab, in the NWFP, in Karachi and in the Northern Areas of Gilgit and Baltistan—but the conflict has been particularly violent in the Punjab, especially in the south of the province.

Much has been written on the internal and external causes of the

---

[1] In the Pakistani context, sectarianism refers to the conflict between Sunnis and Shias.

emergence of the sectarian conflict in Pakistan at the macro level. Therefore, we will neither insist on Zia ul Haq's politics of Islamization and its consequences nor on the regional dimension of the sectarian conflict fuelled by the Iranian revolution and the Iran–Iraq war which assumed the character of a proxy war between Iran and Saudi Arabia on Pakistani soil (Abou Zahab 2002). Such analyses, although relevant, fail to explain why sectarian violence affected some areas of Punjab more than others.

This paper will focus on the Sunni-Shia conflict at the micro level with a study of Jhang, a city of central Punjab where the Anjuman Sipah-e Sahaba (later renamed Sipah-e Sahaba Pakistan, SSP), an extremist Sunni movement, was founded in September 1985.[2] The case study reveals that a multiplicity of factors, most of them not related to religion, have to be taken into account while analysing sectarianism at the grassroots level.

The aim of this paper is to analyse the factors that led to the rise of sectarianism in Jhang. Our assumption is that the sectarian conflict in Jhang is mainly the result of the struggle for political power between the traditional feudal families who are primarily Shia and rural-based and the emergent middle class which is largely Deobandi or Ahl-i-Hadith and urban-based.

This paper will examine the religious dimension, which is not the main reason for the conflict but only a pretext which proved to be a powerful means of mobilization in the 1980s. We try to analyse the complexity of the social conflict in Jhang, which is not limited to a class struggle between feudals and the urban middle class but should also be analysed as a conflict between the locals and the Muhajirs and as a conflict inside the Sunni community between two dominant castes or *biradaris*. We will describe the rise of the SSP which emerged as a credible alternative to the feudals and was instrumentalized both by local Sunni landlords and businessmen and by the Muhajir emergent middle class who used it to mobilize the urban youth in the defense of their own interests. Finally, the criminal dimension (the Islamization of criminality) should not be overlooked as it played a major role in the mobilization of the militants and in the persistence of the violence.

[2]The SSP was banned by President Musharraf on 12 January 2002, along with 4 other jihadi outfits but its militants were not really targeted in the crackdown on extremist groups which followed the ban.

Geographical Context

Jhang is located about 200 kilometres south of Lahore. It had historically a great politico-strategic importance for two reasons: the Sial dynasty was once powerful and Jhang was situated on the main communication line between Lahore and Multan. Parts of the vast district were taken away by the British and later by the Government of Pakistan when they created new districts. Today Jhang consists of three tehsils: Jhang, Chiniot and Shorkot. According to the 1998 census, the total population of the district is 2804 million out of which 655,000 (1/5) live in the urban areas. Jhang itself has a population of 292,000 inhabitants.

The municipal area of Jhang is divided into 3 parts: Jhang City (the walled city known as Jhang Sial), predominantly Hindu before 1947 and where the Muhajirs are in a majority, Jhang Saddar (Jhang Maghiana) with a sizeable Muhajir population (both Sunnis and Shias) and the satellite town with a mixed population. Jhang City and some *mohallas* of Jhang Saddar have also been affected by sectarian violence.

The Social Structure

Jhang is the centre of Punjabi folk culture, the famous epic Hir-Ranjha took place in Jhang where the shrine of Hir attracts many devotees. Many prominent academics and politicians[3] belong to Jhang which was also the home of the only Pakistani Nobel prize winner, Dr Abdus Salam, the nuclear scientist who happened to be an Ahmadi.

Jhang is one of the most backward and feudal districts of Pakistan. The feudals—more precisely the Shah Jewna family[4]—and the Pirs have dominated the political set-up of the district since the days of the Raj; the local population is convinced that they have deliberately

---

[3]Among others, Maulana Tahir ul Qadri, a prominent Barelvi leader.

[4]In true Punjabi fashion, this prominent political family is divided into two rival factions. The first one was led by the late Colonel Abid Hussain and now by his daughter Abida Hussain (former federal minister in Nawaz Sharif's government and ambassador to the USA), her husband Fakhr Imam and their daughter Sughra Imam who started her political career in December 1998 as Chairman of the district council. The other faction is led by Makhdoom Faisal Saleh Hayat who is the *sajjada nashin* of Shah Jewna. A central leader of the PPP, he defected in 2002 to join the PML (QA), he is the current federal minister of Interior. Leaders of both factions contested elections against one another at the local and at the national level in 2001 and 2002.

kept the district backward, refusing the opening of schools and the building of roads. In 1947, a sizeable number of refugees from India, many of them hailing from Panipat, were settled in Jhang;[5] they occupied the properties left by the Hindus and started business activities. The large influx of refugees provoked a negative reaction among the locals, some of whom had occupied the properties of Hindus and Sikhs which were later taken back from them to be distributed to Muhajirs. Contrary to what is generally assumed, even those who settled in the rural areas could never assimilate although they came from East Punjab and shared the same language and culture with the local population. Although they do not identify themselves as Muhajirs, the local population considers them as such. The wounds of Partition have not healed, there is resentment even among those who were born much later, and everybody has a story to tell about who became rich overnight or about the *kammis* (lower caste people) who changed their caste during Partition to become Syed. Relations between the communities were always tense, even if violent clashes were few.

The Religious Communities

Although the majority of the population is Sunni, Jhang district has a sizeable Shia population, probably around 25 per cent (10 per cent in the city itself) although it is very difficult to make an accurate assessment. Shia communities had moved to Punjab and Sind after the conquest of Muhammad bin Qasim. Ismaili missionaries were also active in the area. Under the Abbassides, the governor of Jhang, Umar bin Hafas, was a clandestine supporter of the Fatimid movement and the Batiniya influence spread in Southern Punjab. Then, the Karmats who had established contacts with the Fatimids in Egypt set up an independent dynasty in Multan and ruled the surrounding areas till they were defeated by Mahmud Ghaznavi.[6] The Karamat movement left a deep impact on the local population. The small Shia Muhajir community settled in Jhang Saddar belongs mostly to the educated middle class, is often Urdu speaking, shares the Sunni hatred

---

[5]According to the 1951 census, Muhajirs formed 49 per cent of the population of the district and 65 per cent of the population of the municipal area of Jhang.

[6]Bilal Zubeiri. *Tarikh-e Jhang*. nd, np.

for the feudals and has few contacts with the local Shias who are mostly Siraiki speaking and rural-based.[7]

While Muhajir Sunnis are often Deobandis, most of the local Sunnis are Barelvis, the shrine of Sultan Bahu is located in Jhang district and a Qadiri Pir belonging to the Gilani family who was previously settled in Azam Warsak (Waziristan) has moved to Jhang in the early 1980s. According to Pir Syed Agha Kazem Shah Gilani, known locally as Pir Pathan, he chose Jhang because of the central geographical location of the city which makes it much easier for his *murids* (followers) to visit him than when he was based in Waziristan.

Jhang has a history of sectarian conflict which goes back to pre-Partition days. After 1947, the relocation of the headquarter of the Ahmadi community from Qadian now in Indian Punjab and the transformation of Rabwah (near Chiniot) to an 'Ahmadi Vatican' attracted militant Sunnis originally from Panipat, Rohtak and Hisar in Jhang and Chiniot where they opened *madrasas* and were active in the anti-Ahmadi movement since the 1950s. Maulana Manzoor Ahmed Chinioti, the head of Tehrik-e Khatm-e Nubuwwat, always took the lead of anti-Ahmadi campaigns. The Muhajirs were also in the forefront of anti-Shia and anti-feudal activity but they were not yet economically powerful and they did not have enough support among the locals to challenge the monopoly of the Shia feudals on politics (Ali 1999). The Muhajirs whose religious identity had been sharpened by the revivalist movements of the 1920s in East Punjab[8] and by the sufferings experienced during Partition have always supported religious parties, namely Jamiat-e Ulema-e Pakistan (JUP) and Jamiat-e Ulema-e Islam (JUI).

Elections have been contested on a sectarian basis in Jhang since the 1950–1 provincial elections. Maulana Ghulam Hussain started an anti-Shia crusade in the 1950s; he opposed Colonel Syed Abid Hussain both as a feudal and as a Shia and was utilized by the small Sunni landlords who drew political benefits from this campaign (out of a total of 9 seats, Sunni landlords were able to secure 4 seats in 1951). The elections of 1954 were not fought on a sectarian basis:

[7]The local Shias blame, for instance, the Muhajirs for having introduced Hindu customs in the Muharram processions while many Muhajirs consider the local Shias as uneducated and ignorant of 'true Shiism'.

[8]The Jats of Rohtak were the target of a Shuddi movement launched by the Arya Samaj in the 1920s and was aimed at reconverting them to Hinduism.

Syed Abid Hussain won the only seat from Jhang in the National Assembly and became the federal minister. But in 1970, there was an unprecented mobilization of Sunni *ulema* against the Shia feudals of Jhang due to violent Sunni-Shia clashes in front of Khewa Gate (renamed Bab-e Umar by the Sunnis) during the procession of 7th Muharram (March 1969) which had caused the death of five Sunnis. Syed Abid Hussain was defeated by Ghulam Haider Bhawana, a Sunni landlord, and the three National Assembly seats were won by Sunni candidates elected on a JUP ticket.[9] The political activism of the *ulema* was however short-lived, their attention was focused on the Ahmadis and on Islamization and they soon went back to their *madrasas*. The Sunni-Shia factor receded to the background for some time, the middle class was still very small and too weak to challenge the political monopoly of the Shia feudals. Sunnis supported Sunni landlords but they had a feeling of betrayal as the Sunni landlords were as indifferent to their interests as the Shia landlords[10] and they were not ready to share power with the emergent Muhajir middle class.

By that time, members of the Sunni business class, both Muhajirs and locals, had entered the municipal committee: Sheikh Iqbal, a local who claimed he belonged to the famous trading *biradari* of the Chinioti Sheikhs and who monopolized municipal politics for many years, became Vice-president of the municipal committee in the late 1960s and later the Chairman, a post which he held for almost 25 years. He was elected to the Provincial assembly on a JUI ticket in 1970 and joined the PPP in 1972. Since then, Sunnis have dominated the municipal committee while the district committee remained, except for a very short period, in the hands of the Shia feudals sometimes associated with the *sajjada nashins* of Sultan Bahu as is the case since the local elections held in 2001 under the devolution plan designed by General Musharraf.

In 1974, the Qadianis were declared non-Muslims by a constitutional amendment and in 1977 Zulfiqar Ali Bhutto banned alcohol and declared Friday as a holiday. General Zia ul Haq who took power in July 1977 soon started implementing a program of Islamization.

---

[9]One of them was Sahibzada Nazir Sultan linked to Sultan Bahu shrine who defeated Arif Khan Sial.

[10]Two of the three Sunnis elected in 1970 had joined the ruling PPP and they contested the election in 1977 on PPP tickets (PPP was very much seen as pro-Shia). The number of National Assembly seats in Jhang was increased from 1 in 1965 to 3 in 1970, 5 in 1977 and 6 in 2002.

This emboldened the *ulema* and in the context of Jhang, the Shias were likely to be their next focus. The consequences of Zia ul Haq's politics of Islamization and the politicization of the Shias after the Iranian revolution and the imposition of *zakat*[11] led to a new phase of sectarianism in Jhang.

The formation of the Tehrik-e Nifaz-e Fiqh-e Jaafria (TNFJ) in 1979, later renamed Tehrik-e Jaafria Pakistan (TJP), with a purely religious agenda in the beginning, was a turning point for the sectarian conflict in Pakistan. This party, whose name sounded offensive to Sunnis, became much more militant from 1984 under the leadership of Allama Arif Hussain al Hussaini, a charismatic leader who empowered the Shia community and transformed this religious movement to a political party in July 1987. The young *ulema* who had been educated in prestigious religious schools in Iran promoted a more rationalized and puritan version of Shiism. They were branded as 'Wahabi Shias' by the traditional clergy who accused them of destroying the religion, but surprisingly enough, they soon became very popular among the community and their *majlis*, often politicized, attracted crowds.[12] The young *ulema* opened *madrasas* with Iranian support and became an inspiration for the Shia community, especially for the students who joined the militant Imamia Students Organization (ISO). Although the feudals had no influence on these *ulema* who were financed by Iran, the Sunnis blamed them for the new assertiveness of the Shia community.

It is in this context that the Anjuman Sipah-e Sahaba was founded on 6 September 1985 in Jhang by Maulana Haq Nawaz Jhangvi (1952–90). There are lots of rumours about the role of the agencies in the creation of the SSP—a parallel can be drawn with the foundation of the MQM in Karachi, both parties being the product of the political vacuum created by Zia ul Haq's regime—and about the financing of the party by Iraq and Saudi Arabia and by *zakat* money.[13] It is obvious that the SSP was a retaliation to Shia militancy and that Zia

---

[11]For more details about the politicization of the Shia community, see Mariam Abou Zahab, The politicization of the Shia community in Pakistan in the 1970s and the 1980s (paper presented at the Conference on Images, Representations and Perceptions in the Shia world, Geneva, October 2002 (forthcoming).

[12]This does not mean that the traditional zakirs who often have no formal religious education and who have always been economically dependent on the feudals were marginalized. Both styles of *majlis* coexist in Punjab and attract crowds.

[13]There have also been recent allegations about links between the SSP and Al Qaida networks.

ul Haq was too happy to get an opportunity to teach the Shias a lesson. It can also be assumed that Haq Nawaz, who was at that time vice-amir of the JUI for the Punjab,[14] had political objectives as the SSP was created a few months before the lifting of martial law on 1 January 1986.

The SSP's goals are to defend the honour of the Sahaba (companions of the Prophet), to strive against *rafiziyat* (Shiism) by all legal and constitutional means, to proscribe Muharram processions, Shia *azan* (call to prayer) and all forms of *azadari* and *matam* (chest beating) in public, to get Shias declared as non-Muslims and Pakistan declared a Sunni state, and to make efforts to unite Sunni sects.[15]

Born in a poor rural family of the Khoja (pathfinders) caste of Chela, a village of Jhang district, Haq Nawaz received a *madrasa* education[16] and, in 1973, he became the *khatib* and *imam* of a Deobandi mosque in the mohalla of Piplianwala in Jhang Saddar. Before he started mobilizing Sunnis against Shias, he had participated in the anti-Ahmadi movement and had also denounced Barelvi rituals.[17] Haq Nawaz, who was a fiery orator, launched a crusade against Iran which he accused of supporting the Shias in Pakistan and of wanting to export its revolution, his attacks were as much directed against Khomeini as against Shia beliefs and rituals. Locally, he particularly targeted the Shah Jewna family and the district administration. Besides appealing to anti-Shia sentiments, Haq Nawaz started addressing social problems, becoming involved in *thana-kutcheri* issues, which made him extremely popular even among local Shias. He emerged quickly as a credible alternative to the feudals and won the support of persons who were not otherwise sympathetic to his personality or ideology[18] as he was much more accessible and more efficient than the feudals to solve people's problems.

The class struggle rhetoric of the SSP was largely borrowed from the JUI which remained closely associated with the SSP at least till

[14]Haq Nawaz's militancy against Shias annoyed Maulana Fazlur Rehman who did not want to antagonize his sizeable Shia constituency in Dera Ismail Khan and who opposed his election as amir of the JUI for Punjab.

[15]*Dastur-e Asasi*, Sipah-e Sahaba, nd.

[16]He graduated in 1971 from Khair ul Madaris in Multan, joined the JUI and started teaching in a *madrasa* of Toba Tek Singh in 1972.

[17]See for more details Maulana Mohammad Ilyas Balakoti. *Amir-e Azimat*. Jamia Usmaniya, Jhang Saddar, nd. This tendentious book is the 'official' biography of Haq Nawaz Jhangvi.

[18]Mukhtar Ahmad Ali, 1999.

1989. The SSP denounces the Shia jagirdars who received lands from the British and the 'black laws'[19] and claims that nothing has changed since the days of the Raj as the poor have simply become the slaves of the 'Brown sahibs', that is those feudals who supported the Raj and were the slaves of the British. With such a rhetoric, the SSP attracted the downtrodden who had voted for the PPP in 1970 and had seen their hopes frustrated.

The Causes of the Conflict

The conflict has a religious, or rather a cultural, aspect. Although he had denounced Barelvis till the early 1980s, Haq Nawaz was later careful to avoid antagonizing them and he managed to win their electoral support for the SSP to some extent. Haq Nawaz criticized the peasants for their ignorance of 'true' Islam which he linked to the influence of Shiism, he accused them of being devoid of religious identity and wanted to make them aware of the differences between Sunnis and Shias (Zaman 1998) which are quite blurred in the rural Barelvi society. The SSP wants to convert Sunnis to a rationalized Islam, to replace customary practices by the Islam of urban *ulemas* and *madrasas*, their struggle is directed as much against local rituals seen as Shiism as against the influence of *pirs*, both Sunni and Shia. They want to purify Islam from all external influences and their rhetoric often borrows from the reformist literature of the nineteenth century to which they constantly refer to give legitimacy to their anti-Shia campaigns. The SSP preaches a total social boycott of the Shias, relying on famous fatwas of the founders of Deoband. It denounces Shias as Zionist agents and as the 'other' responsible for all the problems of the country. The SSP's rhetoric equates local forms of religious beliefs and cultural practices to the influence of Shiism. However, these rituals have hardly anything in common with Shia rituals in Iran or Lebanon, they are a local expression of the tragedy of Karbala which is deeply rooted in the Punjabi culture and often evokes Sikh or Hindu rituals. It is true that up to now Sunnis and Shias, and even Ahmadis, participate in Shia rituals in Jhang, just like the Hindus participated before Partition,[20] because they do not equate *majlis* or processions with Shiism but with their local culture. By assassinating

[19]The Punjab Land Alienation Act of 1900.
[20]It is often said that the best zakirs of Jhang were Hindus.

prominent zakirs, the SSP militants are destroying part of the Punjabi culture transmitted orally from father to son. Those zakirs are targeted because they are popular with Barelvis who share the same devotion to the Ahl-i-Bait (the family of the Prophet); they are seen as more dangerous than the Iran-educated zakirs who preach a rationalized form of Shiism which appeals only to a fraction of the Shia community.

This religious aspect is however not the main reason for the conflict: these themes were not new, the Deobandi *madrasas* and *ulema* had been promoting the same anti-Shia sentiments for many years and they had promulgated anti-Shia fatwas but these ideas never penetrated the society in South Punjab and did not lead to large scale violence.

Religion was only a pretext as anti-Shia rhetoric proved to be a powerful means of mobilization in the mid-1980s and also a way to get support both from the state and from foreign sources. The Sunni emergent middle class, both local and Muhajir, who had been trying to enter the political arena made full use of this situation and quickly understood the benefits it could draw from supporting Haq Nawaz. Sunni landlords and the emergent under-class of transporters, contractors,[21] intermediaries and shopkeepers who had benefited from the liberal economic policy of the Zia regime and who supported the SPP to further their own political and economic interests. Most of the Muhajir businessmen dealing in animal skins and distributors of ghee, sugar and flour who had prospered under the Zia regime financed the SSP. Haq Nawaz gained the support, both financial and political, of the rich businessmen of Jhang who wanted an access to the political arena and also wanted to break Sheikh Iqbal's monopoly on municipal affairs. Muhajir businessmen and shopkeepers supported the SSP, either directly or through the powerful Anjuman-e Tajiran (Association of traders). It is not surprising that shops belonging to Sunni Muhajirs were set on fire at the instigation of Shia feudals as retaliation. Those who wanted to stand for the provincial elections against the feudals and could not get a Pakistan Muslim League (PML) ticket also supported the SSP. Sheikh Iqbal[22] and Sheikh Yousaf were competing to support Haq Nawaz. Sheikh Iqbal, who wanted to keep Haq Nawaz away from local politics, financed discreetly his electoral campaign for the national elections of 1988, which ironically gained him the support of the local Shias who shared the same interests.

---

[21] These two professions are often described as powerful mafias.

[22] Sheikh Iqbal's personality is very controversial. In the 1970s, Sheikh Iqbal owned a petrol pump, a hotel, a cinema hall and dozens of buses.

Sheikh Yousaf, once a small contractor of Jhang settled in Lahore, had become very rich in the 1980s. He now owns Hasnain Construction Company to which the contract of the Islamabad-Lahore motorway, among other lucrative contracts, was awarded. This former MPA, well connected in army circles, was the major financier of Haq Nawaz and of the SSP in general, providing Pajeros and the like and financing the election campaigns. Richer than Sheikh Iqbal, he had the support of all those, Sunnis and Shias, who were opposed to Sheikh Iqbal. Haq Nawaz thus became a pawn in this rivalry between local Sunni businessmen and his assassination in February 1990 was most probably perpetrated at the instigation of Sunni leaders as they were competing for the same constituency. Some sources argue that Haq Nawaz wanted to stand for the provincial assembly elections against Sheikh Iqbal and that he resented the fact that Sheikh Iqbal had convinced him to rather contest the National Assembly elections in 1988.

After the assassination of Haq Nawaz, Sheikh Iqbal who was MPA at that time, made a mistake which contributed to the cycle of violence. The police had wanted to launch an operation against the SSP which was postponed at the request of Sheikh Iqbal. When he refused later to finance the purchase of weapons for the SSP activists, they attacked his home.[23] From that time, Sheikh Iqbal and his family have become the enemy of the SSP and have been the target of many acts of violence perpetrated by the SSP militants.[24]

The social conflict has thus several levels: feudals versus the emergent middle class, Shias versus Sunnis, local Shias versus Muhajir Shias, local Sunnis versus Muhajir Sunnis, Syed (local and Muhajir Shias) versus *julahas* and *kammis* (Sunni Muhajirs), Sheikh *biradari* (local Sunnis) versus Arain *biradari* (Muhajir Sunnis) and also competition for power inside the local Sheikh *biradari*. The local-Muhajir conflict can also be analysed in terms of a conflict between two dominant castes (Sheikh versus Arain).[25]

[23]A case was falsely registered against Shias who became martyrs in the eyes of the Shia community.

[24]Sheikh Iqbal was himself assassinated in March 1995 by the SSP. The only son of Sheikh Iqbal, who is a high civil servant, was designated in the FIR registered after the assassination in January 1991 of Isar ul Qasmi, the successor of Haq Nawaz, in which Sheikh Iqbal's family was in fact not involved. Sheikh Iqbal's brother, Sheikh Akram, was elected tehsil nazim in 2001, defeating the SSP candidate, Zahoor Sajid Janjua, brother of late MPA Riaz Hashmat Janjua.

[25]The importance of caste in Jhang can be judged from the fact that our informers always refer to Ibbetson's book 'Punjab Castes' published in Lahore in 1916 and

If the biggest financiers were local, the cadres of the SSP come mostly from the Muhajir community and belong to the Arain *biradari* as did many of the settlers who migrated from East Punjab to the Canal Colonies at the end of the nineteenth century. Many of them have fought in Afghanistan and most of the terrorists who caused a lot of bloodshed between 1990 and 1993 in Jhang were Muhajirs.[26] The SSP militants belong to the emergent 'under-classes', semi-urban, often unemployed, who are at the margin of the middle class, and whom the SSP has empowered by giving them an agressive Sunni identity (Zahab 2002).

During Haq Nawaz's lifetime, there was not such a high level of violence in Jhang as after his death. This can be attributed to the fact that he was a local. His successors as leaders of the SSP were Muhajirs, outsiders imported in Jhang,[27] and it can be said that the SSP thrived on the dead body of Haq Nawaz. The criminalization of the sectarian conflict in Jhang, which could be observed since the creation of the SSP, became much more obvious after the death of Haq Nawaz thanks to the weaponization of society and to the power of the local mafias.[28] Muhajir goondas who had joined the SSP—Anwar alias Gaddu, Haider Butt, Saleem Fauji[29] to name but a few—played a prominent role in the bloodshed which followed the assassination of Haq Nawaz. They became heroes when they vowed to avenge his death. They got political protection from the SSP and a lot of local drug dealers gave them protection money which means that the SSP utilized them to

---

based on the Census Report of 1881. This book is regularly reprinted both in Pakistan and in India and has recently been translated into Urdu.

[26]Mukhtar Ahmad Ali, op. cit. Muhajirs, both Sunnis and Shias, are said to be more assertive and to resort quickly to violence because they do not have the same values and family networks than the locals who have many other ways of resolving conflicts before resorting to violence.

[27]Isar ul Qasmi was from Samundri and Azam Tariq settled in Karachi was born in a village near Chichawatni.

[28]The Punjab government did not move against the SSP between 1988 and 1993 because the Islami Jamhoori Ittihad (IJI) saw it as a potential ally and because the targets of the SSP, namely Ahmadis and Shias, were seen as supporters of the PPP. Benazir Bhutto sought the alliance of the SSP against the PML; Azam Tariq enjoyed a quasi-immunity when the PPP was in power because he was an arch enemy of Abida Hussain who was despised by Benazir Bhutto.

[29]Saleem Fauji was killed in a police encounter in 1992. Azam Tariq attended his funeral and pronounced a very provocative speech describing him as a martyr. His death provoked the attack of a police APC with a 17 mm anti-aircraft gun which caused the death of 4 policemen and provoked a police operation against the SSP.

maintain a certain level of tension in the street. In exchange for financing the SSP, Sheikh Yousaf is also alleged to having used SSP activists and goondas to threaten and sometimes kill people.

The sectarian situation was also manipulated by the drug mafia— Jhang is at the crossroads of drug and arms distribution networks. The drug mafia had an interest in maintaining a certain level of tension and resorted to provocations whenever the situation was too calm for its activities. Heroin smuggling became a main commercial activity in Jhang after the onset of sectarian violence[30] and electoral campaigns were financed by the profits of the drug business. Both sides were involved: a Shia feudal who is an ex-MNA is regularly denounced as one of the drug mafia bosses and the SSP apparently controlled the retail sales with the connivance of the police. When Jhang experienced the worst violences in 1992, drug dealers and drug users were the only persons who could move freely between the different parts of the city.

The SSP tried to get rid of the goondas after Azam Tariq was elected MNA for the first time in a by-election in 1992, and adopted a soft line, insisting on welfare (development projects, Sui gas, etc.) and on the necessity to maintain peace in Jhang. The extremists who felt betrayed, created the Lashkar-e Jhangvi headed by Riaz Basra in 1994 and the violence spread to other districts where it was more of terrorist in nature.

Azam Tariq was elected as an independent MNA in October 2002—the authorities tried, so far in vain, to get his election invalidated—he had spent the whole year either in jail or under house-arrest after the SSP was banned in January 2002. Although Shia feudals have lost some of their influence,[31] Faisal Saleh Hayat, a powerful Shia landlord and *sajjada nashin* of Shah Jiwana, has been rewarded with the Ministry of Interior for having left the PPP to join the PML(Q). Sughra Imam, the daughter of Abida Hussain, has been elected MPA and Asad Hayat, a Shia feudal and brother of Faisal Saleh Hayat, is naib nazim of the district. The results of these elections held in August 2001 demonstrated that, at least at the local level, it is power and the traditional Punjabi rivalry between factions

[30]Drug and alcohol traficking witnessed an increase of 250 to 300 per cent after the outset of sectarian violence. Khalid Hussain. Live and Let Die. *The Friday Times*, 3–9 September 1992.

[31]Abida Hussain, her husband Fakhar Imam, and Amanullah Sial were defeated in the elections.

which count rather than ideology. The SSP supported Sahibzada Sultan Hamid of Sultan Bahu and Asad Hayat, a PPP-backed panel, against Sughra Imam who was defeated. It shows once again that when the game is about power and money, Shia feudals and Barelvi Pirs are acceptable to the SSP.

Local Sunnis have retained their power at the local level as Sheikh Akram, the brother of Sheikh Iqbal, was elected tehsil nazim despite the efforts of the SSP to take over this seat. Given the enmity between Sheikh Akram and the SSP, there is every reason to fear a new outbreak of violence in Jhang.

Conclusions

This short study of the many aspects of the sectarian conflict in Jhang demonstrates that sectarianism is linked with the power struggle and that, due to the lack of confidence in the state and the absence of channels of political participation, primordial identities come to the forefront and are instrumentalized by the protagonists to conflicts involving class, biradari, factions, or ethnic identity. It shows that in the context of Jhang the conflict cannot be explained in religious and ideological terms alone and that it is primarily the result of the socio-economic tensions among different classes of the society. Sectarianism can thus be defined in this particular context as a temporary substitute identity and as a vehicle of social change.

References

Ali, Mukhtar Ahmad. 1999. *Sectarian Conflict in Pakistan: A Case Study of Jhang*', Regional Center for Strategic Studies, Colombo, June 1999.

Zahab Mariam, Abou. 2002. The Regional Dimension of Sectarian Conflicts in Pakistan, in C. Jaffrelot (Ed.), *Pakistan: Nationalism without a Nation?* Manohar, Delhi, 115–28.

——. 2002. 'Sectarianism as a Substitute Identity. Sunnis and Shias in Central and South Punjab in Pakistan', in Sofia Mumtaz, Jean-Luc Racine and Imran Anwar Ali (Eds), *The Contours of State and Society*, Oxford University Press, Karachi, pp. 77–95.

Zaman, Muhammad Qasim. 1998. 'Sectarianism in Pakistan: The Radicalization of Shii and Sunni Identities'. *Modern Asian Studies* 32 (3): 689–716.

8

Languages as a Marker of Religious Difference

Asha Rani

Introduction

I n this paper, I try to posit the semantic and symbolic meanings of the term syncretism—culturally and linguistically defined with particular reference to the category of 'Hindustani'—as it was constructed historically within the nationalist discourse in the early twentieth century colonial north India.* As a theoretical construct, linguistic-cultural syncretism indicates a process of staging, mediating and intervening with social and cultural pluralities moving beyond straight-jacketed binarism and exclusivism. In this manner, a syncretic position defies given structures and processes, and can at times be located in a collectivity having multiple roles and characteristics. Being something more than either this or that, the metaphor of syncretism can help us in understanding the dynamics of cultural and political mobilization and politicization of collective identities broadly typified under the categories of religion, language, caste, class, race and region, etc.

I will analyse the category of 'Hindustani' as a potential syncretic

I thank Professor Imtiaz Ahmad for his critical suggestions and comments on this paper.

category having been given specific linguistic, ideological and cultural sign-system within the nationalist discourse to sublimate the communalization of religious and social differences between Hindu–Muslim and Hindi–Urdu communities. I propose that the category of Hindustani remained ambiguous and fuzzy in content and form while, at the same time, it was used as a category of political mobilization and collectivization of the two communities between 1920–40. The nature and form of linguistic nationalism surrounding the Hindi-Urdu language movement within which the controversy over Hindustani is situated shows us the simultaneity of communalization and nationalization of social identities with their consequences for the processes of community formation in twentieth century colonial India.[1]

The question of language in colonial India was an intensely communal-political one. The Hindi-Urdu linguistic conflict had an explicit religious and cultural agenda to pursue. The Indian nationalists were clearly divided over their choice of a national language and its script—whether to adopt Hindi in the Nagari script or Hindustani in Nagari and/or Persian scripts. In this context, the fight over Hindi, Urdu and Hindustani was clearly a fight over two religions—Hinduism and Islam—and their associated identities with Hindu and Muslim cultures, histories, traditions and beliefs. The discursive-political articulation of Hindustani coincided with deliberations over Hindu and Islamic religious scriptures and their contribution in the making of classical languages of Arabic, Persian, Sanskrit, etc. For Indian nationalists, the language question in colonial India was implicated within cultural and social pluralism of the society, and was often conflated with the religious identities of the communities. It is within this context that the nationalists addressed the language question of Hindustani as a culturally symbolic and ideologically semantic question. They argued and debated over its philological meanings, cultural repertoires, political pragmatism and ideological implications for the broader processes of nation-state and community identity formation in post-colonial India. Hindi-Hindustani as a linguistic identity of the Indian nation and its people—that seemed to be a secularizing

---

[1]I have elaborated on the nationalist discourse and the language question in my dissertation titled 'Politics of Linguistic Identity and Community Formation: North India, 1900–1947', Department of Political Science, University of Chicago, March 2002.

process initially—proved to be gradually an intense communal and sectarian event dividing people along religious and cultural lines. Whether to write it in Nagari and/or Persian script again remained a question of religious and cultural divisions between Hindu and Muslim communities.

Nationalist Discourse on Hindustani

The nationalist discourse on Hindustani posits an implicit symbiotic relationship between language and nation as not naturally given but socially constructed. The category of Hindustani is imagined within the nationalist discourse in three crucial ways—Hindustani as a *discourse*, a *practice* and an *identity*. It was through these three distinctive modes that nationalists planned to institutionalize Hindustani in the spheres of state and civil society. The Indian nationalists intensely argued over the diversity of existing linguistic social order and proposed a number of political programs and strategies to decide the choice of a 'common and/or national language' for the country. What puzzled them most was the question of a 'national language', and whether or not Hindi-Hindustani could qualify for this status. The question of national language divided the Indian nationalists into two major camps: some favouring Hindi and others Hindi-Hindustani. However, specific historical conditions attended their preferences, ideological positions and selective political programmes regarding the choice of a national language for the Indian nation. For some, Hindi exclusively should become the national language of India whereas for others Hindustani could prove to be a more ideal and inclusive linguistic political category to secularize the language question. However, the political programme of the 'making of a national and/or common language' in the nationalist discourse could not be pursued without negotiating with the social and political power of numerous other Indian languages and their communities. Indian nationalists emphasized that the political scaling of language/s—to determine their fate for the national and common language/s—should be equivalent with their social, cultural and political capital. In what follows, I elucidate diverse positions of nationalists over the language question, their dilemmas, anxieties and political strategies with respect to an ideology of linguistic identity for the Indian nation. I begin with Gandhi, the most vocal spokesman on the language question during this period.

For Gandhi, Hindi and Urdu languages represented, as Bakhtin would say, 'a polyglot social reality (Bakhtin 1981).'[2] In his view, all languages are equally important. But he also said, 'some one (language) must become the national language if Indians are to become a nation (GOI 1958–91).' For Gandhi, and for other nationalists as well, the real challenge was to decide which one language could become a 'national language'. Such a choice involved the question of script too—whether it should be Nagari, Persian or any other script. Gandhi wanted to bridge the Hindu-Muslim communal divide politically through Hindustani—a hybrid language combining Hindi and Urdu languages, and written in Nagari and/or Persian script.[3] Gandhi's Hindi was not a Sanskritized Hindi but a simpler and a more vernacularized one. He intended to create a discursive public language through Hindustani, which his contemporary Hindi/Hindu nationalists such as Rajgopalachari, Sampurnanand and P.D. Tandon dismissed as being more Persianized and Urduized.

The years 1935–45 mark the most pragmatic and decisive years for ideological and political changes in Gandhi's position from Hindi to Hindustani. The Hindi nationalists within Congress had started supporting Hindi much more vigorously contesting Gandhi's syncretic and integrative position on Hindi and Urdu languages. Therefore, when Bhartiya Sahitya Parishad (an organization for the promotion of Indian Literature) changed the language of its proceedings from Hindustani to Hindi-Hindustani in its session of 24 April 1936, Muslim nationalists worried about the future of Urdu. Abdul Haq, a member of the Congress party, Gandhi's close associate and the head of Anjuman Taraqqui-e-Urdu (organization for the promotion of Urdu) opposed this change vehemently. Some prominent Muslim leaders wrote letters to Gandhi protesting against this change. Gandhi's unpredictable response to Haq that Muslims could preserve the Urdu script—Quranic in nature—outraged Muslim nationalists. Haq wrote back to Gandhi:

[2]For Bakhtin, languages symbolize mentalities and world-views where a language is 'not a system of abstract grammatical categories but rather conceived as ideologically saturated, language as a world view, even as a concrete opinion insuring a maximum of mutual understanding in all spheres of social life.'

[3]Gandhi sets the following criteria for the national language of India: it should be easy to learn for the government officials, it should be capable of serving as a medium of religious, economic and political affairs and it should be the speech of the majority of people. See *Our Language Problem* by M.K. Gandhi, 1965.

Mahatmaji, you say you have no antipathy towards Urdu; still you openly called it the language of Musalmans, which is written in the Quranic script. You even said the Musalmans may take care of it, if they so please.[4]

This incident led to a deep rift between Gandhi and Abdul Haq even though the latter had supported Gandhi's earlier position during the yeas of 1918–35 when Gandhi had supported Hindi in the Nagari script. But Haq and other Muslim nationalists during the period of 1935–45 began to move away from Gandhi and the Congress party on the language question. During this period, Congress had won the 1937 elections and gained majority of assembly seats in the United Provinces of North India. Muslim League, which had lost considerably in this election, felt more threatened with Congress's dominance after the elections, and started mobilizing Muslims on the basis of religion and language more intensely.[5] M.A. Jinnah, President of the All India Muslim League, said in his presidential speech at the twenty-sixth session of the Muslim League at Patna in December 1938,

Take next the case of Hindi-Hindustani. Is there any doubt now in the mind of anyone that the whole scheme of Hindi-Hindustani is intended to stifle and suppress Urdu (Pirzada 1970).

Muslims and Hindus grew apart and so also the Urdu and Hindi nationalists. The Muslim League not only rejected the proposed category of Hindi-Hindustani but also suspected the discursive and political meaning of the word Hindustani. The shadow of Pakistan had started lurking in the minds of Muslim nationalists by this time, and language became an identity for them as strong as religion. Tariq Rahman quotes Maulana Ashraf Ali Thanavi, a Muslim nationalists during this time,

In the present circumstances, therefore, protection of Urdu language is protection of our religion. Thus this protection is a religious obligation of every Muslim according to his capacity (Rahman 1996).

Now Urdu and Hindi languages were used more forcefully as identity markers for Hindus and Muslims. Muslim League's meetings started debating about Urdu and its future. Individual Muslim leaders like Jinnah and Liaquat Ali Khan started mobilizing Muslims around the language question more strongly than ever before, and Liaquat Ali Khan even said, 'we will speak and write Urdu, educate our children in Urdu and never call our language by any other name except Urdu.' (Ibid.) On the other hand, Gandhi began to move more towards Hindustani, and was joined in his efforts by nationalists such as Nehru and Rajendra Prasad whereas Rajgopalachari and P.D. Tandon favoured a more Sanskritized Hindi, which, in their views, could mobilize the support of Hindus of north India. For Gandhi and his supporters, Hindi-Hindustani became a discursive political category for collectivizing Hindus and Muslims as political communities of an imagined Indian nation-state within the broader ideology of linguistic nationalism as a form of political nationalism.

For over a decade (1935–47), Gandhi strongly argued in favour of Hindustani. During this period, he formulated his vision of an Indian nation incorporating diverse linguistic-cultural traditions, histories and communities. He emphasized that Hindi and Urdu languages were distinguished by differences of script only. The differences of script, Gandhi argued, should not be identified with differences of culture, religion or history of different linguistic communities. He also proposed that Hindustani could be written in either and/or Nagari and Persian script with vocabulary drawn from both Hindi and Urdu languages.

The category of Hindustani had a strong nationalistic political programme for Gandhi since, he emphasized, it is capable of consolidating Hindi and Urdu linguistic communities as cultural and political collectivities. This cultural political formation of linguistic communities in Gandhi's vision will mobilize and unite diverse and different linguistic and social communities of colonial India in their fight against colonialism and communalism.

The Congress party in a resolution at its Kanpur session in 1925 approved Gandhi's initial proposal for the promotion of Hindustani by accepting it as its official language. Till the Kanpur session in 1925, Congress used English as an official language for its proceedings and meetings. It was in 1925, for the first time, that Congress amended Article 33 of its own constitution and specified that the proceedings of Congress should be conducted in Hindustani as much as possible. However, in the meetings of the Congress, a speaker, who was unable to speak Hindustani, was allowed to speak in English or any other provincial language that she or he felt comfortable with. Congress also stated that the proceedings of the Provincial Congress Committees would be conducted in the language of the provinces concerned, and if necessary, Hindustani might be used in both Nagari and Persian scripts.

For the next decade, Hindustani in Nagari or Persian script was gradually accepted as the language of Congress which even proposed that all government and official forms should be printed in both Nagari and Persian scripts.[6] During this period, Congress and most of its members accepted Gandhi's leadership on the language question without much resentment. P.D. Tandon, a member of the Congress party and a strong Hindi nationalist, who otherwise opposed Hindustani, also accepted Gandhi's plan of promoting Hindustani through Congress. Two years later in 1927, Raj Rajeshwari Bali, a Congress nationalist and a close associate of Gandhi, founded Hindustani Academy in Lucknow for the promotion of Hindustani.

During the decade of 1930s, Gandhi and others promoted Hindustani to avoid the possibility of linguistic political division of north India based on Hindi and Urdu languages exclusively. A number of linguistic political struggles had already emerged in other parts of the country opposing the possible hegemony of the Hindi language. For Muslim nationalism, religious identity entailed the preservation of Urdu language whereas for Hindu nationalism, protection of Hindi linguistic identity entailed the religious identity as well. Gandhi's preference for Hindustani in the years of 1935–45 appears strongly in many of his speeches and writings. In his speech at the Nagpur session of Bhartiya Sahitya Parishad in 1936, Gandhi used expressions of *Hindi Yane Hindustani* (Hindi meaning Hindustani) or *Hindi athwa Hindustani* (Hindi or Hindustani) or *Hindi ya Hindustani* (Hindi and/ or Hindustani)—all of which communicated a symbolic identification between Hindi and Hindustani. Consequently, both Hindi and Urdu nationalists saw the possibility of linguistic exclusivism in Gandhi's use of 'Hindi and/or Hindustani' *Hindi ya Hindustani*. For Hindi nationalists, the usage conveyed the message that Hindustani could/ might be an alternative to Hindi in the days to come, and for Urdu nationalists, it was Hindi disguised in the form of Hindustani. Alok Rai suggests that this proposal of Gandhi was misunderstood both by

---

[6]This proposal was made at the Congress Presidents' Urdu conference held on 5 April 1938. *Naya Hindi* (September 1947) p. 298.

Hindi and Urdu supporters. The 'or' in Hindi-Hindustani 'connoted either alterity or identity. It could mean either the Hindi was *same* as Hindustani, in which case the Mullah was up in arms or that Hindustani was alternative to Hindi, in which case the Pandit, quite as suspicious and pugnacious concluded that Hindustani was mere camouflage for Urdu' (Rai 2000). Urdu supporters also feared that Hindustani was a cultural-political ploy used against Urdu. However, for the next ten years, Gandhi's use of Hindustani as a possible common/national language of India continued to be contested and interrogated intensely within the nationalist discourse. Gandhi summarized his own changing position from Hindi to Hindustani at the Indore session of Hindi Sahitya Sammelan in the following manner:

Firstly I joined the Sahitya Sammelan, which propagated Hindi as spoken by Hindus and Muslims. I appreciate Bhadant Konsalyanan's point of view wherein he suggested the learning at present of only one script (Devnagari). At one time, I was opposed to using Urdu words. I did not listen to Dr Abdul Haq or their friends suggesting for the acceptance of Urdu or Hindustani as the national language. But when I was convinced of Hindustani (spoken and understood by the villages) as capable of being the national language, I left the Sahitya Sammelan. Then there was time when I favoured Sanskritized Hindi but now I think we should popularize Hindustani and learn Nagari and Urdu scripts. I desire a Hindu–Muslim unity and it is possible by this step.[7]

Gandhi continued to create an ideological consensus among his fellow nationalists to recognize and legitimize Hindustani within and outside the Congress. He established Hindustani Sangh like his other organizations such as Charkha Sangh and Seva Sangh working towards the goal of Swadeshi. Personally too, Gandhi adopted a multilingual life style. He patronized three newspapers in three different languages- *Young India* (English), *Navjivan* (Gujarati) and *Hindi Navjivan* (Hindi). Apart from Gujarati, Hindi, English and Marathi, he learnt Urdu and wrote in it sometimes. Gandhi urged repeatedly that Hindustani language should first be used in Congress's proceedings, correspondences and political affairs before it be made a language of people. He emphasized that not only Congress should use and introduce Hindustani words and vocabulary in its activities but should also provide a platform to resolve the Hindi and Urdu language

[7]*Amrit Bazar Patrika* (February 29, 1945).

conflict. In other words, he wanted to create a civic public sphere for Hindustani without which, as he said, ' Hindi would remain confined to Hindus and Urdu to Muslims.'[8]

It is important to note here that the contest over Hindustani during this period is situated within a specific historical context characterized by intense political struggles over the identity politics and its communal representation through linguistic, religious and caste identities in different parts of the country. Gandhi had to face a community of nationalists who were either indifferent or opposed to the category of 'Hindi-Hindustani'. A few nationalists supported Hindustani more out of personal loyalty to Gandhi and Congress than due to any ideological reasons. Abdul Haq urged people to notice how the Congress leaders used the two words—Hindi and Hindustani—interchangeably. In his view, such a usage indicated the historical inevitability of Hindi becoming a 'language of the nation'. He further emphasized that the term 'Hindi-Hindustani' symbolized a temporal linguistic political slippage by first adding Hindustani (in this case de-Persianized Urdu) with Hindi under the new rubric of Hindi-Hindustani, which would be replaced by Hindi alone in the near future. Haq thought that the usage of 'Hindi-Hindustani' was a political conspiracy to marginalize the significance of Urdu as a language having equal status to Hindi. Haq writes that when he asked Gandhi, 'why don't you follow the decision of the Congress that the language of the nation will be Hindustani', Gandhi did not reply, and when asked again a second time what he meant by Hindi-Hindustani, Gandhi said, 'that which is going to be Hindustani in future.' Haq recounted that even Nehru, Congress president, who was present during this meeting with Gandhi, did not utter a word and sat silent. Haq emphasized that the only acceptable form of Hindustani for him was the one drawn equally on both Persian and Sanskrit languages, their vocabularies and grammars since, he further suggested, this would keep the legacy of two languages and communities alive 'with the fusion of civilization, socialization, mental work, psychological unity, and a property of ancestors' hard labor.'[9]

On the other hand, Congress leaders like P.D. Tandon, Sampurnanand and Rajendra Prasad personally differed from Gandhi regarding his use of Hindustani but supported him as members of

---

[8]*Collected Works of Mahatma Gandhi*, Vol 68. p. 24.
[9]Abdul Haq's lecture at the Urdu conference in Patna. See *Urdu* (October 1936).

the Congress. Though they ideologically interrogated Gandhi's vision of a Hindustani India, they did not oppose much the institutionalization of Hindustani from within the Congress that Gandhi emphasized. In his correspondence with Kaka Kalelkar, Rajendra Prasad once said, 'Congress should not take up the task of Hindustani in its own hands but should encourage and support Hindustani Prachar Sabha and its branches to promote Hindustani'.[10] In another letter to Ambika Prasad Vajpayee and Seth Govind Das, both of whom favoured Hindi over Hindustani, Rajendra Prasad considered the controversy over Hindi-Hindustani useless while supporting the plans of creating Hindustani by an amalgamation of Arabic, Persian and Sanskrit words in its vocabulary. Similarly, Sampurnanand, a Congress member and a staunch supporter of Hindi, considered Hindustani a disguised form of Urdu and criticized Gandhi for promoting it. He suggested that Hindustani could be accepted only if it incorporates more Sanskrit words in its vocabulary. Other nationalists, who followed the ideological position of Tandon and Sampurnanand on the language question, were Tej Bahadur Sapru and Amarnath Jha who expressed their outrage against the incorporation of Urdu in Hindustani, which, if accepted in their views, should include more words of Sanskrit than Persian/Arabic.

A person who stood behind Gandhi's call for Hindustani was Jawaharlal Nehru who, unlike his fellow Hindi nationalists, contested claims of inherent superiority of Hindi language over Urdu. Like Gandhi, Nehru too supported Hindustani written in both Nagari and Persian scripts as a matter of political necessity for the development of two language communities (*quams*) of Hindus and Muslims. For Nehru, Hindustani was an inclusive linguistic political category, which could unite people socially and politically. It is its content and not form, Nehru emphasized, that one could call it Hindi, Urdu or Hindustani. Nehru said,

The only all India language that is possible is Hindi or Hindustani or whatever it is called. It must be remembered that no language is nearer to Sanskrit than Persian. As I have said that it is the content of a language that counts and not the name so much. The word Hindustani comes nearest to the content of my choice. As for the script, it is clear that the Nagari script will be a dominant script. But again, because I think it wrong to be exclusive

[10]Letter of Rajendra Prasad to Kaka Kalelkar, dated April 6, 1946. *R.P. Papers* (New Delhi: National Archives of India).

both from the cultural and political point of view, I think that the Urdu script should be recognized and thought where desired.[11]

During the decade of 1930 and 1940, Nehru thought and wrote a lot about the language question. He wrote an article titled 'The Question of Language' that first appeared in Bombay Chronicle in 1937. Subsequently, the All India Congress Committee republished it as a pamphlet with a foreword written by Gandhi. Nehru wrote a couple of essays, which were translated in Urdu with the titles of 'Quami Zaban aur Rasmulkhat Pandit Jawaharlal Nehru ke Khayalat' (published in *Humanyu* of September 1936) and 'Pandit Jawaharlal Nehru ka Khat Dr Sayyed Mahmud ke Naam' (*Jamia* of October 1936). Even though Nehru's knowledge of Indian languages was extremely limited and narrow, he started learning Hindi and Urdu languages during his imprisonment in the Ahmednagar fort with Maulana Azad. Robert King writes that Nehru's diaries and letters written to his daughter Indira Gandhi from the Ahmednagar Fort prison during 1943–4 show quotations from Urdu poetry written in both Nagari and Persian scripts. Nehru was concerned about Indira's learning of Indian languages. Therefore, while writing to her from the Bareilly jail in 1932, he advised Indira, who was at Shantiniketan at this time, to choose Hindi and French as two languages for study. Subsequently, again from Almora jail in 1935, he asked her to learn Bengali and Hindi along with French, English and German languages. In Almora jail, Nehru started reading and writing in Hindi, and even wrote a small article titled, 'Literature in Hindi and Other Languages'. For Nehru, Hindustani symbolized 'cultural and political point of view' and it had the capability of combining both Sanskrit and Persian languages. What was needed, in his view, was the right form of linguistic, cultural and political integration—a process to which Gandhi referred as the fusion (and not the negation) of two languages—Hindi and Urdu—to form the Hindustani language.

Alongside Hindustani, the important question was whether Hindi could ever become the 'national language' of India. Indian nationalists

[11]*National Herald*, 13 February 1949. Nehru once wrote that the invitation cards of his sister Krishna's wedding were printed in the Hindustani and Latin letters and not in Nagari or Persian script, which was the convention at that time. He emphasized that Hindustani could be written in the Latin script—a proposal not liked by Gandhi at that time.

differed substantially on this subject indicating a significant ideological move for the linguistic uniformity through the process from
language (*bhasha*) to national language (*rashtra bhasha*)—a process
symbolizing linguistic structures of beliefs, actions, events legitimized
and institutionalized within the ideology of a nation-state formation.
Gandhi changed his ideological position on the language question
several times. He often used Hindi and Hindustani interchangeably denoting primarily the differences of script between these two
languages, and the latter, in his characterization, was identified
with simpler and less Sanskritized Nagari. For a nationalist like
Rajgopalachari, Hindi in the Nagari script could be the national language because of its numerical strength. Rajendra Prasad opined that
Hindi language was easier and could be learnt in three months whereas
learning of Urdu required two years. Hindi/Hindu nationalists often
used these sorts of rhetorical explanations to emphasize the urgency
of recognizing Hindi as the national language. For some of them,
Hindustani could become a workable solution for a short while to
avoid the communalization of linguistic conflict whereas for others,
such as Gandhi, Abdul Haq, Tara Chand, Zakir Husain and Nehru,
Hindustani symbolized a world of common histories, cultural traditions and political kinships. It was Gandhi who emphasized that
learning Hindustani was a 'first step of a true nationalist and a good
citizen'.

Institutionalization of Hindustani

How was Hindustani actualized and practiced? What methods and
strategies were adopted to institutionalize it? The relationship between
language and nation, between language and community and language
and identity was reinforced and began to be institutionalized in a
number of ways by setting up several language organizations, associations and promotional centres to promote Hindi and Urdu as
separate languages and as medium of education and literature. Tara
Chand supported Hindustani and proposed that Hindi and Urdu
language communities should read each other's languages and litera-
tures. Towards this goal, he suggested the compilation of English-
Hindustani dictionary having common words of use for the Hindi
and Urdu writers. A common vocabulary, he suggested, should be
formed drawing partially on Sanskrit, Persian and Arabic languages,
and be compiled in Devnagari or Persian script. Zakir Husain de-

fined Hindustani as a common language for common use in north India with words drawn from the villages, local folktales and proverbs. We see that for Gandhi and Nehru, Hindustani as a language could be written in both scripts with the potential of bridging differences between Hindi and Urdu language communities and the communalization of linguistic identity between Hindus and Muslims. Abdul Haq and Rajgopalachari considered Hindustani as a symbolic reminder of common cultural histories, philological and textual traditions and social relations between Hindus and Muslims. For Tandon and Sampurnanand, Hindustani would never be able to reconcile the differences of script, vocabulary and grammatical structures between Hindi and Urdu languages and their linguistic communities.

Hindustani was institutionalized with the founding of the Hindustani Committee in 1938. The Committee was engaged in determining the nature and form of the Hindustani language and its promotion. It consisted of nationalists like Rajendra Prasad, Sachidanand Sinha, Zakir Husain, Tara Chand, Dr Abdul Haq, Mr Suleiman Naqvi, Narendra Jha, Badri Narayan Verma and B.R. Saran. The Committee considered making of Hindustani a common language of instruction throughout India. In its first meeting held in Patna on 22 March 1938, it resolved to work in the following areas: make Hindustani a language of everyday conversation, compile a dictionary of everyday words in Hindustani and write textbook readers in Hindustani. The task of compiling a Hindustani dictionary was given to Abdul Haq, Tara Chand, Pandit Ram Naresh Tripathi and B.R. Saxsena. Another institution engaged in the mission of spreading Hindustani was Hindustani Prachar Sabha, which was founded by those who had resigned from Rashtra Bhasha Prachar Samiti. It included Mahatma Gandhi, Rajendra Prasad, Kaka Kalelkar, Dada Dharmadhikari, Periben Captain, Gopinath Bardole, Jawaharlal Nehru, Pattabhi Sitaramayya, K.K. Munshi and Tara Chand. It was founded in 1942 in Wardha with the following aims: promoting books written in both Nagari and Persian scripts, to prepare dictionary and grammar books of Hindustani, to prepare school textbooks, to conduct examinations for propagating Hindustani in different parts of the country, to introduce Hindustani as a necessary subject in government educational institutions, municipal boards, national educational institutions and to give donations to libraries and organizations helping to promote Hindustani. The first session of the Sabha chose Rajendra Prasad as chairman, Mahatma Gandhi as

vice-chairman and Srimannarayan as secretary. Gandhi, who presided over the All India Hindustani Prachar Sabha conference in
Wardha, said,

I would like those who oppose but do not wish to waste time in discussing
whether Hindustani language as understood by the villagers, in Devnagari
and Urdu scripts should be learnt or not. Those who approve of this work
may come and join me. The language will be one but scripts two. It is not
difficult to learn 10–12 prominent languages if we give up sluggishness and
idleness. Northerns can learn the Southerner's language and vice versa. He
is unfit to live in India if one says, I can't learn Hindustani. It is easy to learn
Devnagari and Urdu scripts and I can arrange for teaching such other
languages at Sewagram.[12]

Abdul Haq too favoured Gandhi's proposal when he said at this
conference,

Even ladies and servants once spoke in the villages' and bazaars' Urdu. If
Hindustani is accepted, I will see that Muslims approve of it and if they oppose
it, I will turn them out of India.[13]

The nationalists' efforts to enthrone Hindustani as the language
of the nation were carried out by setting up exclusive schools for
imparting education such as Gandhiji's attempts to start Hindustani
Prachar Sangh at Wardha and Tara Chand's Hindustani Academy at
Allahabad. Similarly, specific grammar books, dictionaries, school
textbooks, general awareness books, instructional manuals on
different subjects and historical treatises were written in Hindustani
which was brought into the public sphere along with the existing
hegemonic sacred position of Arabic, Persian, Sanskrit, Pali and
Gurumukhi. Hindustani did not necessarily lead to the desacralization
of either Sanskrit or Arabic in the same way as the processes of
desacralization of Latin took place in Europe, which indicated a move
towards the vernacularization of classical languages, and their gradual
displacement from selected spheres of the society. Schools, burial
grounds, marriage places, streets and entertainment sites, etc. became
important arenas of Hindustani language production and consolidation.
    Unlike Gandhi who genuinely wanted Hindustani to be a language
of the Indian State, other nationalists often invoked the metaphor of

[12]*Amrit Bazar Patrika* (27 February 1945). Several prominent nationalists such
as Tara Chand, Suleiman Naqvi, Pandit Banarsidas Chaturvedi and Pandit Sunderlal
attended the conference.
    [13]Ibid.

Hindustani strategically to deflate the communalization of language question associated with Hindi/Hindu and Urdu/Muslim nationalisms. The term 'Hindustani' connoted multiple meanings ideologically, culturally and socially. It inhabited a political space within the existing communal zones of Hindi/Hindu and Urdu/Muslim identities, and became an integral part of the state rationalization, bureaucratization and modernization.

Hindustani: A Language of Linguistic-Cultural Syncretism

Hindustani as a category of linguistic-cultural syncretism indicated not only the confluence of Hindi and Urdu languages and Nagari and Persian scripts but also Hindu and Muslim cultures, histories, religions and traditions. Furthermore, as a discursive and linguistic-political category, it was mapped and carved along the legal, administrative, cultural, educational, ideological and religious sites as sites of linguistic mediation and construction within and among the Hindi and Urdu linguistic social communities.

Hindustani was a polysemic term having multiple meanings of a vernacular, a local language or a patois. It was addressed by different names such as Moors, Indostan, Hindostanic, Hindwee, Nagree or even a jargon. It gradually became what Bernard Cohn has defined 'a language of command.' Hindustani became a new linguistic-cultural ideology for the new Indian nation-state. The category of Hindustani embedded within the context of an anti-colonial struggle against the hegemonic imperial order of the British rule and its power of language— English—on the one hand, and Sanskritized Hindi and Persianized Urdu as the indigenous hegemons on the other—indicated the capacity to resist all three of them.

The question of linguistic nationalism in India, and South Asia in general, has to deal with the non-elitism and non-exclusivism of language/s as the language/s of power. The nationalist leaders in colonial India subscribed to this view and advocated the use of 'languages of masses'. The linguistic-cultural syncretic position contests the given polarities and defies norms of standardization and uniformity or even stereotyped categorization. As a theoretical construct, it can also symbolize a position of hybridity, ambiguity, marginality and heterogeneity. Syncretism also indicates a degree of collectivization as historically embedded—however fuzzy or enumerative in character it may be. The linguistic-cultural syncretism, as envisioned through the category of Hindustani, also meant the dynamics of social and cultural relationships between Hindi/Urdu and Hindu/Muslim communities and their specific historical location bordering on the margins or boundaries of the state and nation. Whether the goal of Hindustani has moved in the direction of a more Hinduized and Sanskritized Hindi or Persianized Urdu is to yet to be studied and analysed. The linguistic liminalism of Hindustani helps us in understanding the nature and form of linguistic nationalism in colonial north India—a subject inadequately studied and under-theorized in the historiography of colonial and post-colonial India. I suggest that the conflict over Hindustani indicates a complex political, cultural and ideological process through which language is socially mediated, politically mobilized and ideologically structured on the one hand, and represented as identity, community, state and nation on the other. It is within this duality of language as structure and practice, as ideological sign-system (Voloshinov) and dialectical productive activity (Marx) that we need to situate the problematic of linguistic and cultural liminalism of Hindustani in early twentieth century colonial north India. The historical representation and production of Hindustani as a category of social collectivity within the nationalist discourse needs to be situated and understood along with the colonial discourse and its ideology of language as culture and linguistic differences as cultural differences identified with mentalities, ethnicities and identities of the colonized. For the nationalists, on the other hand, Indian languages embodied, to use Balibar's phrase, 'nation-form' and 'nation-ness', and the communicability of language with the nation established, as Walter Benjamin would say, 'a social existence without which the relationship to language is an idea only and not a communication because there is no relationship between mental being and communication' (Benjamin 1986). Hindustani as a category of linguistic-cultural syncretism helps us in moving beyond the binaries defined primarily through religion and culture, and allows us in understanding the dynamics of the historical relationship between Hindi/Hindu and Urdu/Muslim communities as not dichotomous and segmented but mutually commensurate and convergent on questions of linguistic-cultural identity and community formation.

References

Bakhtin, M.M. 1981. *The Dialogical Imagination: Four Essays*, University of Texas Press, Austin.

Benjamin, Walter. 1986. On Language as Such and On the Language of Man, in Peter Demetz (Ed.), *Walter Benjamin: Reflections: Essays, Aphorisms, Autobiographical Writings*, Shocken Books, New York.

Gandhi, M.K. 1965. *Our Language Problem*, Bhartiya Vidhya Bhawan, Bombay.

GOI. 1958–91. *Collected Works of Mahatma Gandhi*, Vol. 65. Publication Division, Ministry of Information and Broadcasting, Government of India, Delhi, pp. 2–27.

Pirzada, S. (Ed.) 1970. *Foundations of Pakistan All India Muslim League Documents, 1925–47, Vol. 2*, National Publishing House, Karachi.

Rahman, Tariq. 1996. *Language and Politics in Pakistan*, Oxford University Press, Karachi.

Rai, Alok. 2000. *Hindi Nationalism*, Orient Longman, New Delhi, p.16.

9

Shared Hindu-Muslim Shrines in Karnataka: Challenges to Liminality

YOGINDER SIKAND

Introduction

A remarkable feature of popular religion in South Asia is the widespread popularity of shared religious traditions which bring together Hindus and Muslims, and in some cases Sikhs as well as Christians in common worship and ritual participation. These traditions are, by nature, ambiguous in terms of clearly defined communal categories, defying the logic of neatly separated and demarcated communities defined on the basis of a reified, scripturalist and essentialized understanding of religious identity (Gottschalk 2001). Faced with religious movements for 'reform', 'orthodoxy', such traditions have increasingly come under attack, as powerful organizations seek to redefine them. Increasingly, 'fuzzy' identities are being replaced by clearly demarcated boundaries, resulting in these traditions gradually being identified as unambiguously 'Hindu' or 'Muslim' or other as the case might be. While the origins of this process may be traced to colonial times, in particular to the introduction of the Census as a tool to map and categorize religious communities and to the politics of competing communalisms, it has, in the post-independence period received added impetus by the active intervention of communal organizations seeking to 'purify' these traditions and their followers of what is seen as their tainted association with the religious beliefs and practices of other communities. In the process, many of these traditions have today emerged as arenas of sharp inter-communal contestation.

This paper analyses this process of transformation of shared religious shrines in contemporary Karnataka, in South India. Of particular concern is the transformation of these traditions from being a means of bringing people from different communities together to arenas of inter-communal rivalry. We argue that this must be seen in the context of the introduction of a notion of community based on a reified, textual understanding of religion, each community being neatly marked off from other similarly constructed communities. A complex interplay of economic and political forces, we show, are forcing the traditions that have developed around these shrines to increasingly identify themselves as unambiguously 'Hindu' or 'Muslim', with all the implications that this has for a rich shared culture that transcends narrowly inscribed community boundaries.

The Spread of Islam in Karnataka and the Emergence of Shared Hindu-Muslim Traditions

One out of eleven people in the state of Karnataka in South India is Muslim, and various Muslim dynasties have ruled this region for centuries. Islam made its advent in the region as early as the tenth century, by when Arab traders had set up settlements all along the Malabar and Konkan coasts. The first Muslim military presence, in what is today Karnataka, dates to the late thirteenth century. In 1296, Alauddin Khilji raided the Yadava capital of Devgiri, later named Daulatabad (the city of riches), ransacked it of its immense treasures and then returned to Delhi in triumph. From the fourteenth century onwards, large parts of north Karnataka came under various Muslim dynasties, often at loggerheads with their Hindu neighbours as well as with the Muslim Emperors of Delhi. These included the Bahmanis, the Adil Shahis of Bijapur, the Barid Shahis of Bidar and the Qutb Shahis of Golconda. They were later followed by the Mughals in the seventeenth century and then by the Nizams of Hyderabad in the eighteenth century, who, till 1948, remained masters of much of present-day north Karnataka. Under Haider Ali and his charismatic son, Tipu Sultan, another powerful centre of Muslim rule emerged at

Srirangapatanam, near Mysore, extending over large stretches of present-day central and southern Karnataka and even beyond, till it was put an end to by the combined forces of the British and the Nizam of Hyderabad in 1799.

It was principally through the agency of the Sufis that Islam spread in Karnataka, a process that has been well-documented in Eaton's classic study of the various Sufi orders in the region (Eaton 1996). Using local motifs and idioms, the Sufis were able to exercise a powerful appeal, making numerous converts to a form of Islam heavily coloured by local influences. In addition, they attracted a large number of Hindus as well, owing principally to their charisma and the widespread belief in their powers as intermediaries with God. Consequently, the traditions that developed around the figures of many of these Sufis came to be shared by Hindus and Muslims alike, although this did not rule out differences in the ways in which they were seen and regarded by Hindus and Muslims.

Living together for centuries, many Hindus and Muslims in northern Karnataka inevitably came to share, to a considerable extent, a common cultural world. At the level of the political elite, a shared Indo-Persian culture emerged, to which both Hindus and Muslims made rich contributions. It was in the Deccan that the Urdu language, which was to become the lingua franca of most educated north Indians in the nineteenth and early twentieth century, first emerged. At the local level, although they maintained a strong sense of a separate identity, Hindus and Muslims often worshipped together at the shrines of Sufi saints (*dargahs*). Many Muslims were but nominal and recent converts to Islam, and as such continued to practice several customs associated with their pre-Islamic past which they shared with their Hindu neighbours, particularly in matters of domestic rituals.

One of the most intriguing features of this popular religious tradition, but one that has gone almost completely unnoticed in the existing literature on the Deccan, is the large number of shared religious figures venerated by Hindus and Muslims alike, on whom both communities today make claims of their own. These figures and the shrines and cults associated with them represent a powerful popular tradition that harks back to an age when notions of monolithic 'Hindu' and 'Muslim' communities were still non-existent, and the boundaries setting apart one community from the other were still fuzzy and unclear. These figures seem to have played a central role in bringing people of various castes, Hindus as well as Muslims, together in common worship in a shared cultural universe, and also played an important role in the conversion of non-Muslim communities to Islam. Today, these figures still command widespread popularity.

All the figures whose shrines are examined in this paper are almost undoubtedly of Muslim origin, although this is a matter of considerable debate and dispute among their followers today. The widespread veneration of Muslim holy figures among Hindus is a phenomenon that is common to almost all parts of India. Sufi saints, seen as powerful beings capable of performing miracles, healing the ill, granting children to barren women, providing a job to the unemployed, averting the evil eye and so on, are widely propitiated as *devtas* or gods by Hindus, who see them as part of their vast pantheon of deities. The cults of the Muslim saints are particularly popular among 'low' caste Hindus in rural areas. Historically, and even today in several places, 'untouchables' and other 'low' caste people are denied access to Hindu temples, and the shrines of Muslim saints are often the only places of worship which they could freely enter. Stories of how these Muslim figures fraternized with the 'low' castes and won them over with their love and compassion abound. Till this day, 'low' caste Hindus vastly outnumber Muslims at many *dargahs*.

For many Hindus, these Muslim figures are incarnations (*avatar*) of one or the other Hindu god, and hence, they are often called by Hindu names and incorporated as Hindu religious figures into the local set of deities. Thus, for instance, Dada Hayat, a Qalandar Sufi whose shrine is located in the Baba Budhan hills in Chikmagalur, is popular among his Hindu devotees as Dattatreya Avatar, an incarnation of the Hindu deity Dattatreya, himself a combination of Vishnu and Shiva. Muslim followers of these figures see them differently, as 'friends' of God (*auliya*), powerful beings, capable of interceding with God to have one's desires met. It appears that the Muslim custodians of the shrines of these figures freely welcomed Hindus to worship therein, and some even popularized stories of their association with Hindu deities in order to win local support and even possibly as a means to preach Islam to them in an idiom and language with which they were familiar. Hence, as a result of Hindus and Muslims worshipping at common shrines and venerating common religious figures, local traditions evolved centred on what were undoubtedly Muslim figures, but who, with the passage of time, became transformed into figures with a dual identity, seen in different ways by their Hindu and Muslim followers.

While in the past such shared traditions served to bring Hindus and Muslims together in common worship, as well as facilitating the gradual Islamization of local non-Muslim communities, today many of them have emerged as centres of inter-communal contestation and conflict. Boundaries between 'Hindus' and 'Muslims', between 'Islam' and 'Hinduism', have been sharply drawn, and shared shrines and their followers are being increasingly defined as unambiguously 'Hindu' or 'Muslim', their ambiguous identity being, as we seek to show, suitably reinterpreted to serve contemporary purposes and agendas.[1]

The Baba Budhan *Dargah* Case

Conflicts over shared shrines in Karnataka today take various forms. In some cases it has led to lengthy court cases, which, in typical Indian fashion, have been fought over for years without the courts delivering any conclusive judgement. In other instances, it has involved outside intervention, in the form of political parties and private militias, resulting in Hindu-Muslim violence and bloodshed. A good example of this is the present controversy over the Baba Budhan *dargah* in Chikmagalur. The *dargah* is said to be the oldest Sufi shrine in Karnataka, the hagiographic works describing Baba Budhan, also known as Hazrat 'Abdul 'Aziz Makki, as one of the companions (*sahabi*) of the Prophet Mohammad.[2] Baba Budhan is said to have fought against the powerful landlords (*palegars*) of the area and to have crusaded against their oppression of the poor, putting an end to the practice of human sacrifice, whose victims were largely from among the 'low' castes. Owing to the stories of his miraculous powers as well as his having fought for the rights of the downtrodden, he gained a large following in the area. Many people converted to Islam

[1]This uneasiness with liminality has been traced to the ways in which British colonial administrators sought to map and categorize their Indian subjects, forcing them, primarily through the instrument of the census, to define themselves as Hindu or Muslim or other. This point is persuasively argued by Harjot Oberoi in his study of the emergence of a distinct Sikh identity in colonial Punjab. Refer to Oberoi, 1994 and Jones, 1987.

[2]Abdul Wasi Asri and S. Abdul Jabbar, *Tazkira-i-Hazrat Dada Hayat Mir Qalandar* (The Story of Hazrat Dada Hayat Mir Qalandar), published by Sayyed Pir Muhammad Shah Qadri, Chikmagalur, n.d. Also, Abdul Wasi Asri, *Qalandar Bar Haq: Tarikh-i-Dada Hayat Mir Qalandar* (The True Qalandar: The History of Dada Hayat Mir Qalandar), published by Sayyed Pir Muhammad Shah Qadri, Chikmagalur, 1996.

at his hands, it is said, while remaining Hindus, began venerating him as a powerful spiritual being, an incarnation of their own principal deity, Dattatreya.

Historical records tell us that the shrine of Baba Budhan was patronized by both Hindu as well as Muslim kings, both of whom endowed it with large land grants. In edicts issued by the Hindu rulers of Mysore the shrine was referred to as the *Sri Dattatreya Swami Baba Budhan Peetha* (The Monastery of the Revered Lord Dattatreya Baba Budhan), while the Muslim custodians of the shrine were granted the honorific title of *jagad guru* or 'Teachers of the World' (Gazetteer of Mysore). They were, in addition, the only Muslim religious heads to be exempted from personal appearance in the civil courts of the state.[3]

It appears that through the centuries Hindus and Muslims freely worshipped at the shrine of Baba Budhan, each approaching him according to their religious preference—as an incarnation of Dattatreya for the Hindus or as a 'friend' of Allah for the Muslims. There is, moreover, no record of any conflict over the shrine or about its Muslim custodians. In the mid-1960s, for the first time a dispute arose over the control of the shrine, setting in motion a process of conflicting claims and counter-claims which has now turned into a major political controversy, causing a sharp deterioration in relations between Hindus and Muslims in the area. The immediate cause for the emergence of the dispute was the claim put forward sometime in the mid-1960s by the Waqf Board, a statutory body set up to administer Muslim shrines and endowed properties in the state, that the Baba Budhan shrine, being a Muslim *dargah*, should be brought under its jurisdiction. This claim was disputed by the Muzrai Department, in-charge of Hindu endowments in the state, which argued that the shrine was not an exclusively Muslim place of worship since it was held in great regard by the local Hindus as well. In 1975, the Government of Karnataka directed that the shrine be vested with the Waqf Board, but five years later this order was struck down by the Chikmagalur District Court, which was later challenged by the Waqf Board. In 1989, the Court of the Commissioner for Religious and Charitable Endowments restored the shrine to the Muzrai Department and upheld the status of the Muslim custodian (*sajjade*) as its sole administrator.

Although the conflict was between two administrative bodies, one

---

[3]*Supplement to the Mysore Muzrai Manual,* 1940. Government of His Highness the Maharaja of Mysore, Bangalore, pp. 500–01.

Muslim and the other Hindu, it did not, at this time, take the form of a Hindu-Muslim communal controversy. Indeed, the Muslim *sajjade* of the shrine actually supported the stand of the Muzrai Department and challenged the claims of the Waqf Board, arguing that the shrine was not an exclusively Muslim one. What is clear from the claims of both the Waqf Board and the Muzrai Department was their inability to deal with the shrine's liminality, and the difficulty that they faced in categorizing the shrine as belonging to one religious community or the other. For both it had to be clearly defined as either 'Hindu' or 'Muslim', and, hence, the controversy soon took on the form of a 'Hindu' versus 'Muslim' dispute.

With the case lingering in the courts, politicians were quick to take up the issue, seeing in it a means to garner political support. From the mid-1980s onwards, militant Hindu groups, encouraged by the mass movement launched to destroy a mosque at the town of Ayodhya in north India and build a temple in its place, grew increasingly active throughout Karnataka. Chikmagalur soon emerged as a powerful base of extreme right-wing Hindu organizations. Some time in the late 1980s, the Vishwa Hindu Parishad (VHP), an all-India organization of Hindu religious leaders allied to the militant and fiercely anti-Muslim Rashtriya Swayamsevak Sangh, launched what they called a campaign to liberate the temple of Dattatreya from Muslim control. VHP activists now put forward the claim that the shrine was actually a temple of the Hindu deity Dattatreya and that the Muslims had falsely claimed it to be the *dargah* of Baba Budhan in order to lay control over its vast properties and income. Accordingly, the VHP set up what it called the *Datta Peetha Samrakshana Samiti* (The Committee for the Liberation of Datta Peetha). In 1989, amidst tight security and in the face of strong Muslim protest, for the first time a Brahminical *puja* was conducted outside the shrine of Baba Budhan by a group of Brahmins affiliated to the VHP. Following the destruction of the mosque at Ayodhya in 1992, the VHP, now further emboldened, began celebrating an annual three-day festival dedicated to Dattatreya at the *dargah*, in complete violation of the court's orders that the traditional rituals associated with the *dargah* be left unchanged.

In order to further galvanize public support for the liberation of the temple from Muslim control, the VHP and its allied private militia, the Bajrang Dal, organized a massive campaign all over Karnataka in late 1998. Some Hindu leaders involved in this campaign publicly announced that they would dispatch suicide squads if need be to rescue the temple. Others predicted that a blood bath was certain if the government failed to deliver the shrine to the Hindus. Passions ran high, and in some places violence between Hindus and Muslims was reported, in which Muslims suffered considerably greater loss of life and property. A massive crowd of Hindutva activists, mostly brought in from outside, gathered at the *dargah* in early December 1998. They tore down the green flags decorated with Islamic motifs at the entrance to the shrine and replaced them with saffron Hindu flags. A three-headed idol, purporting to be that of Dattatreya, was forcibly taken inside the shrine and worshipped. After the *puja*, a public rally was held outside, where militant Hindu leaders demanded that the shrine be handed over to the Hindus, that the Muslim custodian be replaced by a Hindu priest, that Hindu-style *puja* be conducted at the shrine and that the Sufi *urs* festival be stopped with immediate effect. They also insisted that the shrine must be converted into a purely Hindu place of worship.[4]

The intervention of the VHP and allied groups in the controversy only added to the pressure, set in motion by the earlier dispute between the Waqf Board and the Muzrai Commissioner, to clearly identify the shrine as either 'Muslim' or 'Hindu'. To the VHP, like the Muzrai Commissioner and the Waqf Board, a situation of liminality was one that directly challenged their own understanding of community, religion and identity. The construction of the notion of the 'Hindu community' in Hindutva discourses, and, indeed, in dominant varieties of Indian nationalist discourses as well, is premised on a distinction from the Muslim 'other', who is generally characterized in terms befitting an inveterate foe. Quite naturally, then, a situation of religious syncretism and liminality, where boundaries between 'Hindus' and 'Muslims' are blurred, if not completely invisible, forcefully questions the very basis of Hindutva as an ideology. It is thus not surprising that the VHP has been actively seeking to take control of several *dargahs* in various other parts of India, in addition to the Baba Budhan shrine, where Hindus worship along with Muslims, and turning them into temples,[5] seeking to actively discourage Muslim-derived practices among Hindus.

[4]For details see Yoginder Sikand, *The Baba Budhan Giri Dargah Controversy*, Himayat, Bangalore, 2000.

[5]Such as, for instance, the Imam Shahi shrine at Pirana (Gujarat), the Haji Malang *dargah* at Kalyan (Maharashtra) and the Lal Das *dargah* at Dhuli Dub (Rajasthan).

What is particularly significant about the VHP's intervention in the controversy over the Baba Budhan *dargah* is the Brahminization of the Dattatreya tradition that it aggressively promotes, in line with the sternly Brahminical Hinduism that it represents. The Dattatreya image associated with popular Hindu religiosity in the Deccan is one that is clearly non-Brahminical, if not distinctly anti-Brahminical, in its origins. Phadke, in his *Sri Dattachintan*, writes that the *avadhutas*, considered to be incarnations of Dattatreya, were believed to be 'beyond caste, cult and social conventions' (Warren 1999). In the *Markandeya Purana*, Dattatreya appears in the form of an antinomian *yogi*, defying the rituals and rules of purity and pollution so central to Brahminical Hinduism. He is depicted as consorting with women and drinking wine.[6] A subsidiary shrine associated with the Baba Budhan *dargah*, the shrine of Biru at Palang Talab, is looked after by a Dalit priest, thus clearly suggesting the non-Brahminic association of the Dattatreya cult in the region. Many 'low' caste followers of Baba Budhan/Dattatreya see him as having bravely fought against the oppression of their ancestors at the hands of the 'upper' caste *palegars* and Brahmins. In contrast, however, the image of Dattatreya in VHP discourse seeks to place him firmly within the boundaries of Brahminical Hinduism. Thus, for instance, the *pujas* held by the VHP at the Baba Budhan shrine, in violation of the court's orders, were conducted by Brahmin priests and in Brahminical fashion, which would be equally alien for Muslims as it would for the 'low' castes who have their own ways of worship. In other words, the VHP's efforts to 'liberate' the *dargah* of Baba Budhan seem directed equally at the Muslims as at the 'low' castes, challenging both Muslim as well as Dalit representations of Baba Budhan/Dattatreya.

In the Baba Budhan *dargah* case, then, a host of factors have combined to undermine and challenge the centuries-old popular tradition associated with it. Clearly, modern government bureaucracies, in this case the Waqf Board and the Muzrai Department, used to dealing with 'Hindus' and 'Muslims' as two neatly demarcated communities, and with 'Islam' and 'Hinduism' as two rigidly separated religions, fail to understand and appreciate traditions and shrines associated with religious liminality or syncretism. Militant communal organiza-

---

[6]This image of Dattatreya fits in neatly with some of the practices associated with the Baba Budhan shrine. Like the antinomian *yogis* and *sadhus*, many of the Muslim Qalandars associated with the shrine regularly consume intoxicating drugs. Refer to Dange, 1987.

tions, in this case the VHP, too, cannot recognize fluid religious identities that defy any neat categorization, for they forcefully challenge their understanding of 'Hindus' and 'Muslims' as two monolithic blocs permanently at war with each other. The Indian state, now increasingly Hindu in character, has, in some cases, assisted groups like the VHP to take over syncretic shrines and convert them into Hindu temples. In addition, the state as well as groups like the VHP have actively sought to promote a Brahminization of 'low' caste shrines and traditions, absorbing them into the broader Brahminical fold. Consequently, 'low' caste traditions associated with Muslim figures are reinterpreted in purely Brahminical terms that serves to rigidly set 'low' castes and other 'Hindus' against Muslims. In this manner, many shared religious traditions, as the Baba Budhan case shows, are now being transformed in order to serve contemporary political purposes, shaped largely by the growing challenge of Brahminical Hinduism and moulded by modern understanding of religious and community identity.

The Thinthini Mouneshwar/Moinuddin Tradition

Mouneshwar, also known as Moinuddin, is the patron saint of the 'low' caste Hindu Panchals or goldsmiths of Gulbarga, Bagalkot and Bijapur in northern Karnataka. As his twin names, one Hindu and the other Muslim, so strikingly suggest, his identity is ambiguous, claimed as he is by both Hindus as well as Muslims. His shrine at the village of Thinthini, located on the banks of the Krishna river in the Gulbarga district, is built entirely in Muslim fashion, with a round dome topped with the symbol of a crescent, and surrounded by four slender minarets. In the vicinity are located the graves of successive Hindu custodians of the shrine, all constructed in Islamic fashion, covered with green cloths decorated with the insignia of the crescent and the star. The central structure within the shrine complex has two levels. In the basement is a stone platform on which is placed a flask and an axe, said to have been used by Mouneshwar/Moinuddin, under which is said to be the grave of Mouneshwar. On the floor above is a Muslim-style grave, said by some to be the grave of Moinuddin, while others claim it to be the grave of the Prophet Mohammad. For all purposes it appears like any other shrine of a Muslim Sufi.

Little is known about Mouneshwar/Moinuddin. According to one story, he was born in a Hindu goldsmith family but adopted several of the practices associated with Muslim *faqirs*, spending much time in their company visiting mosques and Sufi lodges (Shastri 1998). Another story has it that he was a Muslim, a follower of a noted Sufi, identified variously as Hazrat Khwaja Aminuddin Ala Chishti of Bijapur or Mohammad Sarwar/Kodekkal Basavanna of Gulbarga. According to some sources, he had become a Muslim at the hands of a Muslim Sufi but retained the Hindu name of Mouneshwar in order to more closely identify with the 'low' caste Hindus among whom he lived and preached. According to yet another version, Mouneshwar and Moinuddin were actually two close friends, one a Hindu and the other a Muslim, who lived together and are buried within the same shrine complex. In all these stories while there is considerable confusion about the religious identity of Mouneshwar/Moinuddin, there is no hint at all of Hindu-Muslim conflict (Tarikere 1998).

The Thinthini shrine, like many other similar shrines in the area, has in recent years undergone a process of considerable Brahminization, and, as a result, its Muslim links are now sought to be denied or suppressed. According to Muslim informants this process began in 1948, when the area, which was till then under the rule of the Muslim Nizam of Hyderabad, was incorporated into the Indian Union. The transformation of the tradition is clearly evident in the stories that are now told about Mouneshwar/Moinuddin and his life. According to one of the custodians of the shrine, a young Hindu Panchal, Mouneshwar was actually a Hindu saint. The Muslim-style grave on top of the *samadhi* of Mouneshwar, he says, is that of the Prophet Mohammad. According to him, driven out of Mecca and unable to find shelter anywhere, the Prophet approached Mouneshwar, who, in his generosity, provided him with a grave within his own shrine complex, thus suggesting the superiority of the Hindu over the Muslim. Another popularly recounted story is that Mouneshwar, a Hindu saint, was, like other Hindu religious figures, 'persecuted' by the local Muslim Sultan. After his death, in order to conceal his grave and ward off the threat of destruction from Muslim 'iconoclasts', his disciples constructed his shrine complex in Muslim fashion so that the Muslims would spare it, believing it to be the *dargah* of a Muslim saint.

Both these stories are, of course, completely fanciful, but they show how what was clearly once a liminal tradition centred round a figure whose confessional identity was blurred, but was probably a Muslim, is now being sought to be completely Hinduized. This process of Hinduization has meant that over the years the number of Muslims visiting the shrine has sharply declined. As part of the process of the

Hindu appropriation of the shrine, visible Hindu markers have been employed to give it a clear Hindu appearance. Thus, for instance, an idol purporting to be that of Mouneshwar, has been installed in his shrine, this being a complete break from tradition, for the Mouneshwar/ Moinuddin cult is based on the worship of a formless God, an indication of a distinct Sufi influence. Pictures claiming to represent Mouneshwar are sold at the shrine to throngs of pilgrims, depicting him as a Hindu *sadhu*, donning the 'holy' thread reserved only for 'high' caste Hindus. A massive copper bell has been installed at the entrance of the shrine, and the Hindu holy syllable 'Om' has recently been painted on some structures within the shrine complex.

The custodians of the shrine being Hindus, and Muslims being only a small minority in the area, the Hinduization of the shrine has carried on unhindered, unlike in the case of the Baba Budhan *dargah* where the Muslim custodians have sought to challenge the claims of the VHP and allied groups through the courts. The 'low' caste Panchals seem to have enthusiastically promoted the Hinduization of the Mouneshwar/Moinuddin tradition, for it provides them with a higher status within the Hindu caste hierarchy, as followers of a powerful deity. In order to prove their own claims to 'high' caste status, the orthodox Hindu credentials of the Mouneshwar tradition are forcefully asserted, while his clearly Muslim links are either denied or conveniently explained away.

The Sultan Ahmad Shah Wali Tradition

Bidar, in northern Karnataka, is home to numerous Sufi shrines. Under the Muslim Bahmani Sultans, numerous Sufis were attracted to the area from north India and from as far as Iran and Central Asia. Their *dargahs* are till this day popular places of pilgrimage for Muslims and Hindus alike. One of the most intriguing shrines in Bidar is the massive tomb complex of Sultan Shihabuddin Ahmad Shah Wali (d. 1436), son of the founder of the Bahmani dynasty, Hasan Gangoh, who later took the name of Sultan Alauddin Shah.

Sultan Ahmad was widely known for his piety and generosity and for his Sufi leanings (Rizvi 1978). He was a disciple of the great Chishti saint, Hazrat Gesu Daraz Banda Nawaz.[7] He is said to have been so

---

[7]Shafiuddin Saif, Bidar. Ba-Haisiyat Paya Takht-i-Saltanat-i-Bahmani (Bidar as the Main Centre of the Bahmani Sultanate), in Qayyum Sadiq (Ed.), *Nazr-i-Bidar* (Perspectives on Bidar), Karnataka Adabi Circle, Gulbarga, 1993, p. 23.

just, kind-hearted and tolerant that his Muslim subjects considered him to be a *wali* of God, while the local Lingayats revered him as an incarnation of their saint Allama Prabhu. His fame as a saint is believed to have owed principally to his prayers during a particularly severe drought, which caused it to rain and thereby relieved the people of their misery.[8]

Every year, twenty days after the Hindu festival of Holi, a large fair is held at the massive tomb of Sultan Ahmad at Ashtur, a village on the outskirts of Bidar town. On the occasion, the Lingayat priest of the subsidiary shrine of Sultan Ahmad at the village of Mudiyal comes walking all the way to the shrine, a journey of five days, along with a large procession of Lingayats, Muslims, Hindus and Dalits. He dons a long, green Muslim-style robe and a green and red Muslim-style cap, both of which are believed to have been gifted to one of his ancestors by Sultan Ahmad. He offers coconuts and flowers at the grave of Sultan Ahmad, while the Muslim custodian of the shrine reads the *fatiha*, the opening verse of the Quran, and distributes little pieces of sugar as *tabarruk* to those present.

Sultan Ahmad has several subsidiary shrines dedicated to him at various places in the Bidar and Gulbarga districts. These are believed to actually have been *chillahs* marking places where the Sultan halted on his journeys. Alternately, they may have been *dargah*-like structures dedicated to the Sultan built on lands granted by him to various Lingayat families as *jagirs*. In contrast to the main shrine of the Sultan at Ashtur, whose custodian is a Muslim, these subsidiary shrines are all controlled by Lingayat priests. Till 1948, this area formed part of the vast dominions of the Muslim Nizams of Hyderabad, and Hindus and Muslims would regularly visit these Muslim-style shrines. Since 1948, when the Indian armed forces overran Hyderabad and incorporated it into the Indian Union, in the course of which scores of Muslims were killed, these shrines have been undergoing a rapid process of Hinduization. In 1948, a Shiva *lingam* is said to have been forcibly installed on the Muslim grave-like structure at the subsidiary shrine of Sultan Ahmad at Mudiyal. The shrine of Sultan Ahmad at Jiroli has now been completely Hinduized. Its Muslim-style domes have been torn down, and replaced with a Hindu-style tower (*shikara*).

[8]Sayyed Ahmad, Bidar Mai Bahmani Salatin Ke Adabi Karname 'The Literary Achievements of the Bahmani Sultans in Bidar', in Qayyum Sadiq (Ed.), *Nazr-i-Bidar*, Karnataka Adabi Circle, Gulbarga, 1993, p. 62.

The Muslim-style grave-like structure inside has been converted into a platform with a Shiva *linga* placed on it. At the entrance of the inner chamber of the shrine, pictures and idols of various Hindu deities have been recently installed.[9]

The denial of the cult's Muslim links is apparent in the stories that are now told to explain its origins. The Lingayat custodians of these shrines deny any association with Sultan Ahmad and insist that Allama Prabhu and Sultan Ahmad are two distinct figures. An ingenious argument for some distinctly Muslim practices associated with the cult traces them to a spiritual competition which the Sultan and Allama Prabhu, so it is said, once entered into. The Sultan was defeated, and accepted Allama Prabhu's superiority, and begged him to take him as his disciple, which he did. In gratitude, the Sultan ordered several shrines to be built to perpetuate the memory of his *guru*. Needless to say, this story has no basis in fact, for the Sultan was born at least three centuries after Allama Prabhu is believed to have died. As in the case of the Mouneshwar/Moinuddin tradition, the reworked story points to a radical denial of the Muslim origins of the tradition of Sultan Ahmad, attempting to place it firmly within the Hindu tradition and stress the claim of the superiority of the Hindu over the Muslim.

The Raja Bagh Sawar Tradition

Several shrines dedicated to the fifteenth century Sufi Taj Baba, more popularly known as Raja Bagh Sawar (The King Astride a Tiger), are located at various places in northern Karnataka and neighbouring southern Maharashtra. His principal shrine, where he is buried, is at the town of Basavakalyan in the Gulbarga district. Looked after by a family of hereditary Muslim custodians, the shrine is one of the biggest Sufi *dargahs* in the region.

Taj Baba is said to have been born in Simnan, in present-day Iran, and to have later migrated, along with his family, to India, settling down first at the town of Hansi in the Punjab. There he became a disciple of one of the leading Sufis of his times, Hazrat Qutbuddin Munawwar Hansvi, who, in turn, was a disciple of the famous

[9]These changes are dated to sometime in the mid-1990s, at a time when militant Hindutva groups became increasingly popular in parts of Karnataka.

thirteenth century Chishti Sufi, Hazrat Nizamuddin Auliya of Delhi. After the death of his master, Taj Baba left Hansi and travelled through Gujarat, Khandesh and Andhra, finally arriving in Gulbarga, riding, so the story goes, on a tiger. More than one hundred shrines dedicated to him, big and small, are found all over the Deccan at places that he is said to have visited.[10]

The largest of the subsidiary shrines of Taj Baba is located at the village of Yamanur, near the town of Nawalgund in the Bagalkot district in northern Karnataka. In contrast to the principal shrine at Basavakalyan, this shrine is looked after by a family of hereditary Maratha Hindu priests. In recent years, the shrine has been gradually Hinduized. In the mid-1990s a new wall was built around the shrine, with a Hindu-style entrance topped with idols of Hindu deities. A board was put up at the entrance announcing the shrine as the 'temple' of 'Chang Dev alias Raja Bagh Sawar'. Two statues, purporting to be that of 'Chang Dev' and his 'Brahmin guru', Gyaneshwar, were installed on top of the main gate of the shrine. Lithographed pictures of Raja Bagh Sawar are now sold at shops near the shrine, depicting him as a Hindu *sadhu* riding a tiger, holding a whip made of fierce snakes in one hand and a rein consisting of scorpions in the other.

Inside the shrine, *puja* is now conducted in Hindu-style, with offerings being made to massive copper *alams*, outstretched palms that probably originally represented the 'holy family' (*panjatan pak*) of the Prophet Mohammad, his daughter Hazrat Fatima, her husband Imam Ali and their two sons, Imam Hasan and Imam Hussain. While several customs associated with the shrine are distinctly Muslim, such as, for instance, the recitation of the *fatiha*, the opening verse of the Quran, by a Muslim *faqir* during the *puja*, the Hindu custodians insist that Raja Bagh Sawar (Chang Dev) was a Hindu Brahmin and not a Muslim. As for the Muslim rituals associated with the shrine, these are said to be a result of the patronage given to the shrine by a Muslim king who was defeated in a spiritual contest with the Brahmin 'Chang Dev' and who, suitably humbled, gifted the Brahmin the land on which his shrine today stands. This reworking of the story of Raja Bagh Sawar bears close parallels with the case of both the Sultan Ahmad as well as the Mouneshwar/Moinuddin traditions, seeking to stress the claim of the moral superiority of the Hindu over the Muslim.

[10]Interview with Abul Hasan Shah Afzal Pir Chishti Nizami Sher Sawari, custodian of the shrine of Taj Baba, Basavakalyan, 10 February 2001.

The Koddekkal Basavanna/Mohammad Sarwar Tradition

Located in the Gulbarga district in northern Karnataka is the village of Koddekal, centre of the cult of Muhammad Sarwar/Koddekal Basavanna. Built like a Sufi *dargah*, the shrine is looked after by a family of hereditary Lingayat priests belonging to the 'low' caste Nekar community of weavers. Little is known about the life of Mohammad Sarwar/Koddekkal Basavana. According to the Nekar custodians of the shrine, he was the thirteenth or 'Mohammada' incarnation of Basavanna, the founder of the Lingayat movement[11], or, alternately, of Allama Prabhu, Basavanna's teacher, charged with the special responsibility of bringing Hindus and Muslims together. On the other hand, his Muslim followers insist that he was one of them, a disciple of the famous Sufi, Hazrat Makhdum Jahaniyan Jahangasht. According to this story, he played a leading role in spreading Islam in the area, making seven disciples from among the Nekar Lingayats of the village of Koddekal, from whom the present custodians of his shrine are descended. These seven Nekars are said to have been 'incompletely' converted to Islam, retaining many of their Hindu practices and beliefs even after their change of faith, which accounts for the liminal nature of the tradition that has developed centred on the figure of Mohammad Sarwar.

The grave of Koddekal Basavanna/Mohammad Sarwar is housed in a Muslim-style domed structure with slender minarets topped with the Islamic symbol of the crescent and the star. The grave is constructed in Muslim fashion, covered with a green cloth decorated with the insignia of the crescent and star. Above the grave are large glass domes from which hang long, intricately crafted metal medallions with the Islamic creed of confession, the *shahdah* (There is no god but Allah and Mohammad is the Messenger of Allah) embossed on them. A picture purporting to be that of Kodekkal Basavanna/Mohammad Sarwar, a recent addition, is placed at the entrance. He appears as a *sadhu* draped in a tiger's skin with a cobra under his arm, carrying a pot in one hand, the other hand lifted up in blessing. On one foot he wears a 'Hindu-style' wooden sandal (*padarakshi*) and a 'Muslim-style' leather shoe (*kausi*) on the other.

---

[11]The twelfth century Basavanna, said to have been born in a Brahmin family, launched the powerful Lingayat movement, bitterly critiquing the ritualism of the Brahmins and the caste system and preaching an ethical monotheism. There are several parallels between the Lingayat and the Deccani Sufi traditions.

The followers of Koddekal Basavanna/Mohammad Sarwar include Muslims as well as Nekar Lingayats, the latter forming the vast majority. The cult itself is based on the conception of a formless God. Unlike the other Lingayats, the Nekars associated with the cult do not wear the phallic symbol (*lingam*). In place of the *lingam*, they worship the scripture (*vachana*) of Koddekal Basavanna, which they consider as their *atma lingam* (the *lingam* of the soul). The rituals associated with everyday worship at the shrine are similar to those conducted at other Hindu village shrines. During the two annual festivals associated with the shrine, however, the priest dresses up like a Muslim, plasters the grave of Kodekkal Basvanna/Mohammad Sarwar with a fresh coat of sandalwood paste (a custom associated with most Sufi shrines in India) and then prays after a Muslim *faqir* recites the *fatiha* and asks for blessings on the Prophet Mohammad and his friend (*dost*), Mohammad Sarwar.[12]

The Muslim style of the shrine, the rituals associated with the tradition as well as the extensive ruins of Muslim monuments in the vicinity suggest that Koddekal was probably a major Sufi centre at one time, particularly under the Adil Shahis, lending credence to the Muslim version of the story of the origins of the Koddekal Basavanna cult. However, today, the Lingayats and other Hindu devotees of Koddekal Basavanna tend to deny the Muslim origins of the cult. In contrast to the Sultan Ahmad/Allama Prabhu and Mouneshwar/ Moinuddin case, Hinduization has taken a very different form here. The role of Koddekal Basvanna in promoting harmony between Hindus and Muslims is recognized and even stressed, but he is placed firmly within the framework of the broader Hindu tradition, as an *avatar* of a Hindu/Lingayat deity, albeit one who was also charitable towards the Muslims. The distinctly Muslim grave complexes located

---

[12]This is known as 'offering of the *deen*', the word *deen* meaning 'religion' (Islam) in Arabic. After the *fatiha* is read, the Muslim *faqir* recites the following verse several times aloud:

> *Awwal Mohammad Akhir Mohammad*
> *Zahir Mohammad Batin Mohammad*
> *Mohammad Sarwar Ka Dost Raha Voh Deen*
> *Ek Lakh Assi Hazar Panch Pir-o-Paighambar*

(Mohammad is the First, Mohammad is the Last
Mohammad in his outward aspect, Mohammad in his inner aspect
Mohammad Sarwar is a friend of the religion
Of the one hundred and eighty thousand and five Pirs and Prophets).

in the village are now claimed to be graves of various Hindu saints. The mainstream Lingayat tradition does not recognize incarnations of Basavanna, and, clearly, in this case, a considerable departure has been made from established tradition to deny what seems to be the undeniable Muslim origins of the cult and to incorporate it into the broader Lingayat/Hindu fold.

Conclusion

As these cases of shared Hindu-Muslim shrines in Karnataka show, religious liminality does not necessarily promote inter-communal harmony and understanding. Rather, because of their ambiguous character, many shared shrines have today emerged as arenas of inter-community contestation and rivalry. Liminal traditions in Karnataka, as elsewhere in India, are under considerable pressure today, being forced to define themselves as unambiguously Hindu or Muslim as the case might be.

Several factors have worked to steadily undermine such syncretic traditions. North Karnataka is where the centres of most of the traditions that we have looked at here and elsewhere[13] are located. This area was, till 1948, part of the Muslim kingdom of Hyderabad, and prior to that, was for centuries under the rule of various local Muslim dynasties. With the incorporation of the Nizam's Dominions into the Indian Union after the police action in 1948, Muslim influence in the area was forcefully challenged. Several Muslims were killed in the western districts of the Nizam's Dominions after the Indian forces took control. Then, laws were passed dispossessing large landlords, many of them members of the erstwhile Muslim nobility, of their estates, which were then distributed to their former tenants, mainly Hindus. With the decline of Muslim influence and the restraining power of the Muslim political elite, shared Hindu-Muslim shrines, many of them Sufi *dargahs*, that had Hindu custodians gradually began undergoing a process of Hinduization, subtle in some cases and overt in others. Cultic figures, in many cases of Muslim Sufis, whom both Hindus as well as Muslims had venerated for centuries, were now sought to be presented as unambiguously Hindu, and the rituals and stories associated with them were suitably modified. The

[13]Yoginder Sikand, *Hindu-Muslim Syncretic Shrines in Karnataka*, Himayat, Bangalore, 2001. Here I have examined seventeen such shrines in Karnataka.

gradual spread in the region of the Islamic reformist Tablighi Jamat movement, with its hostility towards popular Sufi cults, which it sees as 'un-Islamic', only helped to further accelerate this process, as fewer Muslims continued to visit these shrines. Muslims who continued to pray at these shrines found themselves too heavily outnumbered to protest against their transformation into temples.[14] From the late 1980s onwards, the Hinduization of syncretic shrines in Karnataka has been particularly noticeable. This must be seen in the context of the growing strength of right-wing and militantly anti-Muslim Hindu groups in the region, coinciding with a well-organized mass mobilizational campaign all over India to generate public support for the destruction of the Ayodhya mosque.[15]

For bureaucrats, politicians as well as a new generation of educated people taught to believe that Hindus and Muslims are two completely separate and well-defined communities, Islam and Hinduism being seen as completely unrelated and neatly bounded bodies of knowledge and forms of ritual practice, shared religious identities are a direct challenge to their ways of seeing the world. Consequently, local communities and traditions that had earlier comfortably existed in a situation of liminality are increasingly forced to identify themselves as either Hindu or Muslim. Outside political interests, as in the case with the ongoing controversy over the Baba Budhan *dargah*, further add to this pressure. Economic factors, too, seem to have played a major role in the marked Hinduization of such shrines. Many of these shrines have followers who number in hundreds of thousands, mostly Hindus from various castes. Several small shared shrines have in the last five decades been converted into large, distinctly Hindu temples, their histories being suitably amended to emphasize their claims to orthodox Hindu status, thus converting them into popular Hindu places of pilgrimage, attracting growing numbers of the devout, who are encouraged to make liberal donations to the 'temples' and their custodians.

In the reworking of the histories of the figures associated with the shrines, the Islamic component is not always denied. Indeed, it can still be retained, although interpreted differently in order to emphasize the claim of the 'superiority' of the Hindu over the Muslim. Thus, for

[14]Thus, several Muslim respondents answered that since the 'government belongs to the Hindus, they are doing what they like'.

[15]In almost all the shrines described here, it was only after the late 1980s that Hindu idols and images were installed or Hindu-style architectural features added.

instance, in the case of the Thinthini shrine, the Muslim-style grave is now claimed to be that of the Prophet Mohammad, who had, so the story now goes, beseeched the Hindu Mouneshwar for a place to lay his head.[16] Or, for instance, the distinctly Muslim rituals associated with the subsidiary shrines of Sultan Ahmad are now interpreted as following from the defeat of the Sultan in a spiritual contest with the Hindu saint Allama Prabhu, after which the Sultan, accepting him as his *guru*, constructed several shrines dedicated to him. The fact that these traditions are entirely oral, with few, if any, records of these shrines dating to their formative period, has meant that it has been possible for them to be suitably moulded to completely transform their basic character and firmly locate them within the broader framework of an ill-defined 'Hinduism'. Integral to this process of reinterpretation is the incorporation of stereotypical notions about the Muslims so integral to a prominent strand in contemporary Hindu discourse: the Muslim 'other' as 'inferior', 'militant' and 'iconoclastic'.

The Hinduization of syncretic shrines may be seen as part of a long historical process of the formation of what is today called 'Hinduism'. As Ilaiah (1996) points out, what we know as 'Hinduism' today is largely an amalgam of local traditions, many of them non-Brahminic, that have, over time, been gradually absorbed into a system defined by an overall Brahminical hegemony. Thus, tribal and 'low' caste deities, such as Shiva, Kali and Krishna, have been suitably Brahminized and incorporated into the Brahminical pantheon of deities. Shrines of 'low' caste deities are taken over by Brahmin or other caste Hindu priests, and stories are woven claiming them to have been the incarnation of one or the other Brahminical deity. The same process of Brahminization is clearly observable in the case of the shared religious shrines and traditions that we have looked at. This process is given further impetus by efforts on the part of 'low' caste groups to rise up within the local caste hierarchy by emulating the practices associated with Brahminical Hinduism. Many of the shared traditions that we have looked at have been historically associated with the 'low' castes, such as the Panchal goldsmiths, the Lingayat peasants and Nekar weavers. As these castes

---

[16]Muslim followers of the cult argue, on the other hand, that because the Muslim-style grave is located above the Hindu-style *samadhi* in the basement, this 'indicates the superiority of Islam over Hinduism'. Some Muslim respondents suggested that the position of the Muslim-like grave indicated that Mouneshwar had accepted a Muslim Sufi as his master, and out of respect for him, had arranged for him to be buried above him.

seek to improve their social standing, their popular religious traditions are suitably modified, giving them an orthodox Hindu pedigree. In this sense, the gradual Hinduization of shared traditions in contemporary Karnataka is hardly a new phenomenon. Rather, it can be seen as part of the historical process of the spread of Brahminical Hinduism through incorporation of non-Brahminic shrines, traditions and cults. Militant Hindutva organizations have today given this process an added impetus, targeting these traditions, suitably reinterpreting them in the process of constructing a Hindu identity based on an unrelenting opposition to the Muslim 'other'.

References

Dange, Sadashiv Ambadas. 1987. *Encyclopaedia of Puranic Beliefs and Practices* (Vol. II), Navrang Publishers, New Delhi, p. 377.

Eaton, M. Richard. 1996. *Sufis of Bijapur 1300–1700: Social Roles of Sufis in Medieval India*, Munshiram Manoharlal, New Delhi.

Gazetteer of Mysore, Government of Mysore, Mysore (Vol. V) p.1137.

Gottschalk, Peter. 2001. The Problem of Defining Islam in Arampur, *Institute for the Study of Islam in the Modern World Newsletter*, no. 8, p. 23.

Ilaiah, Kancha. 1996. *Why I Am Not A Hindu: A Shudra Critique of Hindutva Philosophy, Culture and Political Economy*, Samya, Calcutta.

Jones, W. Kenneth. 1981. Religious Identity and the Indian Census, in Gerald Barrier (Ed.), *The Census in British India: New Perspectives*, Manohar, New Delhi.

Oberoi, Harjot. 1994. *The Construction of Religious Boundaries: Culture, Identity and Diversity in the Sikh Tradition*, Oxford University Press, Delhi, p. 17.

Rizvi, Saiyid Athar Abbas. 1978. *A History of Sufism in India* (Vol. I), Munshiram Manoharlal, New Delhi, p. 252.

Shastri, Mahantesh. 1998. *Thinthini Mouneshwar Mahima Charitre*, (The Life of Thinthini Mouneshwar), P.C. Shabadi Mutt, Gadag.

Tarikere, Rahmat. 1998. *Karnatakakada Sufigalu* (The Sufis of Karnataka), Hampi University, Hospet, pp. 1–50.

Warren, Marianne. 1999. *Unravelling the Enigma: Shirdi Sai Baba in the Light of Sufism*, Sterling Publishers, New Delhi, p. 139.

10

Devotional Practices among Shia Women in South India

DIANE D'SOUZA

Introduction

Muslims account for approximately 30 per cent of the five million inhabitants in the South Indian city of Hyderabad. Of this population, the Shia community is estimated to be nearly 10 per cent of the Muslim population or somewhere between 150,000 and 200,000 people (Howarth 2001).[1] The majority of the community lives in the Old City quarter which, although rich in tradition and culture, remains an economically disadvantaged area. Like Old City Muslims in general, the majority of Hyderabad Shia families live in lower economic conditions, although overseas employment in the Gulf and other circumstances have brought a measure of wealth to some portions of the community.[2] The most common occupation among women of this community tends to be full-time caring for family and home.

[1] Difficulties in population estimates arise from the fact that the Indian census does not require people to name their religious 'sect', and also that in situations of perceived threat, Shias follow a practice of concealing their identity (known ideologically as *taqiyyah*).

[2] To understand Muslims in Hyderabad, one needs to have a sense of the region's history of two dynasties (three centuries) of Muslim rule. At the time of India's independence, the ruler (Nizam) asserted that Hyderabad (at that time a whole state,

In this paper I discuss some of the rituals that form an integral part of the religious experience of Ithna Ashari Shia[3] women. My focus is on two rituals familiar to most Ithna Ashari women: *amal* (lit. 'practice'), a litany of prayer said in times of need or crisis and taking the form of a repeated powerful phrase or Quranic verse (somewhat akin to the Sunni or Sufi practice of *dhikr*); and *dastarkhan* (lit. 'meal cloth'), a special gathering organized by women to remember, revere and seek the intervention of sacred personalities and to commemorate the fulfillment of a vow.[4] These two rituals form a small part of a larger constellation of Shia[5] religious activities. In analysing the form of women's religious expressions, I suggest that efforts to seek out life-enhancing relationships leads many Shia women to participate in rituals which help to develop and maintain relationships in social networks, which includes cosmic figures central to Shia belief.

My research on women's devotional practices springs from over a decade of contact with the community, although the years of most intense interaction have been from 1994 to 2000. Through this extended contact, I have both observed and taken part in hundreds of ritual events, most in all-women environments. I have drawn on this experience in constructing the following two examples of *amal* and *dastarkhan* rituals. Although the descriptions spring from real events which have taken place, I have changed names and certain details to protect the privacy of the women I describe.

---

not simply a city) would not join the Indian Union but would remain a separate and independent state. The Indian Army responded with military intervention in 1948 and the Nizam surrendered rather quickly. The subsequent collapse of the existing feudal system meant that a fairly large 'noble' class of Muslims in Hyderabad (including prominent Shia families) lost their privileged social and economic positions. As a result they, their employees, and others who served the royal court no longer had access to traditional sources of income. A subsequent collective spiral to poverty affected the Hyderabad Muslim community for decades.

[3]This community is often referred to in literature by its literal translation as 'twelver', i.e. believing in twelve *imams* (sinless spiritual successors to the Prophet). It is the majority group, forming roughly ninety per cent of the Shia community in Hyderabad and worldwide.

[4]Known as *sofreh* in other parts of India (e.g. Mumbai), Iran and parts of the Middle East.

[5]In addition to the decision not to use diacritical marks for words translated to English from other languages, I also have chosen not to distinguish between the noun 'Shia' and the adjective 'Shi'a'; I use the word Shia in both cases, as is done in common English usage today.

A Ritual of Intervention in Times of Need

Nur's daughter-in-law is pregnant, but the pregnancy has been difficult. She's been unable to keep much food down and often feels exhausted or giddy. She spent most of her days over the last week in bed. The doctor advises that if she doesn't get stronger she may have to be admitted to the nursing home for a day or two to take some glucose intravenously. Nur is very worried. She remembers her own miscarriage as a young bride and doesn't want the same experience for her son's wife. She goes to the *ashurkhana* (a Shia shrine which houses sacred icons)[6] known as Yadgar Husayni and speaks with a woman named Ismat about what she wants to do (D'Souza forthcoming). Ismat writes down the daughter-in-law's name and a few other details, then confirms that the rate for the requested intercessory litany (*amal*) is Rs 190. After looking at the schedule for the week, she tells Nur that the *amal* will be held the next day at eleven o'clock. Nur leaves the *ashurkhana* happy and relieved.

The following day, Ismat arrives at the *ashurkhana* before eleven. She greets a few women who sit chatting in the vast and airy main hall which opens onto the surrounding courtyard. The hall easily accommodates a thousand women, but such large gatherings are rare outside the main mourning month of Muharram. Along the western wall of the hall, one door is open to the room holding the *ashurkhana's* collection of revered icons. As Ismat stops to remove the embroidered sheet (*chador*) with which she covers herself when going out, a woman with a young child crosses the hall to slip inside the room. The girl is carrying a garland of flowers in a plastic bag. When the two emerge from the inner room, the fragrant flowers are left behind, adorning one of the main icons:[7] an *alam* (battle standard) representing Husain, the grandson of Prophet Mohammad. Three young women talk and laugh as they wash apples and grapes under a gushing tap in the courtyard. A faint smell of incense wafts from the room known as the *niyazkhana* (place for performing rituals known as *niyaz*), where a small group of brightly dressed women are busy

[6]Literally, 'the house of Ashura', Ashura being the tenth of Muharram and the day on which Husain, the grandson of the Prophet, and seventy-two of his family and followers were martyred.

[7]The word for icon is *nishan*, literally 'symbol'. One of the distinguishing hallmarks of Shia Islam as it is practiced in Hyderabad—and to a large extent worldwide—is its relatively extensive use of symbols compared to much of Sunni Islam.

cutting and arranging fruit as they prepare for a celebratory *dastarkhan*.

It is nearly twelve o'clock before all ten women needed to perform the requested *amal* have arrived. Ismat grumbles about people who are late to a friend who has stopped by the shrine for a visit and a chat, and scolds a woman who is sweeping for overlooking a pebble under the mat she uses for prayers. 'What is this? What kind of cleaning is this? This is a *yadgar* (shrine)!' she reprimands. The woman grins in the face of Ismat's scolding, and sweeps vigorously under the white sheet (*farsh*) covering the mats on the floor. Eventually all ten women arrive. Most perform the *wudu* (ablutions) in the courtyard as soon as they enter the *ashurkhana*, several take time to greet or talk with friends or to visit the icons housed in the inner room. Before arranging themselves in rows on the two long prayer carpets which are spread out in the front of the hall, most take a *sajdaga* (prayer tablet)[8] and a *tasbih* (string of prayer beads) from plastic baskets which have been set out near Ismat. A few have brought their own ritual items, which they unwrap from embroidered handkerchiefs or protective pouches and set out on the mat before them. The women also collect a small pile of seeds from Ismat, and a few get a glass of water, setting it down next to them on the mat. Ismat sits cross-legged facing the two rows of women, her back to the closed door of the icon room.

As the ten women continue to settle, Ismat begins reciting from a small book in a clear melodious voice. She is reading *Hadith-i Kisa*, one of the most well-known traditions among Shias which describes an incident understood to confirm the sanctity of the Prophet's family.[9] The Arabic recitation is familiar to the assembled women and at key moments they punctuate it with invocations of praise (*salavat*; lit. 'benedictions') for the mentioned family of the Prophet. When Ismat has finished, the women stand and perform two *rakats* (formulaic sections) of ritual prayer (namaz), their foreheads resting on the earthen *sajdaga* with each prostration.[10] Meanwhile, on directions from Ismat, one of the women distributes money, placing a payment of twelve rupees in front of each woman. By the end of this ritual the money

[8]Known in other circles as a *mohra-i namaz*, according to Howrath, 73.

[9]Literally, 'tradition of the cloak'. This *hadith* narrates the context of the revelation of the Quranic verse of purity (33:33), which Shias understand to refer to Muhammad, Fatima, Ali, Hasan and Husayn and confirm their special status before God.

[10]The *sajdaga* is made of soil from the plains of Karbala, a spot sanctified by the blood of the martyred Husayn and his family and followers more than thirteen hundred years ago.

is grace-filled, a blessing (*barakat*)[11] earned through performing a sacred deed. The women begin their recitations, some silently, others whispering in barely audible tones. All repeat the words, '*Ya Ali madad*', 'Oh Ali, help [us]'. Some of the women are reflective as they do this, some are lost in thought, a few rock gently as they say the words. When the noise in the hall ebbs for a moment, one can hear the slight whispering of their collective prayer. A young child races gaily across the hall, calling loudly, and all eyes move, heads turn, but lips keep moving, the recitation never stopping.

The women keep track of the number of times they repeat the phrase by deftly fingering the beads of the *tasbih*. When a woman has repeated the words one hundred times, she moves aside one seed from the small pile in front of her. When ten seeds have accumulated in a new pile, she sets aside a seed to mark 1000 repetitions and then starts the process again. In less than an hour, the assembled women have called on the help of the revered first Imam 12500 times. As they finish, one by one, most of the women touch the *tasbih* lightly to each eye and then to their lips in a traditional and respectful gesture of greeting or parting. Almost all take a few moments to prostrate with their heads on the *sajdagah* before kissing the stone lightly and either putting it away or rising to return it and the *tasbih* to the baskets at the front of the hall. The '*Ya Ali Madad amal*' is now complete: together the women offered a litany of prayer, calling on the intercession of Ali to bring health and a safe pregnancy to Nur's daughter-in-law.

The Significance of Amal

An *amal* is a believer's call for help, a ritual of intercession which uses words of particular power and blessing. The power of the words can derive from the sacred personality to whom they are addressed, as in the above example where the women call on Ali, the first Imam and a revered 'friend of God', to act as a mediator (*wasilah*) in bringing Nur's intention before God. Power also can derive from the grace-filled source of the words themselves, as in the case where an *amal* involves the repetition of verses or a whole chapter from the Quran.[12]

---

[11]The Urdu word *barakat* is adapted from the Arabic term (*barakah*) and means 'increase, abundance, prosperity, blessing; good fortune, auspiciousness' and 'inherent prosperity which produces success or abundance' (Platts 1977).

[12]*Surah Yasin* and *ayat Karimat* are popular Quranic chapters and verses used

Occasionally women choose to recite the whole of the Quran once in a single sitting; a ritual popularly known as *khatam* (lit. 'finished'). As with *amal*, a number of those who can read Arabic—ten, twelve, fifteen, twenty—come together and simultaneously recite segments of the Quran (*paras*). Thus, within a few hours the whole of the sacred text has been recited. Here again, the source of power is in the revealed words which are identified as coming directly from God. In Hyderabad, men and women tend to perform *khatam* as a ritual of blessing for the dead on various death anniversaries, although women also infrequently use it as a ritual of intercession in affairs of daily life.

In the above example, although Nur requested the ritual, she herself was not present during its performance. Most comfortable at home with her ailing daughter-in-law, Nur had full confidence in the efficacy of the prayer being offered at Yadgar—she did not feel that she needed to be there in order to partake of its power. On other occasions, those who request an *amal* choose to participate in the ritual, although in cases where the repeated words are chapters or verses from the Quran, women need to be able to read or recite Arabic clearly and correctly. This is an important criteria (along with being of 'good character') which organizers like Ismat look for when setting up such events. Ismat will often invite women she doesn't know to sit near her while they participate in the ritual so that she can keep an eye on them and be sure the recitation is done 'properly'.

The volunteers who perform *amal* at Yadgar Husayni are mostly women who have some education and are in need of extra money. Almost all are in limited economic circumstances because their husbands—the traditional income providers—are unemployed, dead or out of the women's lives through divorce or separation (the latter sometimes initiated by the women). But it is not simply the meagre earnings which draw the women to perform this task. The volunteers believe that their participation in the ritual ensures them a measure of blessing (*barakat*); indeed, they consider the money they earn as specially blessed. The women demonstrate their belief in this sense of grace and blessing in different ways. Some keep a glass of water next to them while they perform the *amal*, then drink the water after

---

at Yadgar Husayni. As with the *Ya Ali madad* ritual, the words are recited 125000 times, although since the texts are relatively long, a larger number of women volunteers is needed to complete the recitation in a reasonable period of time (usually under two hours). Because of the extra women involved, Yadgar charges more for these rituals.

the recitation is complete. Ingesting the water is one way to bring into oneself the power of the grace-filled words which, carried on one's breath, transform the water into a medium of blessing. I have seen a woman ask her fellow volunteers to blow into a bag in which she had sweets after they had finished reciting. This food became blessed, for again the belief is that one's very breath is rendered grace-filled through the repetitions of words of divine power.[13]

One does not find *amal* carried out only in Yadgar Husayni: it is sometimes performed at other shrines or in people's homes. In such settings—as was the case in the generation before Yadgar existed—it is knowledgeable older women within an extended family or neighbourhood who usually assume leadership in directing the ritual. At Yadgar, it is grey-haired Ismat who coordinates and oversees all the *amal* rituals which are held. Yadgar remains a popular site for women to conduct this intercessory rite: in 1996 alone, for example, just over ten thousand *amal* were held.[14] When I talked about the popularity of Yadgar with women who use the shrine, they referred to the ease and convenience of performing rituals there. Most clarified that it is not simply the organization and overseeing of details which they appreciate, but the pure (*pak*) setting which Yadgar offers. Ritual purity is essential for holding such an event. At home, it takes considerable work to ensure such an environment—especially when there are children, or only one woman in a nuclear family. With more and more families living in small flats (partially linked with the trend of fewer extended families living under one roof), there are also relatively few women who are able to set aside a separate room which is a 'pure' space for religious icons and rituals. Yadgar, then, provides the ritual purity which allows a woman to offer her intentions in an acceptable and powerful way.

Whatever its setting or form, the *amal* ritual provides women with an opportunity to overcome the sense of powerlessness in the face of difficulty. Women organize the intercession when a family member loses a job, in the aftermath of accident or sickness, when children are writing exams or need to find admittance in a school, and in situations

[13]This is also contested activity, with some women discouraging or downplaying this aspect of ritual. In other words, it is not a universal belief held by all women who participate in *amal* or other rituals.

[14]I have rounded off the figure which is taken from the annual report of the women's organization responsible for the running of Yadgar Husayni: *Anjuman Niswan Barkat-i Aza, Report Salanah* (Hyderabad: *Anjuman Niswan Barkat-i Aza*, 1996), 2.

of marital strain or divorce—to cite the most popular reasons. Offering the ritual is an action women take to help deal with challenging and sometimes overwhelming situations. Also important to rituals like *amal* is the opportunity for women to come together: volunteers spend time at the shrine talking with friends, and those who sponsor or organize the rituals interact with a supportive group of women to whom they tell their story. The ritual known as *dastarkhan*, which we will look at next, in some ways plays a similar role in women's lives.

A Ritual of Celebration and Hope

Razia's house is only a short distance from Yadgar Husayni. Today the household is bustling: Razia's servant spent the previous day giving the main hall a thorough cleaning: all the furniture was moved out, the carpets removed and the stone floor scrubbed. The ceiling fans, picture frames and shelves have been dusted and the cushion covers changed. The large furniture has been pushed to the sides of the hall or temporarily stored in the adjoining bedrooms. The carpets have been rolled up and a thick, soft mat with fresh white sheets (*farsh*) has been laid down. Two new brightly coloured bed sheets have been spread out in different parts of the room as meal cloths. Razia's sister-in-law and a close friend are still working on final preparations in the kitchen along with two women servants. Another friend is setting out five large candles in the centre of each meal cloth.

Razia's husband has left to spend the day at a friend's house. She did not have to ask him to go, for it is understood that it is a time when men are not welcome at home: Razia is arranging a women-only *dastarkhan*, a ritual she vowed to perform at a similar event held just over a year ago if her prayer to Prophet Mohammad's daughter Fatima was answered. Her daughter who was diagnosed with cancer is now in total remission, and the doctors—puzzled by the strength of her recovery—say that all trace of the cancer cells are gone. Razia is ecstatic; it has been a horrendous year with the chemotherapy, the pain of seeing her only daughter so sick, and her own fear and sense of helplessness. Through it all she has drawn heavily on a supportive circle of women and their leadership or assistance in performing rituals which carry her daughter's needs before God. At the *dastarkhan* she attended last year, she lit a candle with a clear prayer for the complete recovery of her daughter. Now she feels the prayer has been answered and is honouring her vow to repeat the ritual.

Razia has invited twenty-seven women friends and relatives to join her on this happy occasion. They arrive singly or in small groups, taking off their sandals before entering the house to greet Razia and others. Those who wear *chador* pause to remove the simple shawl-like cloth which they wrap casually around their head and shoulders. The noise of conversation ebbs and flows as the main hall fills up. When all the women have arrived, Razia encourages them to take their places: fourteen around each meal cloth. The number carries special significance, for it is linked to the fourteen 'pure ones' (*masumin*: i.e. Prophet Mohammad, Fatima, and the twelve *imams* or spiritual successors to the Prophet) of Shia faith. Someone has lit incense, and a powerful floral smell fills the room. One of Razia's friends recites *Hadith-i Kisa*, and voices the intention of performing this *dastarkhan* to remember and honour Zahra ('the resplendent one'), *Bibi* (lady) Fatima. On each meal cloth, the five candles are lit with words of blessing; again the number is meaningful, echoing the five persons (*panjatan* or 'five beings') believed to be closest to God: Prophet Mohammad, Fatima, the Prophet's cousin and son-in-law Ali, and Fatima and Ali's sons Hasan and Husain. Also on the cloths are five different kinds of fruit, carefully cut, and bowls of a sweet made from bread, sugar and *ghee* (clarified butter) known as *malida*. In front of each woman is an unlit candle and a *tasbih*. Razia lights her candle—the one she has saved from the last *dastarkhan*—using the flame of one of the five candles in the centre of the cloth, then passes her candle around so that all may light their own candles from hers. The symbolism is again rich: light comes to the room through the light of the holy five, and it is from them that others receive light—in this case, through the inspiring light of one whose need has been met. The blessing and miracle of this answered prayer becomes a source of hope, for others having their own needs. If a woman wishes to put her need before God, to make a vow, she simply voices it silently within herself—a stated intention in the presence of Bibi Fatima—as she lights the candle. When she goes home later, she takes the candle with her, a reminder of her vow and connection with Fatima.

The *dastarkhan* continues in the room with its twinkling of candle lights. The women recite prayers, including poetic greetings of praise (*salam*) to Bibi Fatima, and then begin a collective repetitive prayer (*dhikr*). The women's voices are barely audible as they slide the hundred-beaded *tasbih* through their fingers, one bead for each call of supplication, '*Ya Fatima adrikni*' (Oh, Fatima, save me/help me).

The women follow their own rhythms, offering a collective prayer numbering in the thousands. Razia's aunt narrates a story of the miraculous intervention of Fatima in the lives of poor but faithful people, following which several women take turns leading the recitation of melodic poetry of praise known as *qasida*. Through most of the ritual Razia cries profusely. She later confesses that she was thinking of her daughter, of all she had gone through, of the difficulties of the situation and her own apprehensions. Some of the other women also are visibly moved, particularly during poetry which obliquely refers to the suffering which Fatima underwent in her life. The women conclude the ritual by blowing out their candles and partaking of the food. The informal conversation over the meal ranges widely, touching on topics including Razia's daughter's recovery, news about different family members and friends, happenings at a local school, the escalating costs of food, and other details of the women's lives.

The Significance of Dastarkhan

As in the case of *amal*, the ritual of *dastarkhan* can take many forms, although the women organizers are quite precise about what needs to be done for the ritual to have efficacy. There are different kinds of food which people see as essential, and a given type of *dastarkhan*, or one regularly organized by a particular family, is usually associated with specific food preparations. Examples include bread and a meat dish, or seven types of fruit, or a special kind of sweet (as in the example above). The food may be on one tray shared by the women or, more commonly, each may serve herself individually. Women will sometimes take the food home to share what is understood as blessed food with others in their families. The ritual may be held in the name of different members of the family of the Prophet, the selected sacred personality being honored by poetry and inspiring stories where he or she is the central character. In Hyderabad, popular personages around which such events are organized include Fatima, Ali, Abbas (the step-brother and close companion of Husain) and certain Imams such as Hasan, Zayn al-Abidin, and Musa (the second, fourth and seventh Imams, respectively). Each *dastarkhan* has its own ritual components, some might include the application of certain cosmetics, the inclusion of a coin or other meaningful symbol in the food (the person receiving it gaining special blessing, or the responsibility to hold a similar event), particular recitations or prayers, or the participation of special groups—

for example, unmarried young women. The elements common to the various kinds of *dastarkhan* are: it is a gathering of only women (even to the extent that if someone is pregnant, she usually will not participate in case the baby she is carrying is male); food is central to the event, and is made blessed through the enacted rituals; it is held in the name of a holy member of the Prophet's family; and women generally organize it in fulfillment of a vow—usually one which had been made previously at a similar type of *dastarkhan*.

Like *amal*, *dastarkhan* is a way for women to realize blessing, to bring one's needs before God (directly or indirectly), and to get together with other women. It differs from *amal* in that it carries a celebratory air, nurturing hope through the stories of answered prayers. Thus it helps to encourage women to persevere in efforts to access holy power as they seek tangible solutions to problems. It is also an opportunity to deepen one's relationship with spiritual personalities by listening to stories of their lives, particularly those which underline the spiritual being's empathy with the suffering of faithful persons and his or her intervention in such people's lives. *Dastarkhan* is part of a larger constellation of rituals popularly known as *niyaz*, which are characterized by the remembrance of a member of the holy family of the Prophet, and include a gathering and some type of edible offering—whether a piece of sugar, or a goat whose meat is cooked and shared or is donated to the poor and needy. Both men and women are involved in *niyaz*, although the organizing of what is largely a home-centered ritual is usually in the hands of women.

Women organize *dastarkhan* rituals in homes and in shrines including Yadgar Husayni. A few families hold them as a regular feature, sometimes on a monthly basis, within the extended family. At Yadgar, women can make use of the *niyazkhana* to hold their event, or—as with the *amal*—can pay a set amount to have a small team of women associated with the shrine do all the preparations. In the latter case, the purchase and preparation of food, the ritual cleaning of the room and even sometimes the overall coordination of the ritual itself can be done by Yadgar 'volunteers', with the women sponsoring the *dastarkhan* needing only to invite guests and come themselves. In 1996 alone, women organized approximately fifteen thousand *dastarkhan* in Yadgar Husayni.[15]

---

[15] *Anjuman Niswan Barkat-i Aza*, 2.

The Ritual Context

I have described examples of two women-led rituals which are practiced fairly frequently within Hyderabad's Ithna Ashari Shia community. They are part of a universe of Shia devotional practices consisting
of women-only rituals, men-only rituals, and those in which both
men and women participate, separately or together. Two of the most
commonly recognized religious activities among women are formal-
ized daily prayer (namaz or *salat*) and fasting (*roza*) during the month
of Ramzan—rituals which are practiced by Shia men, as well as Sunni
men and women who are religiously active. Of central importance for
a vast majority of Shia women are gatherings (*majlis* and *jeshan*) which
honour members of the family of the Prophet, commemorating key
events in their lives, particularly their births and deaths. Men as well
as women organize and attend these gatherings, following an annual
cycle of tragic and joyous remembrance days which are well-known
in a majority of Shia households. Individual families sponsor *majlis*
and *jeshan* (usually held at home) which commemorate days of
special meaning on an annual, weekly or—during the main annual
mourning period—daily basis. These ritualized events also form part
of major life ceremonies, such as weddings and funerals. Women participate in *majlis* and *jeshan* organized by men (in which they usually
occupy a physically and ritually marginalized position), and also
organize, lead and take part in women-only gatherings held at homes
and in shrines. In fact, women-organized remembrance gatherings
outnumber those organized by men.[16]

Another popular activity among women is pilgrimage (*ziyarat*) to
local, national and global sites associated with revered members of
the Prophet's family. Like most Muslims, the majority of Shia women
hope to perform the pilgrimage to Mecca (*hajj*), but the opportunity
to visit other sacred sites is longed for at least as greatly by many.
Such places of pilgrimage include the tombs of the holy personalities,
places important in their lives (like Karbala, the place where Husayn,
his family and followers were martyred), sites associated with their
miraculous appearance, and *ashurkhanas* known to be imbued with
the presence and power of these revered beings. Both men and women
participate in *ziyarat*, although it is women who are generally the more
frequent pilgrims, especially at local sites which some visit on a regular

[16]Howarth, 78.

daily, weekly or monthly basis. The broad canvas of women's devotional activities also includes individual offerings of specialized prayers (of which a wide variety exist; many being available in popular books or booklets containing recommendations about how to use them in specific situations); rituals which help sanctify events in the life cycle (including birth, the first cutting of the hair, engagement before marriage, death of a spouse, etc.); practices particular to special annual days like *shab-i barat* (literally, 'the night of quittancy'), *laylat al-qadr* (the night which commemorates the 'descent' or revelation of the Quran), and new year (*nawroz*); and a wide-ranging variety of rituals which draw on recitation and remembrance—some of which I have mentioned briefly (for example, *khatam* and *niyaz*).

Although men do not perform *amal* and *dastarkhan*, almost all are aware of these rituals, and many see them as part of 'what women do'. Levels of cooperation or support include leaving the home when a ritual requires women-only spaces (as was the case in the cited example of Razia's husband), contributing money for the purchase of items which are necessary for the event, accepting food blessed at a ritual (when the ritual permits) and, infrequently, requesting—directly or indirectly—a female member of the family to perform a ritual for a particular need. In a similar way, women extend levels of cooperation in male-only rituals. For example, in the public processions (*julus*) through Old City streets which are enacted by men during the Muharram period,[17] women play the role of passive or ritually participating (beating one's chest, shedding tears, etc.) audience, helping to inspire processionists as they recite dirges (*nawha*) and perform self flagellation in remembrance of and allegiance to the martyred family of the Prophet. Women also provide practical support—seeing to the preparation of food, the washing of clothes, and the care for wounds and aches—which makes possible men's participation in an intense cycle of ritual activity. There is, thus, a certain level of cooperation taking place between men and women which helps to make single-gender rituals possible.

As with any religious practice, it would be wholly incorrect to assume that all Shia women participate in *amal* and *dastarkhan*, or even that all women share a belief in the efficacy of intervention-

[17]As far as I know, at the present time in Hyderabad there is only one public procession of women; although I've occasionally seen women make use of procession in private *majlis* rituals.

seeking vows (*mannat*). People differ in their degree of religiosity and in the forms of devotion with which they feel affinity. Moreover, people's engagement in religious acts often changes over the course of their lifetimes; women's ritual participation is strongly influenced by the constraints and possibilities attached to different moments in the life cycle, including a woman's attachment to or freedom from household responsibilities (including children), and the degree of independence to travel outside the home (associated at least in part with a woman's age, marital status and social perceptions about sexual availability at particular ages). Within this variability, it is still correct to say that *amal* and *dastarkhan* form an important—although probably not central—part of the devotional lives of a large number of Shia women in Hyderabad. As rituals they are perhaps best understood as part of a constellation of activities which manifest a faith-filled belief in the presence and power of well-known and beloved friends of God.

The Perspective of Relationship

If we observe women's lives carefully, without attempting to force our observations into pre-existing patterns, we discover that an inner sense of connection to others is *the* central organizing feature of women's development ... Women's sense of self and of worth is most often grounded in the ability to make and maintain relationships (Miller and Stiver 1997: 16).

In trying to analyse Shia women's rituals, I find it useful to see women as operating within a two-fold context of relationship: giving and receiving support among family, friends, community; and deepening a supportive relationship with God—particularly through those revered as God's beloved, the *ahl al-bayt*. In the ritual examples which I presented at the beginning of this chapter, women took the needs of ailing family members before the divine, participating in rituals which also brought together a supportive group of women during times of difficulty or celebration. Spiritual expression, then, is inseparable from the social needs and relationships which inhabit their lives. At the same time, the ritual act is grounded on strengthening a relationship which literally spans the cosmos. In many of the religious activities in which Shias take part, including *majlis*, *jeshan* and *dastarkhan*, it is the lives and characters of the revered *masumin* which usually remain an important focus—perhaps to a greater extent in rituals led by women than by men.[18] When women seek divine intervention in solving vexing problems, they often direct their supplications not to some amorphous God, but to holy beings whose lives are as familiar to them as their own friends and relations.[19]

The work of anthropologist Azam Torab (1998), in a study of women's religious activities in the Iranian urban setting, reaches a similar conclusion. Women who regularly meet for neighbourhood religious meetings (*jalaseh*) in southern Tehran form relationships with each other, with the wider social world, and with the divine. Torab notes that 'holy beings' and the spirits of the dead are a vital part of this social world, with the presence of cosmic personalities being crucial in constructing powerful and meaningful religious rituals. Comparing devotional poetry which women and men compose and recite in performative settings, Torab notes that women use simpler language, tend to write verse with a more personal and emotive tone than that of men, and commonly use an informal way of addressing sacred personalities. Their poems, which range from gentle pleading supplications to 'loving, respectful, praising, hyperbolic ... poems, often with cosmic imagery', reflects the close personal relationship which many women have with key members of the Prophet's family:

The poems also revealed the women's intimacy and tender emotions toward the Holy Beings ... The women referred to the Holy Beings as 'friends' ... considered them as part of their extended family, on whom one could rely for protection and resolution of problems, and demonstrated their allegiance (*beyat*), love and friendship (*dusti*) in countless ways. They shared the joys and sorrows of the Holy Beings, as with any of their own friends and relatives, ritually cursing their enemies, or more concretely, by suffering, as they imagined them to have done ... They also identified with the Holy Beings by choosing their names for their own children and showing kindness toward *seyyeds* [those descended from the line of the Prophet]. They visited their shrines and each time the *jalaseh* women met or visited a returning pilgrim, they spoke of their hopes and expectations, of wishes granted, and told and retold the emotional comfort they had derived in the vicinity of the shrines, of the relief ... they had experienced in telling the Holy Beings represented by the shrines their problems ... secrets and requests.[20]

[18] See Howarth, 262.

[19] I do not want to overstate the gender distinction here. Much of the religious behaviour of men which social scientists have described in rural settings within the Muslim world also can be couched within the framework of relationship.

[20] Torab, 317–19.

To understand Shia women's rituals, then, is to understand that for many women, ties with the family of the Prophet are part of a presently existing and mutually supportive network of relationships. For many women these are cosmic friends with whom joys and sorrows are exchanged with a degree of mutuality; where one's problems can be poured out without constraint to an assured listening presence, bringing comfort in the relief of burdens shared and the hope of needs fulfilled. One fifty year-old woman with whom I spoke, a member of the Shia diaspora who had left India for North America when she was a young bride, emphasized the give and take of the relationship with these holy personalities. It was not, she asserted, a 'one-way thing'.

I went through a phase of deeply questioning certain of our practices. I don't know what kissing the *alam* means for me ... why do I have to kiss a piece of fabric? So for several years I didn't. But then I changed. I came to believe that it stands for something. It's not the physical thing itself, it's the things I say in my head as I kiss that fabric and touch it to my eyes. My remembering, my honouring, it all takes place in my head. These are living spiritual teachers. Friends who are there just as we have physical friends. If I ask my friends to come over to my house and help me prepare for a party, they help me. In the same way we can ask for help from these friends. It doesn't mean that we are taking something away from God. You can develop relationships with them, very deep. But it takes time, it depends on how much time you invest, how much you can invest.[21]

The woman speaking is a successful business person from a well respected family of educators. She describes a period in her life when she questioned the common practice of greeting or showing respect to an icon—here an *alam*—associated with a member of the family of the Prophet. This accurately conveys some of the tension which exists for believers, particularly those who are well educated, on the issue of venerating objects seen as holy. Such tension has its root in Quranic injunctions against idolatry, and in historical and contemporary challenges of certain Sunnis (reflected within Shia apologetic discourse) that veneration of anyone but Allah diminishes God's oneness (*tawhid*). We can see this concern also implied in her remark that a relationship with cosmic friends 'doesn't mean that we are taking something away from God'. In very clear terms this woman conveys her present understanding that certain gestures embody a deep respect and honouring of relationship with 'living spiritual teachers'

[21]Interview in Toronto, Canada, 6 April 2001.

who are helpful friends. As she observes, the building and maintaining of such relationships takes time. One gets to know of and, in some ways, participate in the lives of these spiritual friends through various activities. The rituals which the Shia community has evolved to remember—and often express emotions in response to—tragedies and joys in the lives of the *masumin* are part of what helps to deepen these important relationships.

Conclusions

In this paper, we have looked at two distinct sets of devotional rituals organized and performed by Shia women in Hyderabad. Both *amal* and *dastarkhan* are rituals associated with the seeking of divine intervention: *amal* being sponsored when a woman faces a challenging situation she would like to change; *dastarkhan* being held when a woman sees that her prayerful request has been answered, fulfilling her vow to repeat the ritual through which she sought help. There are similarities as well as differences between the two rituals. Both are women-only events: men's participation in *dastarkhan* being impossible by definition, while men organizing and taking part in a ritual like *amal* is conceivable, and may happen in certain settings. Both rituals offer women a chance to talk with others—human friends and holy beings—about the circumstances of their lives, particularly troubling situations they seek to change. The opportunity to engage in supportive social interactions during times of crisis is directly related to reducing the mental and physiological effects of stress, and seems to be typical of how many women cope with worrying situations (Taylor 2002).[22] It is not surprising, then, that participants tend to use ritual settings as opportunities to maintain and deepen social ties.

By offering a single example of *amal* and *dastarkhan*, I was able to give sufficient detail to convey the essence of these rituals, but consequently sacrificed the possibility of giving more than a passing reference to the tremendous variety which exists in how women organize and practice them. There are variations in the recitations, poetry, prayer and stories; in the arrangement and type of ritual objects including food; in the holy being (God or individual members of the

[22]Scientist Shelley E. Taylor notes that, 'the difference between women's and men's inclination to turn to the social group in times of stress ranks with "giving birth" as among the most reliable sex differences there are' (148).

ahl al-bayt) whose powerful intervention is sought; in the length of time, degree of complexity, and numbers of women involved in an individual event. Less variable is the strong belief that how one conducts the ritual is essential to its efficacy. Although women may be aware of some of the variability in how people conduct *amal* and *dastarkhan*, most would insist that for the ritual to be effective one needs to do things in a certain prescribed manner. In other words, few would share the perspective of an academic researcher who sees variability as an interesting and noteworthy fact. For most performers it is a question of right and wrong or, in the very least, preferred versus less acceptable ways of conducting a ritual.[23]

As far as collective beliefs and values which become normative, I would suggest that in addition to well recognized fundamentals of Shia faith, a number of over-arching theological ideas also gain prominence through the rituals of *amal* and *dastarkhan*. These are listed as follows.

Powerful cosmic personalities exist and have the willingness and ability to intervene in people's lives.

There are rituals which, through sacred power, have the ability to transform situations, objects and persons; their efficacy is tied to the power of spiritual beings or sacred words, and their impact on an individual life can be independent of that person's presence at the ritual.

Blessing or grace (*barakat*) is a tangible quality gained through association with things, people or actions perceived as holy, and has the power to inhabit objects including food, the body, icons, books, etc.

In some sense the above represents a 'lowest common denominator' of normative assumptions sustained by women through the rituals we have studied. Strengthened by the collective performance of ritual, they provide a basis for people's belief in their ability to influence the events of their lives with the help of powerful supportive friends.

Does the study of women's religious experiences offer any new insights into how we understand or explain people's devotional lives? In Emile Durkheim's classic work, *The Elementary Forms of the Religious Life* (1915), the pioneering sociologist made three main points which

---

[23]Loeffler (1988: 247) makes a similar observation (although about religious beliefs generally rather than specific rituals) in his study of the religious world views of Iranian peasants.

continue to contribute to our academic understanding of religion: (1) religious rituals create strong emotional states which re-establish and cement social relationships within a community (2) such rituals give normative significance to certain collective beliefs and values, and (3) at its base, religion reflects the human division of the world into two incompatible spheres: the sacred and the profane (Durkheim 1915). Women's ritual expression as exemplified in *amal* and *dastarkhan* offers some insights which may help modify these sociological assertions. First, while rituals clearly contribute to the maintenance of social relationships, it is equally true that relationships help shape the form of ritual. In their practice of *amal* and *dastarkhan*, for example, women conduct rituals because needs arise and incidents occur (or are remembered) among the social network in which they interact. Thus social relationships are not simply an outcome of religious activities; a ritual's form, shape and meaning can be profoundly influenced by the network of relationships which organizers and participants necessarily bring with them. Second, the web of relationships associated with a particular person can sometimes include personally meaningful ties to sacred or cosmic figures. Durkheim's theories of religious practice do not adequately account for people's own subjective experiences and beliefs as they participate in rituals. As we have seen in this paper, there are devout women who see holy beings as 'living' friends or guides and who invest in maintaining these important and supportive relationships. I would argue that most of these women would not share Durkheim's neat division of the world into sacred and profane spaces. In fact, the basis of the ritualized activity which we have studied is that the sacred personality is present in a very real way within the mundane world of the believer, he or she being a sacred yet indivisible part of a woman's network of social relationships.

References

Durkheim, Emile. 1965. (1915). *The Elementary Forms of the Religious Life*, Macmillan Publishing Co., New York.

D'Souza, Diane (forthcoming). Yadgar Husayni: An All Women Shia Shrine in India, in Imtiaz Ahmed (Ed.), *Muslim Practice in India*, Oxford University Press, New Delhi.

Howrath, Toby. 2001. *The Pulpit of Tears: Shi'i Muslim Preaching in India*, Vrije Universiteit, Amsterdam.

Loeffler, Reinhold. 1988. *Islam in Practice: Religious Beliefs in a Persian Village*, State University of New York, Albany.

Miller, Jean Baker and Irene Pierce Stiver. 1997. *The Healing Connection*, Beacon Press, Boston.

Taylor, E. Shelley. 2002. *The Tending Instinct*, Times Books, New York.

T. Platts, John. 1977. *A Dictionary of Urdu Classical Hindi and English* (1884) Oriental Books Reprint Corporation, New Delhi.

Torab, Azam. 1998. '*Neighbourhoods of Piety: Gender and Ritual in South Tehran*, Ph.D. thesis submitted to the University of London, School of Oriental and African Studies, Department of Anthropology and Sociology.

The Presence
of Sufism

11

Liminality and Legality: A Contemporary Debate among the Imamshahis of Gujarat

DOMINIQUE-SILA KHAN

The main shrine at Pirana, a village located near Ahmedabad in Gujarat, registered under the 1950 Bombay Public Trust Act as 'Imam Shah Bawa Rauza', is one of the many Muslim sacred spots of South Asia that attracts devotees of various creeds. Muslims and Hindus belonging to different castes and religious traditions freely mix within the precincts of the *dargah*, particularly during the annual *urs* festival which takes place on 25 Muharram. The shrine thus functions as an open, shared space transcending communal barriers, very much like the famous Ajmer *dargah* dedicated to the Sufi saint, Muinuddin Chishti. Needless to say, the history of the shrine and the identity of the saint who is buried there is of little concern to average pilgrims, as long as they are allowed to worship there. Inside the mausoleum, their common reverence for the *pir* and the belief in his blessing and healing powers enables them to downplay their own caste and religious affiliations.

The Satpanth: A Historical Perspective

The shrine is not only a centre of Sufi and popular piety; it is also the main seat of a particular sectarian tradition referred to as Imamshahi or Satpanth, the followers of which are said to number about 9 lakh

(Khan and Moir 1999). For several years now, its former and present members have been engaged in a series of conflicts that have recently assumed a communal aspect and created an atmosphere that, according to some affiliated Sayyids, 'resembles that of Ayodhya' (petition to the Government of India, dated 20 September 1994). The interest of the Satpanthis or ex-Satpanthis in the shrine is of a totally different nature from that of people seeking non-sectarian devotion, a feature which is common in South Asia and some other countries. Non-sectarian devotion, which has a universal character should be clearly distinguished from the beliefs and practices of the Satpanthis.

The 'composite' nature of the Imamshahi tradition has been largely misunderstood by journalists and lawyers who see in its founder another Kabir: Imam Shah is portrayed as a tolerant Sufi saint of the fifteenth century who, 'fed up with Islamic rigidities', created a sect where elements drawn from various Hindu traditions were associated with Sufi Islamic beliefs and practices. In this way, he is supposed to have attracted both Muslim and Hindu followers without demanding a formal conversion from the latter.[1] The 'official' division of the Satpanthis into Hindus (who make up about 85 per cent of the sect, and of whom the Patidars constitute 75 per cent) and Muslims has been made along these lines.

Although not fully explored to this day, the historical roots of the Satpanth are far from being shrouded in mystery, in spite of the fact that many modern Satpanthis continue to ignore or even deny their origins. The Satpanth is actually an offshoot of South Asian Nizari Ismailism—itself a branch of Shiite Islam—which was also, till recently, referred to as 'Satpanth' and whose members are now mainly known as 'Agakhani Khojas' (Ivanow 1936). A common assumption among the rare scholars who have devoted a few pages or a few lines to the study of this sect is that the Imamshahi Satpanth detached itself from the 'parent body' or mainstream Nizarism at the beginning of the sixteenth century. This was the time when Muhammad Shah, the founder's son, proclaimed that his father and/or himself was the 'real' religious leader of the sect instead of the Persian Imam (Nanji 1978). However, recent research points to the fact that the split may have

[1] See for example, 'Distorting a Tradition', *Rashtriya Sahara*, May 1998, pp. 24–5, and 'The Pirana Shrine becomes a Bone of Contention', *Indian Express*, Ahmedabad, 19 April 1998.

occurred at a much later date, most probably during the late eighteenth or even the early nineteenth century.[2] Be that as it may, it can be demonstrated that until recently, there existed important links as well as sharp controversies between the followers of Imam Aga Khan and the Imamshahi Satpanthis. Some groups of Imamshahis continue to perform the same rituals (*gat-pat*) and share the same literature (*ginans*) as the 'mainstream' Agakhani Nizaris. In this way, the liminality that traditionally characterizes both the Imamshahi and the Nizari Khoja tradition has a common origin.

Liminal Identities

At this juncture, it is important to briefly analyse the causes and consequences of the phenomenon we have chosen to refer to as 'liminality'. But before doing so, we will have to briefly define the term and distinguish it from the concept of 'syncretism' which has been often indiscriminately used by colonial and post-colonial authors to describe all kinds of religious movements that appeared to them as 'hybrid' or 'ambiguous' (Oberoi 1994: 9). As reminded by many scholars, from a historical perspective, all religious movements are naturally syncretistic, and so are civilizations and cultures. On the other hand, in labelling a number of South Asian religious sects in which Hindu and Muslim elements coexist as 'syncretistic' the authors of the British census assumed the existence of 'pure' faiths and viewed these movements as 'hybrid', 'incomplete' or 'distorted' forms of religion (ibid.) that emerged, according to them, as the consequence of ignorance and superstition. Such a vision, it goes without saying, is closely connected with the notion of 'orthodoxy' and the assumption that each religion must possess a normative, 'correct' form in contradistinction to which all other beliefs are regarded as 'heterodox' or 'deviant'.

Although considerably enlarging the concept of 'syncretism' Tazim Kassam yet acknowledges its dynamic aspect in her analysis of an Ismaili text attributed to the famous fourteenth century Satpanthi Nizari missionary of Multan, Pir Shams Sabzwari, (1994: 231–2, 241). However, she still sees this devotional composition as a transitional

[2] I am grateful to Zawahir Moir who generously shared her latest findings with me regarding the history of the Imamshahi sect. We have together started an extensive research project on this tradition.

212 Lived Islam in South Asia

phenomenon and suggests that it enables two different cultures 'to make their transitions with relative ease and continuity' but that 'the existence of foreign elements demands resolution ...'. In this way, she concludes that the syncretism of some South Asian Nizari compositions 'is less an amalgam that results from a compromise reached between two different religious traditions than a conscious, clever and creative strategy to effect a smooth process of conversion' (ibid.). Similarly, although in a different context, M.I. Khan (1994: 2) essentially views the sacred literature of the Kashmiri Rishis not as an alternative form of Islam or an altogether different faith, but as a 'transition to Islam' as the title of his book indicates. For him, 'the syncretic tradition has been the necessary concomitant of the process of Islamization rather than its culmination'. Esmail (2002: 36–7) refuses to apply the term 'syncretism' to the sacred literature of South Asian Nizaris. Rejecting the idea of a conscious strategy of conversion, he asserts that, 'It is the product, rather, of an indigenous "organic" creativity ... the literature of a particular time and place, and displays the culture and conditions peculiar to that setting.'

As for the term 'liminality', first used in the domain of religion by Van Gennep and Turner as Mayaram reminds us (1997: 38), it is linked to the image of the threshold: 'Liminality is used as a shorthand for the intermediary, whether in the form of bridges, gates, doorways, bodies or social margins. These liminal or intermediary locations are points of intersection between the theological discourses' (ibid.). However, understanding that the ideas of liminality themselves may still imply a dualism, the same author rightly expresses her doubt about the relevance of this term: 'I am not sure that liminality avoids being premised upon a binary formulation ...' (ibid.); but she adds that this term is, nonetheless, preferable to that of syncretism in so far as it implies the existence of 'a line of thought that emphasizes "fuzzy" thinking as an alternative to bivalent, either/or logic' and may suggest 'a potentially anti-structural questioning of categorial identities, in this case, "Hindu" and "Muslim"' (ibid.: 37, 39).

In my forthcoming study on the formation of Hindu–Muslim religious identities in South Asia, I have used this concept of liminality in a similar sense, stressing that the image of the 'threshold' that it suggests 'need not ... be viewed only as a temporary space, a kind of limbo out of which one would eventually have to emerge to return to normality. It may be regarded as a permanent opening into a world of multiple values.' Each follower of a 'liminal' tradition should be regarded as a kind of Janus *bifrons*, the faithful custodian of a doorway who, choosing to remain in this intermediary location, thus guarantees the existence of multiple values and the free exchange of ideas in an atmosphere of mutual tolerance. However, as liminal religious identities are less and less accepted in the contemporary world where binary values dominate, the 'people of the threshold' have been forced to cross the doorway or have been walled-in, as the open space is closed and gradually replaced by a boundary wall (ibid.).

At this stage, however, I would add that syncretism and liminality should be used as conceptual tools only if one keeps in mind the fact that both these terms always reflect a particular viewpoint. This is necessarily the perspective of an outsider, whether an ordinary observer or a scholar, whose vision is influenced by the prevalent or taken-for-granted binary categories—even though he may not accept them as a universal truth; for this reason it often does not coincide with the view of the devotees themselves.

The other point I wish to make here is that, even from the same perspective, not all religious beliefs and practices that associate various Hindu and Islamic elements can be subsumed under the label 'liminal'. For instance, the 'non-sectarian' sharing of a sacred space, as described at the beginning of this article, should not be viewed—or referred to—as liminal or syncretistic. In this case, we are confronted with a plurality of identities that do not vanish through a common act of worship: they are rather 'subdued' or recede to the background while sharing a sacred space or time.

The Imamshahi Satpanthi configuration, however, can be termed 'liminal', provided one does not forget that such a categorization implies a particular perspective. A more detailed discussion of this complex issue, which is out of the scope of this paper, may be found in our forthcoming, *Crossing the Threshold*.

Let us now revert to the Imamshahis. Not all scholars agree on the reasons that encouraged the leaders and the followers of the Nizari sect to use Indic and Islamic elements in tandem in their sacred literature and rituals, so as to create what appeared to the British census officers as a 'confused set of beliefs', an 'incomplete' or 'hybrid' form of religion. However, by examining in detail the complex history and the different systems of philosophy developed by the Ismailis, one can surmise that three main factors influenced the origin of the Satpanth, the 'acculturated' Indic form of Nizarism that was referred to in Arabic as *sirat-e mustaqim*.

Firstly, it may be perceived as a carefully planned method of conversion. This should not, however, be interpreted as a kind of Machiavellian and subversive plot fomented to mislead and deceive devotees, as has been understood by some Arya Samaji ideologists at the beginning of the twentieth century (Nanji 1978, Daftary 1990, Shackle and Moir 2000, Asani 2002, Esmail 2002). During the 1920s, influenced by some of his Brahman friends and feeling suddenly ashamed of his traditions, a Satpanthi Patel known as Ram Narayan Limbani renounced his original faith to join the ranks of the Arya Samaj. Limbani was responsible for converting a good number of Patidars to this version of Hinduism. 'Contractor', as he later referred to himself, published a book where he expounded in detail on the idea of a secret conspiracy imagined by the Ismaili preachers to convert the Hindus.[3] According to him, the Nizari mission actually aimed at deceiving the local population by making them believe that they had remained Hindus while adhering to the Islamic Satpanth. Interesting for us is the fact that Contractor referred derogatorily to the Imamshahi sect as a '*kichdia panth*', a rather amusing expression which those who have analysed the phenomena of syncretism and liminality in north India will undoubtedly appreciate.

In reality, a careful study of the old Fatimid *dawa* or mission work shows that this 'strategy' of conversion had different and also deeper implications (Ivanow 1939). The *dawa* should also be viewed in a more realistic historical context when various religious traditions were competing for pre-eminence, but it was also in conformity with the universality, flexibility and tolerance that characterizes Ismaili philosophy as a whole. This leads us to the following point: going further than the Sunni tradition in accepting the message of the prophets of the past and their law as a necessary stage in the history of mankind, the Ismailis have sought to integrate to a certain extent nearly all the important religious currents of their time. In the same way as Zoroaster and his movements were taken into account by the missionaries in Persia, the various Hindu creeds were paid due attention and made to fit into what Henry Corbin calls the Ismaili 'meta-history', leading to a genuinely 'universalizing' perception of religion (Corbin 1983: 37–47). Eventually, religious dissimulation, referred to as *taqiyya*, a major feature of Shiism, was also responsible for the fact that the

---

[3]Contractor, Ram Narayan Limbani, in his *Pirana Satpanth ni pol* (Ahmedabad, 1926), was actually one of the first authors to disclose to the outer world the secret doctrines and practices of the Imamshahis.

Satpanth, whether 'mainstream' or Imamshahi could appear, according to the context, as a Sunni Sufi movement or as a Hindu tradition similar to the numerous local sectarian movements or *panths* prevalent in medieval South Asia (Daftary 1990: 566 and Passim, Nanji 1978: 68, 75). Nearly through the whole of their history in the subcontinent, the Nizaris had to resort to *taqiyya* to protect themselves from the persecution of the Sunni rulers and of their *ulema* who sought to either convert or exterminate them. Those who chose to live in the guise of 'orthodox' Sufis openly interacted with the various local *tariqas*, at times even taking formal initiation into these orders, and remained so inconspicuous that to this day many people regard some famous Ismaili Pirs as 'Sufi shaikhs of Sunni persuasion' (Asani 1983: 50, n. 21). Others were not only allowed, but encouraged by the missionaries, to maintain their original caste identity and continue outwardly with some of their former religious customs. The latter were later on referred to as 'Gupti' or 'the secret ones'. The integration of Indic and Islamic elements into the tradition made it possible for the Satpanth to survive in a hostile environment and at the same to gain many converts who came to share common beliefs expressed in various forms and idioms.

In this way, before historical, political and social circumstances came to challenge this configuration the Satpanthis, both 'mainstream' and Imamshahis, felt no need to define themselves clearly and openly as 'Hindus' or 'Muslims' and survived with various identities that they did not perceive as conflicting or contradictory.

This picture, that was first disturbed with the British census operations, changed drastically with the pressure of Islamic reformists and the activities of Hindu revivalist bodies between the later half of the nineteenth century and our days (Jones 1976 and 1981).

The arrival of the Imam Aga Khan in India, the creation of Hindu and Muslim personal law and the events linked with the Partition were other powerful factors that triggered those transformations. As liminality within Islam was less and less tolerated by Sunni and Twelver Shia organizations, gradual reforms were implemented within the Agakhani Khoja community that brought it closer to 'mainstream' Islam. Among the Imamshahi followers, the Sayyids who claimed to be the descendants of Imam Shah, along with some other converted communities, were gradually led to adopt a stricter Sunni or Twelver Shia identity. Conversely, starting with the Arya Samaj, Hindu revivalists sought to gradually 're-Hinduize' the Imamshahi Gupti communities. As long as Satpanthis who accepted this line severed all links with their sect and adhered to the Arya Samaj, the Sanatan Dharm movement, or the Swami Narayan or Ramanandi orders, the Satpanth was not threatened by communal conflict, although its individual members appeared to outsiders as having totally separate religious identities; the secrecy which surrounded the *panth* prevented them from actually seeing what was at stake.

On the other hand, at the beginning of the twentieth century, while the process of shifting identities was intensifying itself, a prominent leader of the Imamshahi mainstream community, Sayyid Ahmad Ali Khaki who represented the Jalalshahi branch of Sayyids, sought to strengthen the liminality of his tradition; although he was certainly convinced of the truth of his vision, he probably did it mainly to keep his Patidar followers who were more and more attracted into the orbit of the Arya Samaj or the Sanatan Dharm movements, and also to avoid being absorbed into the Agakhani Khoja community as its living Imam sought to reclaim his scattered disciples. Although Khaki had himself adopted an outwardly Sunni identity, he started to publish a series of pamphlets and edited a number of Imamshahi sacred texts, among which was the ritual prayer—a variant of the Nizari Khoja *du'a* to which he gave a new 'Hinduized' title: *Yagya vidhi*. The text itself, which remained largely unchanged beginning with the traditional *Bism'illah* invocation, was provided with extensive footnotes explaining the 'Hindu' meaning of Muslim terms. He was so successful in stressing the Vedic equivalents of Islamic concepts that in 1931 the Hindu Mahasabha declared that the 'Satpanth' should be cleared of any suspicion as it was undoubtedly a 'Vedic' tradition.[4]

Till the eighties, it can be said that the major conflicts that had torn the Imamshahi tradition at its very onset revolved around the issue of spiritual authority, which led to the fragmentation of the Satpanth into various sub-sects. The Imamshahi 'mainstream' (whose Sayyids were themselves divided into three branches), the Athias, Sathias and Panchias gradually built their own separate shrines at Pirana and elsewhere. At the sectarian level, the main conflict was between those who had adopted a Sunni identity and those who appeared outwardly as Twelver Shias (Khan and Moir,1999).

But the actual communal conflict started when, in the late eighties, one of the religious heads of the Imamshahis launched a movement that aimed at reforming the sect in order to integrate it fully into

[4]See 'Hindu Maha Sabha and Satpanthis', *The Times of India*, 15 August,1931: 13.

'mainstream' Hinduism. Karsan Das Kaka, the *mujavar* of the Pirana *rauza* who was the leader of the 'converted' community, undertook a series of reforms by suppressing the Islamic elements that were present in the rituals and literature, leaving only those which were not 'spurious' from this particular point of view. A large group of Guptis, in particular Patidars from Kutch, followed him (Khan, 2006).

We have yet to understand how this process evolved and even, to a certain extent, was silently accepted by the Sayyid who was Karsan's spiritual master of *murshid*, and Khaki's son and successor. First of all, it must be stressed that earlier, outward religious identities within the Satpanth were far from being as clear as it may appear from what we have said above, even from the point of view of *taqiyya* or religious dissimulation. For instance, traditionally the Kakas or heads of the Guptis had two names, a Muslim and a Hindu. Before he renounced the use of this title, Karsan Das himself was also known as 'Pir Karim'. Hindu/Indic customs were prevalent among the Sayyids who posed as Sunni or Shia Muslims. The Kakas sometimes offered prayers (namaz) in the mosque that was built at the beginning of the eighteenth century within the precincts of the *dargah* (it may be understood that they did it for *taqiyya* purpose), while the allegedly Sunni Sayyids were far from being strict in the performance of the obligatory religious duties.

Tampering with the rituals and the sacred literature of the Imamshahis was possible only, needless to say, for those who had a deep knowledge of their original traditions and who, to a certain extent, respected it. Therefore, this task was entrusted to the senior leaders of the community who actually belonged to the Patidar caste. Interestingly enough, these efforts aimed at preserving the originality of the tradition while seeking to give it an 'orthodox Hindu' appearance. This was not too difficult owing to the abundance of Indic terms and concepts that already were an integral part of the tradition (Kassam 1994) and also because, different, and often widely divergent currents have always existed within the broad denomination of 'Hinduism'. What was not possible to change—as, for instance, the shape and the structure of the shrine—was reinterpreted or explained away. The liminal character of the tradition was thus fast disappearing, creating a rift between the members who assumed different outward identities but also among those who did not accept these 'reforms' and transformations.

This paper seeks to explore some complex issues connected with religious identity and liminality by examining a number of civil suits that were filed in Gujarat between 1931 and 1998 by the Satpanthis and the Sayyids who claim to be the descendants of Imam Shah. Contrary to a common assumption, in South Asia, the liminality that historically characterizes the Ismail Nizari movements is very different from the 'composite' or 'acculturated' forms assumed by some Sunni Sufi traditions. The main difference, as I have attempted to demonstrate elsewhere, lies in the fact that the religious identity of the Sunni Sufis affiliated to various orders (*tariqas*) has not generally been questioned, even if these mystics have used concepts and images drawn from various Indic traditions such as Krishnaite *bhakti* or the Nath movement. This type of sacred literature, we will argue, cannot be termed 'liminal'. The examples of some famous Muslim saints, such as Abdul Quddus Gangohi in the sixteenth century or the eighteenth century Punjabi mystic and poet Bullhe Shah could be given here to illustrate the former phenomenon. Similarly, the devotees of the Ajmer saint, Mouinuddin Chishti, who may be classified along diverse religious, sectarian or caste lines, do not feel the need to deny that the Pir they worship belongs to the Sunni-Sufi tradition. In contradistinction to this, the personality of the Nizari preachers, for instance, usually appeared to be elusive to the non-initiated, who would not be able to define them by using the broad categories 'Hindu' or 'Muslim'. That is why the Nizari saints have been often claimed by various religious traditions. In this respect, one must add that their liminality exists only from the point of view of those who do not know the Satpanthi Nizari tradition or try to analyse it from a particular binary perspective. A specialist—or a traditional Nizari himself—could easily classify them as 'different Muslims', followers of a particular Shia tradition within Islam.

A Judicial Jigsaw

The first case that was filed in the twentieth century revolved around the administration of the shrine of Pirana and the rights of the various parties involved. Till 1931, the *dargah* and its land, which was a private property belonging to the alleged descendants of Imam Shah, was administrated by the head of the converted communities who acted as the *mujavar* (*khadim*) of a Sufi shrine and was traditionally referred to by his Persian title of Kaka. The 'ordinary' devotees who had no connection, whether past or present, with the Satpanth were not concerned by the dispute that took place during that period. In

1939, as the final result of this long case (civil suit no 168, Ahmedabad Court) the creation of a Trust was decided on: the Imam Shah Bawa Rauza Sansthan Committee, which consisted of ten members, was to administer the shrine and its lands henceforth. Later, in the fifties, it was registered by the charity commissioner according to the Bombay Public Trust Act of 1950 under category E, which is defined as 'cosmopolitan'.

The 1931 case was filed by a group of Gupti Patidars against the Kaka, Ramji Laxman (also known as Hayat) who was later supported by some Sayyids. The *mujavar* of the shrine, who was also a Patidar, was accused of misusing the funds. The plaintiffs stressed the fact that Imam Shah was the founder of a sect called Satpanth and that they were their followers, referred to as Satpanthis. They demanded the creation of a public charitable trust. The Sayyids denied that the Patidars were Satpanthis and thus, could not have held any interest in the shrine's property: they were Hindus, whereas, Imam Shah, their ancestor, was a Muslim saint. He had himself appointed the first Kaka to administer the shrine and, therefore, they were the only persons entitled to continue this tradition and to certain rights, as the institution of the Rauza had been created for their benefit. The plaintiffs replied that the Satpanthis were indeed Hindus belonging to the Pirana 'Atharva Vedi Dharma'[5] which was founded by Imam Shah. Owing to this historical circumstance, they also had certain rights.

After having heard the different parties, the court ended up by defining three different categories interested in the Pirana Rauza: the 'Gadivala Kaka' (that is to say the *mujavar* who was traditionally a Patidar by caste), the 'Sayyids' (belonging to two branches who were the descendants of Imam Shah) and the 'Satpanthis'. The Trust Committee was constituted according to this classification. It included the Kaka, three Sayyids and seven Satpanthis. The committee had the right to exclude a Satpanthi in case he ceased to follow the Satpanth, a question that was to be determined by the members of the trust. But even after this, no clear definition of the Satpanth itself was suggested by the concerned parties.

The classification and the terminology used was to have far-reaching consequences in the future. For example, there was no mention of the Satpanthis being *murids* or Guptis although they were

[5]One of the many cover names by which the *ginans*, that is to say the Nizari (mainstream and Imamshahi) Sapanthi sacred texts, were referred to was 'Athar Ved' or 'Atharva Veda', the fifth Veda regarded as the final revelation of our times.

traditionally regarded as disciples and descendants of Imam Shah according to Sufi terminology. This was by virtue of having been allowed by their Pir to continue practising some of their original customs as well as to conceal the Islamic elements of their faith for the purposes of *taqiyya*. Similarly, no remark was made on the function of the Kaka as a *mujavar* of the shrine, a term that clearly belongs to the traditional Sufi idiom. Also—and we should add characteristically enough—the Sayyids claimed that they were Muslims and the descendants of Imam Shah who was a Muslim saint, without specifying which kind of Islam he had preached. This shows clearly that at that time, the broad categories 'Muslim' and 'Hindu' had come to be regarded as monoliths and accounts for the fact that in the fifties, shortly after Independence, the Charity Commissioner could only register the shrine under the 'Cosmopolitan' category, as it was not possible to classify it as either 'Hindu' or 'Muslim'.[6]

In 1973, another civil suit was filed to demand some modifications in the administration scheme decided in 1939, and after the judgment of the court in 1975 a series of appeals were made from 1973 onward. The plaintiffs were Satpanthis and the defendants were Kaka Savji (who had succeeded to Ramji on the *gaddi* of Pirana) and some members of the Trust Committee. We will examine the appeal of 1976 in this paper.

The main interest of the appeal of 1976 lies in the fact that it is preceded by a lengthy, although somewhat confusing, description of the sect. It was argued by the Satpanthis that the fifteenth century saint Imam Shah wished to unite the Hindus and the Muslims: he believed in the four Vedas, particularly in the Atharva Veda, and had a special reverence for Nishkalanki Narayan who is the tenth incarnation of Vishnu. Muhammad Shah, Imam Shah's son, is also known as Adi

---

[6]It may not be out of place to mention here the different conclusion made in 1938 by a local district magistrate regarding the religious identity of the shrine dedicated to Laldas, a Meo saint mainly revered by Meos and by other communities of Mewat. See Lakshman Tripathi, 1945, reprinted 1992, *Shri Laldasji* (Alwar: Shri Laldas Dharm Prachar Sangh), pp. 25–6. On the basis of an earlier police report, he states: 'the above mentioned shrine belongs to the Laldasis whose faith is different from that of the Hindus and the Muslims ...'. One should also compare these cases with that of the Sikhs, but also with that of the Ahmadiyas who have officially been declared a non-Islamic sect by the Pakistan Government. Similarly, during the medieval period, Sunni theologians refused to classify the Ismailis among the Muslims. A more detailed discussion on this subject, which is unfortunately beyond the scope of this article, will be included in my next project on the Pranami tradition.

Vishnu and his mother as Adi Shakti.[7] The majority of Imam Shah's disciples are Hindus, mainly Patidars, who follow the tenets of his creed. After their death most Satpanthis are cremated but a part of their bones are kept to be later interred in a grave, whereas the Kaka is directly buried. The plaintiffs also argued that the Sayyids, being the descendants of Imam Shah had propagated the Satpanthi faith earlier, but that they cannot now be considered as Satpanthis, because when they filed the suit in 1973 they were no longer preaching nor practising the Satpanth. Further, the plaintiffs said that the Sayyids, being 'predominantly' Muslims (other adjectives such as 'essentially' and 'basically' Muslims were also used during the case), could not claim any right. They were referred to as 'pure' Muslims who did not render any assistance to the Trust, nor did they do anything for the Satpanth. Consequently, the plaintiffs requested the court to make some changes in the scheme which provided *haqs* or fees for certain religious services performed by the Sayyids. They insisted that their affiliation to the Satpanth should be made a condition for receiving these dues; therefore, the adjective 'Satpanthi' had to be added in the administration scheme before the word 'Sayyids' and the joint committee had to decide to exclude those who would, according to this, cease to be Satpanthis.

Interestingly, although the suit was filed against the Kaka as well, he himself decided to support the plaintiffs by arguing that indeed the Sayyids are not Satpanthis.

The Sayyids replied that their ancestor Imam Shah was a Muslim by birth and had always lived as a Muslim, performing namaz, *roza*, etc.; he was never a Hindu saint. His descendants are, therefore, obviously Muslims and not Satpanthis. So why should they preach the Satpanth? The Sayyids argued that they were entitled to certain rights and privileges in the shrine as the Muslim descendants of Imam Shah whose sacred mausoleum it was, and not as Satpanthis. Actually, the Sayyids stressed their Muslim identity by listing the different dues according to the tasks usually performed by them—*fatia, bismillah*, etc.—rituals that, according to them, proved their Islamic identity beyond doubt. But this was questioned by the Satpanthi Patidars who claimed that earlier, the Sayyids performed '*puja* like the

[7]These elements would be perfectly familiar to any scholar who has studied South Asian Nizarism, as they are prominent motifs of the Ginanic literature: the Imam is equated with the tenth avatar of Vishnu, Fatima with the Goddess as Shakti, etc. See Nanji (1978) and the other publications on the Satpanth mentioned in the references.

Brahmins', conducting the ceremonies of *ghat-pat* which included the use of a vessel (*kalash, ghat*) and of consecrated water.[8] Meanwhile, the plaintiffs claimed that contrary to what the Sayyids do now, they themselves never performed any Muslim rituals or participated in Islamic festivals like Muharram.

The conclusion of the court was revealing. It judged that the Sayyids indeed were not Satpanthis and never were Satpanthis. Nevertheless, they were entitled to certain rights as descendants of the saint buried at Pirana and as performers of a number of services at the *dargah*. As the Sayyids had been defined as a separate group since 1939 and not included in the Satpanthi category, the adjective Satpanthi should not, in any case, be added to the word Sayyid. As a result of this ruling, no major change in the scheme was allowed and the matter was entrusted to the district court of Ahmedabad for deciding whether some minor modifications were necessary.

As one can see, the confusion arises from the creation, in 1939, of arbitrary categories such as 'Sayyids' and 'Satpanthis', the former wishing to be defined as Muslims and the latter as Hindus. Secondly, the parties involved do not take into consideration historical facts such as the evolution of the tradition, nor the elements that explained the nature of this sectarian tradition. These facts and elements could have been easily shown by producing a certain number of documents, mainly the sacred texts of the Imamshahi Satpanthis. In 1866, in the famous Aga Khan court case in Bombay, it was ultimately the *ginan* literature of the Khojas that was instrumental in establishing the specific identity of that community and its link with the Imam Aga Khan.

In reality, both plaintiffs and defendants were concealing certain facts: the former by denying that their beliefs and practices were re-plete with Islamic elements not only pertaining to the particular Nizari Ismaili tradition but, at times, also to the Sunni or Twelver Shia ethos (as when some Kakas performed the namaz in the Pirana mosque or following the Muharram festival). In the same way, it was—and still is—the custom for some Sayyids to conduct the ceremony of *ghat-pat*, etc. It is in fact the interpretation of these customs as 'Muslim' or 'Hindu' that is fraught with error—precisely because, the judges examining the case were unable to take into consideration or acknowl-

---

[8]This is again a typically Satpanthi sacred ceremony which associates Sufi and Indic elements. A modified form of it is still practised by the Agakhani Khojas.

edge the religious phenomenon that we have defined as 'liminality'. This type of liminality would have been, actually, easily understood by examining the history of the Satpanth as a branch of Nizari Ismailism whose followers, initially endowed with 'liminal' personalities were, at that time, gradually shifting to sharply demarcated identities under the influence of various historical factors.

The Communalization of the Pirana Affair

The 1990s mark a turn in the evolution of the Satpanth and its main shrine of Pirana, which is reflected in the particular atmosphere that surrounded the court cases between 1992 and our days. To understand what prompted Kaka Karsan Das, the newly elected *mujavar* of the shrine to start a rapprochement with some Hindutva right wing organizations, one must mention briefly a number of crucial events that took place during the late seventies and the eighties. These events reflected a deep identity crisis within the Satpanthi community, and in particular among the Patidars who form about two-thirds of its followers. In Kutch, for instance, one of the traditional strongholds of the Imamshahis where entire populations of some villages were Satpanthis, an increasing number of Patidars who had been attracted into the orbit of Hindutva ideologists, abandoned their former affiliation and joined the rank of the Sanatani Hindus. They erected numerous temples to Lakshmi-Narayan that enshrined idols strictly prohibited in the Satpanthi tradition. Simultaneoulsy, others who wished to remain faithful to the Satpanth challenged some of its customs and launched what has been referred to as 'the cremation movement'. It is in this light that we should perhaps interpret the attitude of the Kaka. By 'reforming' the rituals and the literature of his sect, he sought to preserve the specificity and the separate identity of the Satpanth while asserting its intrinsic Hindu nature (Khan, 2006). In this way, he was putting an end to the sharp critiques of the exponents of Hindutva and guaranteed the survival of the Satpanth at a time when the numbers of its followers were dwindling alarmingly. This exercise was a kind of acrobatics as it was not easy to achieve the subtle balance that was necessary to preserve the distinct character of the sect while making it appear unmistakably Hindu. On the other hand, the task was made easier by the earlier writings of Ahmad Ali Khaki, as by the original liminality of the tradition. However, some

Sayyids, supported by a few Patidars who had remained faithful to the former ideals, reacted sharply. The most prominent figures among the latter was Pachan Kaka, a former rival of Karsan Das who had been eliminated from the election for the *gaddi* of Pirana, and Ravji ... who posed as a sincere protector of a traditionally 'syncretistic' Satpanth. Interestingly enough, the Gupti leaders of the Athias, a detached branch of the Imamshahis which had established its separate *dargah* and *gaddi* at Pirana supported the opponents of Karsan Das.

A series of civil suits were filed and complaints and petitions sent to the Government of Gujarat and India beginning 1992. In 1992 and 1993, at least five cases were filed by the Sayyids against Karsan Das and the reforming Patidars. In 1994, the Patidar writer, Ravji supported Sayyid Nuruddin who, with Mustafa Miya, was organizing a 'resistance movement' against the Kaka's reforms. In 1994, the Sayyids who had formed a committee referred to as 'Imamshah Sadat Committee' to defend their rights, lodged a criminal complaint with the State Home Minister of India. They alleged that the Kaka and his followers were trying to convert the *dargah* into a Hindu place of worship and therefore demanded protection. It is worth mentioning here a few of the points made in the petition. To begin with, the Sayyids argued that the *rauza* of Pirana was established for Hindu-Muslim alliance and brotherhood, and that Imam Shah had created a religion known as Satpanth whose followers were known as 'Satpanthis', while his descendants were popularly referred to as 'Sayyids'. It was pointed out that the *mujavar* of the shrine, traditionally known as 'Kaka' (which in Persian means 'servant', clearly indicating that he is subordinate to the Sayyids), had arbitrarily assumed the titles of 'Acharya' and 'Mahant'. Besides, although the *rauza* is originally a Muslim place of worship, it has been a shared space from the very beginning and Hindus and Muslims continue to visit it in equal numbers. Karsan Das was accused of having adhered to a right wing Hindutva organization and of trying to 'communalize' this sacred place. Therefore, the Sayyids demanded the protection of the Government of India, that would enable them to preserve the original tradition of the shrine, as well as their own rights and privileges.

The case filed on 13 August 1998 by the Sayyids and supported by the Patidar rival of the present *mujavar*, Pachan Kaka, gives more details about the reforms brought about by the *gaddivala* Kaka and his followers. The plaintiffs tried to demonstrate that these reforms were illegal according to the original scheme framed in 1939. We will examine two major points in this context. Firstly, the definition of the Satpanth that was proposed by the plaintiffs and secondly, the reforms that Karsan Das was accused of having initiated after his election as the *gaddivala* Kaka in 1986.

I will quote here the words used by the Sayyids (the plaintiffs) to describe the Pirana tradition: 'Pir Imam Shah established a religious denomination (order or school of thought) which became popular in the state of Gujarat as Satpanth (the correct path). Consequently, several religious right practices, observances and functions *predominantly Muslim* (italics mine) came to be established which have been customarily performed by Satpanthis for more than five centuries and which have become an integral part of their religion.' Describing the historical development of the shrine complex, the plaintiffs said that apart from the main tomb and subsidiary graves there was a building referred to as the *dholia* which was supposed to have been Imam Shah's housing quarter. The sacred complex also included a mosque and an Imambara (basically a Shia structure erected to enshrine the *taziyas* used for the Muharram festival). The Kaka was accused of having erected a huge shade over the *rauza* which prevented the passage of the *tazias* during Muharram and of having cut the electricity and water supply of the mosque. Sayyids were no longer invited to recite the *fatiha* on different occasions as they did earlier. The Kaka was said to have transformed the *dolia* into a Hindu temple by installing the images of various Hindu gods and goddesses, and had the Hindu symbol *Om* painted on a few walls inside the shrine complex; he was also charged with having tampered with the sacred literature of the sect, among others, by publishing a new version of their *dua* entitled, *Yagya vidhi* that was replacing the former book allegedly known as *Satpanth shastr ane moksh no dvar*. Finally, it was alleged that the head of the Pirana *gaddi* had renamed Muhammad Shah, Imam Shah's son and successor, as Adi Vishnu and the shrine as Prerna Pith instead of Pirana. The Sayyids, therefore, demanded that the earlier religious rites and ceremonies be restored through intervention of the court.

Karsan Das responded to these charges by filing an affidavit in December the same year. He reminded the court that the sacred complex of Pirana was registered at Ahmedabad under the Bombay Public Trust of 1950, under the number E-738. The letter 'E' referred clearly to its 'cosmopolitan' nature. He repeated that it was wrong to assert that the rituals, etc. were 'predominantly' Muslim as the

Satpanthis were Hindus, following the Pirana AtharvaVedi Dharma. However, he insisted that they did not install real tri-dimensional images for worship, the pictures painted on the walls being mere decorations. He demanded that a clear definition of the Satpanth should eventually be included in the administration scheme initially framed in 1939. Further, he declared that the mosque, the Muslim graveyard near it and the *imambara* did not belong to the Trust and had never been registered as a part of the *rauza* complex; the Trust being cosmopolitan had nothing to do with a Sunni mosque and a Shia shrine.

He also mentioned the fact that within the precincts of the Pirana shrine there existed other structures that were managed by different trusts, such as the Nurshahi Momin Jamat Trust which administrated the tomb of one Nur Shah. Finally, to prove that the term *yagya* was not an innovation, he produced the older version published by Sayyid Ahmed Ali Khaki. That version—which had been banned together with the parallel publication of another Sayyid named Kassimali, mentioned by the plaintiffs, but had the advantage of bearing the same title—clearly revealed the 'syncretistic' nature of the *panth* that the accused Kaka was now trying to emphasize: Imam Shah was a great Sufi who had shown the equivalence of the famous utterance of Al Hallaj, the ninth century Mulsim mystic, with the Hindu *Om*— both pointing to the fundamental unity of the human soul with the Divine. To conclude, Karsan Das argued that since matters of faith were essentially subjective, they could not be discussed in court and that the use of adjectives such as 'Muslim' or 'Islamic' was baseless owing to the cosmopolitan nature of the Trust. Consequently, no illegal change had been introduced into the shrine complex nor in its rituals and ceremonies.

One of the remarks made by the charity commissioner with reference to this case was that the shrine, still known as 'Bawa Imam Shah Rauza', should be registered under the Muslim Waqf Board.

The Law and the Lords

We will now look at the arguments produced in court by the rival parties with historical documents and the recent field inquiries, which include our visits to the shrine and the analysis of the existing Satpanthi literature, new and old.

As has been stated earlier, the confusion that arises from the above mentioned court cases results from the failure to acknowledge the complex historical reality of the Satpanth and to examine in detail the various versions of its sacred literature. On the other hand, this failure itself results from the legal definition of religious identities within the secular State of India—a definition that is the product of a long process initially started by the colonial power more than one hundred years ago.

While it can be proved that initially, the Imamshahi Satpanth was an offshoot of Nizari Ismailis, itself an undoubtedly Muslim tradition, it is not difficult to show that this branch of Islam took a distinctive character in the subcontinent, that gave it—from a particular perspective—a 'syncretistic' (in this case, we would rather say 'liminal') appearance, but also made it distinctive as 'heterodox' to other dominant Muslim groups. One should also mention the fact that, for *taqiyya* purpose, a mosque and then an *imambara* were later erected near the *rauza*. On the other hand, the activities of some Sufi orders (such as the Suhrawardi *tariqa*), later completed by the mission conducted by the Tabliqi Jamat, convinced many Sayyids to come closer to Sunni Islam, while Shia organizations, including more recently the Jaffri Federation, sought to convert the Satpanthis to the Ithna Ashari religion. This resulted in a complex setting that can be summed up as follows: some descendants of Imam Shah assumed a full-fledged Sunni or Twelver Shia identity, that is to say they ceased to practice the Satpanthi rituals, although they did not discontinue to visit the *dargah* which was still regarded as a sacred place and to claim certain rights. Others adopted a Sunni or Ithna Ashari identity only partially or outwardly while continuing earlier practices. This latter attitude is, in fact, the continuation of the customary Shia Ismaili *taqiyya*—the religious dissimulation that has been practised by these types of sects for centuries. As for the allegedly Hindu Satpanthis, they are related to the so-called Gupti phenomenon which is a typical feature of the history of Nizarism in South Asia. Therefore, in one sense, one can say that the allegations of both the plaintiffs and the defendants are at once both right and wrong. For instance, while retaining his Ismaili affiliation the Imam was, from the very beginning, considered to be a manifestation of Vishnu and often referred to in the Ginanic literature—whether of the Khojas or of the Imamshahis—as Narayan and Nishkalanki *avatar*. Even the Om symbol was given a dual meaning and was printed on the cover of the Satpanthi books in a form that made it simultaneously appear as the Hindu sacred syllable and as the name Ali when read from right to left. The *murtis* 'installed' in the *dolia* were only wall paintings and not three-dimensional statues, so the accusation of image worship could not hold good.

If on one hand some Sayyids had totally detached themselves from the Satpanth, insisting only on preserving their hereditary rights, others, supported by rival Patidars, started a reactionary movement that was not only reflected in the court cases but also in their activities. While Karsan Das was revising the sacred Satpanthi literature by removing its Islamic elements—an exercise that had its interesting counterpart in the efforts made by the Agakhani Khojas to 're-Islamize' the *ginans* by removing the Hindu elements—his opponents who had remained faithful to the Satpanth started to publish counter-literature. It did not only mean reverting to the old versions of some texts that had been banned by the *gaddivala* Kaka, but also introducing additional elements that could strengthen their viewpoint. However, the judicial tangle had its roots in the colonial power that ultimately opted for clear-cut categories that were later introduced into the Constitution and personal law in Independent India.

In order to understand the complexity of the issue at this juncture, it is necessary to refer to the Aga Khan court cases of the late 1860s that resulted in a definition of the Nizari Khoja community. Masselos (1984) had written on this subject with great clarity, but more recently Shodhan (1999) has given a new dimension to the problem by analysing its relationship with the colonial judiciary system and the consequences it was to have for religious identities in general. A few passages of her article merit full citation. First of all she recalls that initially, different systems were followed by the courts of different regions administered by the Crown. So in the Bombay Presidency, customary law was followed. For example, Justice Conch in 1867 ruled that, 'the law by which the Khojas are governed is not properly speaking Hindu law, but that law modified by their own familiar customs.' This situation continued till the passing of the Shariat Act in 1937. According to it, a codified Muslim law should be made applicable to all Muslims equally: 'This application of a uniform Anglo-Mohammadan Shariat or text-based law was another process in the Indian judicial system which discredited a dispersed and decentralized dispute resolution by local polities ....'

The author shows that when the Bengal model—which favoured the division into uniform blocs, was later adopted, the court gave an authoritative view on what the Khoja religion was on the basis of colonial texts on Islam. Besides, 'the case was entered under the charitable jurisdiction of the court. Thus the properties were seen as trusts endowed with a charitable purpose. The law held that such charitable properties were to be used by those who adhered to the original religion for which the trust was endowed.' Therefore, at a time when the origin and nature of the Nizari Khoja religion was totally unknown in the subcontinent, the court had to discover what were the distinctive beliefs of these people.

The case can be profitably compared to that of the Imamshahis. The 1866 civil suits of the Khojas led to a situation that was very similar and full of paradoxes that, more than once, provoked the laughter of the judges and others who were present in court. For instance, a Khoja witness declared that his religion was Shia, then said that he was Sunni. Similarly, another Nizari, speaking of the sacred texts of his sect, declared that it was neither a Shia nor a Sunni book but simply a good book. As Shodhan reminds us, the decision of the court made many people castigate the Khojas as 'incomplete Muslims', 'partially Hindus' and 'syncretists'. In her conclusion, the author stresses that determining only the acceptable practices amounted to 'freezing' the communities: the individual is supposed to hold a faith that is fixed and unchanging, which 'removes the possibility of recognizing the historicity of actual practices and dissent from within'. These lengthy quotations were necessary for the understanding of the issue raised in this paper, as Shodhan's deep analysis throws considerable light on the subject. The rest is well known: the artificial creation of two uniform blocs referred to as 'Hindus' and 'Muslims' and the sharp division established between them in the Article 25(2) of the Indian Constitution, that must serve as a model in all matters pertaining to personal law.

The Future of Liminal Religious Movements

One would like to ask if there was any chance for communities or sects to retain their liminal character in the present context, where the division into monolithic religious blocs is supported by the legal system?

A remarkable case should be mentioned here—the example of a section of the Imamshahi 'Hindu' *murids*. Having recently declared their allegiance to the Aga Khan, these Imamshahi Hindu *murids* have joined the Ismaili Nizari mainstream (which has itself reformed considerably to come closer to the Sunni mainstream) but continue with their earlier Gupti customs. They have been permitted by the Imam to worship in separate *jamats* and when asked about their identity, generally reply: 'We are both Hindus and Muslims—Hindus by custom and Muslims by religion.'[9]

The example of the Imamshahis and of some other groups that originated from the Nizari Ismaili religion points to the fact that the liminal character of a movement does not necessarily mean an unknown or 'mixed' origin. A tradition may be originally Muslim and its adherents continue to be seen as liminal irrespective of whether they deny their origin or not.

As far as the other Imamshahis are concerned, we can mention the partial success obtained by some of their sub-branches, such as the Athias and the Panchias: to avoid the criticisms and attacks from the Hindutva right wing, they have extensively resorted to the old custom of *taqiyya*. For example, the Athias have published a few booklets in the pure 'Hindu style' meant for a broader readership and built, outside the precinct of their shrine, an allegedly Hindu temple where worship is performed, so to say, 'in case of emergency'. At the same time, they keep their original liminal literature and rituals secret which they are careful not to disseminate outside the close circle of the initiated.

While the opposing Sayyids and Patels are publishing older versions of the *ginans* and a whole 'counter-literature' as a response to the revised publications directed by the *gaddivala* Kaka of Pirana, a prominent Jalalshahi Sayyid who himself practises *taqiyya,* has 'gone underground', secretly continuing to act as his *murshid* as well as the Pir of a few Guptis who refuse to follow the re-Hinduized version of the Satpanth. He also conducts for them the 'original' *ghat-pat* ceremony where the earlier version of the *dua* is recited.

Interestingly enough, the publications of the Kaka's opponents have started, for the first time, to openly refer to the historical origin of the Imamshahi Satpanth as a detached branch of the Nizari Ismailis. These Nizari Ismailis have been said to have separated owing to the fact that, from a certain period onward, they started to recognize a line of Imams that is different from the one accepted by the mainstream Agakhani Khojas. The evidence produced by them is, among others,

[9]For this valuable information, I thank Shafique Virani who has studied in depth the case of a Gupti community of Bhavnagar and generously shared with me the preliminary results of his research.

an article written in 1936 by one of the most eminent scholars of Ismailism, Valdimir Ivanow.

In this way, the long denied historical connection of the Imamshahis with the Nizari Satpanth is being once more openly acknowledged. It remains to be seen if, by referring to this distinct form of Islam which has a long history and a rich philosophical and literary heritage and at the same time also asserting their independence from the Agakhani mainstream, these groups of Imamshahis will be able to survive as the representatives of a religious movement that is characterized—according to the current binary vision—by a strong liminality.

References

Ahmad, Imtiaz. 1978. *Caste and Social Stratification among Muslims in India*, (2nd revised and enlarged edition), Manohar, Delhi.

Asani, Ali S. 1987. The Khojahs of Indo-Pakistan: The Quest for an Islamic Identity, *Journal of the Institute of Muslim Minority Affairs*, Vol. 1, pp. 31–41.

———. 1983. *Ecstasy and Enlightenment*, I.B. Tauris, London.

Corbin, Henry. 1983. *Cyclical Time and Ismaili Gnosis*, Kegan Paul International, London.

Daftary, Farhad. 1990. *The Ismailis: Their History and Doctrines*, Cambridge University Press, Cambridge, Munshiram Manoharlal, Delhi.

Esmail, Aziz. 2002. *A Scent of Sandalwood: Indo-Ismaili Religious Lyrics*, Curzon Press, Richmond.

Ivanow, Vadimir. 1939. The Organization of the Fatimid Progaganda, *Journal of the Bombay Branch of the Royal Asiatic Society* (JBBRAS), Vol. 15, pp. 1–35.

———. 1936. The Sect of Imamshah in Gujarat, *JBBRAS*, Vol. 12, pp. 19–70.

Jones, Kenneth W. 1981. Religious Identities and the Indian Census, Gerald N. Barrier (Ed.), *The Census in British India*, Manohar, Delhi.

———. 1976. *Arya Dharm: Hindu Consciousness in 19th-century Punjab*, University of California Press, Berkeley.

Kassam, Tazim R. 1994. Syncretism on the Model of the Figure-Ground: A Study of Pir Shams 'Brahma Prakasa', in Young K.K. (Ed.), *Hermeneutical Paths to the Sacred Worlds of India: Essays in Honour of Robert W. Stevenson*, Scholars Press, Atlanta, pp. 231–41.

Khan, Dominique-Sila. 1997. *Conversions and Shifting Identities: Ramdev Pir and the Ismailis in Rajasthan*, Manohar, Delhi.

———. 2006. Karsan Das—Un héros vivant: L'identité Patidar et les secte des Satpanthi au Gujarat, in V. Bouillier and C. Le Blanc (Eds),

Usage des héros: Traditions narratives et affirmations identitaires dans le monde indien. Librairie Honore Champion, Paris.

_____ and Moir, Zawahir. 1999. The Sect of Imamshah in Gujarat, *JBBRAS,* Vol. 12, pp. 19–70.

Khan, Mohammad Ishaq. 1994. *Kashmir's Transition to Islam: The Role of Muslim Rishis (Fifteenth to Eighteenth Century),* Manohar, Delhi.

Masselos, J.C. 1984. The Khojas of Bombay: The Defining of Formal Membership Criteria During the Nineteenth Century, in Imtiaz Ahmad (Ed.), pp. 97–116.

Mayaram, Shail. 1997. *Resisting Regimes: Myth, Memory and the Shaping of a Muslim Identity,* Oxford University Press, Delhi.

Moir, Zawahir. 2001. Historical and Religious Debates Amongst Indian Ismailis 1840–1920, in Offredi Mariola (Ed.), *The Banyan Tree,* Manohar, Delhi, pp. 131–53.

Nanji, Azim. 1978. *The Nizari Ismaili Tradition in the Indo-Pakistan Subcontinent,* Caravan Books, Delmar-NY.

_____. 1988. *Shari'at,* Custom and Legal Change, in Katherine P. Ewing (Ed.), *Shari'at and Ambiguity in South-Asian Islam,* OUP, Delhi.

Oberoi, Harjot. 1994. *The Construction of Religious Boundaries: Culture, Identity and Diversity in the Sikh Tradition,* OUP, Delhi.

Rattansi, Diamond. 1987. *Islamization and the Khojah Isma'ili Community in Pakistan,* unpublished thesis, Institute of Islamic Studies, McGill University, Montreal.

Shackle, Christopher and Zawahir Moir. 2000. *Ismaili Hymns from South Asia: An Introduction to the Ginans,* SOAS, 1992, reprinted by Richmond, Curzon Press, London.

Shodhan, Amrita. 1999. Legal Formulation of the Question of Community: Defining the Khoja Collective, in *Indian Social Science Review* 1 (1): 137–51.

_____. 2006. *L'usage des héros. Traditions narratives et affirmations identitaires dans le monde indien,* Librairie Honoré Champion, Paris.

12

Ritual Communication: The Case of the Sidi in Gujarat

HELENE BASU

Introduction

The western state of Gujarat in India is famous as the land of traders, industrialists and global emigrants, but it is also home to Adivasis, Indian migrant labourers and African immigrants. Gujarat is a place where different religious communities have settled side by side for centuries. High and low Hindu castes interacted on various levels of power and dominance with high and low Muslim *jamat* (kinship associations), Jain communities, Parsis and Christians. Rarely did these communities co-exist in a state of hermetical enclosure. Rather, religious pluralism manifested itself through the historical proliferation of context-bound practices that fostered communication across socio-religious boundaries.

Over the last two decades, Gujarat has not only developed into one of the most advanced industrialized Indian states, but also into a society in which Hindu nationalist ideology found its most ardent proponents (Nandy et al. 1995). Hindu nationalist discourse aims to erase plural traditions within Hinduism by inventing a unified image of a bounded Hindu universe (Bhat 2001). A similar trend towards the unification of doctrines and practices is also discernible in the context of Islamic reform movements (van der Veer 1994). Hindu nationalist and Islamic reform discourses mirror each other in their respective constructions of the 'Other', both depend on similar bureaucratic taxonomies of collective identities in terms of reified religious essences. Proponents of Hindu and Muslim fundamentalism are especially adverse to popular understandings of religion that recognize the coexistence of plural transcendent powers. Seen from this perspective, the significance of religion is not primarily tied to the declaration of a politicized identity. Rather, religiosity is manifested in a variety of symbolic systems. These may intersect at some points and differ at others but share the concern for creating moral meanings.

In this paper I explore the latter dimension of religiosity in a local context. My focus is directed at the practical side of religion, at the actions, interactions and forms of behaviour within a symbolic space shared by people of multiple religious backgrounds. More specifically, I look at alternative constructions of boundaries that follow a different logic from bureaucratic and nationalistic taxonomies. Within the context of popular Muslim religiosity expressed in Sufi saint veneration, the making and breaking of boundaries structure religious experiences. The emphasis upon permeability and situational constructedness of symbolic boundaries creates what Geertz in his definition of religion referred to as 'aura of facticity' (Geertz 1973). A sense of reality is produced by and for practitioners across religious boundaries through ritual actions. Here, the concept of rituals is used analytically in the sense of a language or medium of social communication (Douglas 1973; Tambiah 1985). Although the sphere of ritual communication is distinct from non-ritual or everyday domains, both are closely interrelated. The term 'ritualization' coined by Bell provides a useful instrument for taking into account the nature of the relationship between both spheres (Bell 1992). According to Bell, ritualization refers to culturally specific strategies of actions resulting in the proliferation of privileged distinctions between acts (ibid).

Communication through ritual and strategic ritualization lead to the making as well as the breaking of boundaries in terms of the liminal. The notion of liminality stresses movement, transformation, and in-betweenness. It is closely embedded in theories of ritual and did in fact originate in van Gennep's model of rites of passage (1908). In the sixties, Victor Turner extended the concept further to denote ritual situations that are opposed to the socially structured state. These situations that result in unstructured states were called anti-structure (1969). Liminality is a phase in a social process that oscillates between structured and unstructured states. The liminal phase is characterized by ambiguity which allows for transformation and also reflexivity. The liminal state may be marked by inversion (e.g. high–low, pure–impure) or by the transgression of boundaries (e.g. the breaking of taboos). It is transformative (creating fertility, abundance, blessings), fuses incommensurables (e.g. man–woman, god–human, living–dead), and produces ambivalent powers. Such powers are especially attributed to persons who permanently exist in a liminal state referred to as 'threshold people'. Liminal personae form the margins or interstices of social structures and in the neither here nor there of categorical systems. Examples are, itinerant faqirs, court jesters or ritual clowns. Building upon Turner's approach, Don Handelman (1981) theorized the figure of the clown in ritual as a 'symbolic type' (Handelman 1981; 1998). Being inherently defined by ambivalence and ambiguity, the ritual clown as a symbolic type embodies the boundary of ritual and thus stands for the state of liminality itself. Liminal personae such as the symbolic type of the ritual clown redefined by sharing transformative qualities: '... [they] effect a movement of ritual qualities between spaces, subjects, and communities. In doing so, they bring the tangible boons of fertility, life, *baraka*, power, into a community and remove dirt, pollution, decay away from it' (Werbner 2001: 139).

In order to address the question of ritual communication in the context of Sufi religiosity, I shall first outline the ethnographic context in which the specific cult I am dealing with here is situated. In the remaining parts of the paper, I shall present three distinct but related contexts of ritual constructions of boundaries and experiences of liminality. In the first context, a ritual identity of the Sidi faqir community is routinely established through liminal experiences in rituals. In the second context, these faqirs administer liminal experiences of other shrine supplicants. In the third context, faqirs enact a ritual Sufi hierarchy by performatively evoking the boundary of ritual, its frame and very end.

The Sufi Context

In public discourses, the category 'Muslim' is often represented as an undifferentiated, homogenous whole, seen as identical with the ideal—the *umma* as a clearly demarcated religious identity (cf. Hasan 1996:186). The social reality of Muslims, however, is shaped by considerations of status distinctions between kinship associations (*jamat*), inequalities of wealth and ritual hierarchies. The latter are particularly enacted in the field of Sufism. Sufi shrines are sites of institutionalized charisma conceptualized as *baraka* (spiritual power) and *karamat* (miraculous power). In Gujarat, networks of Sufi shrines are linked by high status and low status charismatic ritual agents who move in a religious field in which Muslims creatively deal with the tension between a sacred hierarchy and the proclaimed egalitarianism of Islam. The Sufi field is dominated by high status saints (Pir) who derive their privileged position from notions of descent and routinized charisma. Most of the well-known Sufi shrines in Gujarat are associated with a prestigious spiritual pedigree (*silsila*) of the Chishtia, Qadiria, or Rifai orders. Their shrines are controlled by lineage segments of Sayyid whose high status is based on the claim of being related to the family of the Prophet Mohammad. Living descendants of the *silsila* (spiritual pedigree) of historical Sufi saints are perceived to represent the knowledge, wisdom and specific interpretation of Islam of the original founder. The lower end of the Sufi hierarchy, by contrast, is marked by a range of liminal or threshold people—i.e. faqirs of various orders (e.g. Shah Madari, Musa Suhagi, Malang) of non-Sayyid birth. For faqirs, considerations of descent often give way to notions of individual calling and aptitudes that motivate a person to choose a specific religious path by joining a faqir order.

The faqir organization I am concerned with here has been developed by so-called Sidi people. The name 'Sidi' refers to people whose ancestors have immigrated from East Africa as slaves, seamen or traders (Basu 2000). Over time, a Sidi kinship network emerged in Gujarat which is collectively referred to as *jamat*. The social network of the *jamat* includes both ordinary Sidis and professional faqirs. Situated at the margins of the world of Sunni Muslims, Sidi faqirs administer tasks that contribute to the social regeneration of a regional social milieu at the lower end of the Muslim society. The Sidi and most of their clients belong to the class of have-nots—no money, no high status descent, and no political power.

The Sidi *jamat* numbers approximately ten thousand members most of whom live in oppressive poverty. Still, the specific Sidi cult of Sufi saint veneration enjoys great regional popularity especially amongst the poorer sections of the population. In the Sidi world, religion is understood as an important part of social life—complementing the mundane world. In this sense, religion refers primarily to actions and interactions within established social relationships.

Strategies of ritualization are closely embedded in the overall fabric of socio-economic life. Their cult abounds with liminal phenomena that have a bearing on local constructions of symbolic boundaries.

The Sidi Jamat at the Interface of Social Order and Ritual

The network of the Sidi *jamat* extends from towns in south and mainland Gujarat to Saurashtra and Kutch and also includes a few villages. In almost every town in Gujarat, at least two or three Sidi houses are crammed in between the houses of craftsmen, servants, workers and other inhabitants of urban lower class quarters and shanty towns. Mirroring regional population patterns, Sidis not only live in Muslim but more often in mixed neighbourhoods composed of lower caste Hindus, Adivasis, and Muslim workers. Most Sidi families are engaged in a continuous struggle for making ends meet. Their precarious economic situation is circumscribed by poverty, little education and lack of land or other means of production to secure a regular basis of income. People find employment as domestic servants or work on a contract basis for traders in local handicraft productions. Both men and women are employed by members from all the major religious communities (Hindu, Muslim, Jain, Parsi). In villages, some Sidi may own small plots of land while others work as day labourers. Some are self-employed—riding a rickshaw, hawking, or running a pan shop. On the whole, the Sidi's way of life requires what Jan Breman has called 'wage hunting and gathering' (1994), i.e. searching for casual work of an unskilled and variable nature in the urban sectors of trade and service. People therefore often shift residence between town and village, but only rarely do Sidi leave the state of Gujarat or the shelter of their *jamat*.

In spite of their marginal presence in terms of numbers and economic achievement, in their immediate surroundings Sidis are quite famous. Everywhere they are called *Badshah loko* (king people) which has also become a surname of some families. Sidi Badshah are highly reputed for their ability to joke and make fun as well as for commanding powers over the darker forces of the universe such as evil spirits and demons. It is these qualities that draw members of diverse social backgrounds to their cult and make them visit one of the shrines without which no Sidi settlement is complete. Indeed, a salient feature of the world of the Sidi is the presence of a shrine for an ancestor saint (*kuldada* or *kuldadi*) in every neighbourhood, however small it may be. Varying in size, Sidi shrines provide ritual arenas both for the performative affirmation of a collective Sidi identity as well as for ritualized communication between actors across social and religious boundaries.

In the first sense, shrines are conceptualized as resting places for consecrated male and female ancestors who are said to have led the Sidis from Africa to Gujarat. At the annually held saint's day rituals (*urs*) that are organized by faqirs and attended by the members of kinship networks of the local *jamat*, the ancestor-saints are commemorated. Their journeys, supernatural powers, and emotions are enacted and spiritual bonds between the living and the dead are reaffirmed (cf. Basu 2000). The climax of Sidi *urs*-rituals consists in the 'play' (*khel*) of the ancestors with their Sidi descendants in possession dances referred to as *goma* or *dammal*. Through these practices, a Sidi habitus is inscribed in the body. The Sidi body defined by black skin and curly hair is at the same time taken as a sign of those supernatural powers that have been inherited from the ancestors and enable the living to act as intermediaries between the saints and non-Sidi believers.

Given the precarious economic situation of many Sidi families and individuals, as a last resort people can always turn to what is called 'the work of faqirs' (*faqir nu kam*). The 'work of faqirs' refers to activities performed in the name of the ancestor-saints mediating their powers. Such activities may consist of begging, singing and dancing, writing protective *tawidhs*, performing healing rituals at home or maintaining a shrine. While those who control a shrine take a comparatively privileged position amongst Sidi faqirs, no stigma is attached to begging in the name of the ancestor saints. Those Sidi who are forced to beg see themselves as different from ordinary beggars who are said to beg 'just for the stomach' (cf. Basu 1998). Ritualized begging, by contrast, is interpreted as a privileged action that erases the shame of the beggar.

In the second sense, Sidi shrines are places of holy Muslim men and women imbued with beneficial powers that purify, regenerate and heal individuals afflicted with misfortune of various sorts. Smaller shrines are usually visited by people from the neighbourhood, but the larger ones may attract a regional following. This is particularly the case at the largest shrine in South Gujarat—the conceptual centre of the cult where the principal ancestor-saints are buried. This shrine represents a nodal point of a translocal network of the Sidi *jamat* and a mixed clientele of believers referred to after the name of the eldest saint as *bavagorvale*. Until recently, the spectrum of ritual clients reflected, more or less, the same socio-religious divisions that marked the categories of people with whom Sidi interacted in everyday life too—in the past or in the present. Embedded in economic relations of dominance, Sidi men and women servants work for Parsis, Sayyid, Sunni Bohras and Memons, and also for Rajputs or Hindu and Jain shopkeepers. In the contemporary context of the cult, members of Parsi and Memon communities act as prominent patrons of Sidi ancestor-saints, while the main shrine as well as many of the smaller *dargah*s had been donated by local Rajput chiefs and kings in the past. Another mundane context of interaction consists of the urban neighbourhoods in which Sidi houses are located, Muslim or mixed, from which a large part of the less well-to-do cult adepts are drawn to the regional shrine in South Gujarat. Neighbourhood shrines serve as local satellites attracting actual and potential clients for the main shrine. Thus, besides Muslims, members of pastoralist castes such as Rabaris from Saurashtra and Kutch, low caste Hindus and Bhils (Adivasi) from South Gujarat were also drawn to the Sidi saints. The shrine in South Gujarat—which provides the main focus of this paper—may be said to have been something like a 'cosmopolitan' centre of the lower classes.

The shrine, moreover, marks a fuzzy zone in which shifts of meanings from non-ritual to ritual take place. In contrast to their dominated position at workplaces or the marginal role of Sidi families in urban neighbourhoods, the *dargah* provides a space controlled by Sidi ritual agents or faqirs. Unlike most other Sufi orders, the Sidi faqir organization is not restricted to men but includes women as well. The gendered universe of dead ancestor-saints is mirrored on a practical level by men and women faqirs. Those who are involved in the ritual organization of a shrine are referred to as *mujavar* (caretakers of a shrine). At the main *dargah* in South Gujarat, men take care of the male saint's tombs (Bava Gor, Bava Habash) whereas women look after the tomb of the equally important female saint (Mai Mishra). As in mundane contexts, Sidi men and women perform services for others. But in the context of the shrine, the meaning of service is transformed from being an expression of subordination to one of privileged access to non-mundane powers. At the shrine, hierarchical relationships of status and dominance are reversed. Superiors of the everyday world are levelled with other shrine supplicants who lose their distinctions of rich and poor, high or low when facing the saints and their intermediaries.

Sidi ritual agents act as brokers of various social conflicts and contradictions. Their capacities to mediate are closely tied to their historically constituted social marginality as former African slaves who acted as inventive *bricoleurs* by picking up bits and pieces from diverse religious discourses and weaving them into a new and creolized discourse of their own religious cult. The symbolic construction of the ancestor-saints contain references to and re-interpretations of the broken history of Sidi slaves and they reflect the process of acculturation of former Africans in Gujarat. In their images, multiple strata of identity merge: being descendents of Hazrat Bilal, the famous black companion of the Prophet Mohammad, the Sidi see themselves as firmly embedded in the wider religious community of Muslim believers. This identity, however, is further fractured by linking Sidi saints to superior Sufi orders through the idiom of spiritual discipleship (*pir–murid*). Finally, the assembly of Sidi ancestor-saints recognizes gendered notions of saintly agency. In the context of the cult, Sidi ancestor-saints evolve as hybrid symbolic figures whose veneration draws less on fusing literary traditions as in high status Sufi cults than on the creolization of ritual practices. It is the relatively undetermined, hybrid character of the saints that enables Sidi faqirs as their earthly representatives to move across and in-between the everyday and ritual, mediating non-mundane powers.

The shrine in South Gujarat accommodates the principal ancestor-saints of the Sidi *jamat*. They are represented by an elder and a younger brother and one sister. The two brothers and the sister appear as polysemic symbolic figures whose images combine contradictory moral and mental qualities. Sidi saints simultaneously guard the boundaries of the social order and protect those who transgress them; they represent Islamic piety but demand for their veneration playfulness and fun instead of praying and seriousness. They simultaneously promise the fulfilment of desire, the protection of the poor and the suffering, control over spirits and demons and the power to reveal justice. Opposing mental qualities are attributed to the brothers, while the sister is inherently ambiguous. The eldest brother is perceived as possessing a cool mind, the younger one as hot-tempered and the sister as both cool and hot tempered. While all of them are addressed as masters of spirits (*jinnat na sarkar*), the psychological qualities attributed to each saint, channel individual preferences of the believers and determine the type of rituals performed in each one's name.

Liminal Experiences and Ritual Identity in the Sidi Urs

The first instance of making and breaking of symbolic boundaries is manifested in the context of rituals (*urs*) performed for the ancestor-saints. Saint's day or *urs*-rituals held at the main shrine in South Gujarat are attended by families from all parts of Gujarat. While shrine followers from different religious communities may participate as spectators, *urs*-rituals are actively engaged with mainly by members of the Sidi *jamat* thereby confirming their collective identity in terms of kinship relationships, habitual dispositions and ritual powers. As I have dealt with Sidi *urs* rituals extensively before (1993; 1995; 1996), I shall just summarize the main points relevant for the discussion of Sidi liminal experiences here.

The rituals enacted in the name of the brother- and sister-saints celebrate their passage from life to death and their perpetual existence in the in-between of heaven and earth. The ritual course traverses three distinct phases conceptualized in analogy to heating and cooling processes. The initial phase is marked by a common meal shared by Sidi men, women and children and the ritual tuning of performers by drumming and singing in a sitting position. This is referred to as gradual 'heating' which results in the second or middle phase when participants enter a transitional or liminal zone of ritual action. Performers now leave their sitting positions and begin to dance *goma* in front of the main tomb. According to Sidi notions, *goma* manifests the 'play' (*khel*) of the ancestor-saints with their descendents. Sidi men and women become possessed by a male or female saint. This is conceptualized as a positive form of possession (*hal*) defined in opposition to malevolent spirit possession (*hajri*) that is the fate of those who come to the shrine for a cure. Possession by the ancestor-saints, by contrast, is not considered an illness but a highly empowering experience in the course of which boundaries separating life and death, body and soul, sorrow and joy are temporarily dissolved. The souls of the ancestor-saints are conceived as manifesting themselves in and through the bodies of the living Sidi who experience this state as a kind of 'joyful madness' or ecstasy described as *mast*. The main trajectory of *goma* is the generation of emotions of joy, fun and pleasure. *Mast* refers to an emotional state in which people are no longer confined by the rules of *aql*, or reason. *Aql* belongs to the mundane world governed by norms of the social order that are opposed to experiences of fun (*moj*) and pleasure (*majha*) attained by dancing *goma* in the state of ecstacy (*hal*). *Goma* sessions are characterized by creative chaos and liminality experienced collectively. No implicit or explicit script orders *goma* performances in the middle or transitional phase of Sidi *urs* rituals. Each *goma* session manifests itself as a highly spontaneous and individualized performance that is never exactly replicated at another *urs*. Thus, at this stage possession by an ancestor saint and experiences of *mast* (joyful ecstasy) are not confined to a particular ritual role or to professional faqirs. Neither are the activities of drumming or dancing. Except for the footed drum, the most sacred instrument of Sidi *goma* performances that may be touched exclusively by men, other instruments (drums of various sizes, rattles) are played by both men and women. They are used spontaneously. Some people may be drumming before they are seized by the feeling of *mast* and begin dancing, others may continue drumming the whole night, some dance without being possessed and others might neither dance nor drum but merely watch the whole spectacle. A few people always take care of those who are in such a state of 'heat' that they may be in danger of hurting themselves. Finally, the return from the heated stage of *goma* possession dancing, the 'cooling' and the end of the liminal time of *urs* is achieved by the ritual staging of the engagement ceremony of the sister saint to another local saint of the area.

Sidi *urs* rituals thus both create and dissolve boundaries performatively. By confining the dancing of *goma* to Sidi actors, a boundary between privileged Sidi ritual agents and non-Sidi cult followers is created, while social boundaries that normally structure Sidi social life, especially those pertaining to age and gender, are temporarily dissolved. Or, to put it differently, by affirming the categorical boundary between Sidi and non-Sidi Muslims and others, a ritual space is opened up in which liminal experiences are made to happen that serve to define a specific Sidi ritual identity. Collective liminal experiences reinforce the sense of belonging to the Sidi *jamat*, of sharing the same code and of attaining emotional satisfaction from shared ritual activities. Empowered by *goma* dancing, people return to their respective struggles in the everyday world to face poverty, oppression and powerful superiors, while professional ritual agents have undergone a regeneration that enables them to 'digest' and transform the sorrows of others who visit their shrines.

Sidi Ritual Agents: Brokers of Liminal Experiences of Shrine Supplicants

At the shrine, Sidi ritual agents (*mujavar*) guard the threshold that separates the sphere of power and influence of the saints from non-ritual space. Since the shrine in South Gujarat is one of the few Sidi *dargahs* that is not situated in an urban but in a rural context, the non-ritual surroundings consist in this case of jungle, i.e. the wilderness as the ultimate abode of spirits. Moreover, the ritual arena is not limited to a building but stretches over a hilly area dotted by numerous minor tombs of related Sidi saints. These mark the boundary of the arena charged with the powers of the saints. Each one of these tombs is the seat of one family of Sidi *mujavar* who live in the small village nearby. The ritualization of space is accompanied by the ritualization of time. The principal day for the veneration of saints is Thursday, *jumme rat* or the day before Friday. On Fridays, Sidi men visit the mosque and pray from the Quran while the women cook a feast. The day before, Thursday, is the most busy day of the week for men and women *mujavar*. Tombs being associated with specific family units, they also mark a hierarchy of ritual standing of Sidi ritual agents. Stationed at the tomb of the eldest brother is the ritual head of the *jamat*, the *gaddivaras* (i.e. the one who sits on the throne; elsewhere in Sufi context: *sajjadanishin*, the one who sits on the prayer carpet). He is assisted by his brothers, sons and other men and boys related to him. Not far from this tomb, the ritual heads' wife and daughters post themselves at the tomb of the sister saint. The tomb of the younger brother is situated at the far end of another hill. Here, members of another Sidi family posit themselves, along with a resident non-Sidi faqir. While these tombs mark positions associated with superior tasks of ritual mediation, many other Sidi men and women settle at the remaining tombs scattered over the landscape signifying points of entrance or exit of the ritual arena.

Being stationed literally at the threshold, Sidi ritual agents open up a non-mundane space in which ritualized behaviour allow for the accommodation of difference and experiences of liminality of shrine supplicants. Sidi discourse emphatically stresses the saints' open reception of all who seek their support. Numerous devotional songs (*quawwali*) speak of their welcoming every single person no matter what his or her caste, faith or colour of skin may be. Thursday pilgrims do not speak in one voice nor do they necessarily share the same perceptions of the Sidi saints. Muslim followers may perceive Sidi saints primarily in terms of an exemplary moral personhood of a specific Sufi path whereas Parsi believers may emphasize their mystical qualities. Hindus and Bhils may find the power Sidi saints command over spirits their most attractive feature. Different conceptualizations are accompanied by different practices. Given the diversity of the cult followers' conceptualizations, tolerance according to Sidi notions consists in respecting other people's ways of doing things. The most basic difference between Hindu and Muslim followers consists in the treatment of blessed substances that are distributed to supplicants by Sidi faqirs stationed at the tombs. Ash from a holy fire kept in the name of the eldest brother-saint and rose petals blessed by the contact with a saintly tomb are conceived as carriers of saintly qualities. Muslim followers are expected to orally consume the ash, whereas Hindus put it on their foreheads.

On the level of personal experience and motives, however, distinctions of religious backgrounds disappear. Issues of everyday life such as success in business or school, a good marriage match for son/daughter, or marital fertility are the common and most basic matters for which the protective support of Sidi saints are sought from supplicants of all communities. The same applies to existential and moral predicaments for which relief is sought at the Sidi shrine. Malevolent spirits afflict people across religious boundaries, people ready to commit a theft are not confined by their religion and adultery may occur in any community. In fact, exorcism and the revelation of truth through an ordeal are the most widely acknowledged specific tasks performed by Sidi ritual agents at this shrine. The cure of spirit possession—possession being referred to as *hajri* (presence)—consists of loosely structured ritual acts in between which may lie long stretches of time when the afflicted person is left to oneself. The ordeal to reveal the truth—called *bedi* (iron rings)—on the other hand, is a brief event composed of a series of patterned interactions between a *mujavar* and a person suspected to have committed a moral crime. It is in these contexts that Sidi faqirs act as managers of other people's liminal experiences.

Malevolent spirit possession, theft or adultery are occurrences located in individual actions that are seen as disturbing in any socio-religious community. Aggressive and respectless behaviour towards superiors such as it is often caused by spirits, or violations of property and marital claims are equally experienced as morally disruptive in Hindu, Muslim and other communities. Individuals whose behaviour is defined as the cause for a specific moral disorder are subjected to undergo ritual treatment by those who feel most affected by it, usually members of the same family or community. In these cases, chaos is located in the everyday—in contrast to being actively produced as a temporary release in the liminal phase of the *urs*-ritual. Restoring order in such contexts requires different ways of creating transitions, i.e. a liminal phase that consists of structured acts. This becomes most apparent in the ritual of the ordeal (*bedi*).

The rite performed to identify violators of the moral order is named after the instruments used in it, i.e. iron rings fixed to a rail (*bedi*). They are perceived as instruments through which the eldest brother-saint communicates his judgement on a conflict brought before him. If the rings worn around the accused persons' ankles open during the rite, his or her innocence is proved, but if they remain closed, his or her guilt is established forever. Throughout the year, at least two to three (sometimes up to ten) *bedi*-rituals are performed every Thursday for a variety of reasons. Most common are accusations of theft, adultery and witchcraft. Members of the educated middle class are usually horrified when they are confronted with this practice, while those who turn to the ordeal argue that they have more faith in the judgement of the saint than in regular courts. At modern courts, their grievances would either not be taken serious (as, for example would be the case in accusations of witchcraft) or, being 'small people', they would be at the mercy of corrupt state officials extorting money from them without really finding a solution for their case. These attitudes—that are shared by Hindus, Muslims and Bhils—may be taken to reflect the alienation of the lower classes from modern state institutions and people's resistance to their claims of universal governance. But they also manifest the need for an external authority above religious boundaries who is believed capable of delivering justice and solving conflicts internal to a family or community.

Clients for the *bedi*-ordeal usually arrive in groups consisting of the party of the accusers and one or more suspects. The majority of cases I witnessed concerned accusations of theft, witchcraft and, occasionally, adultery. Hindu and Muslim shopkeepers alike brought employees before the saint suspecting them to have stolen money from the office. Sometimes large groups of Bhils arrived, forcing their old women to undergo the *bedi*-ordeal in order to identify one of them as the witch who was supposedly responsible for the numerous deaths of babies that had recently occurred in their village. Candidates for the *bedi*-ordeal were, moreover, often women accused by their Muslim or Hindu husband of having an illicit sexual affair with another man. The ordeal reveals itself most clearly as a ritualized way of sanctioning and enforcing norms of gender hierarchies across religious boundaries. Thus, the majority of cases tried through the ordeal concerned women.

The process of the *bedi*-ritual begins with profane negotiations of the price for the ordeal. Depending on the conflict and the number of the accused, its performance costs between fifteen and fifty rupees. In order to settle the conditions of the ritual, the whole case has to be spelled out before the *mujavar* responsible for carrying out the rite. The aggrieved party tells of his loss of money or his suspicion against his wife and how he came to bring the accused to the shrine. The *mujavar* then turns to the accused person(s) listening to their version of events and their protestations of innocence. Even before coming to the shrine, a person charged with some violation can hardly refuse the suggestion to undergo the ordeal without thereby admitting his or her guilt. An innocent person, so the logic suggests, does not fear the *bedi*-ordeal. Knowing this, the *mujavar* sometimes refuses to perform the *bedi*-ordeal. For example, once a man accused his wife's mother to have stolen money from him. In order to prove his allegations and in spite her protestations, he forcefully brought her to the shrine. In this case, the *mujavar* refused to perform the ritual and instead accused the man of disrespect towards his mother-in-law by exposing her to public shame. 'These are small matters of the family', he said when sending the party back, 'and you should have given money to your needy mother-in-law. Bava Gor (name of the saint) cannot be troubled with this.'

By way of the *bedi*-ordeal, Sidi faqirs represent the authority of the saint and ritually mediate conflicts between related parties of unequal power. The resolution of the conflict lies with the structurally weaker part, i.e. the accused, who usually takes the subordinate position of employee or wife in the relationship to the dominant employer or husband. In order to restore the disturbed relationship, the weaker part has to move through a liminal phase in which he/she is stripped of all signs of his or her ordinary identity. All *bedi*-initiants have to remove their clothes and cover their bodies instead with rags. So clad they are given a cold-water bath by the *mujavar*. Then they are led to a spot a little below the main tomb where they are made to stand dripping with water and trembling before the *mujavar*. Dressed in impeccable white, the *mujavar* holds a pot filled with burning incense and speaks an oath in the name of the saint which the accused have to repeat. Only then the *mujavar* puts the iron rings around their ankles and makes them hold the rail in hand. Meanwhile, the sounds of a large drum beaten by another *mujavar* announce the most important part of the ordeal. Now the fettered suspects have to follow the hastily striding *mujavar* running through rows of excited onlookers up to the tomb. The tension reaches its climax when the *mujavar* finally declares the suspect proved guilty (rings remained closed)— or innocent (rings opened during the passage). The *bedi*-initiants are allowed to put on their clothes again and then have to face up to the results of the ordeal. If they have been declared guilty, no wailing protestations can help them—the judgement of the saint is unfailingly accepted as truth. Relieved if the ordeal showed them to be innocent, the triumph of the innocent is nonetheless subdued by the recent experience of shame—of having publicly been exposed as a person suspected of being capable of committing a crime or a moral violation.

The Sidi ritual agents tasks ends with the declaration of guilt or innocence. Possible punishments or forgiveness lie in the hands of those who had been aggrieved by the perpetrator. Each community has its own ways of dealing with persons proven to be a thief, a witch or an adultress. The Sidi's role is confined to ritually removing indeterminacies causing conflict and disorder in everyday social relationships. This is done by framing a liminal phase in which indeterminacy is ritually created in order to transform it emotionally and morally. But unlike the liminal indeterminacy produced in Sidi *goma* dancing, this form of the transitional does not inspire emotions of joy and pleasure, but fear and shame in those who experience it. The transformation persons undergo in this case concerns the affirmation of their moral character. Either they are confirmed in what they say they are—good, trustworthy people who do not steal nor violate other norms, or they are exposed as immoral liars.

Sidi Faqirs: Markers of the Boundary of the Sayyid Urs Ritual

The last context of liminality here is set in the wider Muslim/Sufi universe in Gujarat. The hierarchical interdependence of Sayyid Pir and lower level faqirs is routinely evoked during Saint's day celebrations (*urs*). Each high status shrine has not only lay followers but also a range of associated faqir orders whose representatives are invited to perform their specific faqir practices during the festival. Throughout the year, Sidi families travel to an *urs* held at a regional Sayyid shrine. By singing and dancing, Sidi and other faqirs introduce carnevalesque elements into an *urs*-celebration, whereby the focus is directed at the ultimate purpose of the event: to celebrate the liminality of the saint in his grave by evoking his transition from life to death; singing and dancing performances of faqirs mark this passage as a joyful union expressed in the symbolism of marriage. Moreover, in the *urs*-celebrations at a shrine of the Rifai in Vadodara, Sidi faqirs are accorded a ritual role as markers of the boundary of ritual, i.e. of its very end. The sequences and styles of ritual performances draw particular attention to symbolic articulations and affirmations of boundaries pertaining to descent, charisma and distinctions between high and low charismatic persons (faqirs).

The *urs*-rituals at this shrine are orchestrated by different actors. These are: Sayyid, especially the ritual head of the shrine (*sajjada nishin*), who is also the living representative of the Pir (saint), and his relatives and their special guests; Rifai faqirs; Sidi faqirs; crowds of Muslim, Hindu and other lay followers. During the three-day-ritual which is designed to celebrate the liminality of the Pir in his grave, each category of actors moves between the unmarked role of spectator and a marked role of a performer at different stages of the ritual process. Thus, the main performances of the ritual head of the shrine (*sajjada nishin*) consist in leading the procession of shrine followers around the shrine and culminate in purifying the tomb with sandalwood paste—which marks the ritual climax of the ritual process. In the procession, lay followers of different religious backgrounds, faqirs, Sayyid and members of the Rifai lineage join in without following a particular order which would manifest status distinctions. These are levelled for the moment. Similarly, when the Pir purifies the tomb, followers melt into a crowd of excited spectators.

Boundaries between actors are emphasized especially during the nightly performances of Rifai faqirs that manifest the miraculous healing powers of the saint. During the faqir performances, the ritual head of the shrine (*sajjada nishin*) becomes a privileged spectator. Seated on his throne (*gaddi*), he watches the nightlong performances of individual men piercing their bodies with swords or beating themselves with iron chains to the sounds produced by tambourines (*dafs*). At the end of each display, the performer kneels down before the Pir who blesses him by rubbing a little of his saliva on his forehead. This is done, because the healing powers of the saint are said be located in the saliva of members of his spiritual lineage (*silsila*) and transmitted especially by his living spiritual representative, the *sajjada nishin*, the ritual head of the shrine. By representing the spiritual lineage of the saint in his grave, the spiritual head also represents a specific branch of the category of the Sayyid. While he commands the power located in the saliva, neither he nor other members of his lineage are involved in the performative enactment and activation the specific power of the Pir. This is the task of the faqirs of the Rifai order who rarely are of Sayyid status. The distinction between the inherited charisma of the Sayyid-descendants of the saint and the manifestation of this charisma in the world is made visible in the performances of Rifai faqirs who pierce their bodies with swords and iron sticks without bleeding. The performances are delivered as a kind of symbolic tribute which the ritual head of the shrine (*sajjada nishin*) accepts much as a king accepts tribute from his subordinate dependents. For the rest of the spectators, the main spectacle consists in watching this ritual delivery and acceptance of spiritual tribute acknowledging the power of the Rifai. Thus, those who are the source of power by birth are distinguished by the boundary which is created in and through performance from those who are empowered by it.

Throughout the longest part of the ritual process of the Rifai *urs,* Sidi faqirs remain spectators (Basu 1996). The importance of the function which they will ultimately perform, however, is acknowledged by the fact that Sidi are the only faqirs for whom a special corner within the shrine precincts are reserved and marked as Sidi chok (Sidi corner). It is here that Sidi families rest and sleep during the three days of the *urs.* Only at the very end of the ritual do Sidi faqirs perform. In this case, their dancing and singing is interspersed with much grimacing, obscene gesturing, ridiculing respectable behaviour by hyperbolical imitation and clowning. The Sidi performance first takes place in front of the main grave and then moves on to the female spaces within the living quarters of the family of the Rifai *sajjada-nishin,* the ritual head of the shrine. The Sidi are the only faqirs who are allowed to transgress the boundary between male and female spaces which in this case corresponds to the boundary between ritual and non-ritual spheres.

In the context of the wider Muslim social universe, thus, the Sidi represent the lower end, in this case, the very end of the Muslim hierarchy. In doing this, they embody a specific symbolic type, that of the ritual clown. The meaning of this figure has been perceptively analysed by Handelman, who characterizes the clown as a boundary marker:

'... the sacred-clown type can be said to subsume a border, or boundary, within itself, which it straddles, or through which it moves, back-and-forth in a never ending pattern .... Thus, like the liminal frame, the sacred-clown-type is paradoxical: being neither wise nor foolish, being both, but never being wholly either the one or the other. As a paradoxical symbolic type, the ritual-clown evokes inconsistencies of meaning, referential ambiguities and, in a sense, inconsistencies' (1981: 330).

The internal oscillation, which is ascribed to the ritual clown can also be seen as the distinguishing feature of the Sidis' performance at the end of the *urs*. Their performance concludes the ritual, signifying the closure of ritual space and time. Sidi faqirs embody the boundary of ritual, while being situated at the lower threshold or the margins of Muslim society.

Conclusions

As I hope to have shown, Muslim religiosity of the lower classes emerges as intricately interwoven with social relationships within and across community boundaries. In this social context, multiple meanings are communicated through rituals that go beyond the mere assertion of a single, homogenic religious identity. Rather, through ritual interactions the fractured and situational nature of social identities and the accommodation of differences are revealed. Being firmly embedded within the wider field of Sufism, the Sidi cult provides a shared space for the profession of faith based on individual choice and for making experiences that transform and comment upon the everyday world.

Considering the inventive agency of marginal persons like the Sidi who create a religious counter-world by communicating with their social surroundings through rituals also lays bare the dynamic force of liminality. As should have become apparent, liminality does not only imply that symbolic boundaries are broken down, but may also denote shifts and re-structurings of boundaries by which an integrated social and moral order is perceived to operate. Oscillations between chaos and order are salient features of ritual communication. The close intertwinement of crossing, and simultaneously, defining or making boundaries thus plays a crucial role in cross-religious inter-actions. Those who administer and those who seek experiences of liminality in terms of a temporary transgression of boundaries, strive for ritual empowerment that unfolds its efficacy in the non-ritual world. Moreover, the version of Muslim religiosity advocated by the Sidi cult introduces different standards of piety that in addition to respecting the teachings of the Quran allow for the inclusion of a host of local and popular practices. Sufi–Sidi religiosity is directed primarily at subjective needs and experiences. It depends on the active participation of women ritual agents and creates a space for diverse emotional experiences ranging from pleasure, shame and the comical. These features in particular, in connection with their boundary transgressive tendencies provoke the scorn of both Islamic purists and Hindu religious nationalists. The non-permanent, situational and fluid constructions of symbolic boundaries upon which the Sidi cult is built are opposed to and therefore increasingly marginalized by essentialising notions of religious boundaries between Hindus, Muslims and other religious categories that have come to dominate the contemporary political discourse in Gujarat.

To conclude my paper, the ways in which Sidi shrine practices are affected by this discourse must be mentioned briefly. Liminal understandings of boundaries are increasingly perceived as a threat.[1] During the last decade, at the shrine in South Gujarat a growing tendency to close religious boundaries between Hindus and Muslims made itself felt. I have described the process in detail elsewhere, which in the nineties transformed this shrine into a more definite 'Islamic site'. Although Sidi ritual agents and shrine followers tried to resist these pressures, the plural character of the *dargah* clientele slowly gave way to a more homogeneous Muslim clientele. As an effect of the discourse of communalism, Muslims at all levels of society felt compelled to redefine themselves as unambiguously Muslim, which testifies to the notion of boundary as a 'line of demarcation'. Its practical effects are felt also by those at the bottom of society who had managed to subsist in religious niches that were socially removed from middle-class influence. The Sidi *dargah* provided such a niche

---

[1]While Tambiah compares the boundary crossings of a riot mob who plunders and kills the Other to 'the creator of liminal time' (Tambiah 1996: 278), I think there is a fundamental difference in the situations of liminality just described and those of violent encounters between members of different religious communities. In the former situation, people seek to make a liminal experience that restores health, personal well-being, fertility or moral order boundaries by temporarily transgressing boundaries; but one returns from such a situation to the same setting that one has left, even though personally empowered. Violent riots, by contrast, are trajectories for permanent redrawing of boundaries, mixed neighbourhoods are destroyed, people believing in the wrong deities are chased away from their houses or even killed. Thus, there is often no return for those who have been the object of attacks of a riot mob 'temporarily crossing boundaries' (278). As a consequence, the boundary fixed by riots results in further polarization.

for the temporal release of social boundaries, where both claims to hegemonic power could be turned upside down, and social norms were sanctioned. And yet, in contemporary Gujarat, boundaries are still 'at play'. Through plays of liminality, the heterogeneity of Muslim religiosity is displayed in the face of ideological pressures to uniformity.

References

Basu, Helene. 1993. The Sidi and the Cult of Bava Gor in Gujarat, *Journal of the Indian Anthropological Society* 28: 289–300.

_____. 1996. Muslimische Lachkultur in Gujarat/Indien, in Georg Elwert, Jürgen Jensen & Ivan R. Kortt (Eds), *Kulturen und Innovationen: Festschrift für Wolfgang Rudolph*. Duncker & Humblot, Berlin, 161–71.

_____. 1998. Hierarchy and Emotion: Love, Joy and Sorrow in a Cult of Black Saints in Gujarat, India, in Pnina Werbner & Helene Basu (Eds), *Embodying Charisma: Modernity, Locality and the Performance of Emotion at Sufi Shrines*. Routledge & Kegan Paul, London, 117–39.

_____. 2000. Theatre of Memory: Performances of Ritual Kinship of the African Diaspora in Sind/Pakistan, in Aparna Rao & Monika Boeck (Eds), *Culture, Creation and Procreation in South Asia*. Berghahn, Oxford, 243–70.

Bell, Catherine. 1992. *Ritual Theory and Ritual Practice*, Oxford University Press, New York.

Bhat, Chetan. 2001. *Hindu Nationalism: Origins, Ideologies and Modern Myths*. Berg, Oxford.

Breman, Jan. 1994. *Wage Hunters and Gatherers*, Oxford University Press, Delhi.

Douglas, Mary. 1973. *Natural Symbols*. Random House, New York.

Gennep, Arnold van. 1908/77. *The Rites of Passage*, Routledge, London.

Geertz, Clifford. 1973. *The Interpretation of Cultures*, Basic Books, New York.

Handelman, Don. 1981. The Ritual Clown: Attributes and Affinities, *Anthropos* 76: 321–70.

_____. 1998. *Models and Mirrors: Towards an Anthropology of Public Events*, Berghahn, Oxford.

Hasan, Mushirul. 1996. The Myth of Unity: Colonial and National Narratives, in David Ludden (Ed.), *Making India Hindu*, Oxford University Press, Delhi.

Nandy, Ashis; Shikha Trivedi; Shail Mayaram; Achyut Yagnik. 1995. *Creating a Nationality: The Ramjanmabhumi Movement and Fear of the Self*. Oxford University Press, Delhi.

Tambiah, Stanley. 1985. A Performative Approach to Ritual, in *Culture, Thought, and Social Action*, Harvard University Press, Cambridge, Mass.

_____. 1996. *Leveling Crowds: Ethnonationalist Conflicts and Collective Violence in South Asia*, Vistaar Publications, New Delhi.
Turner, Victor. 1969. *Das Ritual: Struktur und Anti-Struktur*, Campus, Frankfurt/M.
van der Veer, Peter. 1994. Syncretism, Multiculturalism and the Discourse of Tolerance, in Charles Stewart and Rosalind Shah (Eds), *Syncretism, Anti-Syncretism*, Routledge & Kegan Paul, London.
Werbner, Pnina. 2001. The Limits of Cultural Hybridity: On Ritual Monsters, Poetic Licence and Contested Postcolonial Purifications, *Journal of the Royal Anthropological Institute* (n.s.) 7: 133–52.

13

The Islamic Mystic Tradition in India: The Madari Sufi Brotherhood

UTE FALASCH

Introduction: Terms and Concepts

The Madaris are a group widely acknowledged to be a part of a shared religious tradition in India. They are street performers who do magic tricks, or walk around with monkeys, bears, or snakes. However, the tradition of the Madaris has been traced back to Badi-ud-Din Shah Madar, who was a Syrian Sufi of the fifteenth century. According to the Sufi tradition, Shah Madar came to India after travelling for many years in the Arabian Peninsula. There, he founded the Sufi brotherhood of the Madaris and settled in Makanpur, a village 60 km northeast of Kanpur. He died around 1436. His tomb, or *dargah*, is venerated by thousands of people to this very day.

While reviewing the various written sources about the Madaris, we are confronted with various terms that have been used to categorize this religious group. Crooke (1975: 397) and Gaborieau (1985: 111), for instance, use the terms, '*be-shar*' and 'unorthodox', Trimingham (1971: 97) uses the word 'syncretic', and the Mughal prince, Dara Shikoh (1900: 187) calls them *ajlaf*, a term that is indicative of the low class of the Madaris. After starting my own field work in the village of Makanpur, the centre of the brotherhood, I was confronted with a different outlook: I found Madaris who could very well be labelled orthodox, pious and learned. The problem was how to fit them within existing religious categories and concepts.

I would like to begin with a brief overview of the existing concepts to clarify their roots and the implicit meanings behind these concepts. This seems important to me, since the term 'liminal' was introduced recently as a possible term to describe groups that transgress religious borders. The question that arises is, to what extent is this connotation of the term 'liminal' based on established categories and to what degree are their implicit meanings acknowledged. In the second part of my paper, I am going to present some material that I have collected on the Madaris over the last few years. This will be followed by a discussion on select descriptive views on the Madaris. Finally, I will discuss the convenience of the above-mentioned concepts on the basis of my empirical research. As my work is still in progress, my ideas on all the discussed categories should by no means be regarded as conclusive.

The term 'liminal', according to me, has been introduced relatively recently to replace the existing categories which define groups like the Madaris by stressing a religious connotation. Theories of 'liminality' in anthropology as developed, for instance, by Victor Turner, deal with rituals, symbols and sited performances as well as the respective actors, that are used by cultures to mark a social, cultural or religious transition. They are described as a threshold, a state of 'in-between' and can neglect or question taken-for-granted hierarchies. These rituals are confined by space and time.

Because of this specific character, 'liminality' is proposed by Shail Mayaram (Beyond Ethnicity: Being Hindu and Muslim in South Asia) in this volume as a possible concept to describe a 'third space': religious communities that are 'in-between'; groups, that cross boundaries and that are part of more than one religious community. As such groups have, at least in most cases, no strong impact on the process of religious decision-making within their communities, they are considered to have a weak identity. However, if such groups can be described as neither 'black' nor 'white', as a logical consequence, there should be an opposite category of 'liminal', which is either black or white and which could be, in this sense, the respective religious 'centre' or the 'mainstream'.

The question that arises here is, how far is it possible to define a religious 'mainstream'. Gudrun Krämer (1999: 24–7), an internationally renowned German scholar of Islamic studies, states that the term 'Islam' cannot be seen as a static entity that is independent from time and space. Moreover, a divergence between theory and practice is imminent. The fundamental problem is that a consensus seems to exist only on basic principles, like the testimony of the oneness of God (*tauhid*) and the five pillars. The Qur'an and the tradition of the Prophet Mohammad are ambiguous. Islamic normativity, based on Qur'an and prophetic tradition, is seen as obligatory, but it is highly adaptable at the same time. There is no institution or community that could claim a monopoly of the right opinion. To refer to the role of consensus does not help, as it is not defined who can apply such a consensus for whom and for what length of time. Especially in modern times, there exists a considerable proportion of educated people theoretically able to provide a consensus. For this reason, however, Islam bears an enormous flexibility. Two 'remedies', necessity (*darura*) and common weal (*maslaha*), permit the adaptation and bending of the doctrine without abandoning it. This flexible character of Islam is unquestioned, but scholars still speak too often of the theory as if it was a monolithic entity. Krämer (1999: 24) sees the main reason for this in the style of writing of Muslim authors. They rarely analyse their own reflections, but speak about 'the "proper", "true", "correctly understood" Islam' instead. (Translation mine.)

I would further argue that this way of interpreting Islam, as the protagonists of Muslim reform movements introduced it, fits very well into our 'western' academic understanding of the world. Aiming to disclose the fundamental and complete features of Islamic principles, norms, and values, while searching at the same time for ways to meet the challenges of the 'modern' time, these protagonists managed to separate dogma from the sphere of magic. Their objective of unveiling a 'purified' religion on the basis of scriptural sources comes quite close to our rational conception of a 'disenchanted world'. We tend to accept judgements unquestioningly which define the hidden powers of saints, their role within the Muslim community, and their veneration as 'improper', because we are not confident about non-rational and non-causal world-views.

The term *be-shar'*, for example, is translated as behaviour not according to the *shari'a*. Mostly, groups of wandering derwishes from the time of the Delhi Sultanate are classified as such. The opposite category is *ba-shar'*—behaviour according to the *shari'a*. This term dates from 'modern' times and is seen as a 'not a wholly satisfactory term' (Digby 1984: 61). It is absent from the standard dictionaries of Urdu and Persian. It was commonly used by British authors of the colonial period to classify religious groups and practices, which were understood to have been influenced by Hindu rituals and concepts. *Be-shar'* is generally translated and used as an equivalent of 'unorthodox' or 'heterodox'. However, an elementary difference has to be pointed out: 'unorthodox/heterodox' refer in a theological way to the right belief, while *be-shar'* does not question the belief and concerns the right behaviour.

The term 'syncretic' is not clearly defined, but one could see it in the widest possible sense as a term that aims to describe religious communities who have assimilated rituals or concepts from other religious communities. 'Syncretism' is described by Peter Van der Veer (1994: 208–9) as only one of all the possible reactions resulting from a confrontation with other religious communities, and as such, is a part of the religious discourse.

Katherine Ewing (1988: 7–8) points out that during the Mughal period, religious behaviour was not judged by adherence to the *shari'a*, as this was considered an unattainable ideal. The hierarchy within the society was indicated through terms like 'proper behaviour' (*adab*), or 'high class' (*ashraf*) and 'low class' (*ajlaf*). The 'understanding of hierarchy rests on a concept of centre, with those closer to the centre perceived as morally and/or socially superior. Thus, the peasant or tribesman who professes Islam but is ignorant of even the most basic tenets is not called an infidel (*kafir*) by the leaders and more educated members of the Muslim community, but simply *be-adab*; he is a Muslim brother nonetheless' (Ewing 1988: 8).

The Muslim reform movements that began from the eighteenth century onwards in reaction to the loss of political power to non-Muslims—Hindus, Sikhs and later the British as well as the upsurge of Shi'ism aimed to purify Indian Islam from Hindu influences, which were seen as un-Islamic. The practice of the veneration of saints and the intermediary role of *pir*s especially came under attack. But this controversy can by no means be regarded as having been resolved by the establishment of consensus. For example, the reformist *ulama'* of the Barelwi school have successfully managed to defend their position on the rightness of the system of saints and *pir*s up to this very day. (See for instance Usha Sanyal 1996.)

The Madari Sufi Tradition

The biographical evidence we have about the founder of the Madari Sufi brotherhood is uncertain; sources differ about his date of birth and family background. The only detailed work from the Mughal period, the *Mir'at-i Madari* (1709: 4), sees him as a Jew who became a Sufi following his conversion to Islam. Later sources trace his genealogy to the family of the Prophet Mohammad (Mohammad Sarwar 1872: 311). It is believed that Shah Madar, as he was called, was a native of Aleppo in Syria. In his spiritual genealogy he is connected to Abu Yazid Bistami (d. 874), but he is regarded as an *uwaisi* too, which indicates a direct guidance through the spirit of the prophet (Dara Shikoh 1900: 187; Mohammad Ghauthi 1652: 37; 'Abd ur-Rahman Chishti 1709: 6).

Shah Madar came to India at a time when Delhi had been ravaged by Timur and many of its inhabitants had migrated to other places. Consequently, towns east of Delhi, like Kalpi and Jaunpur, became centres of Islamic culture and learning, as independent rulers welcomed scholars, Sufis and artisans. Shah Madar came to Kalpi during the reign of Qadir Shah along with prominent Sufis from the Chishti and Suhrawardi brotherhoods (Siddiqui 1982: 219–20). The very few pieces of contemporary information we have describe Shah Madar as a great Sufi, respected for his learning and piety. In the *malfuzat* of Shah Mina, the famous saint of Lucknow, he is called the king of saintly people. Jahangir Ashraf Simnani, with whom he travelled to Mecca, was very much impressed by his learning. It is said that Shah Madar could gather a large number of disciples around him very easily. These disciples spread the Madari way all over India. The two most prominent of these were the scholar and Sufi Qadi Mazhar, whose tomb is in Kalpi (Siddiqui 1982: 220) and Jamal ud-Din, who is buried in Hilsa near Patna.

Shah Madar had shown a keen interest in the physiological concepts of Yogis and, as a result, he incorporated to his own rituals the practice of holding one's breath. Interestingly, the inclusion of the practices of Hindu ascetics seems to have been a widely acknowledged norm during the course of the fifteenth century and we have no source evidence showing that it led to discussions about illegitimate innovations with the '*ulama*' (Siddiqui 1982: 220). The later classification of Madaris as 'heterodox' seems not to be rooted here, since other Sufis, like saints of the Chishti brotherhood, acted in the same manner and, as far as I know, Chishtis are nowhere seriously classified as 'heterodox'.

Shah Madar later went to Jaunpur where he was welcomed by the ruler, Ibrahim Sharqi. A conflict with the Qadi Shihab ud-Din Daulatabadi on an issue concerning the ritual prayer is reported, which was settled later. The saint is said to have avoided any close contacts with the ruling élite and, instead of staying at Jaunpur, he had chosen Makanpur, a remote village, as his abode. (Askari 1949: 46). However, after Shah Madar died, Ibrahim Sharqi built a tomb over his grave.

Sufi biographists and state chroniclers during the Mughal period and after provide references to Shah Madar. The saint is generally depicted as a highly pious and learned man. His extraordinary characteristics are pointed out, like his constant fasting or his remarkable beauty. It is said that he even had to veil his face to prevent people from prostrating themselves in front of him. Several authors recount the legends that are part of Shah Madar's lore ('Abd ul-Haqq Dihlawi 1891: 189; Abu'l Fazl 'Allami 1993: 412; Mohammad Ghauthi 1652: 37–8; Dara Shikoh 1900: 187–8). Dara Shikoh (1900: 188) writes that the Madariya brotherhood was, along with the Qadiriyya, one of the biggest brotherhoods in India: Shah Madar had more followers than the Chishtis and Suhrawardis put together. He also mentions that the Madaris belonged mainly to the class of *ajlaf*. The reason for the scarcity of authentic sources and references on the saint and his order may be seen in this fact, as 'the demarcation of Qadiris from Madaris on class lines helps explain why Persian texts, themselves the literary production of elite groups, focus mainly on the Qadiris, along with the Chishtis and Suhrawardis ..., while largely ignoring the Madaris' (Lawrence 1993: 406). Remarkably, the main corpus of the hagiographic literature on Shah Madar from the Mughal and British periods was written by members of other brotherhoods, like the Chishtis and Naqshbandis.

In later sources, we come across a controversy about the improper behaviour of some of the members of the brotherhood; the neglect of proper dressing is often criticized by sections of the *'ulama'*. But it becomes clear from the sources that only some of the members of the Madaris are being referred to here and that such a behaviour has never been associated with the entire brotherhood (Nadwi 1968: 43–4). The importance of the saint and his shrine was unquestioned. Two mosques have been built at the *dargah* and land endowments have been granted by various rulers (Siddiqui 1971: 17); Aurangzeb even visited it (Munshi Kazim 1868: 241). The mystic teachings of Shah Madar have had a wide dissemination and they have been incorporated at Sufi centres like Kakori, Laharpur and Salon.

Today, the Madaris are active in several areas of Gujarat, Rajasthan, Maharashtra, Madhya Pradesh, Uttar Pradesh, Bihar, Hyderabad and

Kolkata. Some of their earlier centres of influence have declined and are simply forgotten today. This is the case with Bengal, except Kolkata, where the Madaris flourished during the Mughal period. Similarly, the *dargah* of the closest successor of Madar, Jamal ud-Din in Hilsa, a village in Bihar, has suffered. The reasons for the decline are not clear.

Makanpur in Uttar Pradesh is undoubtedly the centre of the brotherhood today. Around 250 families live there, who consider themselves to be the descendants of the nephews of Shah Madar. These Madaris are *sayyids*, as they trace the genealogy of Shah Madar to the Prophet Mohammad. They also use the *nisba* 'Halabi', denoting the birthplace of the saint, the city of Aleppo in northern Syria.

The nephews of Shah Madar were his disciples as well as his legitimate successors, since he granted them permission to initiate disciples themselves. In this manner, the *pir-i muridi* relation is handed down within the Halabis even today. The *pir*s in Makanpur emphasize that they are not living saints, as they have not inherited the *karamat* of Shah Madar. Their position and honour is based on their knowledge of the hidden, esoteric world, which they gained through study and practice and through strict adherence to the *shari'a*. The Madari way propagates the practice of the silent *dhikr*, like the Naqshbandis for instance, but the most apparent feature of their *adab-i dhikr* is the combination of the silent utterances of verses of the Qur'an with alternate holding of the breath (*habs-i dam*).

Regarding the nature of social hierarchy within the Muslim community as discussed by Ewing (1988: 7–10) and Kurin (1983), norms of conduct that define the high status of the *pir* are found in Makanpur. These norms include adherence to Islamic rules of conduct, like praying, keeping the fast, acting and speaking in a proper way or moral regulations laid down for interaction with women. It was said to me on several occasions that being a good Muslim does not mean praying five times a day, but living in the spirit of Islam from the moment of waking up in the morning till sleeping at night. Another norm is the cultivation of good Urdu, something which is exceptional in the context of a village. Because of a difficult economic situation, several *pir*s joined other professions but those who follow the tradition have circles of *murid*s in various places in India.

While doing my field work in Makanpur, I received the impression that due to the large number of *pir*s who legally hold the right to teach, the brotherhood is prevented from acting in an organized manner. For the same reason, the position of the spiritual head at the shrine (*sajjade nashin*) seems to be less institutionalized. This particular feature is barely discernible in other shrines in north India.

The Madaris have developed an elaborate system of explanations for the legends and teachings concerning the biography and spiritual powers of Shah Madar by using Sufi concepts of hierarchy, stages of inner knowledge, spiritual abilities of the friends of God and the related guiding position within the Muslim community. Thus, Shah Madar is the *qutb*, the 'pole' of the saints. This is proved by the direct guidance through the spirit of the Prophet he received, by his extraordinary piety and immense knowledge of the inner and outer worlds. Signs of this high position are, for example, his extraordinarily long life that lasted for 596 years, his constant fasting, his abstainance from all worldly matters, and his exceptional beauty. In the Madari tradition he is older than Mu'in ud–Din Chishti and thus superior to him. Shah Madar is, therefore, the first Sufi who ever came to India. A proof of this is seen in several places in Ajmer, the major centre of the Chishti brotherhood, which are named after Madar.

Karamat legends are a typical feature of most of the accounts of early saints of Indian brotherhoods, but the Madari legends are characterized by a high degree of exaggeration and denial of chronology. This fact seems to be a particular criterion of the Madari hagiographic tradition as reported since the Mughal period. Nevertheless, these legends are most suitable to fulfil several tasks. They are essential for establishing the identity of the Halabis. They define and legitimize the position of the Madaris in relation to the Sufi brotherhoods of India and, finally, they are excellent tools to bind thousands of lay followers from rural and lower class backgrounds to the shrine.

The system of mystical teaching, which revolves around Shah Madar, is commonly handed down orally in the *pir-i muridi* tradition, but the basic features of the saint's life and his powers are recounted even by children in Makanpur. However, there is a scholarly tradition within the *madrasa* of Makanpur as well. After the school got a new, bigger building five years ago, there has been an increase in scholarly activity. The *madrasa* follows the tenets of the *'ulama'* of the Ahl-i Sunnat wa Jama'at. In this context, written texts about Shah Madar and his successors are collected, analysed and published by scholars. Also, I found an increased awareness of the various points of critique offered by the *'ulama'* from reform movements, of which the school of Deoband is most often mentioned. In this case, the controversy on issues like *'urs* celebrations or the role of saints as mediators are the main subjects of discussion. These critiques are completely rejected by the Madaris, who point to their established system of explanation and the important role of the *pir*, who, in turn, is connected to the prophet by the spiritual chain. Through him, the average Muslim can grasp the truth of God. The Sufi teaching is based on Quranic principles, but provides the basis for the appropriate inner attitude which is required to fulfil religious duties. The Madaris do not hesitate to accuse scholars of rival schools as infidels, because they believe these scholars are concerned only with exoteric knowledge and neglect the role of the *wali*, the friend of god, as well as inner knowledge, which are seen as major aspects of Islam.

I would argue that a reaction to 'modern' challenges within the Madari system could clearly be outlined. This reformist strand is combined with an adherence to the principles and values of the Madari Sufi tradition. Important features like the displaying of the miraculous powers of the venerated saints, is very much alive within the Madaris and it is successful, as the following example shows. In the case of the *dargah* of Sayyid Baba Madari in Kolkata, visitors as well as the shrine keepers told me of an incident that had taken place about 25 years ago. A bridge was being erected directly over the tomb of Sayyid Baba. The people at the place told the main engineer, who was said to be a German, that this was not a good idea at all, but he did not listen. The bridge broke down several times, but no one was injured. Eventually, the saint appeared to the engineer in a dream and requested him to build the bridge a little behind the tomb. The engineer complied, and the bridge was erected successfully. This miracle was used to propagate the manifestation of *baraka* of the saint, which led to an increased popularity of the place. The *pir*s of the shrine in Kolkata maintain close contact to the mother shrine in Makanpur and, in turn, are supported by the authority of the main *dargah* of Shah Madar by issuing teaching permission, as well as by the supply of written literature.

The *dargah* in Makanpur is a major religious centre in the region and its popularity has been undiminished through the centuries. Badauni writes about a visit during the reign of Akbar, Francisco Pelsaert (1925: 70) speaks about a huge crowd that gathered in Agra to march to Makanpur for the *'urs* and Mrs Meer Hassan 'Ali (1917: 372–4) gives a figure of half-a-million visitors to the shrine during this festivity.

The *dargah* is a large place with typical features like several courtyards, smaller mosques, two *musafirkhana*s and a Jama Masjid; the last of these was donated by Aurangzeb. The *dargah* is in the possession of the Halabis, the descendants of Shah Madar, who are responsible for its upkeep and all religious functions and who share the income from the shrine. They function as the owners of the *dargah* as well as the spiritual leadership of the brotherhood.

The ritual practice at the *dargah* follows a cyclical rhythm. There are monthly *dhikr* ceremonies in commemoration of the saint and, twice a year, a major *ghusl* (washing of the tomb and changing of the *cadar*s) is performed. However, the most important festival is certainly the *'urs*, which is celebrated during Jumada ul-Awwal. More than one hundred and fifty thousand pilgrims usually come to Makanpur to celebrate this festival. The *dammal* of the Malang, the wandering mendicants of the brotherhood, is, without doubt, the most remarkable ceremony during the *'urs*. During this ritual, some Malangs play a drum. Others, after citing the Surat ul-Fatiha, jump over a fire barefooted, without injuring their feet in any way. I am not certain about the origins of this ritual. The term *dammal* was explained to me as a specific dance of happiness, resembling the hopping of a young camel that sees his mother again. It is traced to Jamal ud-Din, who danced in that manner after he was reunited with his *pir* Shah Madar. Music, however, is not permitted at the shrine, because Shah Madar is said to have disliked it.

The second major festival is celebrated during *basant panchami*. The mela is held for eighteen days, but during the three main days, the *dargah* attracts many Hindu pilgrims. These pilgrims perform the *mundan* ceremony, the first cutting of the hair of a child. The whole *dargah* is full of hair of little children at this time. During the night, *dhikr* ceremonies are held, which are attended by Hindus as well as Muslims. As we can see from this example, the *dargah* offers space for rituals of the other religious community as well. However, there is no attempt, to mix the two religions. In fact, I recognized a clear awareness of the boundaries between the two. It is the comprehension of the concept of the Sufi which is important here for an understanding of this phenomenon. Since one name of God is *rabb ul-'alimin*, the lord of the universe and of all creations, the proper friend of God does not differentiate between human beings on the grounds of their religious creeds. Hindus, thus, are always welcomed as lay followers by Sufi *pir*s who besides teaching, give guidance in daily matters or use their religious knowledge for healing purposes. Actually, this characteristic is not unique to the Madari; it can be found within the *pir-i-muridi* traditions of other brotherhoods as well.

The Malangs of the Madari brotherhood are seen from within the Madari universe, as its respected members. Malangs are organized in the typical *pir-i muridi* relationship. Their spiritual genealogy is traced to Jamal ud-Din, who was one of the most prominent successors of Shah Madar and is said to have been the first Malang within the Madaris. Although some of the elder Malangs are said to have vast mystical knowledge, the group enjoys a special status within the brotherhood, not so much for its learning but for the piety of the members and their close relationship with God. The Malangs can be identified by their dark blue jackets, black turbans and long hair, which they do not cut. As they do not marry and abandon all involvement in worldly affairs, they exist in an external sphere of the community which, in turn, enables them to concentrate fully on religious practices like fasting and praying. The term *mast* or *diwan* (insane) suggests that Malangs are commanded by the order of Allah or a saint but not by their own will. Therefore, they are regarded as the true followers of the Sufi teaching as well as Shah Madar. As far as I know, it is not always a personal decision to become a Malang as parents can offer their children as students to an experienced *pir*.

Malangs are often criticized for not following the laws of the *shari'a* strictly, but this is rejected by the explanation that the *shari'a* regulates the life of the Muslim community, the relations between men and women or the community's economic matters. As Malangs are not part of this community, these rules are not applicable to them (Ewing 1984: 360).

Most of the time, Malangs lead a wandering life, but there are resting places where they frequently return to. These are normally *takyas*, centred around a shrine. Here, Malangs can function as *gaddi nashin*, the spiritual head of the shrine. During the year, they attend the *'urs* festivities of the saints of the Madari as well as other brotherhoods. The greatest festival is undoubtedly the one in Makanpur, but there are other places of importance, for instance the *dargah* of 'Abdul Ghafur in Gwalior. 'Abdul Ghafur, according to the inscription at the shrine, was a Malang of the sixteenth century. More than fifty Malangs come each year to celebrate the *'urs*, and their *dammal* is the main ceremony during the three days of celebrations. For this ceremony, lay followers display the standards of the Malangs in front of the *dargah*, while the Malangs enter the *dargah* in a procession. They perform the *dammal* seven times around the grave and proceed afterwards to the courtyard. Here, they continue the dance to the rhythm of a drum, while visitors throw coins and flour on them. Little children are passed on to them to take part in the dance, which is regarded as a particular blessing. The ceremony concludes after two hours with the procession of the Malangs trooping back to their resting place.

The Malangs have probably been inaccurately used to point a picture of the Madaris as a whole. Katherine Ewing (1984: 359) points out that, 'Many people identify Malangs in terms of the misdeeds of some of their number, labelling them criminals, thieves or—at best—beggars. The *pirs* in their condemnation of them, tend to focus on their "dirty" habits, such as drug taking and the failure to follow the *shari'a*.' Helene Basu (1995: 38) speaks of an ambivalent attitude towards them, as in the case of the Sidi *faqirs*. On the one hand a *faqir* embodies the ideal of the living saint, since he lives in poverty and is unconcerned with worldly matters. On the other, *faqirs* are often seen as useless beggars or performers of black magic.

In the case of the Madari mystical teaching the practice of taking drugs is not considered a ritual that can lead to spiritual trance, as is the case with the Qalandariyya brotherhood. Consequently, *pirs* of the brotherhood fully reject the application of drugs for spiritual purposes. Yet, they are quite aware of the fact that some of the Malangs—about 25 per cent—resort to this habit. Nonetheless, this proves that applying the 'un-Islamic behaviour' of some of the Malangs to the whole brotherhood is questionable. This is supported by the accounts from the seventeenth–nineteenth centuries, where some followers of Shah Madar are criticized for their un-Islamic habits, without discrediting in any way the teachings of the saint and the lifestyles of the majority of his followers.

In an attempt to explain this somewhat conflicting portrait of the Madaris, I would argue that Madaris in the northwest of India, especially in the Punjab, have lost their close connection to Makanpur, where the religious decision-making for the community as a whole takes place. It is possible that the tradition of the Madari street performers is rooted here. On the contrary, a Madari Sufi tradition remains active in other parts of India.

Descriptions of Madaris since the British Period

The first description we find of the Malangs is in the 'Dabistan-i Madhahib'. This major work, on the religions of India, compiled by a

Parsi dates back to the seventeenth century (Askari 1949: 47). The fact that its chronicler was a Parsi is significant for understanding the portrayal of the Malangs in this book. The Malangs are depicted here as Hindus who have given themselves Muslim names. They live in celibacy and because they have heard that *sannyasins* are stratified into classes, they pretend to be subdivided into fourteen groups. The author traces these groups by identifying four sages: Mohammad, Ali, his son Husain, and Hasan al-Basri. Further, he mentions fourteen families who, he believes, have descended from Hasan al-Basri. Among these families, he names the Taifuris, Junaidis, Suhrawardis and the Chishtis (*Shah Dabistan*, 1904: 213). In presenting these persons as imitators of Yogi traditions, the author clearly shows he is unaware of Sufi traditions and the ways in which Sufis trace their spiritual descent from the family and followers of the Prophet. He continues to describe the Madaris as wandering mendicants who go about nearly naked, with their hair entangled, drink *bhang* in excess and always keep a fire near them. They do not pray or keep the fast. These Madaris seem to consider Shah Madar to be even greater than the Prophet because Mohammad had to shout, 'Dam Madar' before he could enter the paradise (Shah 1904: 214). Compared with other sources of the same period, the 'Dabistan' can be considered as an observation of a group of *faqirs*, who lived in the Punjab and seem no longer to have much contact with the community's centre in Makanpur.

Malangs appear, however, relatively well dressed today and one tends to assume that this resulted from the impact of the religious reform movements. But earlier sources provide evidence that this might not have been the case. A *sanad* granted to the Madari *faqir*, Shah Sultan Hasan Burhana by Shah Shuja in 1659 gave several privileges to the saint and his successors concerning their travels in Bengal, Bihar and Orissa. He was permitted to move freely through the country, landlords were obliged to support him, and he was even allowed to confiscate property and land. It seems doubtful to me that such a Mughal *sanad* would have been granted to a half-naked, *bhang*-drinking beggar (Dasgupta 1992: 27–8).

Another description of Madari *faqirs* dates from the end of the eighteenth century. After 1765, the British East India Company introduced significant changes in the economy of Bengal. While relying on the feudal structure of the Mughal society, the Company resorted to increasing profits through the enhancement of land revenue and replacement of the old *zamindars* with new intermediaries. This led to a higher burden on the peasantry but had its impact on *sannyasins* and *faqir*s as well, who were partly holders of rent-free land. As a consequence, the Madari *faqir*s lost their religious endowments as well as other privileges, which had been granted to them by the above-mentioned *sanad* (Dasgupta 1992: 30–51). After a disastrous famine in 1769, most of the peasantry was left starving, but the Company did not lessen the revenue and kept its storehouses closed. The Madari *faqir*s united with the *sannyasins* under the leadership of Majnu Shah, and started an uprising against the Company. Their guerrilla resistance spread all over Bengal, eastern Bihar and parts of Nepal and lasted for 40 years. As they were well armed and very familiar with the territory, they could escape the British troops most of the time. Majnu Shah was never captured; he died in Makanpur. It is reported that the Madaris had been organized on the basis of the *pir-i muridi* relationship and were easily recognizable by their blue jackets (Dasgupta 1992; Ghosh 1930: 107–13).

Today, Madaris refer with pride to this uprising as the first struggle of the Indian people against the British and as a symbol of Hindu-Muslim unity. Nevertheless, it is seen as one of the reasons why Madaris, despite their great numbers, have been on the decline. It was explained to me that because of the uprising, the British pursued the Madaris; to escape, the community members abandoned their Madari identity and pretended to belong to another brotherhood like the Qalandariyya.

William Crooke (1975: 397–408), in his often cited *Tribes and Castes*, seems to have relied largely on the account of the 'Dabistan' for his description of the Madaris, since the similarities between the two are striking. He uses the same descriptive terms, like '*bhang* drinking' and 'half naked', and concludes that the Madaris are an imitation of Hindu sects, having no connection to the genuine Sufi brotherhoods, as Shah Madar was no disciple of any of the mentioned saints nor did he have any disciples. This is quite astonishing, since Crooke continues by giving a detailed version of the account of a shrine keeper in Makanpur on the spiritual genealogy or the *silsila*. I can explain this discrepancy only by the style in which this account is written. While reading, one gets the impression that it is told by an elderly, illiterate man, and Crooke could have assumed that the *khadim* was only talking about some superstitious legends.

The impact Crooke's description had on later works cannot be ignored. In nearly all the following reports and texts from the British period onward, whether they describe the *'urs* in Makanpur or provide some historiographical data about Shah Madar (see, for instance, Rose 1980: 43–4; Ja'far Sharif 1921: 290; Mrs Meer Hassan 'Ali 1917: 372), he is quoted when it comes to unveiling the facts about who the Madaris really are. This reception of Crooke's work continues in recent works.

Madaris are generally neglected in most works on Sufism today, or appear at random under the label 'unorthodox'/'syncretic'/ 'legendary' (see, for instance, Rizvi 1997: 318–20; Mujeeb 1969: 303). Trimingham (1971: 97) gives a short footnote stating that Madaris are more 'a syncretistic sect than an order' and Cole's (1989: 89) work on north Indian Shi'ism repeats Crooke's version. Even some of the latest works on the subject refer to the Madaris in negative terms. For instance, Claudia Liebeskind (1998: 127) wonders how the pious Sufis of Salon could incorporate the Madari way into their culture and Francis Robinson (2001: 18–19), Liebeskind's supervisor at that time, speaks of irreligious Sufis 'who got themselves up like Hindu sannyasis'.

Conclusion

I would like to conclude with an evaluation of the above-mentioned categories and their applicability in the case of the Madaris. The term *be-shar'* is problematic because Islamic normativity is by no means fixed, but depends on consensus over certain interpretations. Even if we consider its use for describing those Malangs who do not dress properly and use hashish, we are still not in a position to apply the term to the Madaris as a whole. Here, the evaluation of the Madari tradition has to be looked upon in a different manner. This is the case for the term 'unorthodox' as well. We have no source-evidence to suggest that the Madari Sufi system is not based on the main principles of Islamic belief. I would like to point here to the impact of British parameters in ethnographic reports and gazetteers which were introduced during the British colonial period. Undoubtedly, they had a tendency to 'emphasize the bizarre features of the native groups' (Lawrence 1984: 120), as well as to construct the society on implemented aspects. I would assume that a change of meaning was introduced in the pattern of representation of the Madaris. This is not to say that British ethnographers invented a classification out of a vacuum. In the Mughal sources, followers of Shah Madar have been labelled mainly as lower class (*ajlaf*) and some of the Madaris have been seen as uneducated and ignorant. But this classification refers to social parameters. In the British sources, a differentiation in religious terms took place; a 'proper' Islamic tradition was distinguished from obscure sects who, out of ignorance, freely mixed religious concepts and rituals.

Regarding the term 'syncretic', we have to state that the Madari tradition was receptive to Hindu practices in medieval times. Today, Hindus do participate in the rituals at the *dargah* of Shah Madar, and they are even considered lay followers of Madari *pirs*. But, there is no intention in either of the religious communities of fusing concepts and values. There is certainly a mutual influence, but on the other hand, since no religious culture exists in a vacuum, none of them is free from influences of other religions.

Finally, 'liminality' in the case of the Madaris is an arbitrary term. Most importantly, 'liminality' does not remove the dichotomy which is implicit in all the former categories. Shail Mayaram speaks of a 'third space' that, in my eyes, needs some elaboration. As I have tried to show, a possible opposite term to 'liminal' in this connotation is the 'centre' or 'mainstream', terms that are already hard to define for the reasons I have outlined above.

In order to explain my point of view on the concept of 'liminality' in a little more detail, I would like to widen it in terms of space, social sphere and demography. As far as the Sufi tradition of India is concerned, Madaris seem to be 'liminal', as Shah Madar had assimilated ritual practices of Hindu *sannyasins*. As far as the *dargah* in Makanpur and the other shrines of the Madaris are concerned, rituals at the shrines, especially those performed by the Malangs, provide a 'liminal' space for the experiences of spirituality to both Hindus and Muslims. On the other hand, the *pirs* of Makanpur are, due to their status as *sayyids*, at the top of the Muslim hierarchy. As one of the biggest brotherhoods in India that managed to spread its influence over large areas of north and central India, the Madari *pirs* and their status are not confined to Makanpur. Madaris have been able to mould their traditions in such a way that they are able to remain in contact with the people of rural areas while, at the same time, maintaining their form of the Islamic mystic tradition. Besides this, the Madaris were able to react to challenges inspired by the religious reform movements as well as by 'modern' society. At the same time, Makanpur has always been considered a centre of religious learning. However, Madaris continue to remain at the bottom of the

Muslim hierarchy as far as educated élites of today are concerned. Sometimes, these elites are not aware of the Madari tradition even if it is actively present in the same area. But this condition seems to be a result of well demarcated social parameters, as Madaris have always been rooted in the lower strata of society.

In that sense, 'liminality', 'heterodox', and 'syncretic', are relative in the context of time, space as well as the social sphere and they should be valued as such. The various religious groups do not remain static entities. 'Liminality' and 'centre', 'orthodox' and 'heterodox' are positions in a disputed field, which are gained and questioned in an ongoing process of debate by means of using various relations of influence and power in the society.

I would argue that to apply a concept or a category it is necessary to show in detail in which historical, sociological or religious context it had developed and the way we would like to place it in the context of space and time. Concepts are mostly the outcome of a subjective comprehension; the observer is part of a common consensus about its own identity and observes from this perspective the 'other'. One consequence of this is that conclusions are often drawn without a detailed study of the 'other' way of looking at the world; without an insight into 'other' values and concepts.

It would be more useful to do a serious study of the field and the written sources and to show the concepts, values and interests of the various groups within their contexts. In that way, we could explain why categories like *be-shar'*, 'syncretic' or 'liminal' are used, but without becoming a part of this classifying system. A value judgement, which is evident in most of the discussed classifications, could be avoided. In that manner, we could recognize so called 'liminal' groups as part of the reality of religious and social discourse and acknowledge that their impulse is not rooted in degeneration, but in legitimate forms of religion.

References

Works in Persian and Arabic

Chishti, 'Abd ur-Rahman. 1709. *Mir'at-i Madari,* 'Abd us-Salam Collection, Aligarh.
Dihlawi, 'Abd ul-Haqq. 1891. *Akhbar ul-Akhyar,* Mujtaba' i Press, Delhi.
Ghauthi, Muhammad. 1652. *Gulzar-i Abrar,* Habib Ganj Collection, Aligarh.

Kazim, Munshi Muhammad. 1868. *Alamgir-Nama,* Asiatic Society of Bengal, Kolkata.

Nadwi, 'Abd ul-Hayy. 1968. *Nuzhat ul-Khawatir,* Vol. 3, Oriental Publication Bureau, Hyderabad (1st ed. 1951).

Sarwar, Muhammad Ghulam. 1873. *Khazinat ul-Asfiya,* Nawal Kishore, Lucknow.

Shah, Mubad. (?) 1904. *Dabistan ul-Madhahib,* Nawal Kishore, Kanpur.

Shikoh, Dara. 1900. *Safinat ul-Auliya,* Nawal Kishore, Lucknow.

Works in English and French and German

'Ali, Meer Hassan. 1917. *Observations on the Mussulmauns of India,* in (Ed.) W. Crooke, *The Tribes and Castes of North-Western India,* London.

'Allami, Abu 'l-Fazl. 1993. *The A'in-i Akbari,* Vol. 3, Transl. by H.S. Jarrett, The Asiatic Society, Kolkata.

Askari, S.H. 1949. The Mausoleum of a Saint of the Madari Order of Sufis at Hilsa, Bihar, *Bengal Past and Present,* Vol. 68.

Basu, H. 1995. *Habshi Sklaven, Sidi-Fakire. Muslimische Heiligenverehrung im westlichen Indien,* Das Arabische Buch, Berlin.

Cole, J.R.I. 1989. *Roots of North Indian Shi'ism in Iran and Iraq: Religion and State in Awadh, 1722–1859,* Delhi.

Crooke, W. 1975. (1896). *The Tribes and Castes of North-Western India,* Vol. 3, New Delhi.

Dasgupta, A.K. 1992. *The Fakir and Sannyasi Uprisings,* K.K. Bagchi, Kolkata.

Digby, S. 1984. Qalandars and Related Groups: Elements of Social Deviance in the Religious Life of the Delhi Sultanate of the Thirteenth and Fourteenth Centuries, in Yohanan Friedmann (Ed.), *Islam in Asia, Vol. 1, South Asia,* The Magnes Press, Jerusalem.

Ewing, K. (Ed.) 1988. *Shari'at and Ambiguity in South Asian Islam,* Berkeley.

———. 1984. *Malangs* of the Punjab: Intoxication or Adab as the Path to God? in Barbara Daly Metcalf (Ed.), *Moral Conduct and Authority,* Berkeley.

Gaborieau, M. 1985. Les ordres mystiques dans le sous-continent indien, in Popopic and G. Veinstein (Ed.), *Les ordres mystiques dans l'Islam,* Paris.

Ghosh, J.M. 1930. *Sannyasi and Fakir Raiders in Bengal,* Bengal Secretary Book Depot, Kolkata.

Ja'far Sharif. 1921. *Qanan-i Islam,* Transl. by M.D. Herklots, Oxford University Press, London.

Krämer, G. 1999. *Gottes Staat als Republik. Reflexionen zeitgenössischer Muslime zu Islam, Menschenrechten und Demokratie.* Nomos, Baden-Baden.

Kurin, R. 1983. The Structure of Blessedness at a Muslim Shrine in Sind, *Middle Eastern Studies,* Vol. 19.

Lawrence, B.B. 1984. Early Indo-Muslim Saints and Conversion, in *Islam in Asia,* Vol. 1, South Asia, Y. Friedmann (Ed.), The Magnes Press, Jerusalem.

_____. 1993. Biography and the 17th Century Qadiriyya of North India, in A.L. Dallapiccola (Ed.), *Islam and Indian Region,* Vol. 1, Stuttgart.

Liebeskind, C. 1998. *Piety on its Knees: Three Sufi Traditions in South Asia in Modern Times,* Oxford University Press, Delhi.

Mujeeb, M. 1995. (1967). *The Indian Muslims,* Munshiram Manoharlal, Delhi.

Pelsaert, F. 1925. *Jahangir's India: The Remonstrantie of Francisco Pelsaert,* Transl. by W.H. Moreland and P. Geyl, Heffer, Cambridge.

Rizvi, S.A.A. 1997. *A History of Sufism in India,* Vol. 1, New Delhi.

Robinson, F. 2001. *The 'Ulama of Farangi Mahall and Islamic Culture in South Asia,* Permanent Black, Delhi.

Rose, H.A. 1980. (1919). *Glossary of the Tribes and Castes of the Punjab and the North-West Frontier Province,* Vol. 3, Delhi.

Sanyal, U. 1996. *Devotional Islam and Politics in British India,* Oxford University Press, Delhi.

Shah, Abd ul-Qadir ibn-i Muluk (Al-Badauni). 1973 (1899). *Muntakhabu't Tawarikh,* Vol. 2, Transl. by W.H. Lowe, Delhi.

Siddiqui, I.H. 1971. *History of Sher Shah Sur,* Aligarh.

_____. 1982. Sufis and Sufism in the Territory of Kalpi: 15th and 16th Centuries, *Studies in Islam,* Vol. 19.

Trimingham, J.S. 2000 (1971). *The Sufi Orders in Islam,* Oxford University Press, Oxford.

Van der Veer, P. 1994, Syncretism, Multiculturalism and the Discourse of Tolerance, in Charles Stuart and Rosalind Shaw (Ed.), *Syncretism/Anti-Syncretism,* London and New York.

14

Jailani: A Sufi Shrine in Sri Lanka

DENNIS B. MCGILVRAY

Introduction

I t may seem a strange topographic irony that the most famous mountain in Sri Lanka, an overwhelmingly Buddhist and Hindu island for well over two millennia, is known to the English-speaking world by a Muslim name, Adam's Peak. However, early Muslim connections with Sarandib[1] are quite well documented. At the summit of this granite pinnacle overlooking the gem district of Ratnapura is a stone impression claimed by Muslim tradition to have been created by the impact of Adam's foot as he fell to earth from the Garden of Eden. Located along a generalized Muslim pilgrimage route that stretches northward from the Arabian Sea ports of Galle and Weligama to the pinnacle of Adam's Peak lies the hermitage shrine

I am grateful to the American Institute for Sri Lankan Studies (AISLS) and the American Institute of Indian Studies (AIIS) for the grant support that made this research possible. I would also like to thank the following individuals who provided invaluable assistance during my ethnographic fieldwork in Sri Lanka and South India: Nilam Hamead and family, Razeen (Murid) Hameedh and family, M.L.M. Aboosally and family, Selvy and Chandran Thiruchandran, Omar Z. Mowlana, Dheen Mohammed, Grant McGilvray, and Kalifa Saheb of Nagoor Dargah. I have also benefited from the comments and scholarly knowledge of Chandra de Silva, K. Sivathamby, Brian Didier, Susan Schomburg, Steve Kemper, and Fred Denny.
[1]Sarandib was the common Arabic name for the island in the medieval period.

of Daftar Jailani,[2] where the Sufi saint, Sheikh Muhiyadeen Abdul Qadir Jilani (d.1166 CE, in Baghdad), renowned throughout South Asia as the founder of the Qadiriya order, is by legend said to have meditated for twelve years after paying his respects to Sri Pada, the Resplendant Foot. Despite opposition from conservative Islamic groups, Jailani today attracts large crowds of Tamil-speaking Muslim devotees to the annual kandoori festival, reflecting the surprising vitality and growth of popular Sufi devotionalism in Sri Lanka.[3] However, in an island nation where sacred geography also maps hostile ethnic boundaries and 'homelands', the growth of the shrine at Jailani has also placed the Sri Lankan Muslims in a potential geo-religious zone of conflict with hostile elements of the Sinhala Buddhist majority.

Jailani as a Muslim Place

Jailani is situated at about 70 km from Adam's Peak, but the terrain is formidable. Roads daringly engineered by British tea planters wind part of the way upward from Ratnapura, 60 km away, and Maskeliya, the most convenient base for climbing the mountain, is a four hour drive from Jailani. Even more isolating is the ethnic and religious environment of the shrine: the nearest town is Balangoda, seat of a 96 per cent Sinhalese parliamentary constituency that encompasses the estate of the Ratwatte family, one of the leading twentieth century Sinhalese Buddhist political dynasties in the island. Unlike *dargahs* located in historic urban Muslim enclaves, such as Galle or Beruwala, or village mosques in the Muslim-dominated agricultural regions of the eastern coast, the shrine at Jailani lies serenely exposed at the edge of a dramatic granite escarpment 22 km southeast of Balangoda, flanked by wet-zone forested hills and surveying Sinhala Buddhist peasant resettlement projects on the Kaltota plain below. A small Muslim community of about thirty families has grown up in the vicinity, but relations with their Sinhala neighbours have been distant and at times hostile (Spencer 1990: 38–9, 50–1). It is a wildly beautiful

[2]Daftar means an official record-book or register in Arabic. The shrine's name implies a visit recorded by Abdul Qadir Jilani.

[3]Muslims form nearly 8 per cent of the Sri Lankan population. The vast majority of these are Tamil-speaking Sunni Muslims (Sri Lankan Moors) of maritime Indo-Arab origin and who belong to the Shafi legal school. There are also small groups of Muslim Malay and Muslim Gujarati communities. For a cultural and historical overview, see McGilvray 1998.

location set midway up the Kandyan Hills, with a commanding view southward toward the coast at Hambantota; a perfect site, it is said, for meditation and mystical gnosis. Although there are some tombs of local *faqirs* and holy men at Jailani, the place is not a mortuary shrine (*dargah*) but a hermitage, a place of saintly visitation and mystical meditation.

The legends linking Jailani to the twelfth century travels (astral or otherwise) of Sheikh Muhiyadeen Abdul Qadir Jilani have been collected elsewhere (Aboosally 1975, 2002), but the plausibility of these traditions is closely linked to the historical evidence of medieval Arab and Persian pilgrimages to Adam's Peak.[4] In my fieldwork, I found it to be a common assumption among Sri Lankan Muslims that the 'logical' route for Arab and Persian pilgrims heading toward South India would be via the Maldive Islands and Sri Lanka, stopping to visit Adam's Peak along the way.[5] Although the modern Sinhalese and Tamil pilgrims who constitute the vast majority of devotees ascending the mountain each year identify it as the footprint of the Buddha or of the Hindu god, Siva, the fourteenth century Arab traveller Ibn Battuta reported that it also attracted a stream of Muslim pilgrims from the Middle East seeking contact with their primordial ancestor, Adam. Gem traders would also have been drawn to the vicinity of Adam's Peak because of its alluvial deposits of precious stones, but Ibn Battuta did encounter a party of Arab and Persian dervishes 'who had come from visiting the Foot' in the Maldive islands (Gibb 1986: 247). Battuta himself made the Adam's Peak pilgrimage soon after, en route to the South Indian city of Madurai.

The Jailani site consists of a steep forested ravine surrounded by three bald granite outcroppings to which the Muslims have given Tamil names: Kappal Malai (ship mountain), Jin Malai (djinn or spirit mountain), and Curankam Malai (cave mountain). The largest and most dramatic of the stone formations is Kappal Malai, which is said to resemble the prow of a petrified ship, and tucked at the base of the rock is an open air mosque built in 1922 that is the centre of festival activities. The overhanging monolith is also referred to as Kaiyadi

---

[4]For a compendium of historical citations of Adam's Peak, see Aksland 2001.

[5]Completing the idealized topography of Muslim pilgrimage to Sri Lanka and South India is the chain of small reefs and islands known as Adam's Bridge, stretching across the Palk Strait from Talaimannar in Sri Lanka to Ramesvaram in Tamilnadu. The tomb of Habil, a son of Adam, is said to be located half a kilometre from the Ramesvaram railway station (Shu'ayb Alim 1993: 3 fn. 5).

Malai (handprint mountain), because it is where the saint and his successors left their handprints in sandalwood paste. Jin Malai is a gentle stone slope with few cultural features apart from an early Arabic inscription[6] and some Muslim flags, but with spectacular views of the Kandyan massif. Curankam Malai is the summit of a sheer granite cliff-face suspended high above the irrigated rice fields of Kaltota, and it is here one finds the cramped but panoramic cave cell where Muhiyadeen Abdul Qadir Jilani is believed to have meditated. Although Jailani is said to have been a place of Muslim refuge and Sufi meditation from the beginning of the fourth century of the Islamic era—and both a discovered dervish tombstone and some Arabic inscriptions would seem to support this view (Aboosally 2002)—all of the infrastructure of the Jailani shrine today is of twentieth century origin.

The site was rediscovered in 1875 through the efforts of an Indian Muslim of Lakshadweep origin who subsequently married and settled in Balangoda. However, it is worth noting that the rediscovery of the Jailani site did not serve to charter an exclusive lineage of saintly caretaker-descendants, such as the hereditary *saheb* shareholders of Nagoor (Saheb 1998) or the *pirzade* families of the Nizamuddin Auliya Dargah in Delhi (Jeffery 1979). Indeed, almost no such established *dargah*-based elite lineages exist in Sri Lanka.[7] Members of the small but prosperous Muslim merchant community in Balangoda began celebrating the Jailani festival annually from 1890, and in 1922 C.L.M. Marikar ('Balangoda Hajiyar') constructed the mosque at the base of the rock that remains the centre of the festival to this day. Seyed Mustafa Abdul Rahuman ('Periya Bawa'), the Lakshadweep maulana who reopened Jailani to popular worship, is buried in a special ziyaram next to the Balangoda Jumma Mosque, and beside him lie his local patrons, Sinna Lebbe Cassim Lebbe and the latter's son, C.L.M. Marikar. The Lakshadweep saint's Balangoda-born son, Seyed Buhari, seems to have been a recognized figure in the 1920s, but he did not perpetuate a local saintly lineage.

In addition to the cliffside cave ledge where Muhiyadeen Abdul

---

[6]The words have been translated as 'Ya Allah Hijri 300' or 907 CE (Aboosally 2002: 61, 87).

[7]A partial exception may be the descendants of Sheikh Mustafa, a nineteenth century Sri Lankan designated to be the hereditary successor of the Yemeni saint Mubarak Maulana. The current hereditary leader of the Mustafaviya order has a comfortable private enclave in Beruwala, although the founders of his order are buried elsewhere.

Qadir Jilani is believed to have meditated, another key location is the *chilla* room,[8] a small enclosed cave-cell built into the overhanging rock above the mosque where it is said the sixteenth century saint Shahul Hamid and his travelling companion Seyed Sahabdeen—whose ziyaram is at the Meera Maccam Mosque in Kandy—meditated in the company of Allah's 'green' servant al-Khidr during an astral journey from his shrine at Nagoor, Tamilnadu. When he returned to Nagoor, Shahul Hamid brought with him an iron chain originally used by Khidr (or, in another version, by the Macedonian hero, Dhul Qarnayn) to bind himself while performing severe austerities at Jailani. A distinctive 'shrinking chain' identified with this legend hangs from the ceiling in front of the tomb of Hazrat Yusuf Saheb, the miraculously conceived son of Shahul Hamid, at the Nagoor Dargah.

The Annual Kandoori Festival

During most of the year, Jailani is a tranquil place to visit, devoid of crowds, and conducive to solitary sightseeing and contemplation. But each year during the kandoori[9] festival commemorating the death anniversary of the Iraqi saint—popularly known in Tamil as Muhiyadeen *Andavar* (Lord Muhiyadeen)—the site fills with Muslim pilgrims from all parts of the island and loudspeakers echo with amplified singing and recitation. During both the inaugural flag raising ceremony and the concluding feast day, the pilgrim shelters are packed; most devotees sleep under the open sky on the plaza, along the footpaths, or under the trees and boulders that surround the central mosque. Tea stalls and eating establishments are crowded, souvenir boutiques cater to pilgrims with children, and the itinerant Bawa *faqirs* are conspicuously installed in their headquarters at the confluence of two walkways leading to the shrine. It is hard to move freely without stepping on some family's sleeping mat or bumping into spectators watching a devotional or curing performance of some kind. The crowd is patient and good-natured; kinship groups remain surprisingly relaxed as they sit jammed together shoulder-to-shoulder. Jailani also affords an opportunity for some rude high-jinks by the children and for some flirtation between large roving groups of young

[8]*Chilla* refers to a 40-day Sufi retreat, or to the place of seclusion where it occurs.
[9]Tamil, *kanturi*, a word meaning 'tablecloth' in Persian. The Arabic term *urs* is seldom used in Sri Lanka.

people. And above it all, from dawn until midnight, the loudspeaker crackles and blares, carrying a steady stream of announcements interspersed with a variety of Muslim recitations, recordings, and *ratibs*.

Flag Raising Ceremony

The opening event of the festival is an all-female recitation of the Talai Fatiha,[10] an intercessory prayer to the wives of the earlier Prophets and to the Prophet Mohammed's daughter Fatima especially composed for the Muslim women of Sri Lanka by the influential nineteenth century South Indian missionary scholar from Kilakkarai known popularly as Mappillai Lebbe Alim (Shu'ayb Alim 1993: 613). The fact that a women's event is first on the programme seems to set a tone of gender equality and co-participation that is felt throughout the festival, despite spatial separation of the sexes within the Jailani mosque itself.[11] However, from the standpoint of sheer religious excitement, it is the late afternoon flag raising ceremony that truly inaugurates the Jailani festival and is the highlight of the entire month-long event. A flag raising ceremony (*kodiyerram*) is a standard feature of Hindu temple and Christian church festivals in Sri Lanka, but flags appear to be especially prominent at Muslim shrines and celebrations. Many pilgrims to Jailani bring with them, or purchase at the site, green pennants with star and crescent markings that they affix to cords and ropes hanging in the mosque, or tie to flagpoles that have been erected on the rocky outcroppings that surround the shrine. The Bawa *faqirs* stage their own special flag raising ceremony directly in front of their headquarters near the bazaar junction. However, it is the consecration and raising of the main mosque flag that generates the greatest anticipation and religious tension among the pilgrims, for it is believed to embody the sacred power or *barakat* of Muhiyadeen Abdul Qadir Jilani, reinforced by the spiritual echo of his latter day follower, the saint of Nagoor.

As sunset approaches, a tense crowd waits at the foot of the stairway leading upward to the rock-enclosed *chilla* room softly intoning the supplicatory invocation, '*muradiya, muradiya*, Sheikh Muhiyadeen *muradiya*[12]...' while the Chief Trustee and a select group of religious

---

[10]'The head or first' *fatiha*.

[11]I would speculate that the assertiveness and independence of mind shown by the Chief Trustee's wife, an educated woman from the matrilineal east coast town of Kalmunai, may have had an impact on the way women are currently incorporated into the Jailani celebrations.

[12]Arabic, *muradiyat*. Fulfillment of one's spiritual wishes or desires.

men, honoured guests, and major patrons crowd into the small chamber where the flag will be consecrated. After a swelling barrage of Arabic invocations by the *kateeb* of the Jailani mosque, the Chief Trustee dips his hands into a bowl of sandalwood paste and places his palm prints on the green embroidered satin flag .What instantly follows is something like a rugby scrum, with everyone else inside the tightly packed room struggling forward to touch the remaining sandalwood paste and the flag itself. After the banner is affixed tightly to a portable wooden pole, a team of muscular men led by the Chief Trustee carry it above their heads from the *chilla* room to the central flagstaff in the mosque, while members of the waiting crowd eagerly jostle and lunge forward to touch the divinely-charged flag as it passes. While everyone is liberally sprinkled with rosewater, the flag crew struggles with pilgrims who impede the hoisting of the flag, seeking to touch it before it is out of reach. In the process, several men fall into a state of religious trance (*hal, jadab*), some of whom are carried back up into the *chilla* room to recover. Women are affected by the divine power of the occasion, too. One prominent female curer known as Kaiyamma is kept busy near the Dervish tomb exorcising malevolent spirits from an array of female patients who range from teenage girls to elderly women.

Once the main flag has been hoisted, most of the crowd relaxes and returns to a variety of personal devotional activities. Inside the mosque, members of the staff assist pilgrims in fastening their individual green pennants, and a steady stream of women signal their vows by tying strips of cloth containing small coins (*kanikkai*), and taking away curative spoonfuls of oil, from a massive brass oil lamp just inside the threshold of the building. In the evening, the shrine kitchen provides a serving of blessed food (*narisa*) to those devotees who have played a direct role in the day's religious programme. The meal I shared consisted of a mixture of dark jaggery-sweetened milk-rice and gram called *kicchadi*, served to groups of six on large metal dishes (*sakan*) or wrapped up for take-away in a dried palm frond parcel called *kidu*.[13]

Ratib *Performances*

In the evening after the flag raising, and on many subsequent nights of the festival, different groups recite mauloods and perform *ratibs*[14]

---

[13]Lit. Tamil *kidaku*, cadjan or dried palm frond.

[14]Arabic, *ratib*, 'that which is fixed.' A Muslim devotional performance, such as a *zikr*.

that celebrate the lives and miracles of the most popular saints. To commemorate the flag raising on 22 June 2001 (the first day of Rabi ul-Akhir), a group of Sufi laymen from Welimada in the central hills performed a carefully rehearsed and choreographed performance of a Rifai *ratib* in the central mosque at Jailani starting around 9 pm. Like other *ratibs* I have witnessed, this performance was staged by two opposing rows of seated men, each with a tambourine (*dahira*, or *daf*), under the leadership of a Kalifa who sang the opening lines and prompted the seated members to respond. The singing started slowly and gradually picked up in tempo until it reached a highly emotional crescendo, accompanied by rapid tambourine rhythms and energetic body movements in perfect unison. Sung in a mixture of Arabic and Urdu, a Rifai *ratib* first recounts the *silsila*, or spiritual genealogy, of the *tariqa* back to its founder, Hazrat Ahmad Kabir Rifai, followed by songs and prayers celebrating the saint's exemplary life and miraculous powers. This distinctive genre of Sufi singing has been introduced from Androth Island in the Lakshadweep archipelago by travelling Rifai *tangals* who have initiated many followers in Sri Lanka over the past 150 years.

The laymen's Rifai *ratib* is a rather mournful form of devotional singing, not the sort of thing that will hold the attention of a restless crowd for very long, particularly when more theatrical feats are being staged nearby. Concurrent with the lay Rifai *ratib*, a professional *ratib* staged by the itinerant Bawas attracts a much larger crowd of onlookers in front of their headquarters near the bazaar junction. The Bawas at Jailani, who mainly come from the east coast towns of Kalmunai and Eravur, depend on donations from the pilgrims for a significant portion of their annual income, and as a result they have worked out a turf-sharing agreement that allows rival Bawas based in Akkaraipattu to have performance rights at other Sufi festivals, such as the shrine to Seyed Sardat Faqir Muhiyadeen at Porvai.[15]

Because the Bawas are members of the Rifai order, their *zikr* performance is also called a Rifai *ratib*, but its content and focus differs markedly.[16] It consists of a circle of 15 or 20 Bawas led by a main

[15]At Jailani in 2001, the Bawas had a lay patron, a businessman from the Colombo Pettah with strong Sufi ties, who provided them with food supplies throughout the entire festival.

[16]There are lay members of the Rifai order at places such as Kappuwatte and Pallimulla on the south coast who perform a self-mortifying *zikr* similar to that of the Bawas, in conjunction with the more devotional form of Rifai *ratib*.

Kalifa and several junior Kalifas, all of whom loudly beat tambourines and shout Muslim invocations (e.g. the declaration of faith: *la illaha illallah* ...) while three or four Bawas take turns performing ecstatic acts of self-mortification as the crowd looks on. After some preliminary singing and a short sermon on the power of the *auliyas* (saints), the first Bawa selects one or more weapons from a large array of daggers, needles, and spikes laid out at the centre of the group. He then presents the implement to his Kalifa for his blessing, which is bestowed by means of verbal invocation and by lightly wetting the tip of the weapon with saliva taken with a swipe of the thumb from deep within the roof of the mouth. Then, accompanied by rhythmic chanting and drumming and copious amounts of incense, the Bawa works himself into a religious trance-like state that may move him to repeatedly slash his chest or tongue with a knife, or perforate his skin with long steel needles, or jab *dabus* spikes with distinctive chain-adorned spherical knobs—similar to those found in Rifai communities stretching from the Balkans to Indonesia—into his skull or his eye sockets. At the conclusion of each individual performance, the Bawa returns to the feet of the Kalifa to receive additional blessings, handshakes, and anointment of his wounds with his Kalifa's saliva. This twenty-first century Rifai *ratib* is quite similar to those reported from Kataragama, Kalkudah, and Colombo in the 1930s (Spittel 1933: 312–21) and to Bawa *ratibs* I attended on the east coast in the 1970s (McGilvray 1988). At the end of each nightly demonstration the Kalifas lead the Bawas in a series of catchy popular Muslim devotional songs while members of the audience are encouraged to step forward to donate money to the Bawa troupe. The Bawa exhibition concludes by midnight, and family groups then retire to their makeshift sleeping areas for the night.

Kandoori Feast

The Jailani festival lasts for a full month, with an intermittent and less intense schedule of *mauloods* and *ratibs* of the sort described during the opening day. The Bawas remain encamped throughout, performing whenever they can attract an audience, but attendance is thinner during the mid-weeks of the festival. The number of pilgrims rises steeply again on the final two days of the festival, the kandoori feast proper, when the kitchen at the shrine serves up huge quantities of food to the pilgrims. From mid-afternoon until noon of the following day, the shrine is alive with a constant stream of amplified prayers, mauloods,

fatihas, *ratibs*, and discourses on Hadith. When I attended the final
day celebrations in July 2001, lay groups from various parts of the
island performed *ratibs* from different Sufi orders, including Jalaliya,
Idroosiya, Qadiriya, and Rifai.[17] A Colombo-based middle class group
known as Hubbul Auliya (Love of the Saints) took the opportunity
to conspicuously demonstrate its mystical devotion and philanthropy
by donating a special calligraphed flag to the shrine. Some of the
more intrepid pilgrims negotiated an arduous footpath to the Uppu
Kulam (salt pond), a small mineral spring under the overhanging stone
cliff where Muhiyadeen Abdul Qadir Jilani meditated. All three of
the monolithic formations that surround the Jailani shrine were dotted
with strolling groups of pilgrims, either ascending or descending,
from dawn to dusk. The temporary souvenir boutiques and tea stalls
carried on a thriving business, and individual traders laid out for
sale a wide array of Islamic literature, prayer beads, inscribed Quranic
amulets, and scented oils. The specially-prepared kandoori food, served
on the final night and once again at noon on the final day, consisted
of six-person servings of rice, peas, lentils, and either beef or chicken.
There was perhaps less anticipation and theatrical excitement than
at the inaugural flag raising ceremony, but the final meal itself seemed
to be strongly imbued with sacred meaning for the pilgrims who
consumed it.

Sri Lanka's Network of Sufi Shrines

Although they are small establishments relative to Sri Lanka's major
urban mosques, four sites can be readily identified as the island's
most well-known Sufi-centred pilgrimage shrines. In addition to
Daftar Jailani, there is the *dargah* of Faqir Muhiyadeen at Porvai
(Godapitiya) near the southern town of Akuressa. In the nineteenth
century, the saint revealed himself in a dream to two Muslim
businessmen from Galle to be a mendicant avatar of Muhiyadeen
Abdul Qadir Jilani. Like Daftar Jailani, the Porvai *dargah* is situated
in a Sinhalese majority area, and it had to be rebuilt (with help from
the British colonial government) after suffering extensive damage in
the Sinhalese-Muslim riots of 1915. The southern coastal towns of

---

[17]The Shaduliya *tariqa* did not appear on the published programme in 2001 and
2002, despite being one of the largest lay Sufi orders in southwestern coastal towns
such as Beruwala and Galle.

Weligama and Matara, only 20 km away, are historic centres of Rifai Sufi allegiance, and the annual festival at Porvai features a strong Rifai presence, including ecstatic 'cutting and stabbing' (*vettukkuttu*) performances by itinerant Bawas from the east coast and sometimes by lay Rifai Sufis as well. Because both Daftar Jailani and Porvai celebrate the death anniversary of the same saint, the two establishments have worked out a coordinated festival calendar that allows both festivals to take place within the same time frame.

The third major Sri Lankan Sufi pilgrimage shrine is the Beach Mosque (Katarkaraippalli) located at Kalmunaikkudy in Amparai District on the east coast of the island. This is an empty or virtual *dargah*—a 'branch office' as local people explained to me in English—of the sixteenth century saint Hazrat Seyid Abdul Qadir Shahul Hamid whose 'head office' tomb is located at Nagoor on the Tamilnadu coast near Nagappattinam. According to local sources, the Beach Mosque shrine was founded by an early nineteenth century South Indian Muslim trader from Kayalpattinam, Muhammad Tambi Lebbe, who was miraculously cured of leprosy at the beach when the Nagoor saint appeared in a vision and instructed him to drink a special mixture of lime juice and sea water. Like similar 'branch office' *dargahs* in Singapore, Penang, and South India, the Beach Mosque celebrates the Nagoor saint's annual festival according to precisely the same ritual calendar, starting with a flag raising ceremony that coincides exactly with the flag raising at Nagoor. A unique feature, however, is the board of matriclan (*kuti*) elders who administer the Beach Mosque in accordance with the matrilineal and matrilocal social system common to Muslims and Hindus in this region of the island (McGilvray 1982, 1989, 1998). The Beach Mosque, too, is a major venue for the Bawas; in fact, it is the site of their annual general meeting presided over by the current head of the island-wide Bawa jamat, Dr Pakeer Jaufar, Ph.D. and Sar Kalifa, a Lecturer in Education at the Open University in Colombo.

A focus on the saints Muhiyadeen Abdul Qadir Jilani (Muhiyadeen Andavar) and Shahul Hamid (Nagoor Andavar) is deeply rooted in Sri Lankan popular Islam. The legends of Daftar Jailani say these two saints combined forces with the scriptural 'green' Prophet al-Khidr—the mysterious servant of Allah also known as Hayat Nabi, an advisor to Moses, who is believed to have a special connection with the world of nature and with the fountain of immortality—and the heroic figure, Dhul Qarnayn (two horns), an Islamic transformation of Alexander the Great. There is an annual celebration at Jailani in the month of Safar solely in honour of Khidr at which *niyattu*,[18] a special form of milk-rice containing extra sugar and raisins, is cooked and distributed at the base of a Khidr flagpole on the eastern parapet overlooking the Kaltota plain and the forested hills to the east. People say that Jailani is the sort of wild location conducive to encountering Khidr, an event that is believed to have occurred when the Baghdad saint, and later the Nagoor saint, visited the site during their astral travels.

However, the Sri Lankan shrine that is most fully dedicated to Khidr is the fourth of the major Sufi sites in the island: Kataragama. While ethnographic attention has focused upon the expanding island-wide Sinhalese and Tamil cult of Kataragama, a Sri Lankan name for the Hindu god, Skanda or Murugan (Obeyesekere 1977, 1978), the Muslim enclave at the Kataragama pilgrimage centre located north of Tissamaharama has also steadily grown over the past century. Muslim oral traditions identify the southeastern quarter of the island as the 'Khidr region' (Hassan 1968: 5). The present day Khidr Taikkya at Kataragama has been steadily enlarged as the centerpiece of a Muslim compound containing the tombs of several north Indian or central Asian *faqirs* who resided at Kataragama to commune with Khidr.[19] One ecumenical Western devotee has even argued that Kataragama is actually 'Khadir-gama,' based on an alternative spelling of Khidr (Harrigan 1998: 109). Another version of the Jailani legend contends that the Nagoor saint was invested with the cloak and title of Qutbul Aktab at Kataragama (Hassan 1968:11). The Bawas make their seasonal appearance here as well, performing their penetrating *zikr* in the area in front of the tomb of the austere vegetarian saint known as Palkudi (milk-drinking) Bawa.

Religion and Politics at Jailani

Challenges from the Muslim Community

A problem of litigious micro-politics is common to religious establishments throughout South Asia, and some of the Sri Lankan Sufi

[18]The literal meaning is 'intention,' but by metaphorical extension it means a kind of food offered with the intention of seeking divine assistance.

[19]Several energetic twentieth century chief trustees have built up the Kataragama Khidr shrine. This includes the current trustee, Mr M.H.A. Gaffar of Galle Fort.

shrines discussed here have suffered their share of managerial conflicts, succession quarrels, and property disputes. A privately published
history of the Kataragama Khidr Taikkya devotes nearly a third of
its pages to recounting the mid-twentieth century succession battles
and court cases that determined legal control of the shrine (Hassan
1968). At Jailani, too, there was a lengthy lawsuit filed in 1922 to
remove a usurping Indian *mastan* who had been charging pilgrims an
entrance fee, and in the early 1970s the government filed a case against
a *faqir* named Trinco Bawa for erecting a shelter at Jailani in defiance
of the Antiquities Ordinance (Aboosally 2002).

Throughout the twentieth century it has been the members of
one family, descendants of a leading Muslim physician who settled
in Balangoda in the nineteenth century, who have been leaders in
protecting and promoting the development of Jailani as a Sufi shrine.
In conversations with the current Chief Trustee, Mr M.L.M. Aboosally,
a retired MP and former government minister, I learned that Jailani
has been a target of criticism from Islamic reformist groups, such as
the Tabliq, Jamat-i-Islami, and Towheed movements, who preach
that Sufi mysticism devalues the fundamental Sharia requirements
and that personal devotion to the saints amounts to *shirk* or idolatry.
However, on my visits to Jailani in 2001 and 2002, I observed no
public opposition to the festival and no printed literature from Islamic
fundamentalist groups. Mr Aboosally says he has dealt with them
repeatedly in the past, however, pointing out that Muslims are free
to stop attending Jailani whenever they wish. As long as pilgrims
continue to come, he feels the shrine serves a religious need in the Sri
Lankan Muslim community. Aboosally is a liberal-minded person,
but there is little doubt that his stature as a highly successful retired
politician, and as a member of one of Balangoda's leading Muslim
families, has given him some needed leverage in this situation. For
their part, the Islamic reformists can discount Jailani as an exotic
rural side-show, a place where Sufi devotionalism is performed far from
the urban gaze. The contrast was stark when I stopped in Balangoda
town to visit the Periya Bawa ziyaram, tomb of Seyed Mustafa Abdul
Rahuman from Lakshadweep and his two local patrons, a small
neglected masonry structure overshadowed by the vast modern
extension of the Jumma Mosque located immediately adjacent. On
the walls of the new mosque were posted notices written in Tamil
announcing meetings and sermons by visiting Islamic reformist
speakers under the sponsorship of the Towheed movement. Inquiring
about events at the Periya Bawa ziyaram, I learned that the annual

kandoori for the local Balangoda saint has not been celebrated for several years because of opposition from a small but highly vocal fundamentalist faction.

Jailani and Buddhist Sacred Geography

It is not the fundamentalists, however, who have posed the most serious threat to the future of Jailani. It was pointed out earlier that Jailani is located in an overwhelmingly Sinhala Buddhist district and that the shrine itself is separated from the Muslim community in Balangoda by 22 km of serpentine road. Adam's Peak is revered by some Muslims, but it is much more sacred today to the Buddhists and the Hindus. Jailani, however, is an exclusively Muslim shrine patronized by the small yet conspicuously prosperous community of Muslim traders and gem dealers in Balangoda, a town located deep in the hinterlands of Dhamma Dipa, the island consecrated to preserving the Buddha's message. During the kandoori festival, Jailani is suddenly flooded with Muslims from all over the island who have no connection to the Balangoda region. In the early 1970s, Jailani began to attract the attention of Sinhala chauvinists and politicized members of the Buddhist sangha as a seeming violation of the island's sacred geography, a religio-spatial error that might be rectified, they thought, with the help of the state Archaeology Department. It is important to note that, while intermittent political friction and communal strife between Sri Lanka's Tamil Hindus and their Tamil-speaking Muslim neighbours in the Eastern Province has always been recognized as a significant and growing problem, especially in the context of the Eelam secessionist conflict, a more submerged but equally dangerous ethnic antagonism has long existed between the Sinhalese Buddhists and the Muslims. Entrenched memories of the traumatic 1915 Sinhalese-Muslim riots can account for much of the twentieth century Muslim political opportunism that Tamil nationalists have considered so disloyal to their Dravidian cultural mission. Because two-thirds of Sri Lanka's Muslim minority live in Colombo and in the Sinhalese towns of the central and southwestern provinces, they are acutely aware of their vulnerability, a fact that has separated them from the more secure Muslim farmers of the eastern coastal districts (McGilvray 1998). Sudden outbreaks of violence against Muslims in Sinhalese towns like Mawanella in recent years have shown that these underlying ethnic embers can easily be fanned into flame.

One such potential flashpoint arose in 1971 during the SLFP

government of Mrs Sirimavo Bandaranaike, herself a member of the powerful, aristocratic Ratwatte family from Balangoda. According to Mr Aboosally, who was the man on the spot, a Muslim petition that had been filed back in the 1940s to obtain permanent legal title to the property at Jailani was eventually denied by the government twenty years later, offering them only a permanent lease. Then, in the context of local political rivalries, a claim was put forward in the early 1970s that Jailani was actually an ancient Buddhist archaeological site requiring urgent government protection and preservation. Abruptly, the Ministry of Cultural Affairs authorized the Archaeology Department to 'reconstruct' a small Buddhist *dagoba* at the summit of Curangam Malai directly above the cave where Muyihadeen Abdul Qadir Jilani is said to have meditated for twelve years, and a Buddhist reclamation of the site seemed imminent. By means of high-level counter-politics, construction of the Buddhist *dagoba*—using locally fired bricks and Kankesanturai cement from Jaffna—was stopped when the Jailani trustees obtained a cabinet order capping the construction at a height of two feet. The unfinished stupa remains on view today, protected by a low metal railing. The Archaeology Department nevertheless erected a permanent trilingual signboard near the Jailani mosque, also visible today, stating that the location, known as Kuragala, was the site of a Buddhist monastery dating to the second century BCE.[20]

Archaeologically stalemated, the proponents of a Sinhala Buddhist take-over of the shrine, including an activist monk from Ratnapura and some members of the Ministry of Cultural Affairs, put together a high-level delegation and demanded to 'inspect' the Jailani site. According to Aboosally's account, the assembled crowd included 30–40 monks from Ratnapura along with their lay supporters, the Cultural Affairs Minister, the Commissioner of Archaeology, and the ruling party MP for Balangoda, Mrs Mallika Ratwatte. With army personnel in position as well, the situation could have become violent if the Muslims had tried to defend their territory by force, but an ugly incident was averted by keeping most of the local Muslims away. On behalf of the Jailani mosque, Mr Aboosally strategically provided all the Buddhist monks with *dana* (ritual presentation of food), and

---

[20]There are Brahmi inscriptions at Jailani dating to the second century BCE, but they appear to assert territorial claims by local political chieftains. According to Aboosally (2002: 62–3) there is no evidence that the site was ever dedicated to the Buddhist sangha.

the only violence was a sharp verbal exchange between Mr Aboosally and Mrs Ratwatte. The conflict was finally resolved at the prime minister's level, when the minister of education (a Muslim) succeeded in persuading the rest of the cabinet to leave the trustees in possession of Jailani. The trustees, for their part, agreed to have the Jailani site gazetted under the Antiquities Ordinance. They also promised to strictly limit any future construction of buildings, and—to reassure the authorities that an expanding *dargah*-necropolis was not envisioned—they agreed to prohibit all further Muslim burials at the sacred site (Aboosally 2002 and personal interviews).

A Muslim Archaeological Ripost

Two years later, trustees of the shrine were gratified to learn that Trinco Bawa had been acquitted of flaunting the Antiquities Ordinance. However, these officially designated, governmentally-gazetted antiquities still do not include the Arabic inscriptions found on tombstones and rock faces at Jailani. 'The Archaeological Department,' observes Mr Aboosally, 'appears to be only interested in Sinhala and Buddhist archaeology' (Aboosally 2002: 85). However, the Muslims at Jailani have since learned something about the symbolic value of rock carving, or what we might call 'lithic politics.' In 1984, a wealthy Muslim donor from Chilaw made it possible for the trustees to hire a local mason to cut an impressive stairway from the living rock leading into the Jailani sacred area, much as the ancient Sinhala kings of Anuradhapura carved steps from the rock at Mihintale to commemorate the conversion of the island to Buddhism. These newly carved steps at Jailani, much more than the Islamic-style arch that frames them, speak the language of religious antiquity and sacred archaeology so popular in Sri Lanka today. They are obviously intended to vouchsafe the footsteps of *future* Muslim pilgrims to the shrine of Daftar Jailani.

References

Aboosally, M.L.M. 1975. Did Shayk Abdul Kader Jilani Visit Adam's Peak in Sri Lanka? *The Muslim Digest* (South Africa), September-October, 167–70.

———. 2002. *Dafther Jailany: A Historical Account of the Dafther Jailani Rock Cave Mosque*, Sharm Aboosally, Colombo.

Aksland, Markus. 2001. *The Sacred Footprint: A Cultural History of Adam's Peak*, Orchid Press, Bangkok.

Gibb, H.A.R. (trans.). 1986. *Ibn Battuta: Travels in Asia and Africa 1325–1354*, Oriental Books Reprint Corporation, New Delhi. Originally published by Routledge & Kegan Paul, London, 1929.

Harrigan, Patrick. 1998. *Kataragama: The Mystery Shrine*, Institute of Asian Studies, Chennai.

Hassan, M.C.A. 1968. *Kataragama Mosque and Shrine*, S.A.M. Thauoos, Colombo.

Jeffery, Patricia. 1979. *Frogs in a Well: Indian Women in Purdah*, Zed Press, Routledge, London and New York.

McGilvray, Dennis B. 1982. Mukkuvar Vannimai: Tamil Caste and Matriclan Ideology in Batticaloa, Sri Lanka, in D.B. McGilvray (Ed.), *Caste Ideology and Interaction*, Cambridge University Press, 34–97.

———. 1988. Village Sufism in Sri Lanka: An Ethnographic Report, *Lettre d'Information* 8:1–12 (January 1988). Programme de Recherches Interdisciplinaires sur le Monde Musulman Peripherique, Centre d'Etudes de l'Inde et de l'Asie du Sud. Paris: EHESS.

———. 1989. Households in Akkaraipattu: Dowry and Domestic Organization among the Matrilineal Tamils and Moors of Sri Lanka, in John Grey and David Mearns (Eds), *Society from the Inside-Out: Anthropological Perspectives on the South Asian Household*, Sage, New Delhi, 192–235.

———. 1998. Arabs, Moors, and Muslims: Sri Lankan Muslim Ethnicity in Regional Perspective, *Contributions to Indian Sociology* 32(2): 433–83. (Reprinted in V. Das, D. Gupta, and P. Uberoi (Eds), *Tradition, Pluralism, and Identity: In Honour of T.N. Madan*, Sage, New Delhi, 1999. Reprinted slightly abridged in T.N. Madan (Ed.), *Muslim Communities of South Asia*. 3rd edition. Manohar, New Delhi, 2001.

Obeyesekere, Gananath. 1977. Social Change and the Deities: The Rise of the Kataragama Cult in Modern Sri Lanka, *Man*, n.s., 12: 377–96.

———. 1978. The Firewalkers of Kataragama: The Rise of Bhakti Religiosity in Buddhist Sri Lanka. *Journal of Asian Studies* 36: 457–76.

Saheb, S.A.A. 1998. A Festival of Flags: Hindu-Muslim Devotion and the Sacralizing of Localism at the Shrine of Nagore-e-Sharif in Tamil Nadu, in Pnina Werbner and Helene Basu (Eds), *Embodying Charisma: Modernity, Locality and the Performance of Emotion in Sufi Cults*, Routledge, London and New York, 55–76.

Shu'ayb Alim, Takya. 1993. *Arabic, Arwi and Persian in Sarandib and Tamil Nadu*, Imamul Arus Trust, Madras.

Spencer, Jonathan. 1990. *A Sinhala Village in a Time of Trouble: Politics and Change in Rural Sri Lanka*, Oxford University Press, Delhi.

Spittel, R.L. 1933. *Far Off Things*, Colombo Apothecaries Co. Ltd., Colombo.

Contributors

IMTIAZ AHMAD
Former Professor of Political Sociology at the Jawaharlal Nehru University, New Delhi.

HELMUT REIFELD
Head of the Planning and Concepts Division within the Department of International Co-operation of KAS.

PETER S. GOTTSCHALK
Professor of Religion at the Wesleyan University, Connecticut, USA.

SHAIL MAYARAM
Professor and Senior Fellow at the Centre for the Study of Developing Societies, New Delhi.

JACKIE ASSAYAG
Anthropologist and Professor of Research at the CNRS affiliated at the Maison Française, Oxford, UK.

SUDHINDRA SHARMA
Executive Director of Interdisciplinary Analysts, a research organization based in Kathmandu, Nepal.

MOHAMMAD ISHAQ KHAN
Former Professor and Head of the Department of History, Kashmir University, Srinagar.

APARNA RAO (1950–2005)*
The Late Associate Professor of Anthropology at the University of
Cologne, Germany.

MARIAM ABOU-ZAHAB
Researcher affiliated with the Sciences Po University, Paris, France.

ASHA RANI
Assistant Professor at the Jawaharlal Nehru University, New Delhi.

YOGINDER SIKAND
Works with the Centre for the Study of Social Exclusion and Inclusive
Social Policy at the National Law School, Bangalore.

DIANE D'SOUZA
Associated with the Henry Martyn Institute of Islamic Studies,
Hyderabad.

DOMINIQUE-SILA KHAN
Independent researcher, associated with the Institute of Rajasthan
Studies, Jaipur.

HELENE BASU
Full Professor at the Westfaelische Wilhelms-Universitaet Muenster,
Germany.

UTE FALASCH
Research Fellow at the Humboldt University, Berlin, Germany.

DENNIS B. MCGILVRAY
Professor of Anthropology at the University of Colorado, Boulder,
USA.

*We are deeply sorry to have to record the passing away of one of our most
talented authors.

The publisher

Index

low, 169
Muslim, 15, 116
tribe, 23
state withdrawal from, 121
caste taboos, 73–4
criticism of, 76, 77
categories/y, *see* Muslim, liminality,
syncretism, xvi, 3
Hindu, 127–8
forms of practice and Muslim,
250–51
of religion, 68
Changadeva/Rajabag Savar saint, 48
Census, 23
enumeration, 124, 125
and mapping of religious community, 166, 170 fn 1, 187 fn 1,
213
change, social, xxi
Chikmagalur, 172
Chisti, 177
Muinuddin, 15, 209, 218
brotherhood, 258
Christian Ashrams, 37
Christian/ity, 34, 116, 123, 129
crisis of western, 35 fn 10
Judaism and, 31
as syncretic, 31–2
Upanisads and truth of, 33, 35
Churaute Muslim practices, 113
circumcision, 113
citizen, nation's model of, 10
classification
challenge of Islam for western,
xviii, 6
evolutionary model of xviii, 4
morphological, 4, 5, 6
phylogenetic, 4, 56
clerics, *see* ulema
deviation from pure Islam, xx, xxi
orthodox Muslim, xx
co-existence, 19, 107
as competitive sharing, 41, 43 fn 4
fundamentalists' aversion to, 234

mutual bonds and, xxi
traditions of in Kashmir, 64 fn 4
colonial, labelling of 'pure' vs deviant
religion, 211
contempt of 'lived' Islam, 98
communication,
computer mediated, 86
communal, 166, 210
harmony, xx, 119
organization, 166
riots, 119
community/ies 48–9
bireligious, xviii, 20, 23
borrowing practices of other,
44
changing relations, xx, 167
consolidation of linguistic, 154
Hindu/Urdu and Hindu–Muslim,
150
Hindunized, 122 for 2
histories of, 20
organic unity of, 48
practices of Islamic, 79
as term, 48–9
'twelver', 188fn 3
virtual online Kashmiri Muslim,
85–103
conflict(s)
ethnic, 18, 53
in Imamshahi tradition, 216
intra/inter religious, xx, 118–20,
129, 210
of Muslim groups/castes, xix, 145;
(Shia-Sunni) 135–48
Muslim emotional, 98
resolving 146 fn 26
Sidi mediation in 246
conversion(s), 45, 110, 210
ban on, 116
as change of heart, 35
to Christianity, 130
incomplete, 181
to Islam, xxi, 15, 21, 77, 78, 168,
170

ethnicity, 18–37
    complex, 23
ethnographers, British, 268
Eucharist, 34
evolutionary paradigm, 5
existence, liminal, xviii
exorcism, 244

fakir, Lallan Shah, 23
    as liminal category, 235, 236
    in Sidi organization, 233–52
Fatima, Prophet's daughter, 194, 196
fertility rate, 110
festival(s) boycott of Hindu, 122, 123
    Kandoori, 274
    of Sufi shrines, 78, 84
feudal families, Shia, 136, 188 fn 2
food, blessed, 193, 195, 197
folk, consciousness, 69, 71
    dancer's oral transmission of Islam,
        77–8
    religion, 120
    theologies (premodern), 32
    tradition, 61
fundamentalist, 234
    onslaught of, 90, 99–100

Gaborieau, Marc, 113, 119
Gandhi, M.K., 32, 151, 152, 153, 155
    multilingual lifestyle of, 156
    rift with Muslim nationalist, 153
Geertz, C., 234
Gellner, David, 125
geography, sacred, xxiii
Gopalraja Vamshavali, 109
god consciousness, 73
groups, affluent Muslim, 110
    conflict, cooperation among, xix,
        41
    dynamic identity of, 49
    ethnic, 123
    religious liminal vs. mainstream,
        255
    roots/routes of, xviii, 4, 13

shared mythic-ritual spaces be-
    tween, 19, 124
syncretic, 124
Gujarat, see Sidi, Satapanthi,
    Imamshahis, xxii, 23
    politically motivated carnage in,
        40
    Sidis in, 233-52
    shrines in, 211–31
gulf country/ies
    employment in, 187
    Muslims from, xx, 116
guru, 28, 73
    –shishye, 36

Hadith-i-kisa, 190
hagiographers, 79, 170
Haj, 116
Haq Navaz Jhangvi, 141, 144–6
    militancy against Iran/Shia, 142
Hazrat Bilal, 240
Hazrat Nizamuddin Aulia of Delhi,
    180
Hebrews, 34
heretic, 20
    syncretic as, 31
heterogeneity, cultural, 52
    of religious practices, 98, 252
    in Nepali Muslim groups, 108–9
heterodox, be-shar' or, 257
    Madaris as, 258
hierarchy, 112
    Sufi and ritual, 235–6
    norms of gender, 245
Hindu,
    –Christian monk, 20, 33
    claims of superiority over Muslims,
        179
    Kashmiri, 88
    as only indigenous religions
        category 12
    philosophy, 70
    nationalist elements, xx, 233
    scriptures, 74

religious identity and, 217
and syncretism, 30–33, 211
shrine's, 172, 176
uneasiness with, 170 fn 1
Linnaeus, C., 4, 9
Literature, hagiological, 71, 79–80, 170
ginans in, 211, 228, 230
Local tradition, evolution of, 167
Low caste's worship
of Baba Budhan, 174
Koddekal Basavanna, 181
Moinuddin—patron saint of, 175–77

Madar Shah, 255
Madari Sufi brotherhood, 254–70
Magars, 122
Madaris, xxii
practice of silent *dhikr*, 260
Malangs in, 264–5
system of mystical teaching, 261
madrasa, 118 (hill), 114
Maithali, 112
Malangs, 264
as Hindus with Muslim names, 266
Makanpur, 266
ritual practice at, 263
mantras, 75
marginality, 27
masumin fourteen 'pure ones', 195
maqam, 19
Mecca, 16, 176
association with pagan rituals, 31
meditation, 90
Meos/Mers, xviii, 20, 21, 28
conflict with Turk's Afghanis, 28, 29
open-ended religious sects of 29–30
middle class, challenge to Shia feudals, 140
Middle East, 9

Middle East Studies Association, 9
Mewati Mahabharat, 28
migrations, 13
to west, 87
to Nepal, 108–10
militant groups, 86 fn 4
Islamic state sponsored, 135
minority position, xix, 119
missionary/ies
Christian, 33
Sufi, 62
miteri relations, 122
modern understanding of religious community identity, 175
Mohammad, 79, 93–4, 175
benedictions (*durud*), 62
bidden for bidden by, 92
sanctity of family of 190, 195, 196
tradition of Prophet, 45, 256
moksha, 32
monotheistic faith, 70
moral life, 244
by *beedi* or deal, 245–6
quest for, 32
mosques
and divisions between Islam, 117
construction of, 79
Hindustani, 109
Shia (Imambara), 109
Mullah, Hindunization of role of, 46
Muharram, 5, 46, 135
Hindu customs in 139 fn 7
as male only ritual, 199
Muhajir, 136
as anti Shia/feudal, 139
emergent middle class, 136
municipal politics
Sunni domination in, 140
Musharraf, P., 140
Muslim(s) *see* Shia Sufi Sunni Satpanthi Sidi Madari
antinomial goal schemes of, 85, 100
as bounded category, 3